THE
Golden Treasury
OF
Children's Literature

The GOLDEN TREASURY
of CHILDREN's LITERATURE

Edited and Selected by

BRYNA and LOUIS UNTERMEYER

GOLDEN · PRESS　NEW · YORK

Western Publishing Company, Inc.

Racine, Wisconsin

Contents

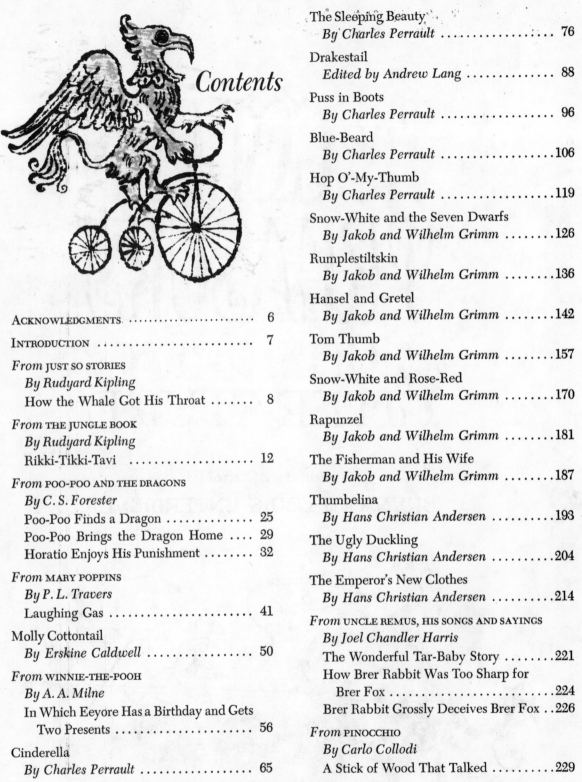

Library of Congress Catalog Card Number: 66-14668

©Copyright 1966, 1962, 1961, 1960, 1959, 1958, 1954, 1952,
1947 by Western Publishing Company, Inc. Printed in the U.S.A.

ACKNOWLEDGMENTS The editors and publishers have made every effort to trace the ownership of all copyrighted material and to secure permission from the holders of the copyright. In the event of any question arising as to the use of any of the selections, the publisher and editors, while expressing regret for any inadvertent error, will be glad to make the necessary correction in future printings. Thanks are due to the following publishers, publications, agents, owners of copyright, and authors for permission to reprint the material indicated.

GEORGE ALLEN & UNWIN LTD. for "An Unexpected Party" from *The Hobbit* by J. R. R. Tolkien.

DOUBLEDAY & COMPANY, INC. for "How the Whale Got His Throat" from *Just So Stories* by Rudyard Kipling.

E. P. DUTTON & CO., INC. for "Eeyore Has a Birthday" from *Winnie-the-Pooh* by A. A. Milne. Copyright 1926, by E. P. Dutton & Co., Inc. Renewal 1954, by A. A. Milne. Drawings by E. H. Shepard.

HARCOURT, BRACE & WORLD, INC. for "Laughing Gas" from *Mary Poppins* by P. L. Travers. Copyright 1934, by Harcourt, Brace & Co.; copyright 1962, by P. L. Travers. Illustrations by Mary Shepard.

DAVID HIGHAM ASSOCIATES, LTD. for "Laughing Gas" from *Mary Poppins* published in England by William Collins Sons & Company. Also for Chapter XIX of *The Sword in the Stone* by T. H. White, published by William Collins Sons & Company.

HODDER AND STOUGHTON LTD. for Chapters XIV, XV, XVI from *The Little White Bird* by J. M. Barrie.

HOUGHTON MIFFLIN COMPANY for "An Unexpected Party" from *The Hobbit* by J. R. R. Tolkien.

LITTLE, BROWN AND COMPANY for "Molly Cottontail" by Erskine Caldwell. Copyright 1931, © 1958, by Erskine Caldwell.

MRS. HUGH LOFTING for "Doctor Dolittle Learns Animal Language" from *The Story of Doctor Dolittle* by Hugh Lofting. Copyright 1920, by Hugh Lofting; renewal 1948, by Josephine Lofting.

HAROLD MATSON COMPANY INC. for Chapters I, II, and VI from *Poo-Poo and the Dragons* by C. S. Forester. Copyright 1942, by C. S. Forester. Also for *Switch on the Night* by Ray Bradbury. Copyright © 1955, by Ray Bradbury.

DAVID McKAY COMPANY, INC. for "Aladdin and the Wonderful Lamp" from *The Blue Fairy Book* and "The Language of Beasts" from *The Crimson Fairy Book,* both edited by Andrew Lang.

METHUEN & CO. LTD. for "Eeyore Has a Birthday" from *Winnie-the-Pooh* by A. A. Milne. Copyright by C. R. Milne. Also for "The River Bank" from *The Wind in the Willows* by Kenneth Grahame. Copyright by The Bodleian Library, Oxford, England.

LAURENCE POLLINGER LIMITED for "Molly Cottontail" by Erskine Caldwell. Copyright 1931, © 1958, by Erskine Caldwell.

G. P. PUTNAM'S SONS for Chapter XIX of *The Sword in the Stone* by T. H. White. Copyright © 1939, by T. H. White.

CHARLES SCRIBNER'S SONS for Chapters XIV, XV, XVI from *The Little White Bird* by J. M. Barrie. Also for "The River Bank" from *The Wind in the Willows* by Kenneth Grahame. Copyright 1908, 1933 by Charles Scribner's Sons.

SIMON & SCHUSTER, INC. for Chapter II from *Bambi* by Felix Salten. Copyright © 1928, 1956, by Simon & Schuster, Inc.

LOUIS UNTERMEYER for his versions of *Aesop's Fables* and *Androcles and the Lion.* Copyright © 1963 and 1965.

VANGUARD PRESS, INC. for *The Amiable Giant* by Louis Slobodkin. Reprinted by permission of the author. Copyright © 1955, by Louis Slobodkin.

A. P. WATT & SON for "How the Whale Got His Throat" from *Just So Stories* and "Rikki-Tikki-Tavi" from *The Jungle Book* by Rudyard Kipling. Reprinted with the permission of Mrs. George Bambridge, the Macmillan Company of Canada, Ltd., and Messrs. Macmillan of England.

JAY WILLIAMS for "Raoul the Owl." Copyright 1962, by Jay Williams.

Introduction

A few years ago the editors assembled
The Golden Treasury of Children's Literature.
The collection ran to ten volumes and
was devoted to the finest and most enduring stories and legends.
In every treasure chest there are certain valuables
a little more precious than others; certain gems
that shine with just a bit more brilliance and color.
It is these gems
that have been picked for this omnibus volume.
The stories have the widest possible range.
Many of them are old favorites; others will be new enjoyments.
There is plenty of adventure here,
a lot of fantasy, and more than a little fun.
All of it is for immediate discovery—
and a lifetime of delight.

Adventure, fantasy, and fun
are the ingredients of the first selection.
It is from Rudyard Kipling's Just So Stories,
which are all about animals.
They are strange stories.
They explain "How the Camel Got His Hump"
and "How the Leopard Got His Spots";
they tell about "The Crab That Played With the Sea"
and "The Cat That Walked By Himself."
Things did not really come about the way
they do in these stories—
the whale did not really get his throat
nor the camel his hump
nor the rhinoceros his skin
nor the leopard his spots
in the manner related.
But every one of Kipling's readers would like
to believe it happened
. . . just so.

How the Whale Got His Throat

From Just So Stories by Rudyard Kipling

Illustrated by NICOLAS

IN THE SEA, once upon a time, O my Best Beloved, there was a Whale, and he ate fishes. He ate the starfish and the garfish, and the crab and the dab, and the plaice and the dace, and the skate and his mate, and the mackereel and the pickereel, and the really truly twirly-whirly eel. All the fishes he could find in all the sea he ate with his mouth—so! Till at last there was only one small fish left in all the sea, and he was a small 'Stute Fish, and he swam a little behind the Whale's right ear, so as to be out of harm's way. Then the Whale stood up on his tail and said, "I'm hungry." And the small 'Stute Fish said in a small 'stute voice, "Noble and generous Cetacean, have you ever tasted Man?"

"No," said the Whale. "What is it like?"

"Nice," said the small 'Stute Fish. "Nice but nubbly."

"Then fetch me some," said the Whale, and he made the sea froth up with his tail.

"One at a time is enough," said the 'Stute Fish. "If you swim to latitude Fifty North, longitude Forty West (that is magic), you will find, sitting *on* a raft, *in* the middle of the sea, with nothing on but a pair of blue canvas breeches, a pair of suspenders (you must *not* forget the suspenders, Best Beloved), and a jack-knife, one shipwrecked Mariner, who, it is only fair to tell you, is a man of infinite-resource-and-sagacity."

So the Whale swam and swam to latitude Fifty North, longitude Forty West, as fast as he could swim, and *on* a raft, *in* the middle of the sea, *with* nothing to wear except a pair of blue canvas breeches, a pair of suspenders (you must particularly remember the suspenders, Best Beloved), *and* a jack-knife, he found one single, solitary shipwrecked Mariner, trailing his toes in the water. (He had his mummy's leave to paddle, or else he would never have done it because he was a man of infinite-resource-and-sagacity.)

Then the Whale opened his mouth back and back and back till it nearly touched his tail, and he swallowed the shipwrecked Mariner, and the raft he was sitting on, and his blue canvas breeches, and the suspenders (which you *must* not forget), *and* the jack-knife. He swallowed them all down into his warm, dark, inside cupboards, and then he smacked his lips—so, and turned round three times on his tail.

But as soon as the Mariner, who was a man of infinite-resource-and-sagacity, found himself truly inside the Whale's warm, dark, inside cupboards, he stumped and he jumped and he thumped and he bumped, and he pranced and he danced, and he banged and he clanged, and he hit and he bit, and he leaped and he creeped, and he prowled and he howled, and he hopped and he dropped, and he cried and he sighed, and he crawled and he bawled, and he stepped and he lepped, and he danced hornpipes where he shouldn't, and the Whale felt most unhappy indeed. (*Have* you forgotten the suspenders?)

So he said to the 'Stute Fish, "This man is very nubbly, and besides he is making me hiccough. What shall I do?"

"Tell him to come out," said the 'Stute Fish.

So the Whale called down his own throat to the shipwrecked Mariner, "Come out and behave yourself. I've got the hiccoughs."

"Nay, nay!" said the Mariner. "Not so, but far otherwise. Take me to my natal-shore and the white-cliffs-of-Albion, and I'll think about it." And he began to dance more than ever.

"You had better take him home," said the 'Stute Fish to the Whale. "I ought to have warned you that he is a man of infinite-resource-and-sagacity."

So the Whale swam and swam and swam, with both flippers and his tail, as hard as he could for the hiccoughs; and at last he saw the Mariner's natal-shore and the white-cliffs-of-Albion, and he rushed half-way up the beach, and opened his mouth wide and wide and wide, and said, "Change here for Winchester, Ashuelot, Nashua, Keene, and stations on the *Fitch*burg Road"; and just as he said "Fitch" the Mariner walked out of his mouth. But while the Whale had been swimming, the Mariner, who was indeed a person of infinite-resource-and-sagacity, had taken his jack-knife and cut up the raft into a little square grating all running criss-cross, and he had tied it firm with his suspenders (*now* you know why you were not to forget the suspenders!), and he dragged that grating good and tight into the Whale's throat, and there it stuck! Then he recited the following *Sloka*, which, as you have not heard it, I will now proceed to relate—

By means of a grating
I have stopped your ating.

10

For the Mariner he was also an Hi-ber-ni-an. And he stepped out on the shingle, and went home to his mother, who had given him leave to trail his toes in the water; and he married and lived happily ever afterward. So did the Whale. But from that day on, the grating in his throat, which he could neither cough up nor swallow down, prevented him eating anything except very, very small fish; and that is the reason why whales nowadays never eat men or boys or little girls.

The small 'Stute Fish went and hid himself in the mud under the Door-sills of the Equator. He was afraid that the Whale might be angry with him.

The Sailor took the jack-knife home. He was wearing the blue canvas breeches when he walked out on the shingle. The suspenders were left behind, you see, to tie the grating with; and that is the end of *that* tale.

No author of animal stories
is more successful than Rudyard Kipling
in communicating the emotional connection
between civilized man and uncivilized nature.
Besides being a poet and novelist, Kipling was one of the
world's greatest story-tellers. Before he died
in 1936 he had been awarded many of the highest honors,
including the Nobel Prize and the Gold Medal
of the Royal Society of Literature.
Kim, *the fascinating narrative of a boy growing up in India,*
and the resounding Barrack-Room Ballads
have been considered Kipling's most
important works; but his most endearing tales
are in Just So Stories *and* The Jungle Book.

Rikki-Tikki-Tavi
From The Jungle Book

BY RUDYARD KIPLING   *Illustrated by* LILIAN OBLIGADO

THIS IS the story of the great war that Rikki-tikki-tavi fought single-handed, through the bath-rooms of the big bungalow in Segowlee cantonment. Darzee, the tailor-bird, helped him, and Chuchundra, the musk-rat, who never comes out into the middle of the door, but always creeps round by the wall, gave him advice; but Rikki-tikki did the real fighting.

He was a mongoose, rather like a little cat in his fur and his tail, but quite like a weasel in his head and his habits. His eyes and the end of his restless nose were pink; he could scratch himself anywhere he pleased, with any leg, front or back, that he chose to use; he could fluff up his tail till it looked like a bottle-brush, and his war-cry, as he scuttled through the long grass, was: *"Rikk-tikk-tikki-tikki-tchk!"*

One day, a high summer flood washed him out of the burrow where he lived with his father and mother, and carried him, kicking and clucking, down a roadside ditch. He found a little wisp of grass floating there, and clung to it till he lost his senses. When he revived, he was lying in the hot sun on the middle of a garden path, very draggled indeed, and a small boy was saying: "Here's a dead mongoose. Let's have a funeral."

"No," said his mother; "let's take him in and dry him. Perhaps he isn't really dead."

They took him into the house, and a big man picked him up between his finger and thumb, and said he was not dead but half choked; so they wrapped him in cotton-wool, and warmed him, and he opened his eyes and sneezed.

"Now," said the big man (he was an Englishman who had just moved into the bungalow); "don't frighten him, and we'll see what he'll do."

It is the hardest thing in the world to frighten a mongoose, because he is eaten up from nose to tail with curiosity. The motto of all the mongoose family is, "Run and find out"; and Rikki-tikki was a true mongoose. He looked at the cotton-wool, decided that it was not good to eat, ran all round the table, sat up and put his fur in order, scratched himself, and jumped on the small boy's shoulder.

"Don't be frightened, Teddy," said his father. "That's his way of making friends."

"Ouch! He's tickling under my chin," said Teddy.

Rikki-tikki looked down between the boy's collar and neck, snuffed at his ear, and climbed down to the floor, where he sat rubbing his nose.

"Good gracious," said Teddy's mother, "and that's a wild creature! I suppose he's so tame because we've been kind to him."

"All mongooses are like that," said her husband. "If Teddy doesn't pick him up by the tail, or try to put him in a cage, he'll run in and out of the house all day long. Let's give him something to eat."

They gave him a little piece of raw meat. Rikki-tikki liked it immensely, and when it was finished he went out into the verandah and sat in the sunshine and fluffed up his fur to make it dry to the roots. Then he felt better.

"There are more things to find out about in this house," he said to himself, "than all my family could find out in all their lives. I shall certainly stay and find out."

He spent all that day roaming over the house. He nearly drowned himself in the bath-tubs, put his nose into the ink on a writing table, and burnt it on the end of the big man's cigar, for he climbed up in the big man's lap to see how writing was done. At nightfall he ran into Teddy's nursery to watch how kerosene-lamps were lighted, and when Teddy went to bed Rikki-tikki climbed up too; but he was a restless companion, because he had to get up and attend to every noise all through the night, and find out what made it. Teddy's mother and father

came in, the last thing, to look at their boy, and Rikki-tikki was awake on the pillow. "I don't like that," said Teddy's mother; "he may bite the child." "He'll do no such thing," said the father. "Teddy's safer with that little beast than if he had a bloodhound to watch him. If a snake came into the nursery now—"

But Teddy's mother wouldn't think of anything so awful.

Early in the morning Rikki-tikki came to early breakfast in the verandah riding on Teddy's shoulder, and they gave him banana and some boiled egg; and he sat on all their laps one after the other, because every well-brought-up mongoose always hopes to be a house-mongoose some day and have rooms to run about in, and Rikki-tikki's mother (she used to live in the General's house at Segowlee) had carefully told Rikki what to do if ever he came across white men.

Then Rikki-tikki went out into the garden to see what was to be seen. It was a large garden, only half cultivated, with bushes as big as summer-houses of Marshal Niel roses, lime and orange trees, clumps of bamboos, and thickets of high grass. Rikki-tikki licked his lips. "This is a splendid hunting-ground," he said, and his tail grew bottle-brushy at the thought of it, and he scuttled up and down the garden, snuffing here and there till he heard very sorrowful voices in a thorn-bush.

It was Darzee, the tailor-bird, and his wife. They had made a beautiful nest by pulling two big leaves together and stitching them up the edges with fibres, and had filled the hollow with cotton and downy fluff. The nest swayed to and fro, as they sat on the rim and cried.

"What is the matter?" asked Rikki-tikki.

"We are very miserable," said Darzee. "One of our babies fell out of the nest yesterday, and Nag ate him."

"H'm!" said Rikki-tikki, "that is very sad—but I am a stranger here. Who is Nag?"

Darzee and his wife only cowered down in the nest without answering, for from the thick grass at the foot of the bush there came a low hiss—a horrid cold sound that made Rikki-tikki jump back two clear feet. Then inch by inch out of the grass rose up the head and spread hood of Nag, the big black cobra, and he was five feet long from tongue to tail. When he had lifted one-third of himself clear of the ground, he stayed balancing to and fro exactly as a dandelion-tuft balances in the wind, and he looked at Rikki-tikki with the wicked snake's eyes that never change their expression, whatever the snake may be thinking of.

"Who is Nag?" said he. "I am Nag. The great god Brahm put his mark upon all our people when the first cobra spread his hood to keep the sun off Brahm as he slept. Look, and be afraid!"

He spread out his hood more than ever, and Rikki-tikki saw the spectacle-mark on the back of it that looks exactly like the eye part of a hook-and-eye fastening. He was afraid for the minute; but it is impossible for a mongoose to stay frightened for any length of time, and though Rikki-tikki had never met a live cobra before, his mother had fed him on dead ones, and he knew that all a grown mongoose's business in life was to fight and eat snakes. Nag knew that too, and at the bottom of his cold heart he was afraid.

"Well," said Rikki-tikki, and his tail began to fluff up again, "marks or no marks, do you think it is right for you to eat fledglings out of a nest?"

Nag was thinking to himself, and watching the least little movement in the grass behind Rikki-tikki. He knew that mongooses in the garden meant death sooner or later for him and his family, but he wanted to get Rikki-tikki off his guard. So he dropped his head a little, and put it on one side.

"Let us talk," he said. "You eat eggs. Why should not I eat birds?"

"Behind you! Look behind you!" sang Darzee.

Rikki-tikki knew better than to waste time in staring. He jumped up in the air as high as he could go, and just under him whizzed by the head of Nagaina, Nag's wicked wife. She had crept up behind him as he was talking, to make an end of him; and he heard her savage hiss as the stroke missed. He came down almost across her back, and if he had been an old mongoose he would have known that then was the time to break her back with one bite; but he was afraid of the terrible lashing return-stroke of the cobra. He bit, indeed, but did not bite long enough, and he jumped clear of the whisking tail, leaving Nagaina torn and angry.

"Wicked, wicked Darzee!" said Nag, lashing up as high as he could reach toward the nest in the thornbush; but Darzee had built it out of reach of snakes, and it only swayed to and fro.

Rikki-tikki felt his eyes growing red and hot (when a mongoose's eyes grow red, he is angry), and he sat back on his tail and hind legs like a little kangaroo, and looked all round him, and chattered with rage. But Nag and Nagaina had disappeared into the grass. When a snake misses its stroke, it never says anything or gives any sign of what it means to do next. Rikki-tikki did not care to follow them, for he did not feel sure that he could manage two snakes at once. So he trotted off to the gravel path near the house, and sat down to think. It was a serious matter for him.

If you read the old books of natural history, you will find they say that when the mongoose fights the snake and happens to get bitten, he runs off and eats some herb that cures him. That is not true. The victory is only a matter of quickness of eye and quickness of foot,— snake's blow against mongoose's jump,— and as no eye can follow the motion of a snake's head when it strikes, that makes things much more wonderful than any magic herb. Rikki-tikki knew he was a young mongoose, and it made him all the more pleased to think that he had managed to escape a blow from behind. It gave him confidence in himself, and when Teddy came running down the path, Rikki-tikki was ready to be petted.

But just as Teddy was stooping, something flinched a little in the dust, and a tiny voice said: "Be careful. I am death!" It was Karait, the dusty brown snakeling that lies for choice on the dusty earth;

and his bite is as dangerous as the cobra's. But he is so small that nobody thinks of him, and so he does the more harm to people.

Rikki-tikki's eyes grew red again, and he danced up to Karait with the peculiar rocking, swaying motion that he had inherited from his family. It looks very funny, but it is so perfectly balanced a gait that you can fly off from it at any angle you please; and in dealing with snakes this is an advantage. If Rikki-tikki had only known, he was doing a much more dangerous thing than fighting Nag, for Karait is so small, and can turn so quickly, that unless Rikki bit him close to the back of the head, he would get the return-stroke in his eye or lip. But Rikki did not know: his eyes were all red, and he rocked back and forth, looking for a good place to hold. Karait struck out. Rikki jumped sideways and tried to run in, but the wicked little dusty gray head lashed within a fraction of his shoulder, and he had to jump over the body, and the head followed his heels close.

Teddy shouted to the house: "Oh, look here! Our mongoose is killing a snake"; and Rikki-tikki heard a scream from Teddy's mother. His father ran out with a stick, but by the time he came up, Karait had lunged out once too far, and Rikki-tikki had sprung, jumped on the snake's back, dropped his head far between his fore-legs, bitten as high up the back as he could get hold, and rolled away. That bite paralysed Karait, and Rikki-tikki was just going to eat him up from the tail, after the custom of his family at dinner, when he remembered that a full meal makes a slow mongoose, and if he wanted all his strength and quickness ready, he must keep himself thin.

He went away for a dust-bath under the castor-oil bushes, while Teddy's father beat the dead Karait. "What is the use of that?" thought Rikki-tikki. "I have settled it all"; and then Teddy's mother picked him up from the dust and hugged him, crying that he had saved Teddy from death, and Teddy's father said that he was a providence, and Teddy looked on with big scared eyes. Rikki-tikki was rather amused at all the fuss, which, of course, he did not understand. Teddy's mother might just as well have petted Teddy for playing in the dust. Rikki was thoroughly enjoying himself.

That night, at dinner, walking to and fro among the wine-glasses on the table, he could have stuffed himself three times over with nice things; but he remembered Nag and Nagaina, and though it was very pleasant to be patted and petted by Teddy's mother, and to sit on Teddy's shoulder, his eyes would get red from time to time, and he would go off into his long war-cry of "*Rikk-tikk-tikki-tikki-tchk!*"

Teddy carried him off to bed, and insisted on Rikki-tikki sleeping under his chin. Rikki-tikki was too well bred to bite or scratch, but as soon as Teddy was asleep he went off for his nightly walk round the house, and in the dark he ran up against Chuchundra, the muskrat, creeping round by the wall. Chuchundra is a broken-hearted little beast. He whimpers and cheeps all the night, trying to make up his mind to run into the middle of the room, but he never gets there.

"Don't kill me," said Chuchundra, almost weeping. "Rikki-tikki, don't kill me."

"Do you think a snake-killer kills muskrats?" said Rikki-tikki scornfully.

"Those who kill snakes get killed by snakes," said Chuchundra, more sorrowfully than ever. "And how am I to be sure that Nag won't mistake me for you some dark night?"

"There's not the least danger," said Rikki-tikki; "but Nag is in the garden, and I know you don't go there."

"My cousin Chua, the rat, told me——" said Chuchundra, and then he stopped.

"Told you what?"

"H'sh! Nag is everywhere, Rikki-tikki. You should have talked to Chua in the garden."

"I didn't—so you must tell me. Quick, Chuchundra, or I'll bite you!"

Chuchundra sat down and cried till the tears rolled off his whiskers. "I am a very poor man," he sobbed. "I never had spirit enough to run out into the middle of the room. H'sh! I mustn't tell you anything. Can't you *hear*, Rikki-tikki?"

Rikki-tikki listened. The house was as still as still, but he thought he could just catch the faintest *scratch-scratch* in the world,—a noise as faint as that of a wasp walking on a window-pane,—the dry scratch of a snake's scales on brickwork.

"That's Nag or Nagaina," he said to himself; "and he is crawling into the bath-room sluice. You're right, Chuchundra; I should have talked to Chua."

He stole off to Teddy's bath-room, but there was nothing there, and then to Teddy's mother's bath-room. At the bottom of the smooth plaster wall there was a brick pulled out to make a sluice for the bathwater, and as Rikki-tikki stole in by the masonry curb where the bath is put, he heard Nag and Nagaina whispering together outside in the moonlight.

"When the house is emptied of people," said Nagaina to her husband, "*he* will have to go away, and then the garden will be our own again. Go in quietly, and remember that the big man who killed Karait is the first one to bite. Then come out and tell me, and we will hunt for Rikki-tikki together."

"But are you sure that there is anything to be gained by killing the people?" said Nag.

"Everything. When there were no people in the bungalow, did we have any mongoose in the garden? So long as the bungalow is empty, we are king and queen of the garden; and remember that as soon as our eggs in the melon-bed hatch (as they may to-morrow), our children will need room and quiet."

"I had not thought of that," said Nag. "I will go, but there is no need that we should hunt for Rikki-tikki afterward. I will kill the big man and his wife, and the child if I can, and come away quietly. Then the bungalow will be empty, and Rikki-tikki will go."

Rikki-tikki tingled all over with rage and hatred at this, and then Nag's head came through the sluice, and his five feet of cold body followed it. Angry as he was, Rikki-tikki was very frightened as he saw the size of the big cobra. Nag coiled himself up, raised his head, and looked into the bath-room in the dark, and Rikki could see his eyes glitter.

"Now, if I kill him here, Nagaina will know; and if I fight him on the open floor, the odds are in his favour. What am I to do?" said Rikki-tikki-tavi.

Nag waved to and fro, and then Rikki-tikki heard him drinking from the biggest water-jar that was used to fill the bath. "That is good," said the snake. "Now, when Karait was killed, the big man had a stick. He may have that stick still, but when he comes in to bathe in the morning he will not have a stick. I shall wait here till he comes. Nagaina—do you hear me?—I shall wait here in the cool till daytime."

There was no answer from outside, so Rikki-tikki knew Nagaina had gone away. Nag coiled himself down, coil by coil, round the bulge at the bottom of the water-jar, and Rikki-tikki stayed still as death. After an hour he began to move, muscle by muscle, toward the jar. Nag was asleep, and Rikki-tikki looked at his big back, wondering which would be the best place for a good hold. "If I don't break his back at the first jump," said Rikki, "he can still fight; and if he fights—O Rikki!" He looked at the thickness of the neck below the hood, but that was too much for him; and a bite near the tail would only make Nag savage.

"It must be the head," he said at last; "the head above the hood; and when I am once there, I must not let go."

Then he jumped. The head was lying a little clear of the water-jar, under the curve of it; and, as his teeth met, Rikki braced his back against the bulge of the red earthenware to hold down the head. This gave him just one second's purchase, and he made the most of it. Then he was battered to and fro as a rat is shaken by a dog—to and fro on the floor, up and down, and round in great circles; but his eyes were red, and he held on as the body cart-whipped over the floor, upsetting the tin dipper and the soap-dish and the flesh-brush, and banged against the tin side of the bath. As he held he closed his jaws tighter and tighter, for he made sure he would be banged to death, and, for the honour of his family, he preferred to be found with his teeth locked. He was dizzy, aching, and felt shaken to pieces when something went off like a thunderclap just behind him; a hot wind knocked him senseless, and red fire singed his fur. The big man had been wakened by the noise, and had fired both barrels of a shot-gun into Nag just behind the hood.

Rikki-tikki held on with his eyes shut, for now he was quite sure he was dead; but the head did not move, and the big man picked him up and said: "It's the mongoose again, Alice; the little chap has saved *our* lives now." Then Teddy's mother came in with a very white face, and saw what was left of Nag, and Rikki-tikki dragged himself to Teddy's bedroom and spent half the rest of the night shaking himself tenderly to find out whether he really was broken into forty pieces, as he fancied.

When morning came he was very stiff, but well pleased with his doings. "Now I have Nagaina to settle with, and she will be worse than five Nags, and there's no knowing when the eggs she spoke of will hatch. Goodness! I must go and see Darzee," he said.

Without waiting for breakfast, Rikki-tikki ran to the thorn-bush where Darzee was singing a song of triumph at the top of his voice. The news of Nag's death was all over the garden, for the sweeper had thrown the body on the rubbish-heap.

"Oh, you stupid tuft of feathers!" said Rikki-tikki angrily. "Is this the time to sing?"

"Nag is dead—is dead—is dead!" sang Darzee. "The valiant Rikki-tikki caught him by the head, and held fast. The big man brought the bang-stick, and Nag fell in two pieces! He will never eat my babies again."

"All that's true enough; but where's Nagaina?" said Rikki-tikki, looking carefully round him.

"Nagaina came to the bath-room sluice and called for Nag," Darzee went on; "and Nag came out on the end of a stick —the sweeper picked him up on the end of a stick and threw him upon the rubbish-heap. Let us sing about the great, the red-eyed Rikki-tikki!" and Darzee filled his throat and sang.

"If I could get up to your nest, I'd roll all your babies out!" said Rikki-tikki. "You don't know when to do the right thing at the right time. You're safe enough in your nest there, but it's war for me down here. Stop singing a minute, Darzee."

"For the great, the beautiful Rikki-tikki's sake I will stop," said Darzee. "What is it, O Killer of the terrible Nag?"

"Where is Nagaina, for the third time?"

"On the rubbish-heap by the stables, mourning for Nag. Great is Rikki-tikki with the white teeth."

"Bother my white teeth! Have you ever heard where she keeps her eggs?"

"In the melon-bed, on the end nearest the wall, where the sun strikes nearly all day. She hid them there weeks ago."

"And you never thought it worth while to tell me? The end nearest the wall, you said?"

"Rikki-tikki, you are not going to eat her eggs?"

"Not eat exactly; no. Darzee, if you have a grain of sense you will fly off to the stables and pretend that your wing is broken, and let Nagaina chase you away to this bush. I must get to the melon-bed, and if I went there now she'd see me."

Darzee was a feather-brained little fellow who could never hold more than one idea at a time in his head; and just because he knew that Nagaina's children were born in eggs like his own, he didn't think at first that it was fair to kill them. But his wife was a sensible bird, and she knew that cobra's eggs meant young cobras later on; so she flew off from the nest, and left Darzee to keep the babies warm, and continue his song about the death of Nag. Darzee was very like a man in some ways.

She fluttered in front of Nagaina by the rubbish-heap, and cried out, "Oh, my wing is broken! The boy in the house threw a stone at me and broke it." Then she fluttered more desperately than ever.

Nagaina lifted up her head and hissed, "You warned Rikki-tikki when I would have killed him. Indeed and truly, you've chosen a bad place to be lame in." And she moved toward Darzee's wife, slipping along over the dust.

"The boy broke it with a stone!" shrieked Darzee's wife.

"Well! It may be some consolation to you when you're dead to know that I shall settle accounts with the boy. My husband lies on the rubbish-heap this morning, but before night the boy in the

house will lie very still. What is the use of running away? I am sure to catch you. Little fool, look at me!"

Darzee's wife knew better than to do *that,* for a bird who looks at a snake's eyes gets so frightened that she cannot move. Darzee's wife fluttered on, piping sorrowfully, and never leaving the ground, and Nagaina quickened her pace.

Rikki-tikki heard them going up the path from the stables, and he raced for the end of the melon-patch near the wall. There, in the warm litter about the melons, very cunningly hidden, he found twenty-five eggs, about the size of a bantam's eggs, but with whitish skin instead of shell.

"I was not a day too soon," he said; for he could see the baby cobras curled up inside the skin, and he knew that the minute they were hatched they could each kill a man or a mongoose. He bit off the tops of the eggs as fast as he could, taking care to crush the young cobras, and turned over the litter from time to time to see whether he had missed any. At last there were only three eggs left, and Rikki-tikki began to chuckle to himself, when he heard Darzee's wife screaming:

"Rikki-tikki, I led Nagaina toward the house, and she has gone into the verandah, and—oh, come quickly—she means killing!"

Rikki-tikki smashed two eggs, and tumbled backward down the melon-bed with the third egg in his mouth, and scuttled to the verandah as hard as he could put foot to the ground. Teddy and his mother and father were there at early breakfast; but Rikki-tikki saw that they were not eating anything. They sat stone-still, and their faces were white. Nagaina was coiled up on the matting by Teddy's chair, within easy striking-distance of Teddy's bare leg, and she was swaying to and fro singing a song of triumph.

"Son of the big man that killed Nag," she hissed, "stay still. I am not ready yet. Wait a little. Keep very still, all you three. If you move I strike, and if you do not move I strike. Oh, foolish people, who killed my Nag!"

Teddy's eyes were fixed on his father, and all his father could do was to whisper, "Sit still, Teddy. You mustn't move. Teddy, keep still."

Then Rikki-tikki came up and cried: "Turn round, Nagaina; turn and fight!"

"All in good time," said she, without moving her eyes. "I will settle my account with *you* presently. Look at your friends, Rikki-tikki. They are still and white; they are afraid. They dare not move, and if you come a step nearer I strike."

"Look at your eggs," said Rikki-tikki, "in the melon-bed near the wall. Go and look, Nagaina."

The big snake turned half round, and saw the egg on the verandah. "Ah-h! Give it to me," she said.

Rikki-tikki put his paws one on each side of the egg, and his eyes were blood-red. "What price for a snake's egg? For a young cobra? For a young king-cobra? For the last—the very last of the brood? The ants are eating all the others down by the melon-bed."

Nagaina spun clear round, forgetting everything for the sake of the one egg; and Rikki-tikki saw Teddy's father shoot out a big hand, catch Teddy by the shoulder, and drag him across the little table with the teacups, safe and out of reach of Nagaina.

"Tricked! Tricked! Tricked! *Rikk-tck-tck!*" chuckled Rikki-tikki. "The boy is safe, and it was I—I—I that caught Nag by the hood last night in the bath-room." Then he began to jump up and down, all four feet together, his head close to the floor. "He threw me to and fro, but he could not shake me off. He was dead before the big man blew him in two. I did it. *Rikki-tikki-tck-tck!* Come then, Nagaina. Come and fight with me. You shall not be a widow long."

Nagaina saw that she had lost her chance of killing Teddy, and the egg lay between Rikki-tikki's paws. "Give me the egg, Rikki-tikki. Give me the last of my eggs, and I will go away and never come back," she said, lowering her hood.

"Yes, you will go away, and you will never come back; for you will go to the rubbish-heap with Nag. Fight, widow! The big man has gone for his gun! Fight!"

Rikki-tikki was bounding all round Nagaina, keeping just out of reach of her stroke, his little eyes like hot coals. Nagaina gathered herself together, and flung out at him. Rikki-tikki jumped up and backward. Again and again and again she struck, and each time her head came with a whack on the matting of the verandah, and she gathered herself together like a watch-spring. Then Rikki-tikki danced in a circle to get behind her, and Nagaina spun round to keep her head to his head, so that the rustle of her tail on the matting sounded like dry leaves blown along by the wind.

He had forgotten the egg. It still lay on the verandah, and Nagaina came nearer and nearer to it, till at last, while Rikki-tikki was drawing breath, she caught it in her mouth, turned to the verandah steps, and flew like an arrow down the path, with Rikki-tikki behind her. When the cobra runs for her life, she goes like a whiplash flicked across a horse's neck.

Rikki-tikki knew that he must catch her, or all the trouble would begin again. She headed straight for the long grass by the thorn-bush, and as he was running Rikki-tikki heard Darzee still singing his foolish little song of triumph. But Darzee's wife was wiser. She flew off her nest as Nagaina came along, and flapped her wings about Nagaina's head. If Darzee had helped they might have turned her; but Nagaina only lowered her hood and went on. Still, the instant's delay brought Rikki-tikki up to her, and as she plunged into the rathole where she and Nag used to live, his little white teeth were clenched on her tail, and he went down with her—and very few mongooses, however wise and old they may be, care to follow a cobra into its hole. It was dark in the hole; and Rikki-tikki never knew when it might open out and give Nagaina room to turn and strike at him. He held on savagely, and struck out his feet to act as brakes on the dark slope of the hot, moist earth.

Then the grass by the mouth of the hole stopped waving, and Darzee said: "It is all over with Rikki-tikki! We must sing his death song. Valiant Rikki-tikki is dead! For Nagaina will surely kill him underground."

So he sang a very mournful song that he made up on the spur of the minute, and just as he got to the most touching part the grass quivered again, and Rikki-tikki, covered with dirt, dragged himself out of the hole leg by leg, licking his whiskers. Darzee stopped with a little shout. Rikki-tikki shook some of the dust out of his fur and sneezed.

"It is all over," he said. "The widow will never come out again." And the red ants that live between the grass stems heard him, and began to troop down one after another to see if he had spoken the truth.

Rikki-tikki curled himself up in the grass and slept where he was—slept and slept till it was late in the afternoon, for he had done a hard day's work.

"Now," he said, when he awoke, "I will go back to the house. Tell the Coppersmith, Darzee, and he will tell the garden that Nagaina is dead."

The Coppersmith is a bird who makes a noise exactly like the beating of a little hammer on a copper pot; and the reason he is always making it is because he is the town-crier to every Indian garden, and tells all the news to everybody who cares to listen. As Rikki-tikki went up the path, he heard his "attention" notes like a tiny dinner-gong; and then the steady "Ding-dong-tock! Nag is dead—dong! Nagaina is dead! Ding-dong-tock!" That set all the birds in the garden singing, and the frogs croaking; for Nag and Nagaina used to eat frogs as well as little birds.

When Rikki got to the house, Teddy and Teddy's mother (she still looked very white, for she had been fainting) and Teddy's father came out and almost cried over him; and that night he ate all that was given him till he could eat no more, and went to bed on Teddy's shoulder, where Teddy's mother saw him when she came to look late at night.

"He saved our lives and Teddy's life," she said to her husband. "Just think, he saved all our lives!"

Rikki-tikki woke up with a jump, for all the mongooses are light sleepers.

"Oh, it's you," said he. "What are you bothering for? All the cobras are dead; and if they weren't, I'm here."

Rikki-tikki had a right to be proud of himself; but he did not grow too proud, and he kept that garden as a mongoose should keep it, with tooth and jump and spring and bite, till never a cobra dared show its head inside the walls.

Hundreds of thousands of people
know C. S. Forester as the author of exciting sea stories.
However, very few admirers of the leading figure of those
stories, the heroic Hornblower, know that his creator also
wrote a most unlikely story for a not too likely reason.
Poo-Poo and the Dragons *was written because his wife
was away on a visit and their son was refusing to eat.*
"It was at the eleventh hour that Poo-Poo came to my rescue.
At each meal time I told the story of Poo-Poo's adventures
with the understanding that the moment the eating stopped,
the story stopped, and was not resumed until
the next mouthful went in."
It worked.
The stories begun to entertain a little boy while
he was eating eventually filled an entire book.
Here are three chapters from it.

Poo-Poo Finds a Dragon

From Poo-Poo and the Dragons

BY C. S. FORESTER
Illustrated by ROBERT J. LEE

ONCE THERE was a boy called Poo-Poo. His other names were HAROLD HEAVYSIDE BROWN, and it might be just as well to remember them. On Saturday morning Poo-Poo (what were his other names?) was wondering what to do, because all his friends were doing something else. First he tried to play inside the house, but his mother (her name was MRS. BROWN) turned him out because she wanted to do the cleaning. Then he went to play at the back of the house, but his father (and his name was MR. BROWN and he was a VERY CLEVER MAN) sent him away because, as he said, he did not feel like answering questions that morning, and then Poo-Poo (what were his other names?) found himself in the front of the house and wondering harder than ever what he should do. So he walked down the street a little way, and around the corner and along the road until he came to a vacant lot—which had a dragon on it.

He was a nice dragon, quite a fair size as dragons go,—something between a duck and a motor bus,—and he was running about in the long grass and swishing his tail and he looked rather like a dachshund who has been taking lessons from a polliwog, and he was not quite as brilliant as dragons sometimes are because he was only black and blue and purple and white and green and red and yellow and orange and violet and magenta with spots of other colors here and there.

The dragon was very pleased to see Poo-Poo (what were his other names?), and he came galloping up to him through the long grass and he skipped about and he swished his long tail and he shot out his long tongue, which would have looked like an eel if it had not looked like a slice of bacon, and he licked Poo-Poo's hand and then he galloped away and he came back and licked Poo-Poo's legs so that they tickled and he ran round in circles and he was a very friendly dragon indeed. So Poo-Poo patted him behind the ears and tried to stroke his back and found it was too spiky and he went on across the field with the dragon galloping round him. And at the far side of the field there was a little wooden building with a sign over it and on the sign were the words: MAXWELL MURRAY McINTOSH,

CHIMNEY POTS CONSTRUCTED.

Inside the building there was a man sitting in a chair making belts out of umbrella handles.

Now Poo-Poo was a very polite boy, so he went up to the man and said: "Excuse me."

And the man said, "Yes, I excuse you."

And Poo-Poo said, "Excuse me, Mr. McIntosh, but is this your dragon?"

And Mr. McIntosh said, "Now do I *look* like a man who has a dragon?"

And Poo-Poo said, "I've never seen anyone who did have a dragon."

"That's a very extraordinary thing," said Mr. McIntosh. "You can't have traveled very far."

"I think I'm going to, one of these days," said Poo-Poo.

"Well, I shan't stop you," said Mr. Mc-

27

Intosh. (Can you remember what Mr. McIntosh's first names were?)

"I should like to know the way home if you please," said Poo-Poo (remember he was always a very polite boy).

"Some think it's one way and some think it's the other," said Mr. McIntosh. "But the one thing to be sure of is that whichever way you go you'll think the other way was the right way. But go whichever way you like and you'll find that you'll come to another place."

"Thank you," said Poo-Poo, still being very polite and rubbing his leg where the dragon had licked it impatiently. "I'll try to remember that. Good morning." And Poo-Poo went on across the field with the dragon skipping and galumphing, clippety-clop round and round him.

And they came to a tremendous big ladder, and Poo-Poo started to climb it, and he had only got a little way up when the dragon came up the ladder with a tremendous rush after him and climbed straight onto Poo-Poo's shoulder, and then went on up the ladder in front of him.

Have you ever seen a dragon running up a ladder? It is one of the most surprising things you could see anywhere. He went up jumping, with all four feet at once, about six rungs at a time; and at every jump he made the ladder spring in and out and all the spines on his back went "rattle-rattle," and on the end of his tail there was a spike like a big arrowhead which shook in Poo-Poo's face every time the dragon made a jump, so that Poo-Poo had to hold on very tight to the ladder and shout up to the dragon:—

"Take your silly old tail out of my face and don't jump so much!"

Poo-Poo only had to say it once, and then the dragon coiled up his tail in a neat roll and walked up the ladder the way respectable dragons walk up a ladder, with Poo-Poo climbing up behind him and needing to puff a little bit as the ladder went on and on and on.

When they got to the top there was the end of a big iron pipe sticking out of the ground with a waterfall running into it. And the dragon drew his head in and made his neck very short and held his legs up close to his body and put his tail down underneath him and all the way along to the front so that he could hold the spike in his mouth, and when he had made himself look as much like a length of pole as any dragon can look, he tucked the front end of himself into the pipe and the water pushed him on and Poo-Poo came on after him. So they went swish down the length of the pipe with the water foaming all around them and it was a very exciting experience until they came out splash into the lake at the end. The dragon twirled his tail round and round so that it made the finest propeller you ever saw, and he went across that lake like lightning so that Poo-Poo had to swim very hard to keep up with him.

And at the other side the dragon scrambled out and shook himself and swung his tail about so that he made Poo-Poo quite wet with all the water he shook off himself. And they went along the street a little way and up another path, and before Poo-Poo could think where he was they were at the back door of his house and he was wondering what his mother would say about the dragon.

Poo-Poo Brings the Dragon Home

Poo-Poo's mother was in the kitchen beside the back door when Poo-Poo came in, and she said, "Oh, there you are," the way she often did say, and then she saw the dragon, and she said:—

"What have you brought that dragon home for?"

And Poo-Poo said, "I like him," and the dragon wagged his tail and squirmed and wriggled and started coming in through the door.

Poo-Poo's mother said: "We don't want dragons in this house."

And Poo-Poo said: "But he's a very nice dragon."

And Poo-Poo's mother said, "All the same, I don't want him in this house."

Then Poo-Poo's father came out, and he stopped and looked at the dragon as he squirmed and wriggled halfway through the door.

"Poo-Poo's brought a dragon home with him," said Poo-Poo's mother.

"That's what it looks like," said Poo-Poo's father. "Where did you find him, son?"

"He was on a vacant lot beside the house of the man who mends chimney pots," said Poo-Poo, "Mr.——Mr.——"

But Poo-Poo could not remember the name of the man who constructed chimney pots. I wonder if you can.

"Well," said Poo-Poo's father, "I think you'd better take him back where he came from."

"Oh," said Poo-Poo disappointed, "but I don't think he could possibly get up the pipe."

"Up the pipe?" said Poo-Poo's father.

"Well that was the way we came," said Poo-Poo.

This time it was Poo-Poo's father who

said "Oh!" And he felt in his pockets and brought out a cigarette and then he began to look for a match, and he felt first in his trouser pockets and then in his coat pockets and then he began to look around the room, and as he did that the dragon opened his mouth with a click like a cigarette lighter and a long flame came out of his mouth the way it does with dragons.

"That's very convenient," said Poo-Poo's father, lighting his cigarette.

And the dragon shut his mouth and put the flame out and wagged his tail with pleasure.

"There—you see?" said Poo-Poo. "Can't I keep him?"

"Not if your mother—" said Poo-Poo's father—"And don't you expect me to go into any argument about it because I've got all that lawn to mow, and I'm not in a fit state to argue."

And then Poo-Poo's father looked out of the kitchen window and he stopped suddenly and he took his cigarette out of his mouth and he said, "My golly!" And Poo-Poo's mother looked out of the window and Poo-Poo peeked round the door, and they saw that the dragon's long wriggling tail had mowed that lawn as close as a billiard table.

"Now there's something to be said for a dragon that can mow lawns," said Poo-Poo's father looking at Poo-Poo's mother. "I've always said I'd rather go to the dentist three times a week than mow lawns."

"But all the same we don't want any dragons here," said Poo-Poo's mother. "He'd only mean a lot of work and bother."

And while she said this the front half of the dragon that was in the kitchen door went on squirming and wriggling first this way and then the other.

"You see," said Poo-Poo's mother, "I just couldn't have a dragon in the house who did that."

But then she looked and she saw that the floor that the dragon had been wriggling on was polished up by the dragon's wriggles so brightly that you could see your face in it without stooping.

"Well," said Poo-Poo's mother, "that's very nice, but—"

"I'm sure he'll work very hard," said Poo-Poo. "Please let me keep him."

"Oh, very well," said Poo-Poo's mother.

And Poo-Poo began to jump about the floor and the dragon began to wriggle harder than ever until Poo-Poo's mother had to say, "Now stop it, this minute!"

"What shall we call him?" asked Poo-Poo.

"Well," said Poo-Poo's father (do you remember that he was a very clever man?), "he looks as if his name was HORATIO."

And he had no sooner said the name when the dragon nodded and smiled and was just going to start wriggling all over again, when he remembered Poo-Poo's mother and left off hurriedly.

"Yes," said Poo-Poo's father, "that's it. HORATIO HEAVYSIDE DRAGON. It's quite a good name."

(If I were you I should try to remember what the dragon's name is.)

"It's dinnertime," said Poo-Poo's mother, "and I don't know what dragons eat."

But of course Poo-Poo's father knew what dragons had for dinner.

"Oh—this and that," said Poo-Poo's father. "On Tuesdays they have to have the other thing, and on Fridays they have to have something else; and on Sundays, it's just as well to give them something different; and you must think up something new for Mondays and Wednesdays. On Saturdays it doesn't matter much, and on Thursdays they'll eat anything that's going."

"Well, that's all right then," said Poo-Poo's mother. "We'd better have dinner right away."

So they had dinner, and the dragon ate first one thing and then the other, and he had a second helping of something else, and he finished up with whatever there was, and his manners were as good as gold as he sat on the floor with his chin on the table and his tail stretching out through the door out into the street. And every time they called him Horatio (I hope you remember what his other names were) he nodded and smiled. Whenever Poo-Poo's father made a joke he laughed politely, and whenever Poo-Poo's mother wanted anything out of the kitchen he turned his head around and shot out his long neck and brought it in quicker than lightning.

Horatio Enjoys His Punishment

IN THE summertime Poo-Poo's mother used to like to have dinner in the garden. Poo-Poo used to like that, because in the garden somehow it was not quite such bad manners to get up and walk about between mouthfuls. Nobody stopped to ask Poo-Poo's father whether he liked it or not.

One day they were all having dinner in the garden when a man in a white apron came in by the garage and walked up towards them, and as soon as Horatio saw him he got up very quietly and went and hid behind a tree. "Good afternoon, folks," said the man with the white apron.

"Good afternoon," said Mr. Brown. "I seem to remember your face, but you will pardon me if I don't remember your name." (You see, although Mr. Brown was a very clever man he was not half as clever at remembering names as you are.)

"I am JAMES PONSONBY AUCHINLECK," said the man in the white apron, "and I am your grocer."

"Of course, Mr.—Mr.—Auchinleck," said Mr. Brown. "And what can we do for you today?"

"It's that dragon of yours," said Mr. Auchinleck very grimly.

"Oh dear," said Poo-Poo's mother. "I'm sure he's been doing something naughty."

"You're quite right, madam," said the grocer (whose name I expect you've forgotten already); "something very naughty indeed."

"What is it?" asked Poo-Poo's father.

"*He's been stealing watermelons,*" said the grocer, leaning forward so as to make quite sure Poo-Poo's father realized what a terrible thing this was.

"Has he indeed?" said Poo-Poo's father. "Here, Horatio, what have you got to say about this? . . . Horatio—bless my soul, where has that dragon gone?"

"He's hiding behind that tree," said Mr. Auchinleck (perhaps now you'll remember his name), "he knows perfectly well he's been doing what he shouldn't."

"Come out from there," said Poo-Poo's father. "I don't know what the world's coming to. First I have to have my dinner out of doors, and as if that wasn't bad enough, I have grocers and dragons and goodness knows what else coming to spoil it for me—what there is left to spoil after the wind has made it cold, and the ants have eaten half of it, and the twigs have fallen into the stew. Come here, Horatio."

And Horatio came out from behind the tree with his ears hanging down and his tail trailing along the ground.

"Now let's hear what you have to say, Mr. Auchinleck," said Poo-Poo's father, "now that Horatio is present to hear the accusation."

"Well," said Mr. Auchinleck, "this morning I was dusting my watermelons and putting them out, and I thought I put out three, and when I fetched another I found there were only two. And so I went and got another one, and when I came back there were still only two. And when I fetched another one, there were still only two. So I hid behind a pile of apples and I peeped out, and in a minute or two I saw a head come round the corner on a long neck, and then—snap—there was another watermelon gone. And that was

your dragon, Mr. Brown."

"Dragons can't ever resist watermelons," said Mr. Brown. "It says so in my encyclopedia. I ought to have thought of it at this time of year. What have you got to say about this, Horatio?"

Horatio never did have anything to say, but this time he clearly had less to say than ever: he just hung his head and looked down at the ground.

"There, you see?" said the grocer.

"I'm afraid I *do* see," said Mr. Brown sadly. "How many watermelons were missing?"

"I don't really know," said Mr. Auchinleck; "there you have me. I couldn't say for sure. But judging by those bulges in that dragon, we ought to be able to tell quickly enough."

"So we ought," said Mr. Brown. "Come here, Horatio."

And he began to try to count the bulges down Horatio's side, but of course dragons are terribly ticklish and the moment he began to do that, Horatio threw himself down on the ground and wriggled and struggled and lashed his tail about until Mr. Brown had to give it up.

"I'm afraid we'll never be able to find out, Mr. Auchinleck," said Poo-Poo's father. "What do you propose that we do? I'm afraid I can't offer to pay you for an unknown number of watermelons."

"Something must be done," said Mr. Auchinleck.

"Well, the only thing to do is to see what Horatio says," said Mr. Brown (you remember that he was a very clever man). "Horatio, did you have one watermelon?"

And Horatio shook his head as it hung down.

"Two?" said Mr. Brown. "Three? . . .

Four? . . . Five? . . ."

And each time Horatio shook his head and let it drop farther and farther down until at last Mr. Brown said, "Fourteen?"

And then Horatio nodded his head and looked very guilty indeed.

"Fourteen watermelons," said Mr. Auchinleck.

"Seeds and rind and all!" said Mrs. Brown, quite shocked.

"How much do fourteen watermelons cost?" asked Mr. Brown. "I shall have to stop it out of his pocket money."

"Well, I wasn't thinking of money," said Mr. Auchinleck. "I was thinking that perhaps the dragon would take it out in work. I'm a bit busy these days and I could do with a dragon helping me around the store."

"That's a very good idea," said Mr. Brown. "Fourteen watermelons—that means fourteen days' work. Horatio, you will start tomorrow and work for Mr. Auchinleck."

And that is just what Horatio had to do. He had to get up very early each morning and run down to the store. (Can you tell me what was the name written up on the top?) And as soon as he had tied his apron on, he was very busy indeed. You have no idea what a lot there is to be done in a grocery store. He had to crack all the apple nuts and take the apples out and stack them up in pyramids ready for sale, and he had to drop all the peas into the pods and stick the pods together, and he had to paint all the radishes red (sometimes he would miss one or two and people would find white radishes in the bunches just as you do).

He had to take all the artichoke leaves and stick them together the way you ex-pect to see artichokes, and he had to wrap the bananas up in their skins, and he had to put all the carrots into the pencil sharpener so as to put points on them. He had to dip the bunches of asparagus so as to make the ends green, and he had to roughen the tops of the cauliflower and make the green cabbages purple and the purple cabbages green, and roll up the celery stalks. The fire from his mouth was very useful for singeing the whiskers off the tomatoes so as to make them smooth. And when he had done all that, he had to sweep up all the mess he had made (which was simply terrific)—although he did it quickly enough with his tail.

When Mr. Auchinleck was tying up a parcel, poor Horatio had to be handy so that Mr. Auchinleck could cut the string on the sharp part of his back. Horatio had to deliver groceries to people's houses. And he had to help unload the trucks; and then whenever he had any spare time he could always use it sawing up the packing cases for kindling with the sharp edge of his tail.

One way and another, Horatio was kept pretty busy all the time he was working for the grocer (whose name of course you remember). And Poo-Poo saw very little of him, and was quite unhappy.

But the fourteen days that Horatio had to work came to an end at last, and Mr. Auchinleck said to him:—

"We must celebrate this occasion. Let's go next door and have an ice-cream soda."

And so they went next door, and Mr. Auchinleck said to MR. QUENTIN FAZACKELY (that was the name of the man who owned the soda fountain):—

"Set 'em up, Mr. Fazackely. This is a great day and I don't mind the expense."

So Mr. Fazackely made up a great big double-dip ice-cream soda for Horatio, and Mr. Auchinleck had a smaller one, and he and Horatio picked up their glasses—and Mr. Auchinleck said:—

"Skin off your nose and mud in your eye!"

And they drank their sodas off quick like pioneers.

It's a great sight to see a dragon drinking an ice-cream soda. When the ice-cream and the cold soda get right down inside where the fire is, there is a bubbling and a hissing and a steaming, and

with this big ice-cream soda, the hissing was just terrific, and Horatio disappeared for a moment in the clouds of steam that surrounded him. The man behind the counter (people who knew him slightly used to call him Quentin Fazackely, but Mrs. Fazackely usually called him Q, which was much more convenient) peered at Horatio through the cloud of steam and said:—

"My golly, does that always happen when you drink a soda?"

And Horatio nodded proudly, and Mr. Auchinleck said:—

"Yes, he's a very remarkable dragon indeed."

Because during the last fourteen days Mr. Auchinleck had grown very fond of Horatio, and was proud of him as well.

"I would like to see it happen again," said Q. (That was what his wife called him, but of course you know better.) And he started in and mixed another double-dip ice-cream soda with pineapple flavoring and strawberry and rocky road ice cream, and he pushed it across the counter to Horatio. And Horatio didn't mind at all. He picked up the glass, and anybody could see that if he had been able to talk he would have said:—

"Skin off your nose and mud in your eye!"

And then up went the glass and down went the soda, and once again there was such a hissing and a bubbling and clouds of steam, as if every fire brigade in the country were trying to put out every fire there had been for the last six months.

"That's quite an advertisement for your ice-cream soda," said Mr. Auchinleck to Mr. Fazackely. And Mr. Fazackely said:—

"Yes, I was thinking much the same sort of thing, in fact I have a very great idea."

He turned and looked at Horatio again very earnestly.

"It looks to me," he said, "as if you liked ice-cream sodas."

And Horatio nodded his head, so Mr. Fazackely went on.

"How would you like all the ice-cream sodas you could drink?"

And Horatio nodded his head more eagerly than ever. So Mr. Fazackely went on:—

"The idea I've got is that you should sit in the window here where people in the street can see you, and whenever there's a little crowd around there, you drink a soda for them to see what happens."

And Horatio nodded again, and so it was settled. And Mr. Fazeckely hurriedly made out a big poster like this:—

FAZACKELY'S SODAS

Watch and see! This is the way they cool this dragon. Just imagine what they'll do to you!!!

And he went outside and hung it over the window, and Horatio settled down behind the glass. And all this of course was very naughty of Horatio, because he was supposed to go straight home every night after working for the grocer and

Poo-Poo's mother was growing quite worried about him.

But Mr. Fazackely's experiment was a very successful one indeed, because quite a big crowd collected in front of the window, and Mr. Fazackely was kept very busy making ice-cream sodas, and every time Horatio drank one there was a big "Oo—oo—oo—" from the crowd just as if a rocket had gone up, and more and more people came into the shop for ice-cream sodas.

After a time, Mrs. Brown at home said to Poo-Poo's father:—

"It's nearly bedtime, and I'm worried about that dragon."

And Mr. Brown said, "Bother the dragon, can't I sit and be peaceful for the first time today? And without having to worry about a dragon?" But all the same he got out of his armchair, and Poo-Poo and he and Mrs. Brown all got into the car and drove down the hill to Mr. Auchinleck's shop to see what had happened to Horatio. As they turned the corner, Poo-Poo said:

"Just look at that crowd outside the soda fountain." And Mr. Brown said:—

"I shouldn't be surprised if that young vagabond of a dragon hasn't got something to do with that."

And of course Mr. Brown was right, the way he always was, being a very clever man, because when they parked the car and found the crowd, they could see Horatio behind the window in a cloud of steam. And as they watched, Mr. Fazackely gave Horatio another ice-cream soda, and Horatio upped with the glass and downed with the soda; but this time there was not nearly so much sizzling and steaming, and Mr. Brown said:—

"This is very serious indeed."

And he started to make his way through the crowd and into the soda fountain, with Mrs. Brown behind him, and Poo-Poo behind Mrs. Brown.

Mr. Fazackely had been very disappointed at the poor results of the last ice-cream soda, and hurriedly mixed another one, so that Horatio could really show what he could do; and he was just giving it to Horatio when Mr. Brown came round behind the counter through the crowd and said, "Stop!" very loudly, and took away the glass just before Horatio could take hold of it.

Mr. Brown was very angry indeed, in fact Poo-Poo had never seen him so angry before.

"You've been taking advantage of the innocence of a poor, dumb dragon," said Mr. Brown to Mr. Fazackely.

"And as for you, Horatio, I thought you had more sense. Don't you know there's a limit to what the best-constructed dragon can stand? Supposing you had put your fire out? Where would you have been then? As it is, I don't expect there's much left of it. Let's see if you can light my cigarette for me."

Horatio looked very ashamed, and he clicked open his mouth, and he clicked it open again, and he clicked it open again, and everybody grew more and more worried until at last, when they had given up hope, there was just a little tiny gleam of flame right down inside, which you could only just see when you peeped down him.

"There, you see?" said Mr. Brown, looking angrily at Mr. Fazackely. And there was quite a murmur through the crowd.

"I've a good mind to tell the Society for

the Prevention of Cruelty to Animals about you," said Mr. Brown; "but still, I suppose it was only ignorance. But don't you ever let me find you giving dragons more than seven ice-cream sodas again, because then there'll be no excuse for you. Come along, Horatio."

And so they went out of the shop, and Horatio was all shivering and shaking with the cold of the ice cream inside, and his skin was all out in gooseflesh.

"There isn't a moment to spare," said Mr. Brown. "Run home as fast as you can, and when you get there, turn around and run back again to meet us, and then run home again, and so on until we get there. Go on, run!"

So Horatio went galloping up the street as fast as ever he could, and Mr. Brown and Poo-Poo and his mother got in the car, and Mr. Brown stepped right on the gas, and up the hill he went. And halfway up they met Horatio tearing down again, and he skidded to a stop with his claws tearing up the road, and spun around and knocked down a lampost with his tail ("I hope nobody notices that," said Mr. Brown), and went dashing up the hill again in front of the car, and down again and up again until at last they reached home. And there was Horatio, stretched out on the lawn with his sides heaving and his tongue hanging out, and great puffs of smoke coming out of his mouth, so that Mr. Brown was able to say:—

"That's all right. Let this be a lesson to you, young Horatio Heavyside Dragon."

(You see Mr. Brown was a very clever man, and could always remember what the dragon's name was.)

*Mary Poppins is the leading character in a wonderful book
called Mary Poppins. It is difficult to explain
much about her because she is a most mysterious person.
She appeared mysteriously—the East wind brought her
to the house of Jane and Michael Banks—
and she stayed as their nursemaid.*

*Everything that happened while she lived with them
was as unexpected and queer as she looked and was.
She was not exactly a witch but a kind of present-day
magic-maker, and what she did was always exciting,
sometimes frightening, and also glorious fun.
"Laughing Gas," the story of a visit to Mary Poppins' uncle,
is one of the many amazing adventures in this
remarkable book.*

Laughing Gas

From Mary Poppins

BY P. L. TRAVERS

Illustrated by MARY SHEPARD

"ARE YOU quite sure he will be at home?" said Jane, as they got off the Bus, she and Michael and Mary Poppins.

"Would my Uncle ask me to bring you to tea if he intended to go out, I'd like to know?" said Mary Poppins, who was evidently very offended by the question. She was wearing her blue coat with the silver buttons and the blue hat to match, and on the days when she wore these it was the easiest thing in the world to offend her.

All three of them were on the way to pay a visit to Mary Poppins's uncle, Mr. Wigg, and Jane and Michael had looked forward to the trip for so long that they were more than half afraid that Mr. Wigg might not be in, after all.

"Why is he called Mr. Wigg—does he wear one?" asked Michael, hurrying along beside Mary Poppins.

"He is called Mr. Wigg because Mr. Wigg is his name. And he doesn't wear one. He is bald," said Mary Poppins.

"And if I have any more questions we will just go Back Home." And she sniffed her usual sniff of displeasure.

Jane and Michael looked at each other and frowned. And the frown meant: "Don't let's ask her anything else or we'll never get there."

Mary Poppins put her hat straight at the Tobacconist's Shop at the corner. It had one of those curious windows where there seem to be three of you instead of one, so that if you look long enough at them you begin to feel you are not yourself but a whole crowd of somebody else. Mary Poppins sighed with pleasure, however, when she saw three of herself, each wearing a blue coat with silver buttons and a blue hat to match. She thought it was such a lovely sight that she wished there had been a dozen of her or even thirty. The more Mary Poppins the better.

"Come along," she said sternly, as though they had kept *her* waiting. Then they turned the corner and pulled the bell of Number Three, Robertson Road. Jane and Michael could hear it faintly echoing from a long way away and they knew that in one minute, or two at the most, they would be having tea with Mary Poppins's uncle, Mr. Wigg, for the first time ever.

"If he's in, of course," Jane said to Michael in a whisper.

At that moment the door flew open and a thin, watery-looking lady appeared.

"Is he in?" said Michael quickly.

"I'll thank you," said Mary Poppins, giving him a terrible glance, "to let *me* do the talking."

"How do you do, Mrs. Wigg," said Jane politely.

"Mrs. Wigg!" said the thin lady, in a voice even thinner than herself. "How dare you call me Mrs. Wigg? No, thank you! I'm plain Miss Persimmon *and* proud of it. Mrs. Wigg indeed!" She seemed to be quite upset, and they thought Mr. Wigg must be a very odd person if Miss Persimmon was so glad not to be Mrs. Wigg.

"Straight up and first door on the landing," said Miss Persimmon, and she went hurrying away down the passage saying: "Mrs. Wigg indeed!" to herself in a high, thin, outraged voice.

Jane and Michael followed Mary Poppins upstairs. Mary Poppins knocked at the door.

"Come in! Come in! And welcome!" called a loud, cheery voice from inside. Jane's heart was pitter-pattering with excitement.

"He *is* in!" she signalled to Michael with a look.

Mary Poppins opened the door and pushed them in front of her. A large cheerful room lay before them. At one end of it a fire was burning brightly and in the centre stood an enormous table laid for tea—four cups and saucers, piles of bread and butter, crumpets, coconut cakes and a large plum cake with pink icing.

"Well, this is indeed a Pleasure," a huge voice greeted them, and Jane and Michael looked round for its owner. He was nowhere to be seen. The room appeared to be quite empty. Then they heard Mary Poppins saying crossly:

"Oh, Uncle Albert—not *again*? It's not your birthday, is it?"

And as she spoke she looked up at the ceiling. Jane and Michael looked up too and to their surprise saw a round, fat, bald man who was hanging in the air without holding on to anything. Indeed, he appeared to be *sitting* on the air, for his legs were crossed and he had just put down the newspaper which he had been reading when they came in.

"My dear," said Mr. Wigg, smiling down at the children, and looking apologetically at Mary Poppins, "I'm very sorry, but I'm afraid it *is* my birthday."

"Tch, tch, tch!" said Mary Poppins.

"I only remembered last night and there was no time to send you a postcard asking you to come another day. Very distressing, isn't it?" he said, looking down at Jane and Michael.

"I can see you're rather surprised," said Mr. Wigg. And, indeed, their mouths were so wide open with astonishment that Mr. Wigg, if he had been a little smaller, might almost have fallen into one of them.

"I'd better explain, I think," Mr. Wigg went on calmly. "You see, it's this way. I'm a cheerful sort of man and very disposed to laughter. You wouldn't believe, either of you, the number of things that strike me as being funny. I can laugh at pretty nearly everything, I can."

And with that Mr. Wigg began to bob up and down, shaking with laughter at the thought of his own cheerfulness.

"Uncle Albert!" said Mary Poppins, and Mr. Wigg stopped laughing with a jerk.

"Oh, beg pardon, my dear. Where was I? Oh, yes. Well, the funny thing about me is—all right, Mary, I won't laugh if I can help it!—that whenever my birthday falls on a Friday, well, it's all up with me. Absolutely U.P.," said Mr. Wigg.

"But why——?" began Jane.

"But how——?" began Michael.

"Well, you see, if I laugh on that particular day I become so filled with Laughing Gas that I simply can't keep on the ground. Even if I smile it happens. The first funny thought, and I'm up like a balloon. And until I can think of something serious I can't get down again." Mr. Wigg began to chuckle at that, but he caught sight of Mary Poppins's face and stopped the chuckle, and continued:

"It's awkward, of course, but not unpleasant. Never happens to either of you, I suppose?"

Jane and Michael shook their heads.

"No, I thought not. It seems to be my own special habit. Once, after I'd been to the Circus the night before, I laughed so much that—would you believe it?—I was up here for a whole twelve hours, and couldn't get down till the last stroke of midnight. Then, of course, I came down with a flop because it was Saturday and not my birthday any more. It's rather odd, isn't it? Not to say funny?

"And now here it is Friday again and my birthday, and you two and Mary P. to visit me. Oh, Lordy, Lordy, don't make me laugh, I beg of you——" But although Jane and Michael had done nothing very amusing, except to stare at him in astonishment, Mr. Wigg began to laugh again loudly, and as he laughed he went bouncing and bobbing about in the air, with the newspaper rattling in his hand and his spectacles half on and half off his nose.

He looked so comic, floundering in the air like a great human bubble, clutching at the ceiling sometimes and sometimes at the gas-bracket as he passed it, that

Jane and Michael, though they were trying hard to be polite, just couldn't help doing what they did. They laughed. *And* they laughed. They shut their mouths tight to prevent the laughter escaping, but that didn't do any good. And presently they were rolling over and over on the floor, squealing and shrieking with laughter.

"Really!" said Mary Poppins. "Really, *such* behaviour!"

"I can't help it, I can't help it!" shrieked Michael as he rolled into the fender. "It's so terribly funny. Oh, Jane, *isn't* it funny?"

Jane did not reply, for a curious thing was happening to her. As she laughed she felt herself growing lighter and lighter, just as though she were being pumped full of air. It was a curious and delicious feeling and it made her want to laugh all the more. And then suddenly, with a bouncing bound, she felt herself jumping through the air. Michael, to his astonishment, saw her go soaring up through the room. With a little bump her head touched the ceiling and then she went bouncing along it till she reached Mr. Wigg.

"*Well!*" said Mr. Wigg, looking very surprised indeed. "Don't tell me it's *your* birthday, too?" Jane shook her head.

"It's not? Then this Laughing Gas must be catching! Hi—whoa there, look out for the mantelpiece!" This was to Michael, who had suddenly risen from the floor and was swooping through the air, roaring with laughter, and just grazing the china ornaments on the mantelpiece as he passed. He landed with a bounce right on Mr. Wigg's knee.

"How do you do," said Mr. Wigg, heartily shaking Michael by the hand. "I call this really friendly of you—bless my soul, I do! To come up to me since I couldn't come down to you—eh?" And then he and Michael looked at each other and flung back their heads and simply howled with laughter.

"I say," said Mr. Wigg to Jane, as he wiped his eyes. "You'll be thinking I have the worst manners in the world. You're standing and you ought to be sitting—a nice young lady like you. I'm afraid I can't offer you a chair up here, but I think you'll find the air quite comfortable to sit on. I do."

Jane tried it and found she could sit down quite comfortably on the air. She took off her hat and laid it down beside her and it hung there in space without any support at all.

"That's right," said Mr. Wigg. Then he turned and looked down at Mary Poppins.

"Well, Mary, we're fixed. And now I can enquire about *you*, my dear. I must say, I am very glad to welcome you and my two young friends here today—why, Mary, you're frowning. I'm afraid you don't approve of—er—all this."

He waved his hand at Jane and Michael, and said hurriedly:

"I apologise, Mary, my dear. But you know how it is with me. Still, I must say I never thought my two young friends here would catch it, really I didn't, Mary! I suppose I should have asked them for another day or tried to think of something sad or something——"

"Well, I must say," said Mary Poppins primly, "that I have never in my life seen such a sight. And at your age, Uncle——"

"Mary Poppins, Mary Poppins, do come up!" interrupted Michael. "Think of something funny and you'll find it's quite easy."

"Ah, now do, Mary!" said Mr. Wigg persuasively.

"We're lonely up here without you!" said Jane, and held out her arms towards Mary Poppins. "*Do* think of something funny!"

"Ah, *she* doesn't need to," said Mr. Wigg sighing. "She can come up if she wants to, even without laughing—and she knows it." And he looked mysteriously and secretly at Mary Poppins as she stood down there on the hearth-rug.

"Well," said Mary Poppins, "it's all very silly and undignified, but, since you're all up there and don't seem able to get down, I suppose I'd better come up, too."

With that, to the surprise of Jane and Michael, she put her hands down at her sides and without a laugh, without even the faintest glimmer of a smile, she shot up in the air and sat down beside Jane.

"How many times, I should like to know," she said snappily, "have I told you to take off your coat when you come into a hot room?" And she unbuttoned Jane's coat and laid it neatly on the air beside the hat.

"That's right, Mary, that's right," said Mr. Wigg contentedly, as he leant down and put his spectacles on the mantelpiece. 'Now we're all comfortable——"

"There's comfort *and* comfort," sniffed Mary Poppins.

"And we can have tea," Mr. Wigg went on, apparently not noticing her remark. And then a startled look came over his face.

"My goodness!" he said. "How dreadful! I've just realised—that table's down there and we're up here. What *are* we going to do? We're here and it's there. It's an awful tragedy—awful! But oh, it's terribly comic!" And he hid his face in his handkerchief and laughed loudly into it. Jane and Michael, though they did not want to miss the crumpets and the cakes, couldn't help laughing too, because Mr. Wigg's mirth was so infectious.

Mr. Wigg dried his eyes.

"There's only one thing for it," he said. "We must think of something serious. Something sad, very sad. And then we shall be able to get down. Now—one, two, three! Something *very* sad, mind you!"

They thought and thought, with their chins on their hands.

Michael thought of school, and that one day he would have to go there. But even that seemed funny today and he had to laugh.

Jane thought: "I shall be grown up in another fourteen years!" But that didn't sound sad at all but quite nice and rather funny. She could not help smiling at the thought of herself grown up, with long skirts and a hand-bag.

"There was my poor old Aunt Emily," thought Mr. Wigg out loud. "She was run over by an omnibus. Sad. Very sad. Unbearably sad. Poor Aunt Emily. But they saved her umbrella. That was funny, wasn't it?" And before he knew where he was, he was heaving and trembling and bursting with laughter at the thought of Aunt Emily's umbrella.

"It's no good," he said, blowing his nose. "I give it up. And my young friends here seem to be no better at sadness than I am.

Mary, can't *you* do something? We want our tea."

To this day Jane and Michael cannot be sure of what happened then. All they know for certain is that, as soon as Mr. Wigg had appealed to Mary Poppins, the table below began to wriggle on its legs. Presently it was swaying dangerously, and then with a rattle of china and with cakes lurching off their plates on to the cloth, the table came soaring through the room, gave one graceful turn, and landed beside them so that Mr. Wigg was at its head.

"Good girl!" said Mr. Wigg, smiling proudly upon her. "I knew you'd fix something. Now, will you take the foot of the table and pour out, Mary? And the guests on either side of me. That's the idea," he said, as Michael ran bobbing through the air and sat down on Mr. Wigg's right. Jane was at his left hand. There they were, all together, up in the air and the table between them. Not a single piece of bread-and-butter or a lump of sugar had been left behind.

Mr. Wigg smiled contentedly.

"It is usual, I think, to begin with bread-and-butter," he said to Jane and Michael, "but as it's my birthday we will begin the wrong way—which I always think is the *right* way—with the Cake!"

And he cut a large slice for everybody.

"More tea?" he said to Jane. But before she had time to reply there was a quick, sharp knock at the door.

"Come in!" called Mr. Wigg.

The door opened, and there stood Miss Persimmon with a jug of hot water on a tray.

"I thought, Mr. Wigg," she began, looking searchingly round the room, "you'd be wanting some more hot —— Well, I never! I simply *never*!" she said, as she caught sight of them all seated on the air round the table. "Such goings on I never did see. In all my born days I never saw such. I'm sure, Mr. Wigg, I always knew *you* were a bit odd. But I've closed my eyes to it—being as how you paid your rent regular. But such behavior as this—having tea in the air with your guests—Mr. Wigg, sir, I'm astonished at you! It's that undignified, and for a gentleman of your age—I never did——"

"But perhaps you will, Miss Persimmon!" said Michael.

"Will what?" said Miss Persimmon haughtily.

"Catch the Laughing Gas, as we did," said Michael.

Miss Persimmon flung back her head scornfully.

"I hope, young man," she retorted, "I have more respect for myself than to go bouncing about in the air like a rubber ball on the end of a bat. I'll stay on my own feet, thank you, or my name's not Amy Persimmon, and—oh dear, oh *dear*, my goodness, oh *DEAR*—what *is* the matter? I can't walk, I'm going, I—oh, help, *HELP*!"

For Miss Persimmon quite against her will, was off the ground and was stumbling through the air, rolling from side to side like a very thin barrel, balancing the tray in her hand. She was almost weeping with distress as she arrived at the table and put down her jug of hot water.

"Thank you," said Mary Poppins in a calm, very polite voice.

Then Miss Persimmon turned and went wafting down again, murmuring as she went: "So undignified—and me a well-behaved, steady-going woman. I must see a doctor——"

When she touched the floor, she ran hurriedly out of the room, wringing her hands, and not giving a single glance backwards.

"So undignified!" they heard her moaning as she shut the door behind her.

"Her name can't be Amy Persimmon, because she *didn't* stay on her own feet!" whispered Jane to Michael.

But Mr. Wigg was looking at Mary Poppins — a curious look, half-amused, half-accusing.

"Mary, Mary, you shouldn't—bless my soul, you shouldn't, Mary. The poor old body will never get over it. But, oh, my Goodness, didn't she look funny waddling through the air—my Gracious Goodness, didn't she?"

And he and Jane and Michael went off again, rolling about the air, clutching their sides and gasping with laughter at the thought of how funny Miss Persimmon had looked.

"Oh dear!" said Michael. "Don't make me laugh any more. I can't stand it! I shall break!"

"Oh, oh, oh!" cried Jane, as she gasped for breath, with her hand over her heart. "Oh, my Gracious, Glorious, Galumphing Goodness!" roared Mr. Wigg, dabbing his eyes with the tail of his coat because he couldn't find his handkerchief.

"IT IS TIME TO GO HOME." Mary Poppin's voice sounded above the roars of laughter like a trumpet.

And suddenly, with a rush, Jane and Michael and Mr. Wigg came down. They landed on the floor with a huge bump, all together. The thought that they would have to go home was the first sad thought of the afternoon, and the moment it was in their minds the Laughing Gas went out of them.

Jane and Michael sighed as they watched Mary Poppins come slowly down the air, carrying Jane's coat and hat.

Mr. Wigg sighed, too. A great, long, heavy sigh.

"Well, isn't that a pity?" he said soberly. "It's very sad that you've got to go home. I never enjoyed an afternoon so much—did you?"

"Never," said Michael sadly, feeling how dull it was to go down on the earth again with no Laughing Gas inside him.

"Never, never," said Jane, as she stood on tiptoe and kissed Mr. Wigg's withered-apple cheeks. "Never, never, never, never . . . !"

They sat on either side of Mary Poppins going home in the Bus. They were both very quiet, thinking over the lovely afternoon. Presently Michael said sleepily to Mary Poppins:

"How often does your Uncle get like that?"

"Like what?" said Mary Poppins sharply, as though Michael had deliberately said something to offend her.

"Well—all bouncy and boundy and laughing and going up in the air."

"Up in the air?" Mary Poppin's voice was high and angry. "What do you mean, pray, up in the air?"

Jane tried to explain.

"Michael means—is your Uncle often full of Laughing Gas, and does he often go rolling and bobbing about on the ceiling when——"

"Rolling and bobbing! The idea! Rolling and bobbing on the ceiling! I'm ashamed of you for suggesting such a thing!" Mary Poppins was obviously *very* offended.

"But he did!" said Michael. "We saw him."

"What, roll and bob? How dare you! I'll have you know that my uncle is a sober, honest, hardworking man, and you'll be kind enough to speak of him respectfully. And don't bite your Bus ticket. Roll and bob, indeed—the idea!"

Michael and Jane looked across Mary Poppins at each other. They said nothing, for they had learnt that it was better not to argue with Mary Poppins, no matter how odd anything seemed.

But the look that passed between them said: "Is it true or isn't it? About Mr. Wigg. Is Mary Poppins right or are we?"

But there was nobody to give them the right answer.

The Bus roared on, wildly lurching and bounding.

Mary Poppins sat between them, offended and silent, and presently, because they were very tired, they crept closer to her and leant up against her sides and fell asleep, still wondering. . . .

None of Jane and Michael's adventures is like any other, for Mary Poppins is full of surprises. When you finish Mary Poppins' first book, you can find many more astonishing happenings in Mary Poppins Comes Back, Mary Poppins Opens the Door, and Mary Poppins in the Park.

*Many stories have meanings
beyond the tales themselves.
They show the reader new ways of looking at things
and teach him deeper understanding.
This is one of them.*

Molly Cottontail

BY ERSKINE CALDWELL

Illustrated by GLORIA KAMEN

JOHNNY'S AUNT Nellie had come down South to visit his parents and they were all sitting around the fireplace talking. Aunt Nellie did most of the talking, and Johnny's mother did the rest of it. His father came in occasionally for a few minutes at a time and then went out again to walk around the house and sit in the barnyard. He and Aunt Nellie did not get along together at all. Aunt Nellie was sure she was smarter than anybody else and Johnny's father did not want to get into an argument with her and lose his temper.

Aunt Nellie's husband had gone down to Florida on a hunting trip and she came as far as Carolina while he was away. Johnny's uncle was crazy about hunting and spent all his spare time away from home gunning for game.

"Bess," Aunt Nellie asked Johnny's mother, "does Johnny like to hunt?" She nodded impersonally toward him where he sat by the fireplace.

50

His mother said he did not. And that was true. He liked to catch rabbits and squirrels for pets, but he did not want to kill them. He had a pet hen right then. She had been run over by a buggy wheel when she was growing up and one of her legs was broken.

Johnny hid her in the barn so his father would not know about her. She stayed there about two weeks and when the leg healed he let her out in the yard with the other chickens. When his father did find her he said she would not have to be killed if Johnny would take care of her and feed her because she could not scratch for worms like the other chickens. Her leg healed all right, but it was crooked and she limped with every step.

"Well," Aunt Nellie said to Johnny's mother, "that is a shame. If he doesn't like to hunt he won't grow up to be a real Southern gentleman."

"But, Nellie," his mother protested for him, "Johnny does not like to kill things."

"Nonsense," Aunt Nellie said. "Any man who is a real Southern gentleman likes to hunt. The Lord only knows what he will turn out to be."

Johnny knew his father would have taken up for him too if he had been in the room just then. His father did not like to kill things either.

"I'm disappointed in having a nephew who is not a real Southern gentleman. He will never be one if he never goes hunting." Aunt Nellie always talked a long time about the same thing once she got started.

Johnny was not greatly interested in being a real Southern gentleman when he grew up, but he did not want her to talk about him that way. Every summer she wrote his mother a letter inviting him up to her home in Maryland, and he wanted to go again this year.

When Johnny's father came in and heard what she said he went out in the back yard and threw pebbles against the barnside.

Johnny went into the dining room where the shotgun was kept and took it off the rack. The gun was fired off to scare crows when they came down in the spring to pull up the corn sprouts in the new ground. Johnny's father never aimed to kill the crows: he merely fired off the shotgun to make the crows so gun-shy they would not come back to the cornfield.

Taking the shotgun and half a dozen shells, Johnny went out the front door without anybody seeing him leave. He went down the road towards the schoolhouse at the crossroads. He had seen dozens of rabbits down at the first creek every time he went to school and came home. They were large rabbits with gray backs and white undercoats. All of them had long thin ears and a ball of white fur on their tails. He liked them a lot.

At the first creek he stopped on the bridge and rested against the railing. In a few minutes he saw two rabbits hop across the road ahead. Picking up the gun, he started after them. A hundred yards from the bridge the road had been cut down into the hill and the banks on each side were fifteen and twenty feet high. At this time of year, when there was nearly always a heavy frost each morning, the bank facing the south was the warmer one because the sun shone against it most of the day. Johnny had seen several rabbits sitting in holes in the bank and he was sure that was where these rabbits were going now.

Sure enough, when he got there a large gray-furred rabbit was sitting on the sunny bank, backed into a hole. When Johnny saw the rabbit he raised the shotgun to his shoulder and took good aim. The rabbit blinked her eyes and chewed a piece of grass she had found under a log somewhere. Johnny was then only ten or twelve feet away, but he thought he had better get closer so that he would be certain to kill her. He would take the rabbit home and show her to his aunt. He wanted her to invite him to spend the summer at her house again.

Johnny edged closer and closer to the rabbit until he stood in the drain ditch only three feet from her. She blinked her eyes and chewed on the grass. He hated to kill her because she looked as if she

wanted to live and sit on the sunny bank chewing grass always. But his Aunt Nellie thought a boy should be a sportsman and kill everything in sight.

There was nothing else he could do. He would have to shoot the poor rabbit and take her back for his aunt to see.

He took steady aim along the center of the doubled-barreled shotgun, shut both his eyes, and pulled the triggers one after the other.

When he opened his eyes the rabbit was still sitting there looking at him. He was so glad after the gun went off that the rabbit was not dead that he dropped the gun and crawled up the bank and caught the rabbit by her long ears. He lifted her in his arms and held her tightly so she could not run away. She was so frightened by the gunshots she was trembling all over like a whipped dog.

When he held her in his arms she snuggled her nose against his sweater and stopped quivering while he stroked her fur.

Holding the rabbit tight in his right arm, he picked up the shotgun and ran home as fast as he could.

His father was still sitting in the back yard when he got there.

"What's that you've got under your arm?" he asked.

"A rabbit," Johnny told him.

"How did you catch it?"

"I shot at her and missed her. Then I caught her by the ears and brought her home."

"Look here, Johnny," he said. "You didn't shoot at that rabbit while it was sitting down, did you?"

"I guess I did," Johnny admitted, adding hastily, "but I didn't hit her, anyway."

"Well it's a good thing you didn't hit it. A good sportsman never shoots at a rabbit when it is sitting down. A good sportsman never shoots at a bird until it flies. A real sportsman always gives the game he is after a chance for its life."

"But Aunt Nellie said I had to kill something and she didn't say not to kill things standing still."

"You stop paying any attention to your Aunt Nellie. She doesn't know what she's talking about, anyway."

Johnny let his father hold the rabbit while he fixed a box to keep her in. When it was ready he put her in it and shut her up tight.

"What are you going to do with the rabbit?" Johnny's father asked him.

"Keep her."

"I wouldn't put her in a box," he said with a queer look on his face. "If it wants to stay it won't run off. And if it doesn't want to stay it will worry itself to death in that box all the time. Turn it loose and let's see what it will do."

Johnny was afraid to turn his rabbit loose because he did not want her to run away. But his father knew a lot more about rabbits then he did. Just then Aunt Nellie and his mother came out on the back porch.

"What have you got there in the box?" Aunt Nellie asked him.

"A rabbit," Johnny said.

"Where did you get it?"

"I shot at her with the gun, but I didn't hit her and she didn't run away, so I brought her home."

His aunt turned to his mother in disgust.

"There you are, Bess! What did I tell you?"

Johnny did not hear what his mother said. But his father got up and went down to the barn. Aunt Nellie went into the house and slammed shut the door behind her. Johnny's mother stood looking at him for several minutes as if he had done the right thing after all.

Taking the rabbit out of the box, he went down to the barn where his father was. He was sitting against the barnside shelling an ear of corn for half a dozen chickens around him. Johnny sat down beside him and turned the rabbit loose. The rabbit hopped around and around and then sat down and looked at them.

"Why don't you name it Molly Cottontail?" Johnny's father suggested, throwing a handful of shelled corn to the chickens.

"What does that mean?" Johnny asked.

"There are two kinds of rabbits around here: jack rabbits and molly cottontails. That one has a cottontail—see the ball of white fur on its tail that looks like a ball of cotton?"

The rabbit hopped around and around again and sat down on her cottontail. The chickens were not afraid of her. They went right up to where she sat and scratched for corn just as if she were a chicken too.

"Why don't you go into the garden and get a head of lettuce for it? Get a good tender one out of the hotbed. All rabbits like lettuce," Johnny's father said.

Johnny got the lettuce and gave it to his rabbit. She hopped up to where they sat against the barnside, asking for more. Johnny gave her all he had and she ate out of his hand.

"If you had killed that rabbit with the gun you would be sorry now," his father said. Anybody could see that he was beginning to like the rabbit a lot.

She hopped around and around in front of them, playing with the chickens. The chickens liked her, too.

"I'd lots rather have her living than dead," Johnny said.

Molly hopped up between them and nibbled at Johnny's father's hand. He reached to stroke her fur with his hand, but she hopped away.

"Whoa there, sooky," he soothed, reaching for their rabbit.

"Eeyore's Birthday" is part of
a much-loved book called Winnie-the-Pooh.
The book is about a boy named Christopher Robin
and his living, animal-like toys. Pooh is really a teddy bear.
Piglet is, of course, a pig,
and Eeyore gets his name from the sound made by a donkey.
Pooh is a foolish little bear and
is always doing foolish things—
but in a most amusing manner.
Eeyore always looks on the sad side of things—
but in a very lovable way.
To Christopher Robin they are all dear companions.
They will be to you, too.

In Which Eeyore Has a Birthday and Gets Two Presents

From Winnie-the-Pooh

BY A. A. MILNE
Illustrated by E. H. SHEPARD

EEYORE, the old grey Donkey, stood by the side of the stream, and looked at himself in the water.

"Pathetic," he said. "That's what it is. Pathetic."

He turned and walked slowly down the stream for twenty yards, splashed across it, and walked slowly back on the other side. Then he looked at himself in the water again.

"As I thought," he said. "No better from *this* side. But nobody minds. Nobody cares. Pathetic, that's what it is."

There was a crackling noise in the bracken behind him, and out came Pooh.

"Good morning, Eeyore," said Pooh.

"Good morning, Pooh Bear," said Eeyore gloomily. "If it *is* a good morning," he said. "Which I doubt," said he.

"Why, what's the matter?"

"Nothing, Pooh Bear, nothing. We can't all, and some of us don't. That's all there is to it."

"Can't all *what*?" said Pooh, rubbing his nose.

"Gaiety. Song-and-dance. Here we go round the mulberry bush."

"Oh!" said Pooh. He thought for a long time, and then asked, "What mulberry bush is that?"

"Bon-hommy," went on Eeyore gloomily. "French word meaning bonhommy," he explained. "I'm not complaining, but There It Is."

Pooh sat down on a large stone, and tried to think this out. It sounded to him like a riddle, and he was never much good at riddles, being a Bear of Very Little Brain. So he sang *Cottleston Pie* instead:

> Cottleston, Cottleston, Cottleston Pie,
> A fly can't bird, but a bird can fly.
> Ask me a riddle and I reply:
> *"Cottleston, Cottleston, Cottleston Pie."*

That was the first verse. When he had finished it, Eeyore didn't actually say that he didn't like it, so Pooh very kindly sang the second verse to him:

> Cottleston, Cottleston, Cottleston Pie,
> A fish can't whistle and neither can I.
> Ask me a riddle and I reply:
> *"Cottleston, Cottleston, Cottleston Pie."*

Eeyore still said nothing at all, so Pooh hummed the third verse quietly to himself:

> Cottleston, Cottleston, Cottleston Pie,
> Why does a chicken, I don't know why.
> Ask me a riddle and I reply:
> *"Cottleston, Cottleston, Cottleston Pie."*

"That's right," said Eeyore. "Sing. Umty tiddly, umty-too. Here we go gathering Nuts and May. Enjoy yourself."

"I am," said Pooh.

"Some can," said Eeyore.

"Why, what's the matter?"

"*Is* anything the matter?"

"You seem so sad, Eeyore."

"Sad? Why should I be sad? It's my birthday. The happiest day of the year."

"Your birthday?" said Pooh in great surprise.

"Of course it is. Can't you see? Look at all the presents I have had." He waved a foot from side to side. "Look at the birthday cake. Candles and pink sugar."

Pooh looked—first to the right and then to the left.

"Presents?" said Pooh. "Birthday cake?" said Pooh. "*Where?*"

"Can't you see them?"

"No," said Pooh.

"Neither can I," said Eeyore. "Joke," he explained. "Ha ha!"

Pooh scratched his head, being a little puzzled by all this.

"But is it really your birthday?" he asked.

"It is."

"Oh! Well, many happy returns of the day, Eeyore."

"And many happy returns to you, Pooh Bear."

"But it isn't *my* birthday."

"No, it's mine."

"But you said 'Many happy returns'—"

"Well, why not? You don't always want to be miserable on my birthday, do you?"

"Oh, I see," said Pooh.

"It's bad enough," said Eeyore, almost breaking down, "being miserable myself, what with no presents and no cake and no candles, and no proper notice taken of me at all, but if everybody else is going to be miserable too—"

This was too much for Pooh. "Stay there!" he called to Eeyore, as he turned and hurried back home as quick as he could; for he felt that he must get poor Eeyore a present of *some* sort at once, and he could always think of a proper one afterwards.

Outside his house he found Piglet, jumping up and down trying to reach the knocker.

"Hallo, Piglet," he said.

"Hallo, Pooh," said Piglet.

"What are *you* trying to do?"

"I was trying to reach the knocker," said Piglet. "I just came round—"

"Let me do it for you," said Pooh kindly. So he reached up and knocked at the door. "I have just seen Eeyore," he began, "and poor Eeyore is in a Very Sad Condition, because it's his birthday, and nobody has taken any notice of it, and he's very Gloomy—you know what Eeyore is—and there he was, and— What a long time whoever lives here is answering this door."

And he knocked again.

"But Pooh," said Piglet, "it's your own house!"

"Oh!" said Pooh. "So it is," he said. "Well, let's go in."

So in they went. The first thing Pooh did was to go to the cupboard to see if he had quite a small jar of honey left; and he had, so he took it down.

"I'm giving this to Eeyore," he explained, "as a present. What are *you* going to give?"

"Couldn't I give it too?" said Piglet. "From both of us?"

"No," said Pooh. "That would *not* be a good plan."

"All right, then, I'll give him a balloon. I've got one left from my party. I'll go and get it now, shall I?"

"That, Piglet, is a *very* good idea. It is just what Eeyore wants to cheer him up. Nobody can be uncheered with a balloon."

So off Piglet trotted; and in the other direction went Pooh, with his jar of honey.

It was a warm day, and he had a long way to go. He hadn't gone more than half-way when a sort of funny feeling began to creep all over him. It began at the tip of his nose and trickled all through him and out at the soles of his feet. It was just as if somebody inside him were saying, "Now then, Pooh, time for a little something."

"Dear, dear," said Pooh, "I didn't know it was as late as that." So he sat down and took the top off his jar of honey. "Lucky I brought this with me," he thought. "Many a bear going out on a warm day like this would never have thought of bringing a little something with him." And he began to eat.

"Now let me see," he thought, as he took his last lick of the inside of the jar, "where was I going? Ah, yes, Eeyore." He got up slowly.

And then, suddenly, he remembered. He had eaten Eeyore's birthday present!

"*Bother!*" said Pooh. "What *shall* I do? I *must* give him *something.*"

For a little while he couldn't think of anything. Then he thought: "Well, it's a very nice pot, even if there's no honey in it, and if I washed it clean, and got somebody to write 'A *Happy Birthday*' on it, Eeyore could keep things in it, which might be Useful." So, as he was just passing the Hundred Acre Wood, he went inside to call on Owl, who lived there.

"Good morning, Owl," he said.

"Good morning, Pooh," said Owl.

"Many happy returns of Eeyore's birthday," said Pooh.

"Oh, is that what it is?"

"What are you giving him, Owl?"

"What are *you* giving him, Pooh?"

"I'm giving him a Useful Pot to Keep Things In, and I wanted to ask you—"

"Is this it?" said Owl, taking it out of Pooh's paw.

"Yes, and I wanted to ask you—"

"Somebody has been keeping honey in it," said Owl.

"You can keep *anything* in it," said Pooh earnestly. "It's Very Useful like that. And I wanted to ask you—"

"You ought to write 'A Happy Birth-day' on it."

"*That* was what I wanted to ask you," said Pooh. "Because my spelling is Wobbly. It's good spelling but it Wobbles, and the letters get in the wrong places. Would *you* write 'A Happy Birth-day' on it for me?"

"It's a nice pot," said Owl, looking at it all round. "Couldn't I give it too? From both of us?"

"No," said Pooh. "That would *not* be a good plan. Now I'll just wash it first, and then you can write on it."

Well, he washed the pot out, and dried it, while Owl licked the end of his pencil, and wondered how to spell "birthday."

"Can you read, Pooh?" he asked a little anxiously. "There's a notice about knocking and ringing outside my door, which Christopher Robin wrote. Could you read it?"

"Christopher Robin told me what it said, and *then* I could."

"Well, I'll tell you what *this* says, and then you'll be able to."

So Owl wrote...and this is what he wrote:

Pooh looked on admiringly.

"I'm just saying 'A Happy Birthday'," said Owl carelessly.

"It's a nice long one," said Pooh, very much impressed by it.

"Well, *actually*, of course, I'm saying 'A Very Happy Birthday with love from Pooh.' Naturally it takes a good deal of pencil to say a long thing like that."

"Oh, I see," said Pooh.

While all this was happening, Piglet had gone back to his own house to get Eeyore's balloon. He held it very tightly against himself, so that it shouldn't blow away, and he ran as fast as he could so as to get to Eeyore before Pooh did; for he thought that he would like to be the first one to give a present, just as if he had thought of it without being told by anybody. And running along, and thinking how pleased Eeyore would be, he didn't look where he was going...and suddenly he put his foot in a rabbit hole, and fell down flat on his face.

BANG!!!???***!!!

Piglet lay there, wondering what had happened. At first he thought that the whole world had blown up; and then he thought that perhaps only the Forest part of it had; and then he thought that perhaps only *he* had, and he was now alone in the moon or somewhere, and would never see Christopher Robin or Pooh or Eeyore again. And then he thought, "Well, even if I'm in the moon, I needn't be face downwards all the time," so he got cautiously up and looked about him.

He was still in the Forest!

"Well, that's funny," he thought. "I wonder what that bang was. I couldn't have made such a noise just falling down. And where's my balloon? And what's that small piece of damp rag doing?"

It was the balloon!

"Oh, dear!" said Piglet. "Oh, dear, oh, dearie, dearie, dear! Well, it's too late now. I can't go back, and I haven't another balloon, and perhaps Eeyore doesn't *like* balloons so *very* much."

So he trotted on, rather sadly now, and down he came to the side of the stream where Eeyore was, and called out to him.

"Good morning, Eeyore," shouted Piglet.

"Good morning, Little Piglet," said Eeyore. "If it *is* a good morning," he said. "Which I doubt," said he. "Not that it matters," he said.

"Many happy returns of the day," said Piglet, having now got closer.

Eeyore stopped looking at himself in the stream, and turned to stare at Piglet.

"Just say that again," he said.

"Many hap—"

"Wait a moment."

Balancing on three legs, he began to bring his fourth leg very cautiously up to his ear. "I did this yesterday," he explained, as he fell down for the third time. "It's quite easy. It's so as I can hear better.... There, that's done it! Now then, what were you saying?" He pushed his ear forward with his hoof.

"Many happy returns of the day," said Piglet again.

"Meaning me?"

"Of course, Eeyore."

"My birthday?"

"Yes."

"Me having a real birthday?"

"Yes, Eeyore, and I've brought you a present."

Eeyore took down his right hoof from his right ear, turned round, and with great difficulty put up his left hoof.

"I must have that in the other ear," he said. "Now then."

"A present," said Piglet very loudly.

"Meaning me again?"

"Yes."

"My birthday still?"

"Of course, Eeyore."

"Me going on having a real birthday?"

"Yes, Eeyore, and I brought you a balloon."

"*Balloon?*" said Eeyore. "You did say balloon? One of those big coloured things you blow up? Gaiety, song-and-dance, here we are and there we are?"

"Yes, but I'm afraid—I'm very sorry, Eeyore—but when I was running along to bring it you, I fell down."

"Dear, dear, how unlucky! You ran too fast, I expect. You didn't hurt yourself, Little Piglet?"

"No, but I—I—oh, Eeyore, I burst the balloon!"

There was a very long silence.

"My balloon?" said Eeyore at last.

Piglet nodded.

"My birthday balloon?"

"Yes, Eeyore," said Piglet sniffing a

little. "Here it is. With—with many happy returns of the day." And he gave Eeyore the small piece of damp rag.

"Is this it?" said Eeyore, a little surprised.

Piglet nodded.

"My present?"

Piglet nodded again.

"The balloon?"

"Yes."

"Thank you, Piglet," said Eeyore. "You don't mind my asking," he went on, "but what colour was this balloon when it—when it *was* a balloon?"

"Red."

"I just wondered.... Red," he murmured to himself. "My favourite colour. ... How big was it?"

"About as big as me."

"I just wondered.... About as big as Piglet," he said to himself sadly. "My favourite size. Well, well."

Piglet felt very miserable, and didn't know what to say. He was still opening his mouth to begin something, and then deciding that it wasn't any good saying *that*, when he heard a shout from the other side of the river, and there was Pooh.

"Many happy returns of the day," called out Pooh, forgetting that he had said it already.

"Thank you, Pooh, I'm having them," said Eeyore gloomily.

"I've brought you a little present," said Pooh excitedly.

"I've had it," said Eeyore.

Pooh had now splashed across the stream to Eeyore, and Piglet was sitting a little way off, his head in his paws, snuffling to himself.

"It's a Useful Pot," said Pooh. "Here it is. And it's got 'A Very Happy Birthday with love from Pooh' written on it. That's what all that writing is. And it's for putting things in. There!"

When Eeyore saw the pot, he became quite excited.

"Why!" he said. "I believe my Balloon will just go into that Pot!"

"Oh, no, Eeyore," said Pooh. "Balloons are much too big to go into Pots. What you do with a balloon is, you hold the balloon—"

"Not mine," said Eeyore proudly. "Look, Piglet!" And as Piglet looked sorrowfully round, Eeyore picked the balloon up with his teeth, and placed it carefully in the pot; picked it out and put it on the ground; and then picked it up again and put it carefully back.

"So it does!" said Pooh. "It goes in!"

"So it does!" said Piglet. "And it comes out!"

"Doesn't it?" said Eeyore. "It goes in and out like anything."

"I'm very glad," said Pooh happily, "that I thought of giving you a Useful Pot to put things in."

"I'm very glad," said Piglet happily, "that I thought of giving you Something to put in a Useful Pot."

But Eeyore wasn't listening. He was taking the balloon out, and putting it back again, as happy as could be....

People have always loved fairy tales.
No one will ever know who told the first one—
it was so long ago.
They are told differently in different countries.
But they all have one thing in common.
Whether the stories are about
poor little drudges like Cinderella,
or princesses like the Sleeping Beauty,
they take us to another world—
a land of wonder, where surprising and
magical things are always happening.

Cinderella

BY CHARLES PERRAULT—ADAPTED BY LOUIS UNTERMEYER

Illustrated by GORDON LAITE

Once upon a time there lived a man whose first wife had died and who was now married to the haughtiest and meanest woman ever seen. This second wife had two daughters who were exactly like her, and even more spiteful, if that were possible. By his first wife the husband had one daughter, a lovely child with the sweetness and good temper of her mother, who was the finest creature in the world.

No sooner was the wedding over than the step-mother began to show

her bad temper. She could not bear her step-daughter's good qualities because they made her own daughters seem even worse than they were.
Accordingly she compelled the poor girl to do all the hard work of the
household. It was she who washed the dishes, and scrubbed the stairs,
and polished the floors and waited on the two ugly daughters, while the
latter slept on soft feather beds in elegant rooms, furnished with full-length
looking-glasses. Meanwhile their sister lay in a wretched garret on an old
straw mattress. Yet the poor thing bore this ill treatment very patiently and
did not complain to her father, who was completely under the influence
of his wife.

When her work was done, she used to sit in the chimney-corner among
the cinders, which had caused the nickname of *Cinderella* to be given her
by the family. Yet, for all her shabby clothes, Cinderella was a hundred
times prettier than her sisters, although they dressed themselves ever so
magnificently.

It happened that the king's son gave a ball, to which he invited all the
nobility. Since our two young ladies made a great to-do in the world, they
were also invited. They began to plan, and grew busy choosing what headdress and which gown would be the most becoming. Here was still more

work for poor Cinderella: for it was she who had to starch their ruffles and iron all their fine linen. Nothing but dress was talked about for days together.

They sent for a skillful hair-dresser to train their hair and to prepare the double rows of quilling for their caps, and they bought patches to put on their cheeks. They called in Cinderella and asked her advice, as she had such good taste, and Cinderella not only advised them well, but offered to dress their hair, which they were only too willing to let her do. While she was doing this, the sisters said: "And pray, Cinderella, how would you like to go to the ball?"

"You are mocking me," replied the poor girl; "it is not for such as I to go there."

"True enough," they said. "Folks would laugh to see a Cinderella at a court ball!"

Any other but Cinderella would have dressed their hair badly to punish them, but she was so good-natured that she dressed them most becomingly.

The two sisters were so delighted that they scarcely ate a morsel for two days. They spent the whole time before a looking-glass, and they laced themselves tight, to make their waists as slender as possible. More than a dozen staylaces were broken in the attempt.

The long-wished-for evening came at last, and these proud misses stepped into the carriage and drove away to the palace. Cinderella looked after the coach until it was out of sight; then she returned to the kitchen and burst into tears. She continued crying in the corner of the chimney, until a rapping at the kitchen door roused her, and she got up to see what it was. It was a little old beggar-woman, who said:

"Dearie me! why all these tears, my child?"

"Alas, I wish..." sighed Cinderella.

"You wish to go to the ball. Is it not so?" said her godmother, who was a fairy.

"Alas, yes," replied Cinderella.

"And you *shall* go if you do as I tell you. First go to the garden and bring me a pumpkin."

Cinderella wondered how a pumpkin could bring her to the ball; nevertheless, she fetched the largest pumpkin she could find. Her godmother took the pumpkin, and scooped out the inside of it, leaving nothing but the rind. Then she struck it with her wand, and it instantly became the most elegant gilt carriage.

Next she sent Cinderella into the pantry, and told her to bring two little mice, which she would find in the mousetrap.

Cinderella raised the trap door, and as the mice came running out, the old woman touched them with the wand, and transformed them into fine prancing mouse-colored carriage horses, with long manes and handsome tails.

"Now, my dear good child," said the fairy, "here you have a coach and horses. But we have no coachman to take care of them. Run and bring the rat-trap to me."

Cinderella did not lose a moment. Soon she returned with the trap, in which there were three large rats. The fairy chose the one with the largest whiskers and he, too, was touched with the wand. Immediately he became a jolly-looking coachman in full finery.

Her godmother then said: "Dear child, go into the garden again. Keep to the right side, and close to the wall you will see a watering-pot. Look behind it, and you will find six lizards. Bring them to me immediately."

Cinderella found the six lizards, which she put into her apron and brought to the fairy. Another touch of the wand converted them into six spruce footmen in dashing liveries.

The fairy said to Cinderella: "Well, my dear girl, is not this a fine carriage to take you to the ball? Tell me, are you pleased with it?"

"O yes, dear godmother," replied Cinderella. "But how can I go among finely-dressed people in these rags?"

The old woman touched Cinderella with her magic wand, and her clothes were instantly changed into a magnificent ball dress, ornamented with the most costly jewels. The fairy also produced a pair of glass slippers, the prettiest in the whole world.

Thus attired Cinderella was ready. Two footmen opened the carriage door, and assisted the now beautifully dressed Cinderella into it. Before she took leave, her godmother commanded her on no account to stay at the ball after the clock had struck twelve. If she stopped a single moment beyond that time, her fine coach, horses, coachman, and footman, and fine clothes would all return to their original shapes of pumpkin, mice, rats, lizards, rags.

Cinderella promised faithfully to leave the ball before midnight, and drove away overcome with joy.

When she arrived at the court, information reached the king's son that a beautiful young lady, evidently some princess, was in waiting. His Royal Highness hastened to the door, welcomed Cinderella, and handed her out of the carriage. He then led her into the ball-room, where a great company was assembled. The moment she appeared, all conversation stopped; the violins ceased playing, people left off dancing, so great was the sensation produced by the stranger's beauty. A confused murmur of admiration fluttered through the crowd: "How beautiful she is!"

The king's son handed Cinderella to the place of honor and asked to have the pleasure of dancing with her. As they danced, Cinderella looked so graceful that she was more and more admired; the eyes of the whole company were fixed upon the beautiful pair.

When the dance was ended, a magnificent feast was served, but the young prince was so taken with Cinderella, that he did not eat one morsel.

Cinderella went and sat with her sisters. In her goodness of heart she offered them the delicacies which she had received from the prince, but they did not recognize her.

When Cinderella heard the clock strike a quarter to twelve, she made a curtsy to the whole assembly and ran off as fast as she could.

Reaching home, she found her godmother; and after thanking her, she said she wished she might go to the ball the next evening, as the prince had asked her to do.

She was still telling her godmother all that had happened at court, when her two sisters knocked at the door. Cinderella went and let them in, pretending to yawn and stretch herself.

"How late you are!" she said.

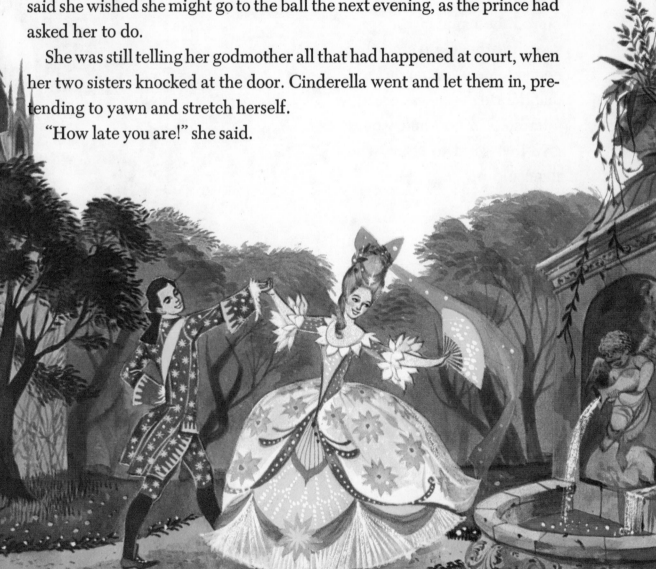

"If you had been to the ball," said one of the sisters, "you would not have thought it late. There came the most beautiful princess ever seen, who loaded us with polite attentions, and gave us oranges and citrons."

Cinderella could scarcely contain her delight, and inquired the name of the princess. But they answered that nobody knew her name, and that the king's son was greatly interested in her, and would give the world to know who she could be.

The next evening the sisters again went to the court ball, and so did Cinderella, dressed even more magnificently than before. The king's son was always at her side, and kept paying her most endearing attentions. The young lady was flattered; she loved to listen to him. So it came to pass that she forgot her godmother's instructions and, before she realized it, the clock struck the first stroke of midnight. She rose hastily, and flew away like a frightened fawn. The prince followed, but she was too swift for him. Only, as she flew, she dropped one of her glass slippers, which he picked up eagerly.

Cinderella reached home out of breath, without either coach or footmen, and with only her rags on her back; nothing remained of her finery but a little glass slipper, fellow to the one she had lost. The guards at the palace gate were closely questioned as to whether they had not seen a princess coming out. But they answered they had seen no one except a shabbily dressed girl, who looked more like a country wench than a lady.

When the two sisters returned from the ball, Cinderella asked them whether they had a pleasant time and whether the beautiful lady had been there. They told her yes, but that she had run away as soon as midnight had struck, and so quickly as to drop one of her dainty glass slippers, which the king's son had picked up, and was looking at it most fondly during the remainder of the ball. Indeed, it was certain that he was deeply in love with the beautiful creature to whom it belonged.

What they said was true. A few days later, the king's son caused a proclamation to be made by sound of trumpet all over the kingdom, to the effect that he would marry her whose foot should be found to fit the slipper exactly. So the slipper was first tried on all the princesses, then on all the duchesses, and next on all the ladies belonging to the court. But in vain. It was then brought to the two sisters, who tried with all their might to force their feet into the tiny slipper. But with no better success. Cinderella who was present, recognized her slipper, laughed, and said: "Suppose you let me try."

Her sisters scorned and began to mock her. But the gentleman who was chosen to try the slipper looked attentively at Cinderella and saw how beautiful she was. He said that it was only fair she should have her chance, as he had orders to try it on every maiden in the kingdom. Accordingly Cinderella sat down, and she no sooner put the slipper to her little foot than she drew it on, and it fitted perfectly. The sisters were amazed; but they were ten times as astonished when Cinderella drew the other slipper out of her pocket, and put it on. Her godmother then came in, and touched Cinderella's clothes with her wand. In an instant, they became even more magnificent than those she had previously worn.

Her two sisters now recognized her for the beautiful stranger they had seen at the ball. Falling at her feet they begged her forgiveness for their ill treatment which they had made her suffer. Cinderella raised them, saying, as she embraced them, that she not only forgave them with all her heart, but wanted them to love her. She was then taken to the palace of the young prince, who thought her more lovely than before, and who married her shortly after.

Cinderella, who was as good as she was beautiful, gave her sisters a home in the palace, and married them, that same day, to two lords belonging to the court.

The Sleeping Beauty

BY CHARLES PERRAULT—ADAPTED BY LOUIS UNTERMEYER
Illustrated by ADRIENNE SÉGUR

Once upon a time there lived a king and queen who were unhappy because they had no children. They tried the waters everywhere, made vows and pilgrimages, and did everything that could be done, but without success. At last, however, the queen gave birth to a daughter.

There was a grand christening, and all the fairies that could be found in the kingdom—there were seven—were invited to be godmothers to the little princess. This was done so that each fairy, according to fairy custom, would bestow gifts upon the princess which would make her not only lovely but the very spirit of perfection.

When the christening was over, the company returned to the king's palace, where a great feast was held for the fairies. Covers were laid for them in magnificent style, and in front of each was placed a solid gold casket containing a spoon, fork, and knife of fine gold, set with diamonds and rubies. But as they were sitting down, an ancient fairy came into the hall. No one had remembered to invite her, because she had stayed in her tower more than fifty years, and people thought she was dead.

The king ordered a place prepared for her, but it was impossible to give her a golden casket like the others, because only seven had been made for the seven fairies. The old fairy believed that she was slighted on purpose and muttered threats between her teeth.

She was overheard by one of the young fairies, who was seated near by. Guessing that some mischievous gift might be bestowed upon the little princess, the young fairy hid behind the tapestry as soon as the company left the table. Her intention was to be the last to speak, and so to undo any harm which the old fairy might do.

Soon the fairies began to bestow their gifts upon the princess. The youngest promised that she should be the most beautiful person in the world; the next, that she should have the nature of an angel; the third, that she should do everything with wonderful grace; the fourth, that she should dance to perfection; the fifth, that she should sing like a nightingale; and the sixth, that she should play fine music.

It was now the turn of the old fairy. Shaking her head, more with spite than infirmity, she declared that the princess would prick her hand with a spindle, and die of the

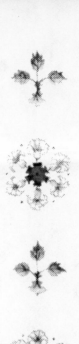

wound. A shudder ran through the company at this terrible threat. All eyes filled with tears.

At this moment the young fairy stepped from behind the tapestry and said in a loud voice, "Take comfort, your Majesties, your daughter shall not die. My power, it is true, is not great enough to undo all that my aged kinswoman has decreed. The princess will indeed prick her hand with a spindle. But instead of dying, she shall merely fall into a deep sleep that will last a hundred years. At the end of that time a king's son shall come to awaken her."

The king, in an attempt to avoid the tragedy threatened by the old fairy, at once published an order forbidding all persons, under pain of death, to use a spindle.

About fifteen or sixteen years later, the king and queen happened one day to be away. The princess was running about the castle, and going upstairs from room to room she came to a garret at the top of a tower, where an old woman sat alone with her spinning. This good woman had never heard about the king's proclamation forbidding the use of spindles.

"What are you doing?" asked the princess.

"I am spinning, my pretty child," replied the old woman, not knowing who she was.

"Oh, what fun!" cried the princess. "How do you do it? Give it to me. Let me try and see if I can do it."

Partly because she was too hasty, partly because she was a little heedless, or perhaps because the fairy had ordained it, no sooner had she seized the spindle than she pricked her hand and fell down in a faint.

Much alarmed, the good dame cried out for help. People came running from every quarter. They threw water on

her face, rubbed her with their hands, and sprinkled cologne on her forehead. But nothing would restore her.

Then the king, who rushed upstairs as soon as he heard the noise, remembered the fairy prophecy. Knowing that what had happened could not be avoided, he gave orders that the princess should be carried to the finest apartment in the palace and placed upon a bed embroidered in gold.

One would have thought her an angel, she was so lovely. The trance had not taken away the brightness of her complexion. Her cheeks were delicately flushed, her lips were like coral. It is true that her eyes were shut, but her gentle breathing could still be heard, and it was plain that she was not dead. The king commanded that she should be left to sleep in peace until the time came for her to awake.

The good fairy who had saved her life by letting her sleep a hundred years was told of this accident by a little dwarf who had a pair of seven-league boots. The fairy set off at once and arrived within an hour.

Being gifted with great foresight, she thought that when the princess was awakened, she might be distressed to find herself all alone in the old castle. This, then, is what she did.

She touched with her wand everybody (except the king and queen) who was in the castle—governesses, maids of honor, scullions, guards, porters, pages, footmen. She also touched all the horses in the stables, with their grooms, the big dogs in the courtyard, and little Fluff, the pet dog of the princess, who was lying on the bed beside his mistress. The moment she touched them they all fell asleep, to awaken at the same moment as their mistress, ready to wait upon her. The very spits before the fire, loaded with partridges and pheasants, stopped and fell asleep; so did the fire. All this was done in a moment, for fairies do not take long.

Then the king and queen kissed their dear child without waking her, and left the castle. Orders were issued, forbidding any to approach it. But the warnings were not needed, for within a quarter of an hour there grew up all round the park such a quantity of trees big and small, with twining brambles and thorns, that neither man nor beast could penetrate them. Nothing but the tops of the castle towers could be seen, and these only from a distance. No one could doubt that this was the fairy's work, done so that, while the princess slept, she should have nothing to fear from prying eyes.

After a hundred years had passed, and another king was ruling the land, the king's son—who was no relation to the princess—returned from a hunt. He noticed, for the first time, the tops of the towers standing above the thick woods and asked what they might be. He was given various answers in reply. Some said it was an old castle haunted by ghosts. Others said that all the witches of the country gathered there to hold their midnight meetings. But most of them believed that it was the home of an ogre, and that he brought there all the children he could catch.

The prince did not know what to believe. It was then that an old countryman came forward and spoke:

"May it please your royal highness, my father told me more than fifty years ago that there was in this castle an enchanted princess, the most beautiful princess in the world. He said that this princess was under a spell, that she had to sleep one hundred years, and that she would be awakened by a king's son, whose bride she would be."

When he heard this, the young prince was all on fire. Thinking nothing of the difficulties, he pushed forward, full of love and adventure and high spirits.

He had only gone a few feet into the tangled woods when the brambles and bushes gave way; even the trees made a path to let him pass through. The prince did not hesitate. He walked straight on toward the castle which seemed to be at the end of a long avenue. The only thing that surprised him was that none of his people followed him—for, as soon as he had passed, the trees and bushes closed in again and formed a thick barrier.

As he approached the outer courtyard, he saw something which might have frozen with terror the blood of the most fearless person. Everything was stone-silent; the feeling of death was everywhere. Nothing could be seen but bodies of men and animals, all stretched out, all seemingly dead. Then he noticed the red faces of the porters and their goblets, which still held some drops of wine—so he knew that they had fallen asleep in the very act of drinking.

Next he crossed the courtyard itself, a place all paved with marble. He mounted the staircase and entered a long hall, where guards were drawn up in a row, their guns upon their shoulders, snoring for all they were worth. He passed through several rooms full of lords and ladies, some standing, some sitting down, but all asleep.

Finally he came into a golden room, and saw upon a bed, the curtains of which were open, the most beautiful sight he had ever beheld—a lovely girl, who seemed to be about fifteen or sixteen years old, whose beauty shone with unearthly radiance. Trembling, he drew close.

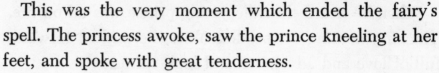

This was the very moment which ended the fairy's spell. The princess awoke, saw the prince kneeling at her feet, and spoke with great tenderness.

"Is it you, my prince?" she said. "You have been a long time coming."

Thrilled by these words, and especially by the manner in which they were said, the prince scarcely knew how to show his delight and gratitude.

His words were faltering, which pleased her all the more. And if he was more at a loss for words than she— no wonder. The princess had had time to think of what to say to him, for it seems (although we cannot be certain of this) that the good fairy lightened her long sleep with pleasant dreams. In short, the young couple talked together for four hours, and in that time they did not say half of what was in their hearts.

In the meantime the palace had awakened. Everyone suddenly remembered his particular business—and, as most of the people were not in love, they were starved. The head lady of honor, as famished as anyone, grew impatient and announced that supper was served.

All then went into a great hall hung with mirrors, and were served with supper by the stewards of the household. The violins and oboes played some old music—and played it remarkably well, considering they had not played at all for exactly one hundred years. A little later, when supper was over, the chaplain married them in the chapel; and in due course they retired to rest.

They slept very little, however. The princess, naturally, had not much need of sleep, and as soon as morning came the prince took his leave of her. He returned to the city,

Adrienne Ségur 1951

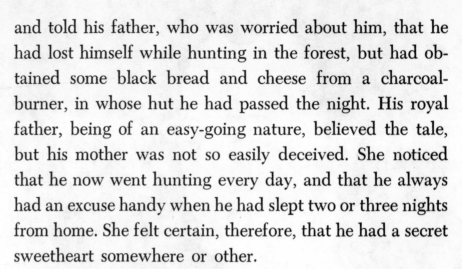

and told his father, who was worried about him, that he had lost himself while hunting in the forest, but had obtained some black bread and cheese from a charcoal-burner, in whose hut he had passed the night. His royal father, being of an easy-going nature, believed the tale, but his mother was not so easily deceived. She noticed that he now went hunting every day, and that he always had an excuse handy when he had slept two or three nights from home. She felt certain, therefore, that he had a secret sweetheart somewhere or other.

Two years passed since the marriage of the prince and princess, and during that time they had two children. The first, a daughter, was called Dawn, while the second, a boy, was named Day.

Many a time the queen told her son that he ought to be content with life at court, and tried to make him confide in her, but he did not dare trust her with his secret. Despite the affection which he bore her, he was afraid of his mother, for she came of a race of ogres, and the king had married her only for her wealth.

It was even whispered at the court that she had ogrish instincts, and that when little children were near her she had great difficulty keeping herself from pouncing on them. No wonder the prince feared to tell her about his wife.

At the end of two years the king died, and the prince found himself on the throne. He then made public announcement of his marriage, and went in state to fetch his queen from her castle. With her two children beside her she made a royal entry into the capital of her husband's realm.

Some time afterwards the young king declared war on a neighboring emperor. He left the government to his mother, entrusting his wife and children to her.

It looked as if the war would last all summer, and soon after the young king departed for the front, the old queen sent her daughter-in-law and the two children to a country house in the forest. A few days later she went there herself, and in the evening summoned the chief steward.

"For dinner tomorrow," she told him, "I will eat little Dawn."

"Oh, madam!" exclaimed the steward.

"It is my will," said the queen. "You will serve her with sharp sauce."

The poor man, seeing that it was useless to argue with an ogress, took his long knife and went up to little Dawn's chamber. She was then four years old, and she came running with a smile to greet him, throwing her arms around his neck and coaxing him to give her some candy. Whereupon he burst into tears, and let the knife fall from his hand. Going to the back-yard, he killed a small lamb. This he served to the queen with such a spicy sauce that she declared she had never tasted anything so delicious in all her life. At the same time the steward brought little Dawn to his wife, and told her to hide the child.

About a week later, the wicked queen summoned her steward and said, "This time I will have little Day for my supper."

The steward did not make any reply, for he decided to deceive her, as he had done before. Searching for little Day, he found him with a tiny sword in his hand—although he was only three years old—fencing with a huge

ape. Taking the child up in his arms, he carried the boy to his wife, who hid him with his sister. Instead of little Day, the steward cooked a young kid, which the ogress found delicious.

So far all had gone well. But one evening the wicked queen announced, "Now I will eat the young queen. Serve her with the same sauce I had with her children."

The steward was in despair. He could not imagine how to deceive her again. The young queen was twenty years old (not counting the hundred years she had been asleep), and he knew he could never find an animal with flesh so white and fine and firm. In order to save his own life, he knew that he would have to take the life of the young queen. Gritting his teeth, he drew his knife and went grimly up to the young queen's room. There he told her of the order he had received from the ogress queen.

"Do it! Do it!" she cried, offering him her neck. "Carry out the cruel command! Then at least I shall see my children again, my poor children whom I loved so much"— for, since the steward had not told her what he had done, she believed them dead.

"No, no madam," cried the steward, his eyes filling with tears and his heart softening. "You shall not die. And you shall see your children again. They are in my lodgings, where I have hidden them. I shall deceive the old queen once more, for instead of you, I shall slaughter and serve a young hind."

Without another word, he took her to his lodgings, where he left her to take her children in her arms, while he went to prepare the animal. The old queen ate it with just as much relish as if it had been her young daughter-in-law. By this time she was well pleased with her cruel deeds, and she made up a story to tell the king when he returned: how some hungry wolves had broken into the palace and had devoured the young queen and her children.

One evening while, according to her habit, the ogress was roaming around sniffing for fresh meat, she heard little Day whimpering because he had been naughty; at the same time she heard little Dawn beg her mother to forgive him.

The ogress recognized the voices of the queen and her children, and was furious to find she had been tricked. The next morning, in tones so terrible that all trembled, she ordered a huge vat to be brought into the middle of the courtyard. This she filled with vipers and toads, with all sorts of snakes and serpents, in order to cast into it the queen and her children, and the steward with his wife and serving-girl. By her command they were all brought forward, with their hands tied behind their backs.

They were brought out, ready for the end, and the executioners were about to throw them into the vat when the young king rode up on horseback. He demanded to know what was the meaning of this horrible sight.

No one dared to speak. And suddenly the ogress, who realized that everything would be found out, knew her end had come. She cast herself into the vat of poisonous toads and hissing serpents, and was immediately devoured by the very creatures she had put there to kill the others.

The king could not help but be sorry, for after all, she was his mother. But he consoled himself with the future, united with his beautiful wife and his adorable children.

Drakestail

EDITED BY ANDREW LANG
Illustrated by RICHARD SCARRY

DRAKESTAIL was very little, that is why he was called Drakestail; but tiny as he was he had brains, and he knew what he was about, for having begun with nothing he ended by amassing a hundred crowns. Now the King of the country, who was very extravagant and never kept any money, having heard that Drakestail had some, went one day in his own person to borrow his hoard; and, my word, in those days Drakestail was not a little proud of having lent money to the King. But after the first and second year, seeing that they never even

dreamed of paying the interest, he became uneasy, so much so that at last he resolved to go and see His Majesty himself and get repaid. So one fine morning Drakestail, very spruce and fresh, takes the road, singing: "Quack, quack, quack, when shall I get my money back?"

He had not gone far when he met friend Fox, on his rounds that way.

"Good-morning, neighbour," says the friend, "where are you off to so early?"

"I am going to the King for what he owes me."

"Oh! take me with thee!"

Drakestail said to himself: "One can't have too many friends.". . ."I will," says he, "but going on all-fours you will soon be tired. Make yourself quite small, get into my throat—go into my gizzard and I will carry you."

"Happy thought!" says friend Fox.

He takes bag and baggage and presto! is gone like a letter into the post.

And Drakestail is off again, all spruce and fresh, still singing: "Quack, quack, quack, when shall I have my money back?"

He had not gone far when he met his lady-friend Ladder, leaning on her wall.

"Good-morning, my duckling," says the lady friend, "whither away so bold?"

"I am going to the King for what he owes me."

"Oh! take me with thee!"

Drakestail said to himself: "One can't have too many friends.". . ."I will," says he, "but with your wooden legs you will soon be tired. Make yourself quite small, get into my throat—go into my gizzard and I will carry you."

"Happy thought!" says my friend Ladder, and nimble, bag and baggage, goes to keep company with friend Fox.

And "Quack, quack, quack." Drakestail is off again, singing and spruce as before. A little farther he meets his sweetheart, my friend River, wandering quietly in the sunshine.

"Thou, my cherub," says she, "whither so lonesome, with arching tail, on this muddy road?"

"I am going to the King, you know, for what he owes me."

"Oh! take me with thee!"

Drakestail said to himself: "One can't have too many friends.". ".I will," says he,

"but you who sleep while you walk will soon be tired. Make yourself quite small, get into my throat—go into my gizzard and I will carry you."

"Ah! happy thought!" says my friend River.

She takes bag and baggage and glou, glou, glou, she takes her place between friend Fox and my friend Ladder.

And "Quack, quack, quack." Drakestail is off again singing.

A little farther on he meets comrade Wasp's-nest, manoeuvring his wasps.

"Well, good-morning, friend Drakestail," said comrade Wasp's-nest, "where are we bound for so spruce and fresh?"

"I am going to the King for what he owes me."

"Oh! take me with thee!"

Drakestail said to himself, "One can't have too many friends.". . ."I will," says he, "but with your battalion to drag along, you will soon be tired. Make yourself quite small, go into my throat—get into my gizzard and I will carry you."

"By jove! that's a good idea!" says comrade Wasp's-nest.

And left file! he takes the same road to join the others with all his party. There was not much more room, but by closing up a bit they managed. . . . And Drakestail is off again singing.

He arrived thus at the capital and threaded his way straight up the High Street, still running and singing "Quack, quack, quack, when shall I get my money back?" to the great astonishment of the good folks, till he came to the King's palace.

He strikes with the knocker: "Toc! toc!"

"Who is there?" asks the porter, put-

ting his head out of the wicket.

" 'Tis I, Drakestail. I wish to speak to the King."

"Speak to the King! . . . That's easily said. The King is dining, and will not be disturbed."

"Tell him that it is I, and I have come he well knows why."

The porter shuts his wicket and goes up to say it to the King, who, with all his ministers, was just sitting down to dinner.

"Good, good!" said the King laughing. "I know what it is! Make him come in and put him with the turkeys and chickens."

The porter descends.

"Have the goodness to enter."

"Good!" says Drakestail to himself, "I shall now see how they eat at court."

"This way, this way," says the porter. "One step further. . . . There, there you are."

"How? what? in the poultry yard?"

Fancy how vexed Drakestail was!

"Ah! so that's it," says he. "Wait! I will compel you to receive me. Quack, quack, quack, when shall I get my money back?" But turkeys and chickens are creatures who don't like people that are not as themselves. When they saw the newcomer and how he was made and when they heard him crying too, they began to look black at him.

"What is it? What does he want?"

Finally they rushed at him all together to overwhelm him with pecks.

"I am lost!" said Drakestail to himself, when by good luck he remembers his comrade friend Fox, and he cries:

"*Reynard, Reynard, come out of your earth,*
Or Drakestail's life is of little worth."

Then friend Fox, who was only waiting for these words, hastens out, throws himself on the wicked fowls, and quick! quack! he tears them to pieces; so much so that at the end of five minutes there

was not one left alive. And Drakestail, quite content, began to sing again, "Quack, quack, quack, when shall I get my money back?"

When the King who was still at table heard this refrain, and the poultry woman came to tell him what had been going on in the yard, he was terribly annoyed.

He ordered them to throw this tail of a drake into the well, to make an end of him.

And it was done as he commanded. Drakestail was in despair of getting himself out of such a deep hole, when he remembered his lady friend, the Ladder.

*"Ladder, Ladder, come out of thy hold,
Or Drakestail's days will soon be told."*

My friend Ladder, who was only waiting for these words, hastens out, leans her two arms on the edge of the well, then Drakestail climbs nimbly on her back, and hop! he is in the yard, where he begins to sing louder than ever.

When the King, who was still at table and laughing at the good trick he had played his creditor, heard him again reclaiming his money, he became livid with rage.

He commanded that the furnace should be heated, and this tail of a drake thrown into it, because he must be a sorcerer.

The furnace was soon hot, but this time Drakestail was not so afraid; he counted on his sweetheart, my friend River.

*"River, River, outward flow,
Or to death Drakestail must go."*

My friend River hastens out, and errouf! throws herself into the furnace, which she floods with all the people who had lighted it; after which she flowed growling into the hall of the palace to the height of more than four feet.

And Drakestail, quite content, begins to swim, singing deafeningly, "Quack, quack, quack, when shall I get my money back?"

The King was still at table and thought himself quite sure of his game; but when he heard Drakestail singing again and when they told him all that had passed, he became furious and got up from table brandishing his fists.

"Bring him here, and I'll cut his throat! bring him here quick!" cried he.

And quickly two footmen ran to fetch Drakestail.

"At last," said the poor chap, going up the great stairs, "they have decided to receive me."

Imagine his terror when, on entering, he sees the King as red as a turkey cock, and all his ministers attending him, standing sword in hand. He thought this time it was all up with him. Happily, he remembered that there was still one remaining friend, and he cried with dying accents:

*"Wasp's-nest, Wasp's-nest, make a sally,
Or Drakestail nevermore may rally."*

Hereupon the scene changes.

"Bs, bs, bayonet them!" The brave Wasp's-nest rushes out with all his wasps. They threw themselves on the infuriated King and his ministers, and stung them so fiercely in the face that they lost their heads, and not knowing where to hide themselves they all jumped pell-mell from the window and broke their necks on the pavement.

Behold Drakestail much astonished, all alone in the big saloon and master of the field. He could not get over it.

Nevertheless, he remembered shortly what he had come for to the palace, and improving the occasion, he set to work to hunt for his dear money. But in vain he rummaged in all the drawers; he found nothing; all had been spent.

And ferreting thus from room to room he came at last to the one with the throne in it and feeling fatigued, he sat himself down on it to think over his adventure. In the meanwhile the people had found their King and his ministers with their feet in the air on the pavement, and they had gone into the palace to know how it had occurred. On entering the throne-room, when the crowd saw that there was already someone on the royal seat, they broke out in cries of surprise and joy:

"The King is dead, long live the King!
Heaven has sent us down this thing."

Drakestail, who was no longer surprised at anything, received the acclamations of the people as if he had never done anything else all his life.

A few of them certainly murmured

that a Drakestail would make a fine King; those who knew him replied that a knowing Drakestail was a more worthy King than a spendthrift like him who was lying on the pavement. In short, they ran and took the crown off the head of the deceased, and placed it on that of Drakestail, whom it fitted like wax.

Thus he became King.

"And now," said he after the ceremony, "ladies and gentlemen, let's go to supper. I am so hungry!"

Puss in Boots

BY CHARLES PERRAULT
ADAPTED BY LOUIS UNTERMEYER
Illustrated by J. P. MILLER

There was once a miller who was so poor that when he died he had nothing to leave his three sons but his mill, his ass, and his cat. These things were quickly shared by the sons—no lawyer was needed to settle the estate. The eldest son took the mill, the second took the ass, and so the third and youngest received nothing but the cat. Really, he was not very happy about it.

"My brothers," said he to himself, "may make a living by joining forces. But what can I do? Even if I eat the cat and make a muff of its skin, I still will have to die of hunger."

The cat, who pretended not to have been listening, heard all this. He spoke up seriously:

"Don't worry, master. Just get me a bag, and have a pair of little boots made for me. Then you will see that I'm not such a bad bargain, after all."

The cat's master did not expect much. But he had seen how clever the cat was catching rats and mice—he had noticed how he had hung by his heels, pretending he was dead, or hid himself in the flour-bin—so he was not without hope that something good would come of it.

After the cat had received what he asked for, he pulled on the little boots and strutted around in them. Then he put the bag around his neck, holding the string between his two front paws, and went to a piece of ground where there were large numbers of rabbits. He put some bran and lettuce in the bag, and stretched himself out pretending he was dead.

The sly puss had just settled himself when things worked out according to plan. A frisky and foolish young rabbit put his head into the bag and started to nibble the food. Puss immediately pulled the string tight and had his catch.

Proud of his prize, he went straight to the king's palace and asked to speak to his majesty. He was ushered into the royal apartment, where he bowed low and said to the king:

"Your majesty, I have brought you a rabbit from the fields of my master, the marquis of Carabas"—for that was the title which puss had conferred upon his master.

"Tell your master," said the king, "that I thank him, and that I am pleased with his gift."

Sometime later, puss hid himself among tall grain, a place much visited by birds. He held his bag open until a couple of partridges flew in. Again he went to the palace and presented the birds to the king, who received them with even greater pleasure, and gave the cat a little present for himself.

The cat continued doing this sort of thing for two or three months, each time taking game to the king as a gift from his master. Finally, there came a day when the cat learned that the king was to go for an outing along the riverside with his daughter, the most beautiful princess in the world.

It was then that the cat said to his master, "The time has come. If you do what I tell you, your fortune is made. All you have to do is bathe in the river, at a spot which I shall point out to you. Leave the rest to me."

The young man had no idea what was going to happen, but he did exactly what puss had advised. While he was bathing, the king came along and the cat cried out:

"Help! help! My lord marquis of Carabas is drowning!"

At these cries the king stuck his head out of the carriage window. He recognized the cat who had brought him so many appetizing gifts, and commanded his guards to hurry to the aid of the marquis of Carabas.

While they were helping the poor marquis out of the river, the cat came up to the carriage and told the king that, while his master was bathing, some robbers had stolen his clothes, although he had tried to stop them by calling, "Stop, thief!" at the top of his voice. (The cunning cat had hidden the clothes under a stone.)

The king received the young man with great kindness, and immediately ordered the officers of his wardrobe to run and bring one of his finest suits for the marquis of Carabas. The rich clothes fit him extremely well, for he was a handsome fellow, and the king's daughter took an instant fancy to him. In fact the young man had looked at her shyly but tenderly only a few times before she was completely in love with him.

The king insisted that the young marquis enter the carriage and drive with them. The cat, delighted with the way his scheme was working

out, went on ahead. Soon he came to a place where some farmers were mowing a meadow, and he said to them:

"My good people, be sure to tell the king that the meadow you are mowing belongs to the marquis of Carabas. If you don't, you will be chopped into mincemeat."

Just as the cat had expected, when the carriage came along, the king asked the mowers to whom the meadow belonged.

"To my lord marquis of Carabas," replied the mowers, for they were taking no chances at the cat's threat.

"You have a very fine estate here," said the king to the marquis.

"You can see for yourself, your majesty," replied the young man. "This meadow yields a rich harvest every year."

Still keeping ahead of the carriage, the cat saw some reapers in a field, and said to them:

"My good people, be sure to tell the king that the field you are reaping belongs to the marquis of Carabas. If you don't, you will be chopped into mincemeat."

A few minutes later the king passed by and asked who was the owner of all the fields.

"My lord marquis of Carabas," replied the reapers.

The cat, still going ahead of the royal carriage, told everyone he met to say the same thing, and the king was amazed at the size of the estate of the young marquis of Carabas.

Puss came at last to a large castle, owned by the richest ogre ever known, for all the land which the king had passed belonged to this ogre. The cat had already found out who this ogre was, and what magic things he could do. So he asked to speak with him, saying that he wished to pay his respects to so rich and great a magician. The ogre received him politely—at least as politely as an ogre could—and asked him to sit down.

"They tell me," said the cat, "that you have the power to change yourself into all sorts of animals; that you can, for example, turn yourself into a lion or an elephant."

"That is true," said the ogre gruffly, "and to prove it I shall now turn into a lion."

The cat was so frightened at the sight of a lion so close to him that he scrambled onto the roof—and it was none too easy for him, because his boots were not meant for walking on such a slippery surface. Soon the ogre turned himself back, and puss confessed that he had been terrified.

"Had I not seen that, I would not have believed it. But," continued the cat, "I've also been told that you have the still greater power to change yourself into the shape of little animals—that you can, for example, change yourself into a rat or even a small mouse. That must be quite impossible."

"Impossible!" growled the ogre. "You shall see!" At the same time the ogre transformed himself into a mouse and scurried about the floor. The next moment puss pounced upon him and quickly ate him up.

A little later the king came along, saw the magnificent castle, and wished to visit it. Puss, hearing the carriage rumble across the drawbridge, ran out and said:

"Welcome, your majesty, welcome to the castle of my lord marquis of Carabas."

"What! My dear marquis!" cried the king. "Does this castle also belong to you? Nothing I have seen is finer than this courtyard and the stately building around it. Let us look at the inside, if you please."

The marquis gave his hand to the princess and followed the king, who went first. They passed into a huge hall where a magnificent feast had been spread by the ogre for certain friends of his. The other ogres were afraid to enter the castle now that the king was there.

The king was won over by the charm and fine figure of the marquis. As for his daughter, the young princess had fallen madly in love with

him. So, having drunk five or six glasses of wine, and seeing the vast estate all about him, the king said:

"My dear marquis, if you wish to be my son-in-law—it rests entirely with you."

Bowing very low, the marquis accepted the honor bestowed upon him. The very same day he was married to the princess.

Puss became a person of great importance at court. Never again did he chase a mouse—except for fun.

Blue-Beard

BY CHARLES PERRAULT
ADAPTED BY LOUIS UNTERMEYER
Illustrated by KANAKO TANABE

Once upon a time there was a very rich man, who had town and country houses and lived in a magnificent castle. He had great quantities of gold and silver, and precious stones and rich furniture, and great gilded coaches. But he was hideously ugly, and what made him most disagreeable was that he had an enormous blue beard, which looked so strange and frightful that all the ladies ran away from him.

One of his neighbors, a fine lady, had two very handsome daughters. Blue-Beard asked for one in marriage, leaving the lady to choose which she would give him. The daughters did not like him at all, neither being able to make up her mind to marry a man who had a blue beard. What made them like him even less was that he had already married several wives, and nobody knew what had become of them.

To become better acquainted, Blue-Beard invited them, with their mother and some young people of the neighborhood, to his castle, where they stayed eight whole days.

They spent their time walking, hunting, fishing, dancing and feasting. They played games and stayed up most of the night. At last all went on so well that the younger daughter began to think that the master of the house was not such a bad fellow after all, and that his beard was not really so blue. In fact before the week was ended, she had consented to become his wife.

At the end of a month, Blue-Beard told his wife that he must go away for at least six weeks on important business. He wished her to enjoy herself while he was away, to invite some of her friends, and to live as happily as possible.

"Here," said he, "are the keys of the two great storerooms. Here are those for the gold and silver plate, which is not used every day. Here are the keys of my strongboxes where I keep my gold and silver. Here are the keys of my caskets, where I keep my jewels. And here is the master-key to all the rooms. But this little key is to the small room at the end of the passage on the ground floor. Examine everything; go everywhere you wish—but I forbid you to open this one little room. And I warn you that if you disobey, your punishment will be more severe than you can imagine."

She promised strictly to obey everything he had commanded, and he set out on his journey.

The friends and neighbors did not wait long for an invitation to call upon the young wife. They were eager to see all the splendors of her house, not having dared to come

while her husband was there, because his blue beard frightened them. They were soon running through the chambers, closets, and store-rooms, each of which seemed richer than the others. They went upstairs to the wardrobes, where they admired the number and beauty of the tapestries, the stately beds, the elegant sofas, the tastefully carved stands and tables, the shining mirrors where they could see themselves from head to foot, and the frames of which, made of gold and silver, were handsomer than any they had ever seen before. They did not cease to praise and admire the good fortune of their friend. But she was not as pleased as the others at seeing all these fine things, because she was longing to examine the small room on the ground floor.

At length her curiosity became so great that, without considering how impolite it was to leave her company alone, she hurried down the back staircase, with such eager haste that she was more than once in danger of breaking her neck.

She was almost breathless when she reached the threshold of the chamber, and a sudden fear seemed to check her as she called to mind the ominous warning of her husband, and the terrible punishment he might inflict if he discovered her disobedience. But the temptation was so strong that she could not resist it. She seized the little key and, with a trembling hand, opened the door.

On entering the room, she at first saw nothing, as the shutters were closed. But on opening them and admitting the daylight, a frightful spectacle met her view. The floor was covered with blood, and along the walls were strung up the bodies of several murdered women. "These, then," she thought in her agony, "are those former wives of Blue-Beard who so mysteriously disappeared." Almost fainting with terror, she tried to replace the key in the lock from which she had withdrawn it on entering, but her hand was so unsteady that it fell upon the floor of the apartment. Hastily picking it up and locking the door, she hurried to her own chamber, and tried to compose herself. But the shock had been so terrible that it took a long time. To add to her worry, she now perceived that the key, which had fallen, was stained with blood. She washed it with soap, and scoured it with sand and stone. But the

blood would not come off; it remained as visible as ever. The truth was, though she did not know it, that the key was a magic key, so that when the stains were gone from one side, they would reappear on the other.

Blue-Beard unexpectedly returned from his journey the same evening, and said that he had received letters telling him that the business which had taken him from home had been settled in his favor. His wife tried to appear as if nothing had disturbed her, as if she were really overjoyed at seeing him so soon again. The following morning her fears were suddenly reawakened when Blue-Beard demanded his keys. After hesitating a moment, she produced them; but her husband remarked that her hand trembled as she gave them to him, and he at once guessed what had happened.

"How is it, my dear," he said, very politely, "that the key of the little room is not among the rest?"

"Isn't it?" she replied, as if surprised. "I must have left it upstairs on my table."

"Be so good as to fetch it, then, without delay," said Blue-Beard, with forced calmness.

After many delays and excuses she was forced to bring him the key. He examined it carefully. Then, eyeing her very sternly, he asked, "How is it, madam, that I see blood-stains on the key?"

"I know nothing about it," she faltered, turning pale.

"You know nothing about it, eh, madam?" returned Blue-Beard, with a sneer. "Then I shall tell you all about it. You determined to pay a visit to the forbidden little room. Very well. You shall visit it again, and at once! And you will take your place with the women you found there."

She threw herself at his feet, and, weeping bitterly, begged for forgiveness. But all in vain.

"If I *must* die, then," said she, looking at him with tearful eyes, "give me a little time to say my prayers." She was so beautiful and sorrowful, she would have melted a rock. But Blue-Beard's heart was harder than any stone.

"I will give you," he said, "exactly one quarter of an hour, but not a moment more."

As soon as she was alone, she called out to her sister, and said, "Sister Anne, go up, I pray you, to the top of the tower, and see if my brothers are coming. They promised me they would come to visit me today. And if you see them, give them a signal to hasten."

Her sister went up to the top of the tower, and the wife called out: "Anne, sister Anne, do you see anybody coming?"

And her sister replied: "I see nothing but the burning sun and the waving grass."

Meantime, Blue-Beard, holding a great cutlass, cried out at the top of his voice: "Come down at once or I shall come after you."

"Just one moment more," cried his wife; and then called very softly: "Anne, sister Anne, do you see anybody coming?"

"I see," replied sister Anne, "a great cloud of dust, which is moving this way."

"Is it my brothers?"

"Alas, no, my sister; it is a flock of sheep."

"Will you come down?" shouted Blue-Beard.

"Only one moment more," she cried; and then called out: "Anne, sister Anne, do you see anybody coming?"

"I see two horsemen coming this way but they are yet very far off."

"Thank God!" she cried out. "They are my brothers!"

"I will give them a signal to hasten," said her sister.

Blue-Beard now cried out so loud that the whole house trembled. His terrified wife came down, and threw herself at his feet, weeping, her hair tumbling over her shoulders.

"It's no use," said he. "You must die." Then, taking her by the hair with one hand, and raising his cutlass in the other, he was about to cut off her head. Turning tearful eyes upon him, she begged him to give her one more moment to recover herself. "Not an instant," roared Blue-Beard. He raised his arm, but there came so loud a knocking at the gate that he stopped short. The gate was thrown open and two horsemen rushed in brandishing swords, and flew furiously at Blue-Beard. He recognized them as the brothers of his wife, and tried to make his escape. But before he could do so, they fell upon him, and ran their swords through his body.

Blue-Beard had no heirs, and so his wife became the owner of all his possessions. She used some of the fortune to marry her young sister Anne to a gentleman whom she had loved for a long time. Another portion was used to buy captains' commissions for her brothers. And the rest she kept for herself, for she married an honorable man, whose goodness made her forget the terrible time she had with Blue-Beard.

"Hop O'-My-Thumb" is a popular folk tale—
the following version is by the French storyteller,
Charles Perrault. It also appears in a German
version recorded by Jakob and Wilhelm Grimm a hundred
and fifty years ago. Five stories from their
famous collection follow "Hop O'-My-Thumb."
A word about "Hansel and Gretel:"
Like "Tom Thumb" and "Hop O'-My-Thumb,"
it is about the family of a poor woodcutter.
As in "Hop O'-My-Thumb," the father
and mother sadly conclude that,
since they can no longer feed their children,
they had better get rid of them. From that
point on, "Hansel and Gretel" takes
an entirely different course.
The story's appeal became even more widespread
when it was made into an opera by Engelbert Humperdinck
and enjoyed by adults as well as children.

Hop O'-My-Thumb

BY CHARLES PERRAULT ADAPTED BY LOUIS UNTERMEYER
Illustrated by MAE GERHARD

Once upon a time there was a woodcutter and his wife who had seven children, all boys. They were very poor, and their seven children were a great worry to them, because none of them was yet able to earn his own living. What troubled them most was that the youngest son was very delicate and small. When born he was no larger than a man's thumb; so everybody called him Hop O'-My-Thumb.

There came a famine in the land, and these people, having no food for their children, resolved to get rid of them. One night, when the children were asleep in bed, the woodcutter said to his wife as they sat before the fire, "You see that we can no longer provide for our children. I cannot see them die of hunger. Tomorrow while they are with us, tying up the twigs, we must lose them in the woods."

"Ah!" cried the woodcutter's wife. "How can we!"

"We cannot find even enough food for one!"

Finally, however, she agreed that she could not bear to see the children die of hunger, and so she consented to his plan, and went weeping to bed.

Hop O'-My-Thumb had heard all that had been said. Listening to the voices, he had crept out of bed and had hidden himself under his father's chair, where he could not be seen. After his parents had finished talking he went back to bed. But he did not sleep a wink that night; he kept on thinking what he would have to do. Finally, he decided on a plan.

The next morning he got up early and went to the brook-

side. There he picked up a lot of white pebbles, filled his pockets with them, and returned home.

Soon after, they entered a thick wood. The woodcutter began to chop wood and, when the children began to gather up the sticks, the mother and father crept off.

When the children found themselves alone, they began to cry. But Hop O'-My-Thumb had dropped the white pebbles all along the way. After letting them cry awhile, he told them to cheer up, for he would lead them back again. So they followed him, and he led them home by the same road by which they came. At first they did not dare to go in, but stood at the door to hear what their parents were saying.

The very moment the woodcutter and his wife arrived home, they received a sum of money which had long been due them for their work. The wife went straight to the butcher's, and got so much meat that when the two had eaten enough, there was still a great deal left, and the woman said, "Alas! where are our poor children? Here is food enough left for them all. I told you it was wrong to leave them in the forest. Perhaps wolves have already eaten them!"

At last she cried so loud that the children heard her, and answered all together, "Here we are! Here we are!"

She ran to the door and, throwing it open, began to embrace them, saying, "How happy I am to see you again, my dear children; how tired and hungry you must be. Come in. You must be starved!"

Their father and mother were well pleased to see them eat, and to hear their voices again.

Everyone talked at once, and there was nothing but joy.

But this happiness did not last. The money was soon spent, and the parents started worrying again. They fell back upon their first plan; but this time they decided to take the children much deeper into the forest.

Hop O'-My-Thumb found out all about it as before. He got up early in the morning to get the pebbles as before; but he found the door locked, so he could not get out. At first he did not know what to do, but they each had a piece of bread for breakfast, and he thought he could mark the road by strewing crumbs along as he had done with the pebbles. So he put his bread into his pocket. Their father and mother led them into the darkest and most tangled part of the forest, and then stole off and left them as before. Hop O'-My-Thumb was not worried. He supposed he could find his way back by the pieces of bread, but he was mistaken; the birds had eaten every crumb.

They were now in great trouble. They wandered deeper into the forest, and were so frightened by the howling of wolves and the rain and wind that they were afraid to speak. Hop O'-My-Thumb climbed to the top of a tree to see what he could discover. At last, looking everywhere, he spied a light beyond the forest. He came down again, and, after walking toward it with his brothers for some time, they at last came to a house.

They knocked at the door, and a woman, bearing a lamp, appeared. She asked what they wanted. Hop O'-My-Thumb told her they were poor children lost in the forest, and had come to beg a night's rest. The woman, who pitied their forlorn condition, began to cry, and said, "Alas, my children, you have come to the house of an ogre!"

"Oh, madam," he replied, trembling with fear, as did

his brothers, "what shall we do? The wolves will certainly eat us up if we stay in the forest, and we would rather take a chance with an ogre. Perhaps your husband, when he sees us, may take pity on us, and spare our lives."

The ogress, hoping she might be able to conceal them, let them come in. While they were warming themselves at a huge fire, before which was a whole sheep roasting for the ogre's supper, they heard three or four heavy blows at the door. It was the ogre, who had come home. The ogress hastily concealed them under the bed, and admitted the ogre, who asked if his supper was ready, and sat down at the table. He began to eat, staring to the right and left, saying: "I smell fresh meat."

"It must be," said the ogress, "that you smell the veal which I am dressing."

"I smell *fresh* meat," roared the ogre. And so saying, he jumped up and went straight to the bed.

"So, madam," said he to his wife, "this is the way you try to deceive me. I would eat you, too, if you were not so tough. This supply of game comes very well to feed three ogres whom I expect in a few days."

He dragged the children out from under the bed; they fell on their knees, and begged for mercy. But he was an unusually hard-hearted ogre. He sharpened his great knife, and seized one of them, when his wife said, "Why such haste? You have a great deal of meat on hand already."

"You are right," said he, "give them plenty to eat. Fatten them up and put them to bed." The ogress was delighted and gave them a good supper; but they were so frightened they could scarcely eat.

This ogre had seven young daughters. Although they

had fine complexions, they had beak-like noses and long sharp teeth. They were not yet wicked, but they were growing up to resemble their father, and they had already bitten several small children. They had gone to bed early, in one large bed, each girl having on her head a golden crown. There was another bed just like it in which the boys were put.

Hop O'-My-Thumb, fearing the ogre would come and kill them during the night, got up after all was quiet, took his brothers' caps and his own, and put them on the heads of the little girls. Then, taking their golden crowns, he put them on the heads of his brothers and himself.

Just as he had expected, the ogre, waking up in the night, was sorry he had put off killing them, and so, taking his great knife, he went upstairs. He groped his way in the dark room, and went to the bed where the little boys lay. He passed his hands over all their heads, and, feeling the crowns, said, "Why, this is strange!"

He then went to the other bed, and, feeling the boys' caps on his daughters' heads, said, "Ah! here you are, my boys!" and in a moment cut the throats of his daughters.

As soon as he was back in bed and snoring, Hop O'-My-Thumb told his brothers to get up and dress themselves and follow him. They went down softly into the garden and jumped over the wall. They ran all the rest of the night, trembling and fearful, not knowing where they were.

In the morning the ogre told his wife to go up and dress the little boys. She was much surprised at his kindness, thinking he meant her to put on their clothes. She went to the room, and, seeing her seven daughters bathed in blood, fainted at the sight. The ogre, getting impatient at his wife's delay, went up himself, and was astonished at the frightful sight.

"Ah!" said he, "what have I done? The wretches shall pay for this!"

He then revived his wife and told her to bring his seven-league boots, so that he might pursue the children. He set out, and, after going in every direction, at last came into the same road where the children were walking, not a hundred rods from their father's house. They saw the ogre striding over the country, and, finding a hollow rock, crept behind it, and waited for him to pass. Being very tired from his long walk (for the boots were quite hard to wear), the ogre happened to sit down on the very rock behind which the little boys were concealed. Weary with fatigue, he went to sleep. Hop O'-My-Thumb, taking courage, told his brothers to run home while the ogre was snoring, which they did.

Then Hop O'-My-Thumb crept out, went quietly to the ogre, softly pulled off his seven-league boots, and put them on himself. They were very clumsy, but, since they were magic boots, they had the power of growing large or small to fit the foot of the wearer. He went straight to the ogre's house and told his wife that the ogre had been seized by a band of robbers who had threatened his life, unless he should give up all his gold and silver. "He told me to wear these boots, and to come for all his treasures."

The ogress, terribly alarmed, gave him the key to all the ogre's wealth. Hop O'-My-Thumb took as much as he could carry, and went straight home, where he was received with great joy, and they lived in ease ever after.

"Snow-White and the Seven Dwarfs"
is one of the best-known stories
from the collection made by Jakob and Wilhelm Grimm.
These brothers wrote down
more than two hundred folk-tales and legends
which had been told in Germany for hundreds of years.
No book for young people is complete
without some of them.

Snow-White and the Seven Dwarfs

BY JAKOB AND WILHELM GRIMM
Illustrated by WILLIAM SHARP

It was in the middle of winter, when the broad flakes of snow were falling around, that the queen of a country far away sat working at her window. The frame of the window was made of fine black ebony; and as she was looking out upon the snow, she pricked her finger, and three drops of blood fell upon it. Then she gazed thoughtfully upon the red drops that sprinkled the white snow, and said, "Would that my little daughter may be as white as that snow, as red as that blood, and as black as this ebony window frame!"

And so the little girl really did grow up. Her skin was as white as snow, her cheeks as rosy as blood, and her hair as black as ebony; and she was called Snow-White.

But this queen died; and the king soon married another wife, who was very beautiful, but so vain that she could not bear to think that anyone could be handsomer than she was. She had a magical mirror, to which she used to go and gaze upon herself in it, and say,

> *"Mirror, Mirror on the wall,*
> *Who is fairest of us all?"*

And the glass had always answered,

> *"Thou, Queen, art the fairest in all the land."*

But Snow-White grew more and more beautiful; and when she was seven years old, she was as bright as the day, and fairer than the queen herself. Then the glass one day answered the queen, when she went to look in it as usual,

> *"Thou, Queen, art fair and beauteous to see,*
> *But Snow-White is fairer far than thee."*

When the queen heard this she turned pale with rage and envy and called to one of her servants and said, "Take Snow-White away into the wide wood, that I may never see her any more." Then the servant led Snow-White away; but his heart melted when she begged him to spare her life, and he said, "I will not hurt thee, thou pretty child." So he left her by herself, and though he thought it most likely that the wild beasts

would tear her in pieces, he felt as if a great weight were taken off his heart when he had made up his mind not to kill her, but to leave her to her fate, with the chance of someone finding and saving her.

Then poor Snow-White wandered along through the wood in great

fear; and the wild beasts roared about her, but none did her any harm.
In the evening she came to a little cottage, and went in there to rest
herself, for her little feet would carry her no farther. Everything was
spruce and neat in the cottage. On the table was spread a white cloth,

and there were seven little plates with seven little loaves, and seven little glasses, with wine in them; and knives and forks laid in order; and by the wall stood seven little beds. As she was very hungry, she picked a little piece off each loaf, and drank a very little wine from each glass; and after that she thought she would lie down and rest. So she tried all the little beds; but one was too long, and another was too short, till at last the seventh suited her; and there she lay down, and went to sleep.

By and by in came the masters of the cottage, who were seven little dwarfs that lived among the mountains, and dug and searched about for gold. They lighted up their seven lamps, and saw at once that all was not right. The first said, "Who has been sitting on my stool?" The second, "Who has been eating off my plate?" The third, "Who has been picking my bread?" The fourth, "Who has been meddling with my spoon?" The fifth, "Who has been handling my fork?" The sixth, "Who has been cutting with my knife?" The seventh, "Who has been drinking my wine?"

Then the first looked round and said, "Who has been lying on my bed?" And the rest came running to him, and every one cried out that somebody had been upon his bed. But the seventh saw Snow-White, and called all his brethren to come and see her; and they cried out with wonder and astonishment, and brought their lamps to look at her, and said, "Good heavens! what a lovely child she is!" And they were very glad to see her, and took care not to wake her; and the seventh dwarf slept an hour with each of the other dwarfs in turn, till the night was gone.

In the morning Snow-White told them all her story; and they pitied her, and said if she would keep all things in order, and cook and wash, and knit and spin for them, she might stay where she was, and they would take good care of her. Then they went out all day long to their work, seeking for gold and silver in the mountains; but Snow-White remained at home; and they warned her, and said, "The queen will soon find out where you are, so take care and let no one in."

But the queen, now that she thought Snow-White was dead, believed that she must be the handsomest lady in the land; and she went to her mirror and said,

> *"Mirror, Mirror on the wall,*
> *Who is fairest of us all?"*

And the mirror answered,

> *"Queen, thou art of beauty rare,*
> *But Snow-White living in the glen*
> *With the seven little men,*
> *Is a thousand times more fair."*

Then the queen was very much frightened; for she knew that the glass always spoke the truth, and was sure that the servant had betrayed her. And she could not bear to think that anyone lived who was more beautiful than she was; so she dressed herself up as an old pedlar and went her way over the hills to the place where the dwarfs dwelt. Then she knocked at the door, and cried, "Fine wares to sell!" Snow-White looked out at the window, and said, "Good-day, good woman; what have you to sell?" "Good wares, fine wares," said she; "laces and bobbins of all colors." "I will let the old lady in; she seems to be a very good sort of body," thought Snow-White; so she ran down, and unbolted the door. "Bless me!" said the old woman, "how badly your stays are laced! Let me lace them up with one of my nice new laces." Snow-White did not dream of any mischief; so she stood up before the old woman, who set to work so nimbly, and pulled the lace so tight, that Snow-White lost her breath, and fell down as if she were dead. "There's an end to all your beauty," said the spiteful queen, and went away home.

In the evening the seven dwarfs returned; and I need not say how grieved they were to see their faithful Snow-White stretched upon the ground as if she were quite dead. However, they lifted her up, and when they found what ailed her, they cut the lace; and in a little time she began to breathe, and soon came to life again. Then they said, "The old woman was the queen herself; take care another time, and let no one in when we are away."

When the queen got home, she went straight to her glass, and spoke to it as usual; but to her great grief it still said,

> *"Queen, thou art of beauty rare,*
> *But Snow-White living in the glen*
> *With the seven little men,*
> *Is a thousand times more fair."*

Then the blood ran cold in her heart with spite and malice to see that Snow-White still lived; and she dressed herself up again, but in quite another dress from the one she wore before, and took with her a poisoned comb. When she reached the dwarfs' cottage, she knocked at the door, and cried, "Fine wares to sell!" But Snow-White said, "I dare not let anyone in." Then the queen said, "Only look at my beautiful combs"; and gave her the poisoned one. And it looked so pretty that Snow-White took it up and put it into her hair to try it. But the moment it touched her head the poison was so powerful that she fell down senseless. "There you may lie," said the queen, and went her way.

But by good luck the dwarfs returned very early that evening, and when they saw Snow-White lying on the ground, they guessed what had happened, and soon found the poisoned comb. When they took it away, she recovered, and told them all that had passed; and they warned her once more not to open the door to anyone.

Meantime the queen went home to her glass, and shook with rage when she received the very same answer as before; and she said, "Snow-White shall die, if it costs me my life." So she went by herself into a chamber, and prepared a poisoned apple. The outside looked very rosy and tempting, but whoever tasted it was sure to die. Then she dressed herself up as a peasant's wife, and travelled over the hills to the dwarfs' cottage, and knocked at the door; but Snow-White put her head out of the window and said, "I dare not let anyone in, for the dwarfs have told me not to." "Do as you please," said the old woman, "but at any rate take this pretty apple; I will give it to you." "No," said Snow-White, "I dare not take it." "You silly girl!" answered the other, "What are you afraid of? Do you think it is poisoned? Come! Do you eat one part, and I will eat the other."

Now the apple was so prepared that one side was good, though the other side was poisoned. Then Snow-White was much tempted to taste, for the apple looked so very nice; and when she saw the old woman eat, she could wait no longer. But she had scarcely put the piece into her mouth, when she fell down dead upon the ground. "This time nothing will save you," said the queen, and she went home to her glass and at last it said,

"Thou, Queen, art the fairest in all the land."

And her wicked heart was glad, and as happy as such a heart could be.

When evening came, and the dwarfs returned home, they found Snow-White lying on the ground. No breath came from her lips, and they were afraid that she was quite dead. They lifted her up, and combed her hair, and washed her face with wine and water; but all was in vain, for the little girl seemed quite dead. So they laid her down upon a bier, and all seven watched and bewailed her three whole days; and then they thought they would bury her; but her cheeks were still rosy, and her face looked just as it did while she was alive. So they said, "We will never bury her in the cold ground." And they made a coffin of glass, so that they might still look at her, and wrote upon it in golden letters what her name was, and that she was a king's daughter. And the coffin was placed upon the hill, and one of the dwarfs always sat by it and watched. And the birds of the air came too, and bemoaned Snow-White; first of all came an owl, and then a raven, and at last a dove, and sat by her side.

And thus Snow-White lay for a long, long time, and still looked as though she were only asleep; for she was even now as white as snow, and as red as blood, and as black as ebony. At last a prince came and called at the dwarfs' house. He saw Snow-White, and read what was written in golden letters. Then he offered the dwarfs money, and prayed and besought them to let him take her away; but they said, "We will not part with her for all the gold in the world." At last, however, they had pity on him, and gave him the coffin; but the moment he lifted it up to carry it home with him, the piece of apple fell from between her lips, and Snow-White awoke, and said, "Where am I?" And the prince answered, "You are quite safe with me."

Then he told her all that had happened, and said, "I love you far better than all the world. Come with me to my father's palace, and you shall be my wife." And Snow-White consented, and went home with the prince; and everything was got ready with great pomp and great splendour for their wedding.

To the feast was asked, among the rest, Snow-White's old enemy, the queen; and as she was dressing herself in fine rich clothes, she looked in the glass, and said,

> *"Mirror, Mirror on the wall,*
> *Who is fairest of us all?"*

And the glass answered,

> *"O Queen, although you are of beauty rare*
> *The young bride is a thousand times more fair."*

When she heard this, she started with rage; but her envy and curiosity were so great that she could not help setting out to see the bride. And when she got there, and saw that it was no other than Snow-White, who, as she thought, had been dead a long while, she choked with rage, and fell down and died. But Snow-White and the prince lived and reigned happily over that land many, many years. And sometimes they went up into the mountains and paid a visit to the little dwarfs who had been so kind to Snow-White in her time of need.

"Rumpelstiltskin" is another of the tales
collected by the Brothers Grimm. It is a queer story.
Perhaps the queerest part of it
is the name of the dwarf, one of the strangest
—and most unforgettable—names
you have ever heard.

Rumpelstiltskin

BY JAKOB AND WILHELM GRIMM
Illustrated by WILLIAM SHARP

By the side of a wood, in a country a long way off, ran a fine stream of water; and upon the stream there stood a mill. The miller's house was close by, and the miller, you must know, had a very beautiful daughter. She was, moreover, very shrewd and clever; and the miller was so proud of her, that he one day told the king of the land, who used to come and hunt in the wood, that his daughter could spin gold out of straw. Now this king was very fond of money; and when he heard the miller's boast, his greediness was raised, and he sent for the girl to be brought before him. Then he led her to a chamber in his palace where there was a great heap of straw and gave her a spinning-wheel, and said, "All of this must be spun into gold before morning, as you love your life." It was in vain that the poor maiden said that it was only a silly boast of her father, or that she could do no such thing as spin straw into gold; the chamber door was locked, and she was left alone.

She sat down in one corner of the room, and began to bewail her hard fate; when on a sudden the door opened, and a droll-looking little man hobbled in and said, "Good morrow to you, my good lass; what are you weeping for?" "Alas!" said she. "I must spin this straw into gold, and I know not how." "What will you give me," said the hobgoblin, "to do it for you?" "My necklace," replied the maiden. He took her at her word and sat himself down to the wheel and whistled and sang,

"Round about, round about,
Lo and behold!
Reel away, reel away,
Straw into gold!"

And round about the wheel went merrily; the work was quickly done, and the straw was all spun into gold.

When the king came and saw this, he was greatly astonished and pleased; but his heart grew still more greedy of gain, and he shut up the poor miller's daughter again with a fresh task. Then she knew not what to do, and sat down once more to weep; but the dwarf soon opened the door, and said, "What will you give me to do your task?" "The ring on my finger," said she. So her little friend took the ring, and began to work at the wheel again, and whistled and sang,

"Round about, round about,
Lo and behold!
Reel away, reel away,
Straw into gold!"

till, long before morning, all was done again.

The king was greatly delighted to see all this glittering treasure; but still he had not enough: so he took the miller's daughter to a yet larger heap, and said, "All this must be spun tonight; and if it is, you shall be my queen." As soon as she was alone the dwarf came in, and said, "What will you give me to spin gold for you this third time?" "I have nothing left," said she. "Then say you will give me," said the little man, "the first little child that you may have when you are queen." "That may never be," thought the miller's daughter: and as she knew no other way to get her task done, she said she would do what he asked. Round went the wheel again to the old song, and the manikin once more spun the heap into gold. The king came in the morning, and, finding all he wanted, was forced to keep his word; so he married the miller's daughter, and she really became queen.

At the birth of her first little child she was very glad, and forgot the dwarf, and what she had said. But one day he came into her room, where she was sitting playing with her baby, and put her in mind of it. Then

she grieved sorely at her misfortune, and said she would give him all the
wealth of her kingdom if he would let her off, but in vain; till at last her
tears softened him, and he said, "I will give you three days' grace, and if
during that time you tell me my name, you shall keep your child."

Now the queen lay awake all night, thinking of all the odd names that she had ever heard; and she sent messengers all over the land to find out new ones. The next day the little man came, and she began with TIMOTHY, ICHABOD, BENJAMIN, JEREMIAH, and all the names she could remember; but to all and each of them he said, "Madam, that is not my name."

The second day she began with all the comical names she could hear of, BANDY-LEGS, HUNCH-BACK, CROOK-SHANKS, and so on; but the little gentleman still said to every one of them, "Madam, that is not my name."

The third day one of the messengers came back, and said, "I traveled two days without hearing of any other names; but yesterday, as I was climbing a high hill, among the trees of the forest where the fox and the hare bid each other good-night, I saw a little hut; and before the hut burnt a fire; and round about the fire a funny little dwarf was dancing upon one leg, and singing,

> "'Merrily the feast I'll make.
> To-day I'll brew, to-morrow bake;
> Merrily I'll dance and sing,
> For next day will a stranger bring.
> Little does my lady dream
> Rumpelstiltskin is my name!'"

When the queen heard this she jumped for joy, and as soon as her little friend came she sat down upon her throne and called all her court round to enjoy the fun; and the nurse stood by her side with the baby in her arms, as if it was quite ready to be given up. Then the little man began to chuckle at the thoughts of having the poor child, to take home with him to his hut in the woods; and he cried out, "Now, lady, what is my name!" "Is it JOHN?" asked she. "No, madam!" "Is it TOM?" "No, madam!" "Is it JEMMY?" "It is not." "Can your name be RUMPELSTILTSKIN?" said the lady slyly. "Some witch told you that!—some witch told you that!" cried the little man, and dashed his right foot in a rage so deep into the floor, that he was forced to lay hold of it with both hands to pull it out.

Then he made the best of his way off, while the nurse laughed and the baby crowed; and all the court jeered at him for having had so much trouble for nothing, and said, "We wish you a very good morning, and a merry feast, MR. RUMPELSTILTSKIN!"

Hansel and Gretel

BY JAKOB AND WILHELM GRIMM
Illustrated by ELOISE WILKIN

Near a great forest there lived a poor woodcutter and his wife, and his two children. The boy's name was Hansel and the girl's, Gretel. They had very little to bite or to sup, and once, when there was much want in the land, the man could not even earn the daily bread.

As he lay in bed one night thinking of this, and turning and tossing, he sighed heavily, and said to his wife, who was the children's step-mother,

"What will become of us? We cannot even feed our children; there is nothing left for ourselves."

"I will tell you what, husband," answered the wife; "we will take the children early in the morning into the forest, where it is thickest; we will make them a fire, and we will give each of them a piece of bread, then we will go to our work and leave them alone; they will never find the way home again, and we shall be quit of them."

"No, wife," said the man, "I cannot do that; I cannot find it in my heart to take my children into the forest and to leave them there alone; the wild animals would soon come and devour them."

"Oh you fool," said she, "then we will all four starve; you had better get the coffins ready," and she left him no peace until he consented.

The two children had not been able to sleep for hunger, and had heard what their stepmother had said to their father. Gretel wept bitterly, and said to Hansel,

"It is all over with us."

"Do be quiet, Gretel," said Hansel, "and do not fret; I will manage something." When the parents had gone to sleep, Hansel got up, put on his little coat, opened the back door, and slipped out. The moon was shining brightly, and the white pebbles that lay in front of the house glistened like pieces of silver. Hansel stooped and filled the little pocket of his coat as full as it would hold. Then he went back again, and said to Gretel,

"Be easy, dear little sister, and go to sleep quietly; God will not forsake us," and laid himself down again in his bed.

When the day was breaking, and before the sun had risen, the wife came and awakened the two children, saying,

"Get up, you lazy bones! We are going into the forest to cut wood."

Then she gave each of them a piece of bread, and said,

"That is for dinner, and you must not eat it before then, for you will get no more."

Gretel carried the bread under her apron, for Hansel had his pockets full of pebbles. Then they set off all together on their way to the forest.

When they had gone a little way Hansel stood still and looked back toward the house, and this he did again and again, till his father said to him,

"Hansel, what are you looking at? Take care not to forget your legs."

"Oh Father," said Hansel, "I am looking at my little white kitten, who is sitting up on the roof to bid me good-bye."

"You foolish boy," said the woman, "that is not your kitten, but the sunshine on the chimney pot."

Of course Hansel had not been looking at his kitten, but had been taking every now and then a pebble from his pocket and dropping it on the road.

When they reached the middle of the forest the father told the children to collect wood to make a fire to keep them warm; and Hansel and

Gretel gathered brushwood enough for a little mountain; and it was set on fire, and when the flame was burning quite high the wife said,

"Now lie down by the fire and rest yourselves, you children, and we will go and cut wood; and when we are ready we will come and fetch you."

So Hansel and Gretel sat by the fire, and at noon they each ate their pieces of bread. They thought their father was in the wood all the time, as they seemed to hear the strokes of the ax, but really it was only a dry branch hanging to a withered tree that the wind moved to and fro.

So when they had stayed there a long time their eyelids closed with weariness, and they fell fast asleep. When at last they woke it was night, and Gretel began to cry, and said,

"How shall we ever get out of this wood?" But Hansel comforted her, saying,

"Wait a little while longer, until the moon rises, and then we can easily find the way home."

And when the full moon came up, Hansel took his little sister by the hand, and followed the way where the pebbles shone like silver, and

showed them the road. They walked on the whole night through, and at the break of day they came to their father's house. They knocked at the door, and when their stepmother opened it and saw that it was Hansel and Gretel she said,

"You naughty children, why did you sleep so long in the wood? We thought you were never coming home again!"

But the father was glad, for it had gone to his heart to leave them both in the woods alone.

Not very long after that there was again great scarcity in those parts, and the children heard their stepmother say to their father,

"Everything is finished up; we have only half a loaf, and after that the tale comes to an end. The children must be off, we will take them farther into the wood this time, so that they shall not be able to find the way back again. There is no other way to manage."

The man felt sad at heart, and he thought,

"It would be better to share one's last morsel with one's children."

But the wife would listen to nothing that he said, but scolded and reproached him.

But the children were not asleep, and had heard all the talk. When the parents had gone to sleep, Hansel got up to go out and get more pebbles as he did before, but the stepmother had locked the door, and Hansel could not get out, but he comforted his little sister, and said,

"Don't cry, Gretel, and go to sleep quietly, and God will help us."

Early the next morning the wife came and pulled the children out of bed. She gave them each a little piece of bread—less than before; and on the way to the wood Hansel crumbled the bread in his pocket, and often stopped to throw a crumb on the ground.

"Hansel, what are you stopping behind and staring for?" said the father.

"I am looking at my little pigeon sitting on the roof, to say good-bye to me," answered Hansel.

"You foolish boy," said the wife, "that is no pigeon, but the morning sun shining on the chimney pots."

Hansel went on as before, and strewed bread crumbs all along the road.

The woman led the children far into the wood, where they had never been before in all their lives. And again there was a large fire made, and the stepmother said,

"Sit still there, you children, and when you are tired you can go to sleep; we are going into the forest to cut wood, and in the evening, when we are ready to go home, we will come and fetch you."

So when noon came Gretel shared her bread with Hansel, who had strewed his along the road.

Then they went to sleep, and the evening passed, and no one came for the poor children. When they awoke it was dark night, and Hansel comforted his little sister, and said,

"Wait a little, Gretel, until the moon gets up; then we shall be able to see our way home by the crumbs of bread that I have scattered along the road."

So when the moon rose they got up, but they could find no crumbs of bread, for the birds of the woods and of the fields had come and picked them up. Hansel thought they might find the way all the same, but they could not.

They went on all that night, and the next day from the morning until the evening, but they could not find the way out of the wood, and they were very hungry, for they had nothing to eat but the few berries they could pick up. And when they were so tired that they could no longer drag themselves along, they lay down under a tree and fell asleep.

It was now the third morning since they had left their father's house. They were always trying to get back to it, but instead of that they only found themselves farther in the wood, and if help had not soon come they would have been starved. About noon they saw a pretty snow-white bird sitting on a bough, and singing so sweetly that they stopped to listen. And when he had finished, the bird spread his wings and flew before them, and they followed after him until they came to a little house, and the bird perched on the roof, and when they came nearer they saw that the house was built of gingerbread, and roofed with cakes; and the window was of transparent sugar.

"We will have some of this," said Hansel, "and make a fine meal.

"We will have some of this," said Hansel, "and make a fine meal. I will eat a piece of the roof, Gretel, and you can have some of the window—that will taste sweet."

So Hansel reached up and broke off a bit of the roof, just to see how it tasted, and Gretel stood by the window and gnawed at it. Then they heard a thin voice call out from inside,

"Nibble, nibble, like a mouse,
Who is nibbling at my house?"

151

And the children answered,

"*Never mind,*

It is the wind."

And they went on eating, never disturbing themselves. Hansel, who found that the roof tasted very nice, took down a great piece of it, and Gretel pulled out a large round windowpane, and sat her down and began upon it. Then the door opened, and an aged woman came out, leaning upon a crutch. Hansel and Gretel felt very frightened, and let fall what they had in their hands. The old woman, however, nodded her head, and said,

"Ah, my dear children, how come you here? You must come indoors and stay with me. You will be no trouble."

So she took them each by the hand, and led them into her little house. And there they found a good meal laid out, of milk and pancakes, with sugar, apples, and nuts. After that she showed them two little white beds, and Hansel and Gretel laid themselves down on them, and thought they were in heaven.

The old woman, although her behavior was so kind, was a wicked witch, who lay in wait for children, and had built the little house on purpose to entice them. When they were once inside she used to kill them, cook them, and eat them, and then it was a feast-day with her. The witch's eyes were red, and she could not see very far, but she had a keen scent, like the beasts, and knew very well when human creatures were near. When she knew that Hansel and Gretel were coming, she gave a spiteful laugh, and said triumphantly,

"I have them, and they shall not escape me!"

Early in the morning, before the children were awake, she got up to look at them, and as they lay sleeping so peacefully with round rosy cheeks, she said to herself,

"What a fine feast I shall have!"

She grasped Hansel with her withered hand, and led him into a little stable, and shut him up behind a grating; and call and scream as he might, it was no good. Then she went back to Gretel and shook her, crying,

"Get up, lazy bones! Fetch water, and cook something nice for your brother; he is outside in the stable, and must be fattened up. And when he is fat enough, I will eat him."

Gretel began to weep bitterly, but it was of no use. She had to do what the wicked witch bade her.

And so the best kind of victuals was cooked for poor Hansel, while Gretel got nothing but crab shells. Each morning the old woman visited the little stable, and cried,

"Hansel, stretch out your finger, that I may tell if you will soon be fat enough."

Hansel, however, held out a little bone, and the old woman, who had weak eyes, could not see what it was, and supposing it to be Hansel's finger, wondered very much that it was not getting fatter. When four weeks had passed and Hansel seemed to remain so thin, she lost patience and could wait no longer.

"Now then, Gretel," cried she to the little girl, "be quick and draw water. Be Hansel fat or be he lean, tomorrow I must kill and cook him."

Oh, what a grief for the poor little sister to have to fetch water, and how the tears flowed down over her cheeks!

"Dear God, pray help us!" cried she. "If we had been devoured by wild beasts in the wood, at least we should have died together."

"Spare me your lamentations," said the old woman. "They are of no avail."

Early next morning Gretel had to get up, make the fire, and fill the kettle.

"First we will do the baking," said the old woman. "I have heated the oven already, and kneaded the dough."

She pushed poor Gretel towards the oven, out of which the flames were already shining.

"Creep in," said the witch, "and see if it is properly hot so that the bread may be baked."

And Gretel once in, she meant to shut the door upon her and let her be baked, and then she would have eaten her. But Gretel perceived her intention, and said,

"I don't know how to do it. How shall I get in?"

"Stupid goose," said the old woman, "the opening is big enough, do you see? I could get in myself!" and she stooped down and put her head in the oven's mouth. Then Gretel gave her a push, so that she went in farther, and she shut the iron door upon her, and put up the bar. Oh, how frightfully she howled! But Gretel ran away, and left her in the oven. Then Gretel went straight to Hansel, opened the stable door and cried,

"Hansel, we are free! The old witch is dead!"

Then out flew Hansel like a bird from its cage as soon as the door is opened. How rejoiced they both were! How they fell each on the other's neck! And danced about, and kissed each other! And as they had

155

nothing more to fear, they went over all the old witch's house, and in every corner there stood chests of pearls and precious stones.

"This is something better than pebbles," said Hansel, as he filled his pockets. And Gretel, thinking she also would like to carry something home with her, filled her apron full.

"Now, away we go," said Hansel, "if we only can get out of the witch's wood!"

When they had journeyed a few hours they came to a great piece of water.

"We can never get across this," said Hansel. "I see no stepping-stones and no bridge."

"And there is no boat either," said Gretel. "But here comes a white duck; if I ask her, she will help us over." So she cried,

> *"Duck, duck, here we stand,*
> *Hansel and Gretel on the land,*
> *Stepping-stones and bridge we lack,*
> *Carry us over on your nice white back."*

And the duck came accordingly, and Hansel got upon her and told his sister to come too.

"No," answered Gretel, "that would be too hard upon the duck; we can go separately, one after the other."

And that was how it was managed, and after that they went on happily, until they came to the wood, and the way grew more and more familiar, till at last they saw in the distance their father's house. Then they ran till they came up to it, rushed in at the door, and fell on their father's neck. The man had not had a quiet hour since he left his children in the wood; but his wife was dead. And when Gretel opened her apron, the pearls and precious stones were scattered all over the room, and Hansel took one handful after another out of his pocket. Then was all care at an end, and they lived in great joy together.

Tom Thumb

BY JAKOB AND WILHELM GRIMM
Illustrated by WILLIAM DUGAN

There was once a poor woodman sitting by the fire in his cottage, and his wife sat by his side spinning. "How lonely it is," said he, "for you and me to sit here by ourselves without any children to play about and amuse us, while other people seem so happy and merry with their children!" "What you say is very true," said the wife, sighing and turning round her wheel; "how happy should I be if I had but one child! and if it were ever so small, and, if it were no bigger than my thumb, I should be very happy, and love it dearly."

Now it came to pass that this good woman's wish was fulfilled just as she desired; for, some time afterwards, she had a little boy who was quite healthy and strong but not much bigger than my thumb. So they said, "Well, we cannot say we have not got what we wished for, and, little as he is, we still love him dearly;" and they called him Tom Thumb.

They gave him plenty of food, yet he never grew bigger, but remained just the same size as when he was born. Still his eyes were sharp and sparkling, and he soon showed himself to be a clever fellow.

One day, as the woodman was getting ready to go into the wood to cut fuel, he said, "I wish I had someone to bring the cart after me, for I want to make haste." "O father!" cried Tom, "I will take care of that; the cart shall be in the wood by the time you want it." Then the woodman laughed, and said, "How can that be? You cannot reach up to the donkey's bridle." "Never mind that, father," said Tom. "If my mother will only harness the donkey, I will get into his ear, and tell him which way to go." "Well," said the father, "we will try for once."

When the time came, the mother harnessed the donkey to the cart, and put Tom into his ear; and as he sat there, the little man told the beast how to go, crying out "Go on!" and "Stop!" as he wanted; so the donkey went on just as if the woodman had driven it himself into the wood. It happened that, as the donkey was going a little too fast, and Tom was calling out "Gently! gently!" two strangers came up. "What an odd thing that is!" said one. "There is a cart going along, and I hear a carter talking to the donkey, but can see no one." "That is strange," said the other. "Let us follow the cart and see where it goes."

So they went on into the wood till at last they came to the place where the woodman was. Then Tom Thumb, seeing his father, cried out, "See, father, here I am, with the cart, all right and safe; now take me down." So his father took hold of the donkey with one hand, and with the other took his son out of the ear; then he put him down upon a straw, where he sat as merry as you please.

The two strangers were all this time looking on, and did not know what to say for wonder. At last one took the other aside, and said, "That little urchin will make our fortune if we can get him, and carry him about from town to town as a show; we must buy him."

So they went to the woodman and asked him what he would take for the little man. "He will be better off," said they, "with us than with you." "I won't sell him at all," said the father. "My own flesh and blood is dearer to me than all the silver and gold in the world." But Tom,

hearing of the bargain they wanted to make, crept up his father's coat to his shoulder, and whispered in his ear, "Take the money, father, and let them have me, I'll soon come back to you."

So the woodman at last agreed to sell Tom to the strangers for a large piece of gold. "Where do you like to sit?" said one of them. "Oh! put me on the rim of your hat, that will be a nice gallery for me; I can walk about there, and see the country as we go along." So they did as he wished; and when Tom had taken leave of his father, they took him away with them.

They journeyed on till it began to be dusky, and then the little man said, "Let me get down, I'm tired." So the man took off his hat and set him down on a clod of earth in a ploughed field by the side of the road. But Tom ran about amongst the furrows, and at last slipped into an old mouse-hole. "Good-night, masters," said he, "I'm off! Mind and look sharp after me the next time." They ran directly to the place, and and poked the ends of their sticks into the mouse-hole, but all in vain; Tom only crawled farther and farther in, and last it became quite dark, so that they were obliged to go their way without their prize, as sulky as you please.

When Tom found they were gone, he came out of his hiding-place.

"What dangerous walking it is," said he, "in this ploughed field! If I were to fall from one of these great clods, I should certainly break my neck." At last, by good luck, he found a large empty snail-shell. "This is lucky," said he. "I can sleep here very well," and in he crept. Just as he was falling asleep he heard two men passing, and one said to the other, "How shall we manage to steal that rich parson's silver and gold?" "I'll tell you!" cried Tom. "What noise was that?" said the thief, frightened. "I am sure I heard someone speak."

They stood still listening, and Tom said, "Take me with you, and I'll soon show you how to get the parson's money." "But where are you?" said they. "Look about on the ground," answered he, "and listen where

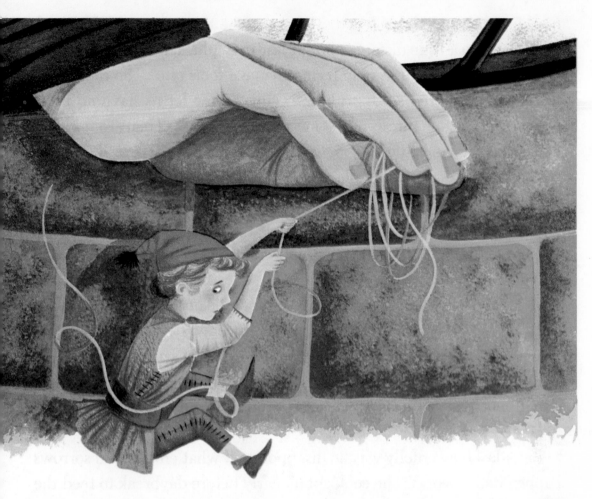

the sound comes from." At last the thieves found him out, and lifted him up in their hands. "You little urchin!" said they. "What can you do for us?" "Why, I can get between the iron window-bars of the parson's house and throw you out whatever you want." "That's a good thought," said the thieves; "come along, we shall see what you can do."

When they came to the parson's house, Tom slipped through the window-bars into the room, and then called out as loud as he could bawl, "Will you have all that is in here?" At this the thieves were frightened, and said, "Softly, softly! Speak low that you may not awaken anybody." But Tom pretended not to understand them, and bawled out again, "How much will you have? Shall I throw it all out?"

Now the cook lay in the next room, and hearing a noise she raised herself in her bed and listened. Meantime the thieves were frightened, and ran off to a little distance; but at last they plucked up courage, and said, "The little urchin is only trying to make fools of us." So they came back and whispered softly to him, saying, "Now let us have no more of your jokes, but throw out some of the money." Then Tom called out as loud as he could, "Very well: hold your hands, here it comes!" The cook heard this quite plain, so she sprang out of bed and ran to open the door.

The thieves ran off as if a wolf were at their tails; and the maid, having groped about and found nothing, went away for a light. By the time she returned, Tom had slipped off into the barn; and when the cook had looked about and searched every hole and corner, and found nobody, she went to bed, thinking she must have been dreaming with her eyes open. The little man crawled about in the hayloft, and at last found a glorious place to finish his night's rest in; so he laid himself down, meaning to sleep till daylight, and then find his way home to his father and mother.

But, alas! how cruelly was he disappointed! what crosses and sorrows happen in this world! The cook got up early before daybreak to feed the cows: she went straight to the hay-loft, and carried away a large bundle of hay with the little man in the middle of it fast asleep. He still, however, slept on, and did not awake till he found himself in the mouth of the cow, who had taken him up with a mouthful of hay.

"Lack-a-day!" said he. "How did I manage to tumble into the mill?" But he soon found out where he really was, and was obliged to have all his wits about him in order that he might not get between the cow's teeth, and so be crushed to death. At last down he went into her stomach. "It is rather dark here," said he; "they forgot to build windows in this room to let the sun in: a candle would be no bad thing."

Though he made the best of his bad luck, he did not like his quarters at all; and the worst of it was that more and more hay was always coming down, and the space in which he was became smaller and smaller. At last he cried out as loud as he could, "Don't bring me any more hay! Don't bring me any more hay!" The maid happened to be just then milking the cow, and hearing someone speak and seeing nobody, and yet being quite sure it was the same voice that she had heard in the night, she was so frightened that she fell off her stool and overset the milkpail. She ran off as fast as she could to her master the parson, and said, "Sir, sir, the cow is talking!" But the parson said, "Woman, thou art surely mad!" However, he went with her into the cowhouse to see what was the matter.

Scarcely had they set their foot on the threshold when Tom called out, "Don't bring me any more hay!" Then the parson himself was frightened; and thinking the cow was surely bewitched, ordered that she should be killed directly. So the cow was killed, and the stomach, in which Tom lay, was thrown out upon a dunghill.

Tom soon set himself to work to get out, which was not a very easy task; but at last, just as he had made room to get his head out, a new misfortune befell him; a hungry wolf sprang out, and swallowed the whole stomach, with Tom in it, at a single gulp, and ran away. Tom, however, was not disheartened. Thinking the wolf would not dislike having some chat with him as he was going along, he called out, "My good friend, I can show you a famous treat." "Where's that?" said the wolf. "In such and such a house," said Tom, describing his father's house; "you can crawl through the drain into the kitchen, and there you will find cakes, ham, beef, and everything your heart can desire." The wolf did not want to be asked twice; so that very night he went to the house and crawled through the drain into the kitchen, and ate and drank there to his heart's content.

As soon as he was satisfied, he wanted to get away; but he had eaten so much that he could not get out the same way as he came in. This was just what Tom had reckoned upon; and he now began to set up a

great shout, making all the noise he could. "Will you be quiet?" said the wolf. "You'll awaken everybody in the house." "What's that to me?" said the little man: "you have had a frolic; now I've a mind to be merry myself;" and he began again singing and shouting as loud as he could.

The woodman and his wife, being awakened by the noise, peeped through a crack in the door. When they saw that the wolf was there, you may well suppose that they were terribly frightened; and the woodman ran for his axe, and gave his wife a scythe. "Now do you stay behind," said the woodman, "and when I have knocked him on the head, do you rip up his belly for him with the scythe."

Tom heard all this, and said, "Father, father! I am here; the wolf

has swallowed me;" and his father said, "Heaven be praised! we have found our dear child again;" and he told his wife not to use the scythe, for fear she should hurt him. Then he aimed a great blow, and struck the wolf on the head, and killed him on the spot; and when he was dead they cut open his body and set Tom free.

"Ah!" said the father, "what fears we have had for you!" "Yes, father," answered he, "I have traveled all over the world since we parted, in one way or other; and now I am very glad to get fresh air again." "Why, where have you been?" said his father. "I have been in a mouse hole, in a snail shell, down a cow's throat, and in the wolf's belly; and yet here I am again safe and sound." "Well," said they, "we will not sell you again for all the riches in the world." So they hugged and kissed their dear little son, and gave him plenty to eat and drink. And that night, the townspeople gathered to hear the wondrous adventures of Tom Thumb.

Snow-White and Rose-Red

BY JAKOB AND WILHELM GRIMM
Illustrated by GORDON LAITE

THERE was once a poor widow who lived in a lonely cottage. In front of the cottage was a garden wherein stood two rose trees, one of which bore white and the other red roses. She had two children who were like the two rose trees, and one was called Snow-White, and the other Rose-Red. They were as good and happy, as busy and cheerful as ever two children in the world were, only Snow-White was more quiet and gentle than Rose-Red. Rose-Red liked better to run about in the meadows and fields seeking flowers and catching butterflies; but Snow-White sat at home with her mother, and helped her with her house-work, or read to her when there was nothing to do.

their mother would add, "What one has she must share with the other."

They often ran about the forest alone and gathered red berries, and no beasts did them any harm, but came close to them trustfully. The little hare would eat a cabbage leaf out of their hands, the roe

The two children were so fond of each other that they always held each other by the hand when they went out together, and when Snow-White said, "We will not leave each other," Rose-Red answered. "Never so long as we live," and

grazed by their side, the stag leapt merrily by them, and the birds sat still upon the boughs, and sang whatever they knew.

No mishap overtook them; if they had stayed too late in the forest, and night came on, they laid themselves down near one another upon the moss, and slept until morning came, and their mother knew this and had no distress on their account.

Once when they had spent the night in the wood and the dawn had roused them, they saw a beautiful child in a shining white dress sitting near their bed. He got up and looked quite kindly at them, but said nothing and went away into the forest. And when they looked round they found that they had been sleeping quite close to a precipice, and would certainly have fallen into it if they had gone only a few paces further. And their mother told them that it must have been the angel who watches over good children.

Snow-White and Rose-Red kept their mother's little cottage so neat that it was a pleasure to look inside it. In the summer Rose-Red took care of the house, and every morning laid a wreath of flowers by her mother's bed before she awoke, in which was a rose from each tree. In the winter Snow-White lit the fire and hung the kettle on its iron hook above the hearth. The kettle was of copper and shone like gold, so brightly was it polished. In the evening, when the snowflakes fell, the mother said, "Go, Snow-White, and bolt the door," and then they sat round the hearth, and the mother took her spectacles and read aloud out of a large book, and the two girls listened as they sat and spun. And close by them lay a lamb upon the floor, and behind them upon a perch sat a white dove with its head hidden beneath its wings.

One evening, as they were thus sitting comfortably together, someone knocked at the door as if he wished to be let in. The mother said, "Quick, Rose-Red, open the door; it must be a traveler who is seeking shelter." Rose-Red went and pushed back the bolt, thinking that it was a poor man, but it was not; it was a bear that stretched his broad, black head within the door.

Rose-Red screamed and sprang back, the lamb bleated, the dove fluttered, and Snow-White hid herself behind her mother's bed. But the bear began to speak and said, "Do not be afraid, I will do you no harm! I am half-frozen, and only want to warm myself a little beside you."

"Poor bear," said the mother, "lie down by the fire, only take care that you do not burn your coat." Then she cried, "Snow-White, Rose-Red, come out, the bear will do you no harm, he means well." So they both came out, and by-and-by the lamb and dove came nearer, and were not afraid of him.

The bear said, "Here, children, knock the snow out of my coat a little." So they brought the broom and swept the bear's hide clean; and he stretched himself by the fire and growled contentedly and comfortably. It was not long before they grew quite at home, and played tricks with their clumsy guest. They tugged his hair with their hands, put their feet upon his back and rolled him about, or they took a hazel-switch and beat him, and when he growled they laughed. But the bear took it all in good part, only when they were too rough he called out, "Leave me alive, children,

"Snowy-White, Rosy-Red,
    Will you beat your lover dead?"

When it was bed time, and the others went to bed, the mother said to the bear, "You can lie there by the hearth, and then you will be safe from the cold and the

172

bad weather." As soon as day dawned the two children let him out, and he trotted across the snow into the forest.

Henceforth the bear came every evening at the same time, laid himself down by the hearth, and let the children amuse themselves with him as much as they liked; and they got so used to him that the doors were never fastened until their black friend had arrived.

When spring had come and all outside was green, the bear said one morning to Snow-White, "Now I must go away, and cannot come back for the whole summer."

"Where are you going, then, dear bear?" asked Snow-White.

"I must go into the forest and guard my treasures from the wicked dwarfs. In the winter, when the earth is frozen hard, they are obliged to stay below and cannot work their way through; but now, when the sun has thawed and warmed the earth, they break through it, and come out to pry and steal. And what once gets into their hands, and in their caves, does not easily see daylight again."

Snow-White was quite sorry for his going away, and as she unbolted the door for him, and the bear was hurrying out, he caught against the bolt and a piece of his hairy coat was torn off, and it seemed to Snow-White as if she had seen gold shining through it, but she was not sure about it. The bear ran away quickly, and was soon out of sight behind the trees.

A short time afterwards the mother sent her children into the forest to get fire-wood. There they found a big tree

which lay felled on the ground, and close by the trunk something was jumping backwards and forwards in the grass, but they could not make out what it was. When they came nearer they saw a dwarf with an old withered face and a snow-white beard a yard long. The end of the beard was caught in a crevice of the tree, and the little fellow was jumping backwards and forwards like a dog tied to a rope, and did not know what to do.

He glared at the girls with his fiery red eyes and cried, "Why do you stand there? Can you not come here and help me?"

"What are you about there, little man?" asked Rose-Red.

"You stupid, prying goose!" answered the dwarf; "I was going to split the tree to get a little wood for cooking. The little bit of food that one of us wants gets burnt up directly with thick logs; we do not swallow so much as you coarse, greedy folk. I had just driven the wedge safely in, and everything was going as I wished; but the wretched wood was too smooth and suddenly sprang asunder, and the tree closed so quickly that I could not pull out my beautiful white beard. So now it is tight in and I cannot get away, and the silly, sleek, milk-faced things laugh! Ugh! how odious you are!"

The children tried very hard, but they

could not pull the beard out, it was caught too fast. "I will run and fetch someone," said Rose-Red.

"You senseless goose!" snarled the dwarf; "why should you fetch someone? You are already two too many for me; can you not think of something better?"

"Don't be impatient," said Snow-White, "I will help you," and she pulled her scissors out of her pocket, and cut off the end of the beard.

As soon as the dwarf felt himself free he laid hold of a bag which lay amongst the roots of the tree, and which was full of gold, and lifted it up, grumbling to himself, "Uncouth people, to cut off a piece of my fine beard. Bad luck to you!" and then he swung the bag upon his back, and went off without even once looking at the children.

Some time after that Snow-White and

Rose-Red went to catch a dish of fish. As they came near the brook they saw something like a large grasshopper jumping towards the water, as if it were going to leap in. They ran to it and found it was the dwarf. "Where are you going?" said Rose-Red; "you surely don't want to go into the water?"

"I am not such a fool!" cried the dwarf; "don't you see that the accursed fish wants to pull me in?" The little man had been sitting there fishing, and unluckily the wind had twisted his beard with the fishing-line. Just then a big fish bit, and the feeble creature had not strength to pull it out. The fish kept the upper hand and pulled the dwarf towards him. He held on to all the reeds and rushes, but it was of little good, he was forced to follow the movements of the fish, and was in urgent danger of being dragged into the water.

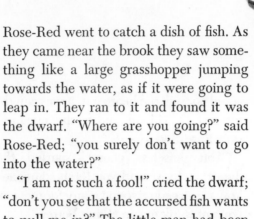

The girls came just in time; they held him fast and tried to free his beard from the line, but all in vain; beard and line were entangled fast together. Nothing was left but to bring out the scissors and cut the beard, whereby a small part of it was lost. When the dwarf saw that, he screamed out, "Is that civil, you toadstool, to disfigure one's face? Was it not enough to clip off the end of my beard? Now you have cut off the best part of it. I cannot let myself be seen by my people. I wish you had been made to run the soles off your shoes!" Then he took out a sack of pearls which lay in the rushes, and without saying a word more he dragged it away and disappeared behind a stone.

It happened that soon afterwards the mother sent the two children to the town to buy needles and thread, and laces and ribbons. The road led them across a heath upon which huge pieces of rock lay strewn here and there. Now they noticed a large bird hovering in the air, flying slowly round and round above them; it sank lower and lower, and at last settled near a rock not far off. Directly afterwards they heard a loud, piteous cry. They ran up and saw with horror that the eagle had seized their old acquaintance the dwarf, and was going to carry him off.

The children, full of pity, at once took tight hold of the little man, and pulled against the eagle so long that at last he let his booty go. As soon as the dwarf had recovered from his first fright he cried with his shrill voice, "Could you not have done it more carefully! You dragged at my brown coat so that it is all torn and full of holes, you helpless clumsy creatures!" Then he took up a sack full of precious stones, and slipped away again under the rock into his hole. The girls, who by this time were used to his thanklessness, went on their way and did their business in the town.

As they crossed the heath again on their way home they surprised the dwarf,

who had emptied out his bag of precious stones in a clean spot, and had not thought that anyone would come there so late. The evening sun shone upon the brilliant stones; they glittered and sparkled with all colors so beautifully that the children stood still and looked at them. "Why do you stand gaping there?" cried the dwarf, and his ashen-gray face became copper-red with rage. He was going on with his bad words when a loud growling was heard, and a black bear came trotting towards them out of the forest. The dwarf sprang up in a fright, but he could not get to his cave, for the bear was already close. Then in the dread of his heart he cried, "Dear Mr. Bear, spare me, I will give you all my treasures; look, the beautiful jewels lying there! Grant me my life; what do you want with such a slender little fellow as I? You would not feel me between your teeth. Come, take these two wicked girls, they are tender morsels for you, fat as young

quails. For mercy's sake eat them!" The bear took no heed of his words, but gave the wicked creature a single blow with his paw, and he did not move again.

The girls had run away, but the bear called to them, "Snow-White and Rose-Red, do not be afraid; wait, I will come with you." Then they knew his voice and waited, and when he came up to them suddenly his bearskin fell off, and he stood there a handsome man, clothed all in gold. "I am a King's son," he said, "and I was bewitched by that wicked dwarf, who had stolen my treasures. I have had to run about the forest as a savage bear until I was freed by his death. Now he has got his well-deserved punishment."

Snow-White was married to him, and Rose-Red to his brother, and they divided between them the great treasure which the dwarf had gathered together in his cave. The old mother lived peacefully and happily with her children for many years. She took the two rose trees with her, and they stood before her window, and every year bore the most beautiful roses, white and red.

Rapunzel

BY JAKOB AND WILHELM GRIMM

Illustrated by GORDON LAITE

THERE once lived a man and his wife, who had long wished for a child, but in vain. Now there was at the back of their house a little window which overlooked a beautiful garden full of the finest vegetables and flowers; but there was a high wall round it, and no one ventured into it, for it belonged to a witch of great might, who was feared by all the world. One day that the wife was standing at the window, and looking into the garden, she saw a bed filled with the finest rampion; and it looked so fresh and green that she began to wish for some; and at length she longed for it greatly. This went on for days, and as she knew she could not get the rampion, her desire grew greater and greater, until she pined away, and grew pale and miserable. Then her husband was uneasy, and asked,

"What is the matter, dear wife?"

"Oh," answered she, "I shall die unless I can have some of that rampion to eat that grows in the garden at the back of

our house." The man, who loved her very much, thought to himself,

"Rather than lose my wife I will get some rampion, cost what it will."

So in the twilight he climbed over the wall into the witch's garden, hastily plucked a handful of rampion and brought it to his wife. She made a salad of it at once; and ate of it to her heart's content. But she liked it so much, and it tasted so good, that the next day she longed for it thrice as much as she had done before. If she was to have any rest the man must climb over the wall once more. So he went in the twilight again; and as he was climbing back, he saw, all at once, the witch standing before him, and was terribly frightened, as she cried, with angry eyes,

"How dare you climb over into my garden like a thief, and steal my rampion! You shall suffer for this!"

"Oh," answered he, "be merciful rather than just, I have only done it through necessity; for my wife saw your rampion out of the window, and became possessed with so great a longing that she would have died if she could not have had some." Then the witch said,

"If it is all as you say you may have as much rampion as you like, on one condition—the child that your wife will shortly bring into the world must be given to me. And I will care for it like a mother."

In his distress of mind the man promised everything; and when the time came when the child was born the witch appeared, and giving the child the name of Rapunzel (which is the same as rampion), she took it away with her.

Rapunzel was the most beautiful child in the world. When she was twelve years old the witch shut her up in a tower in the midst of a wood, and it had neither steps nor door, only a small window high above. When the witch wished to be let in, she would stand below and cry,

> *"Rapunzel, Rapunzel,*
> *Let down your golden hair."*

Rapunzel had beautiful long hair that shone like gold. When she heard the voice of the witch she would undo the fastening of the upper window, unbind the plaits of her hair, and let it down twenty ells below, and the witch would climb up by it.

After they had lived thus a few years it happened that as the King's son was riding through the wood, he came to the tower; and as he drew near he heard a voice singing so sweetly that he stood still and listened. It was Rapunzel in her loneliness trying to pass away the time with sweet songs. The King's son wished to go in to her, and sought to find a door in the tower, but there was none. So he rode home, but the song had entered into his heart, and every day he went into the wood and listened to it. Once, as he was standing there under a tree, he saw the witch come up, and listened while she called out,

"*Rapunzel, Rapunzel,*
Let down your golden hair."

Then he saw how Rapunzel let down her long tresses, and how the witch climbed up by them and went in to her, and he said to himself.

"Since that is the ladder I will climb it, and try my luck." And the next day, as soon as it began to grow dusk, he went to the tower and cried,

"*Rapunzel, Rapunzel,*
Let down your golden hair."

And she let down her hair, and the King's son climbed up by it.

Rapunzel was greatly terrified when she saw that a man had come in, for she had never seen one before. But the King's son began speaking so kindly to her, and told how her singing had entered into his heart, so that he could have no peace until he had seen her. Then Rapunzel forgot her terror, and when he asked her to take him for her husband, and she saw that he was young and beautiful, she thought to herself,

"I certainly like him much better than old mother Gothel," and she put her hand into his hand, saying,

"I would willingly go with thee, but I do not know how I shall get out. When thou comest, bring each time a silken rope, and I will make a ladder, and when it is quite ready I will get down by it out of the tower, and thou shalt take me away on thy horse." They agreed that he should come to her every evening, as the old woman came in the day-time. So the witch knew nothing of all this until once Rapunzel said to her unwittingly,

"Mother Gothel, how is it that you climb up here so slowly, and the King's son is with me in a moment?"

"O wicked child," cried the witch, "what is this I hear! I thought I had hidden thee from all the world, and thou hast betrayed me!"

In her anger she seized Rapunzel by her beautiful hair, struck her several times with her left hand, and then grasping a pair of shears in her right—snip, snap —the beautiful braids lay on the ground. And she was so hard-hearted that she took Rapunzel and put her in a lonely desert place, to live in loneliness and misery.

The same day on which she took Rapunzel away she went back to the tower in the evening and made fast the severed braid of hair to the window hook. Then the King's son came and cried,

"Rapunzel, Rapunzel,
Let down your golden hair."

Then she let the hair down, and the King's son climbed up, but instead of his dearest Rapunzel he found the witch looking at him with glittering eyes.

"Aha!" cried she, mocking him, "you

came for your darling, but the sweet bird sits no longer in the nest, and sings no more; the cat has got her, and will scratch out your eyes as well! Rapunzel is lost to you; you will see her no more."

The King's son was beside himself with grief, and in his agony he sprang from the tower. He escaped with his life, but the thorns on which he fell put out his eyes. Then he wandered blind through the wood, eating nothing but roots and berries, and doing nothing but lament and weep for the loss of his lovely bride.

So he wandered several years in misery until at last he came to the desert place where Rapunzel was living. At first he heard a voice that he thought he knew, and when he reached the place from which it seemed to come Rapunzel knew him, and fell on his neck and wept. And when her tears touched his eyes they became clear again, and he could see with them as well as ever.

Then he took her to his kingdom, where he was received with great joy, and there they lived long and happily.

The Fisherman and his Wife

BY JAKOB AND WILHELM GRIMM
Illustrated by W. T. MARS

THERE was once a fisherman who lived with his wife in a ditch, close by the seaside. The fisherman used to go out all day long a-fishing; and one day, as he sat on the shore with his rod, looking at the shining water and watching his line, all of a sudden his float was dragged away deep under the sea; and in drawing it up he pulled a great fish out of the water. The fish said to him, "Pray let me live. I am an enchanted prince, put me in the water again, and let me go." "Oh!" said the man, "you need not make so many words about the matter; I wish to have nothing to do with a fish that can talk; so swim away as soon as you please." Then he put him back into the water, and the fish darted straight down to the bottom and left a long streak of blood behind him.

When the fisherman went home to his wife in the ditch, he told her how he had caught a great fish, and how it had told him that it was an enchanted prince, and that on hearing it speak he had let it go again. "Did you not ask it for anything?" said the wife. "No," said the man; "what

187

should I ask for?" "Ah!" said the wife, "we live very wretchedly here in this nasty stinking ditch; do go back, and tell the fish we want a little cottage."

The fisherman did not much like the business: however, he went to the sea, and when he came there the water looked all yellow and green. And he stood at the water's edge, and said:

> "O man of the sea!
> Come listen to me,
> For Alice my wife,
> The plague of my life,
> Hath sent me to beg a boon of thee!"

Then the fish came swimming to him, and said, "Well, what does she want?"

"Ah!" answered the fisherman, "my wife says that when I had caught you, I ought to have asked you for something before I let you go again; she does not like living any longer in the ditch, and wants a little cottage." "Go home, then," said the fish; "she is in the cottage already." So the man went home; and saw his wife standing at the door of the cottage. "Come in, come in," said she; "is not this much better than the ditch?" And there was a parlor, and a bed-chamber, and a kitchen; and behind the cottage there was a little garden with all sorts of flowers and fruits, and a court-yard full of ducks and chickens. "Ah!" said the fisherman, "how happily we shall live!" "We will try to do so at least," said his wife.

Everything went right for a week or two, and then Dame Alice said, "Husband, there is not room enough in this cottage, the courtyard and garden are a great deal too small; I should like to have a large stone castle to live in; so go to the fish again, and tell him to give us a castle." "Wife," said the fisherman, "I don't like to go to him again, for perhaps he will be angry; we ought to be content with the cottage." "Nonsense!" said the wife; "he will do it willingly; go along and try."

The fisherman went; but his heart was very heavy: and when he came to the sea it looked blue and gloomy, though it was quite calm, and he went close to it, and said:

"O man of the sea!
Come listen to me,
For Alice my wife,
The plague of my life,
Hath sent me to beg a boon of thee!"

"Well, what does she want now?" said the fish. "Ah!" said the man very sorrowfully, "my wife wants to live in a stone castle." "Go home, then," said the fish; "she is standing at the door of it already." So away went the fisherman, and found his wife standing before a great castle. "See," said she, "is not this grand?" With that they went into the castle together, and found a great many servants there, and the rooms all richly furnished and full of golden chairs and tables; and behind the castle was a garden, and a wood half a mile long, full of sheep, and goats, and hares, and deer; and in the courtyard were stables and cowhouses. "Well!" said the man, "now will we live contented and happy in the beautiful castle for the rest

of our lives." "Perhaps we may," said the wife; "but let us consider and sleep upon it before we make up our minds." So they went to bed.

Then next morning, when Dame Alice awoke, it was broad daylight, and she jogged the fisherman with her elbow, and said, "Get up, husband, and bestir yourself for we must be king of all the land." "Wife, wife," said the man, "why should we wish to be king? I will not be king." "Then I will," said Alice. "But, wife," answered the fisherman, "how can you be king? The fish cannot make you a king." "Husband," said she, "say no more about it, but go and try; I will be king!" So the man went away, quite sorrowful to think that his wife should want to be king. The sea looked a dark-gray color, and was covered with foam as he cried out:

"O man of the sea!
Come listen to me,
For Alice my wife,
The plague of my life,
Hath sent me to beg a boon of thee!"

"Well, what would she have now?" said the fish. "Alas!" said the man, "my wife wants to be king." "Go home," said the fish; "she is king already."

Then the fisherman went home; and as he came close to the palace, he saw a troop of soldiers, and heard the sound of drums and trumpets; and when he entered in, he saw his wife sitting on a high throne of gold and diamonds, with a golden crown upon her head; and on each side of her stood six beautiful maidens, each a head taller than the other. "Well, wife," said the fisherman, "are you king?" "Yes," said she, "I am king." And when he had looked at her for a long time, he said, "Ah, wife! what a fine thing it is to be king! now we shall never have anything more to wish for." "I don't know how that may be," said she; "never is a long time. I am king, 'tis true, but I begin to be tired of it, and I think I should like to be emperor." "Alas, wife! why should you wish to be emperor?" said the fisherman. "Husband," said she, "go to the fish; I say I will be emperor." "Ah, wife!" replied the fisherman, "the fish cannot make an emperor, and I should not like to ask for such a thing." "I am king," said Alice, "and you are my slave, so go directly!" So the fisherman was obliged to go; and he muttered as he went along, "This will come to no good, it is too much to ask, the fish will be tired at last, and then we shall repent of what we have done." He soon arrived at the sea, and the water was quite black and muddy, and a mighty whirlwind blew over it; but he went to the shore, and said:

> "O man of the sea!
> Come listen to me,
> For Alice my wife,
> The plague of my life,
> Hath sent me to beg a boon of thee!"

"What would she have now?" said the fish. "Ah!" said the fisherman, "she wants to be emperor." "Go home," said the fish; "she is emperor already."

So he went home again; and as he came near he saw his wife sitting on a very lofty throne made of solid gold, with a great crown on her head full two yards high, and on each side of her stood her guards and attendants in a row, each one smaller than the other, from the tallest giant down to a little dwarf no bigger than a finger. And before her stood princes, and dukes, and earls: and the fisherman went up to her and said, "Wife, are you emperor?" "Yes," said she, "I am emperor."

"Ah!" said the man as he gazed upon her, "what a fine thing it is to be emperor!" "Husband," said she, "why should we stay at being emperor? I will be pope next." "Oh wife, wife!" said he, "how can you be pope? There is but one pope at a time in Christendom." "Husband," said she, "I will be pope this very day." "But," replied the husband, "the fish cannot make you pope." "What nonsense!" said she; "if he can make an emperor, he can make a pope, go and try him." So the fisherman went. But when he came to the shore the wind was raging, and the sea was tossed up and down like boiling water, and the ships were in the greatest distress and danced upon the waves most fearfully; in the middle of the sky there was a little blue, but towards the south it was all red, as if a dreadful storm was rising. At this the fisherman was terribly frightened, and trembled so that his knees knocked together; but he went to the shore and said:

> "O man of the sea!
> Come listen to me,
> For Alice my wife,
> The plague of my life,
> Hath sent me to beg a boon of thee!"

"What does she want now?" said the fish. "Ah!" said the fisherman, "my wife wants to be pope." "Go home," said the fish, "she is pope already."

Then the fisherman went home, and found his wife sitting on a throne that was two miles high; and she had three great crowns on her head, and around stood all the pomp and power of the Church and on each side were two rows of burning lights, of all sizes, the greatest as large as the highest and biggest tower, and the least no larger than a small rushlight. "Wife," said the fisherman, as he looked

at all this grandeur, "are you pope?" "Yes," said she, "I am pope." "Well, wife," replied he, "it is a grand thing to be pope; and now you must be content, for you can be nothing greater." "I will consider of that," said the wife. Then they went to bed: but Dame Alice could not sleep all night for thinking what she should be next. At last morning came, and the sun rose. "Ah!" thought she as she looked at it through the window, "cannot I prevent the sun rising?" At this she was very angry, and wakened her husband, and said, "Husband, go to the fish and tell him I want to be lord of the sun and moon." The fisherman was half asleep, but the thought frightened him so much, that he started and fell out of bed. "Alas, wife!" said he, "cannot you be content to be pope?" "No," said she, "I am very uneasy, and cannot bear to see the sun and moon rise without my leave. Go to the fish directly."

Then the man went trembling for fear; and as he was going down to the shore a dreadful storm arose, so that the trees and the rocks shook; and the heavens became black, and the lightning played, and the thunder rolled, and you might have seen in the sea great black waves like mountains with a white crown of foam upon them; and the fisherman said:

> "O man of the sea!
> Come listen to me,
> For Alice my wife,
> The plague of my life,
> Hath sent me to beg a boon of thee!"

"What does she want now?" said the fish. "Ah!" said he, "she wants to be lord of the sun and moon." "Go home," said the fish, "to your ditch again!" And there they live to this very day.

One of the loveliest fairy tales of all time
was written in Denmark more than a hundred years ago.
Thumbelina was as good as she was beautiful.
Most of all she was unbelievably tiny.
She was born in a tulip; she was rocked to sleep in
a walnut shell; a leaf was her boat; a beetle carried her away.
The smallest things seemed huge to her.
It was a long time before she found a companion her own size.

Thumbelina

BY HANS CHRISTIAN ANDERSEN
Illustrated by ADRIENNE SEGUR

THERE was once a woman who wished for a very little child; but she did not know where she should procure one. So she went to an old witch, and said:

"I do very much wish for a little child! Can you not tell me where I can get one?"

"Oh! that could easily be managed," said the witch. "There you have a barleycorn: that is not of the kind which grows in the countryman's field, and which the chickens get to eat. Put that into a flower pot, and you shall see what you shall see."

"Thank you," said the woman; and she gave the witch twelve shillings, for that is what it cost.

Then she went home and planted the barleycorn, and immediately there grew up a great handsome flower, which looked like a tulip; but the leaves were tightly closed, as though it were still a bud.

"That is a beautiful flower," said the woman; and she kissed its yellow and red leaves. But just as she kissed it the flower opened with a pop. It was a real tulip, as one could now see; but in the middle of the flower there sat upon the green velvet stamens a little maiden, delicate and graceful to behold. She was scarcely half a thumb's length in height, and therefore she was called Thumbelina.

A neat polished walnut shell served Thumbelina for a cradle, blue violet leaves were her mattresses, with a rose leaf for a coverlet. There she slept at night; but in the daytime she played upon the table, where the woman had put a plate with a wreath of flowers around it, whose stalks stood in water; on the water swam a green tulip leaf, and on this the little maiden could sit, and row from one side of the plate to the other, with two white horsehairs for oars. That looked pretty indeed! She could also sing, and, indeed, so delicately and sweetly that the like had never been heard.

Once as she lay at night in her pretty bed, there came an old Toad creeping through the window, in which one pane was broken. The Toad was very ugly, big, and damp: it hopped straight down upon the table, where Thumbelina lay sleeping under the rose leaf.

"That would be a handsome wife for my son," said the Toad; and she took the walnut shell in which Thumbelina lay asleep, and hopped with it through the window down into the garden.

There ran a great broad brook; but the margin was swampy and soft, and here the Toad dwelt with her son. Ugh! he was ugly, and looked just like his mother. "Croak! croak! brek-kek-kex!" that was all

he could say when he saw the graceful little maiden in the walnut shell.

"Don't speak so loud, or she will wake," said the old Toad. "She might run away from us, for she is as light as a bit of swan's-down. We will put her out in the brook upon one of the broad water-lily leaves. That will be just like an island for her, she is so small and light. Then she can't get away, while we put the State room under the marsh in order, where you are to live and keep house together."

Out in the brook there grew many water-lilies with broad green leaves, which looked as if they were floating in the water. The leaf which lay farthest out was also the greatest of all, and to that the old Toad swam out and laid the walnut shell upon it with Thumbelina. The little tiny Thumbelina woke early in the morning, and when she saw where she was, she began to cry very bitterly; for there was water on every side of the great green leaf, and she could not get to land at all. The old Toad sat down in the marsh, decking out her room with rushes and yellow weed—it was to be made very pretty for the new daughter-in-law; then she swam out, with her ugly son, to the leaf on which Thumbelina was. They wanted to take her pretty bed, which was to be put in the bridal chamber before she went in there herself. The old Toad bowed low before her in the water, and said:

"Here is my son; he will be your husband, and you will live splendidly together in the marsh."

"Croak! croak! brek-kek-kek!" was all the son could say.

Then they took the delicate little bed, and swam away with it; but Thumbelina sat all alone upon the green leaf and wept, for she did not like to live at the nasty Toad's, and have her ugly son for a husband. The little fishes swimming in the water below had seen the Toad, and had also heard what she said; therefore they stretched forth their heads, for they wanted to see the little girl. So soon as they saw her they considered her so pretty that they felt very sorry she should have to go down to the ugly Toad. No, that must never be! They assembled together in the water around the green stalk which held the leaf on which the little maiden stood, and with their teeth they gnawed away the stalk, and so the leaf swam down the stream; and away went Thumbelina far away, where the Toad could not get at her.

Thumbelina sailed by many cities, and the little birds which sat in the bushes saw her, and said, "What a lovely little girl!" The leaf swam away with her, farther and farther; so Thumbelina travelled out of the country.

A graceful little white butterfly always fluttered round her, and at last alighted on the leaf. Thumbelina pleased him, and she was very glad of this, for now the Toad could not reach them; and it was so beautiful where she was floating along —the sun shone upon the water, and the water glistened like the most splendid gold. She took her girdle and bound one end of it round the butterfly, fastening the other end of the ribbon to the leaf. The leaf now glided onward much faster, and Thumbelina too, for she stood upon the leaf.

There came a big Cockchafer flying up; and he saw her, and immediately clasped his claws round her slender waist, and flew with her up into the tree. The green leaf went swimming down the brook, and the butterfly with it; for he was fastened to the leaf, and could not get away from it.

Mercy! how frightened poor little Thumbelina was when the Cockchafer flew with her up into the tree! But especially she was sorry for the fine white butterfly whom she had bound fast to the leaf, for, if he could not free himself from it, he would be obliged to starve. The Cockchafer, however, did not trouble himself at all about this. He seated himself with her upon the biggest green leaf of the tree, gave her the sweet part of the flowers to eat, and declared that she was very pretty, though she did not in the least resemble a cockchafer. Afterward came all the other cockchafers who lived in the tree to pay a visit: they looked at Thumbelina, and said:

"Why, she has not even more than two legs!—that has a wretched appearance."

"She has not any feelers!" cried another.

"Her waist is quite slender—fie! she looks like a human creature—how ugly she is!" said all the lady cockchafers spitefully.

And yet Thumbelina was very pretty. Even the Cockchafer who had carried her off saw that; but when all the others declared she was ugly, he believed it at last, and would not have her at all—she might go whither she liked. Then they flew down with her from the tree, and set her upon a daisy, and she wept, because she was so ugly that the cockchafers would have nothing to say to her; and yet she was the loveliest little being one could imagine, and as tender and delicate as a rose leaf.

The whole summer through poor Thumbelina lived quite alone in the great wood. She wove herself a bed out of blades of grass, and hung it up under a shamrock, so that she was protected from the rain; she plucked the honey out of the flowers for food, and drank of the dew which stood every morning upon the leaves. Thus summer and autumn passed away, but now came winter, the cold long winter. All the birds who had sung so sweetly before her flew away; trees and flowers shed their leaves; the great shamrock under which she had lived shrivelled up, and there remained nothing of it but a yellow withered stalk; and she was dreadfully cold, for her clothes were torn, and she herself was so frail and delicate—poor little Thumbelina! she was nearly frozen. It began to snow, and every snowflake that fell upon her was like a whole shovelful thrown upon one of us, for we are tall, and she was only an inch long. Then she wrapped herself in a dry leaf, and that tore in the middle, and would not warm her—she shivered with cold.

Close to the wood into which she had now come lay a great cornfield, but the corn was gone long ago, only the naked dry stubble stood up out of the frozen ground. This was just like a great forest for her to wander through; and, oh! how she trembled with cold. Then she arrived at the door of the Field Mouse. This mouse had a little hole under the stubble. There the Field Mouse lived, warm and comfortable, and had a whole roomful of corn—a glorious kitchen and larder. Poor Thumbelina stood at the door just like a poor beggar girl, and begged for a little bit of barleycorn, for she had not had the smallest morsel to eat for two days.

"You poor little creature," said the Field Mouse—for after all she was a good old Field Mouse—"come into my warm room and dine with me."

As she was pleased with Thumbelina, she said, "If you like you may stay with me through the winter, but you must keep my room clean and neat, and tell me little stories, for I am very fond of those."

And Thumbelina did as the kind old Field Mouse bade her, and had a very good time of it.

"Now we shall soon have a visitor," said the Field Mouse. "My neighbor is in the habit of visiting me once a week. He is even better off than I am, has great rooms, and a beautiful black velvety fur. If you could only get him for your husband you would be well provided for. You must tell him the prettiest stories you know."

But Thumbelina did not care about this; she thought nothing of the neighbor, for he was a Mole. He came and paid his visits in his black velvet coat. The Field Mouse told how rich and how learned he was, and how his house was more than twenty times larger than hers; that he had learning, but that he did not like the sun and beautiful flowers, for he had never seen them.

Thumbelina had to sing, and she sang "Cockchafer, fly away," and "When the Parson goes Afield." Then the Mole fell in love with her, because of her delicious voice; but he said nothing, for he was a sedate man.

A short time before, he had dug a long passage through the earth from his own house to theirs; and Thumbelina and the Field Mouse obtained leave to walk in this passage as much as they wished. But

he begged them not to be afraid of the dead bird which was lying in the passage. It was an entire bird with wings and beak. It certainly must have died only a short time before, and was now buried just where the Mole had made his passage.

The Mole took a bit of decayed wood in his mouth, and it glimmered like fire in the dark; and then he went first and lighted them through the long dark passage. When they came where the dead bird lay, the Mole thrust up his broad nose against the ceiling, so that a great hole was made, through which the daylight could shine down. In the middle of the floor lay a dead Swallow, his beautiful wings pressed close against his sides, and his head and feet drawn back under his feathers: the poor bird had certainly died of cold. Thumbelina was very sorry for this; she was very fond of all the little birds, who had sung and twittered so prettily before her through the summer; but the Mole gave him a push with his crooked legs, and said, "Now he doesn't pipe any more. It must be miserable to be born a little bird. I'm thankful that none of my children can be that: such a bird has nothing but his 'tweet-weet,' and has to starve in the winter!"

"Yes, you may well say that, as a clever man," observed the Field Mouse. "Of what use is all this 'tweet-weet' to a bird when the winter comes? He must starve and freeze. But they say that's very aristocratic."

Thumbelina said nothing; but when the two others turned their backs on the bird, she bent down, put the feathers aside which covered his head, and kissed him upon his closed eyes.

"Perhaps it was he who sang so prettily before me in the summer," she thought. "How much pleasure he gave me, the dear beautiful bird!"

The Mole now closed up the hole through which the daylight shone in, and accompanied the ladies home. But at night Thumbelina could not sleep at all; so she got up out of her bed, and wove a large beautiful carpet of hay, and carried it and spread it over the dead bird, and laid the thin stamens of flowers, soft as cotton, and which she had found in the Field Mouse's room, at the bird's sides, so that he might lie soft in the ground.

"Farewell, you pretty little bird!" said she. "Farewell! and thanks to you for your beautiful song in the summer, when all the trees were green, and the sun shone down warmly upon us." And then she laid the bird's head upon her heart. But the bird was not dead; he was only lying there torpid with cold; and now he had been warmed, and came to life again.

In autumn all the swallows fly away to warm countries; but if one happens to be belated, it becomes so cold that it falls down as if dead, and lies where it fell, and then the cold snow covers it.

Thumbelina fairly trembled, she was so startled; for the bird was large, very large, compared with her, who was only an inch in height. But she took courage, laid the cotton closer round the poor bird, and brought a leaf that she had used as her own coverlet, and laid it over the bird's head. The next night she went to him again—and now he was alive, but quite weak; he could only open his eyes for a moment, and look at Thumbelina, who stood before him with a bit of decayed wood in her hand, for she had not a lantern.

"I thank you, you pretty little child," said the sick Swallow; "I have been famously warmed. Soon I shall get my strength back again, and I shall be able to fly about in the warm sunshine."

"Oh," she said, "it is so cold without. It snows and freezes. Stay in your warm bed, and I will nurse you."

Then she brought the Swallow water in the petal of a flower; and the Swallow drank, and told her how he had torn one of his wings in a thorn bush, and thus had not been able to fly so fast as the other swallows, which had sped away, far away, to the warm countries. So at last he had fallen to the ground, but he could remember nothing more, and did not know at all how he had come where she had found him.

The whole winter the Swallow remained there, and Thumbelina nursed and tended him heartily. Neither the Field Mouse nor the Mole heard anything about it, for they did not like the poor Swallow. So soon as the spring came, and the sun warmed the earth, the Swallow bade Thumbelina farewell, and she opened the hole which the Mole had made in the ceiling. The sun shone in upon them gloriously, and the Swallow asked if Thumbelina would go with him; she could sit upon his back, and they would fly away far into the green wood. But Thumbelina knew that the old Field Mouse would be grieved if she left her.

"No, I cannot!" said Thumbelina.

"Farewell, farewell, you good, pretty girl!" said the Swallow; and he flew out into the sunshine. Thumbelina looked after him, and the tears came into her eyes, for she was heartily and sincerely fond of the poor Swallow.

"Tweet-weet! tweet-weet!" sang the bird, and flew into the green forest. Thumbelina felt very sad. She did not get permission to go out into the warm sunshine. The corn which was sown in the field over the house of the Field Mouse grew up high into the air; it was quite a thick wood for the poor girl, who was only an inch in height.

"You are bethrothed now, Thumbelina," said the Field Mouse. "My neighbor has proposed for you. What great fortune for a poor child like you! Now you must work at your outfit, woollen and linen clothes for both; for you must lack nothing when you have become the Mole's wife."

Thumbelina had to turn the spindle, and the Mole hired four spiders to weave for her day and night. Every evening the Mole paid her a visit; and he was always saying that when the summer should draw to a close, the sun would not shine nearly so hot, for that now it burned the earth almost as hard as a stone. Yes, when the summer should have gone, then he would keep his wedding day with Thumbelina. But she was not glad at all, for she did not like the tiresome Mole. Every morning when the sun rose, and every evening when it went down, she crept out at the door; and when the wind blew the corn ears apart, so that she could see the blue sky, she thought how bright and beautiful it was out here, and wished heartily to see her dear Swallow again. But the Swallow did not come back; he had doubtless flown far away, in the fair green forest. When autumn came on, Thumbelina had all her outfit ready.

"In four weeks you shall celebrate your wedding," said the Field Mouse to her.

But Thumbelina wept, and declared she would not have the tiresome Mole.

"Nonsense," said the Field Mouse; "don't be obstinate, or I will bite you with my white teeth. He is a very fine man whom you will marry. The Queen herself has not such a black velvet fur; and his kitchen and cellar are full. Be thankful for your good fortune."

Now the wedding was to be held. The Mole had already come to fetch Thumbelina; she was to live with him, deep under the earth, and never to come out into the warm sunshine, for that he did not like. The poor little thing was very sorrowful; she was now to say farewell to the glorious sun, which, after all, she had been allowed by the Field Mouse to see from the threshold of the door.

"Farewell, thou bright sun!" she said, and stretched out her arms toward it, and walked a little way forth from the house of the Field Mouse, for now the corn had been reaped, and only the dry stubble stood in the fields. "Farewell!" she repeated, twining her arms round a little red flower which still bloomed there. "Greet the little Swallow from me, if you see him again."

"Tweet-weet! tweet-weet!" a voice suddenly sounded over her head. She looked up; it was the little Swallow, who was just flying by. When he saw Thumbelina he was very glad; and Thumbelina told him how loath she was to have the ugly Mole for her husband, and that she was to live deep under the earth, where the sun never shone. And she could not refrain from weeping.

"The cold winter is coming now," said the Swallow; "I am going to fly far away into the warm countries. Will you come with me? You can sit upon my back, then we shall fly from the ugly Mole and his dark room—away, far away, over the mountains, to the warm countries, where the sun shines warmer than here, where it is always summer, and there are lovely flowers. Only fly with me, you dear little Thumbelina, you who saved my life when I lay frozen in the dark earthy passage."

"Yes, I will go with you!" said Thumbelina, and she seated herself on the bird's back, with her feet on his outspread wing, and bound her girdle fast to one of his strongest feathers; then the Swallow flew up into the air over forest and over sea, high up over the great mountains, where the snow always lies; and Thumbelina felt cold in the bleak air, but then she hid under the bird's warm feathers, and only put out her little head to admire all the beauties beneath her.

At last they came to the warm countries. There the sun shone far brighter than here; the sky seemed twice as high; in ditches and on the hedges grew the most beautiful blue and green grapes; lemons and oranges hung in the woods; the air was fragrant with myrtles and balsams, and on the roads the loveliest children ran about, playing with the gay butterflies. But the Swallow flew still farther, and it became more and more beautiful. Under the glorious green trees by the blue lake stood a palace of dazzling white marble, from the olden time. Vines clustered around the lofty pillars; at the top were many swallows' nests, and in one of these the Swallow lived who carried Thumbelina.

"That is my house," said the Swallow; "but it is not right that you should live there. It is not yet properly arranged by a great deal, and you will not be content with it. Select for yourself one of the splendid flowers which grow down yonder, then I will put you into it, and you shall have everything as nice as you can wish."

"That is capital," cried she, and clapped her little hands.

A great marble pillar lay there, which had fallen to the ground and been broken into three pieces; but between these pieces grew the most beautiful great white flowers. The Swallow flew down with Thumbelina, and set her upon one of the broad leaves. But what was the little maid's surprise? There sat a little man in the midst of the flower, as white and transparent as if he had been made of glass: he wore the neatest of gold crowns on his head, and the brightest wings on his shoulders; he himself was not bigger than Thumbelina. He was the angel of the flower. In each of the flowers dwelt such a little man or woman, but this one was king over them all.

"Heavens! how beautiful he is!" whispered Thumbelina to the Swallow.

The little Prince was very much frightened at the Swallow; for it was quite a gigantic bird to him, who was so small. But when he saw Thumbelina, he became very glad; she was the prettiest maiden he had ever seen. Therefore he took off his golden crown, and put it upon her, asked her name, and if she would be his wife, and then she should be Queen of all the flowers. Now this was truly a different kind of man to the son of the Toad, and the Mole with the black velvet fur. She therefore said, "Yes," to the charming Prince. And out of every flower came a lady or a lord, so pretty to behold that it was a delight: each one brought Thumbelina a present; but the best gift was a pair of beautiful wings which had belonged to a great white fly; these were fastened to Thumbelina's back, and now she could fly from flower to flower. Then there was much rejoicing; and the little Swallow sat above them in his nest, and was to sing the marriage song, which he accordingly did as well as he could; but yet in his heart he was sad, for he was so fond, oh! so fond of Thumbelina, and would have liked never to part from her.

"You shall not be called Thumbelina," said the Flower Angel to her; "that is an ugly name, and you are too fair for it—we will call you Maia."

"Farewell, farewell!" said the little Swallow, with a heavy heart; and he flew away again from the warm countries, far away back to Denmark. There he had a little nest over the window of the man who can tell fairy tales. Before him he sang, "Tweet-weet! tweet-weet!" and from him we have the whole story.

The Ugly Duckling

BY HANS CHRISTIAN ANDERSEN

Illustrated by LILIAN OBLIGADO

IT WAS glorious out in the country. It was summer, and the cornfields were yellow, and the oats were green; the hay had been put up in stacks in the green meadows, and the stork went about on his long red legs, and chattered Egyptian, for this was the language he had learned from his good mother. All around the fields and meadows were great forests, and in the midst of these forests lay deep lakes. Yes, it was really glorious out in the country. In the midst of the sunshine there lay an old farm, surrounded by deep canals, and from the wall down to the water grew great burdocks, so high that little children could stand upright under the loftiest of them. It was just as wild there as in the deepest wood. Here sat a Duck upon her nest, for she had to hatch her young ones; but she was almost tired out before the little ones came; and then she so seldom had visitors. The other ducks liked better to swim about in the canals than to run up to sit down under a burdock, and cackle with her.

At last one egg shell after another burst open. "Piep! piep!" it cried, and in all the eggs there were little creatures that stuck out their heads.

"Rap! rap!" they said; and they all came rapping out as fast as they could, looking all round them under the green leaves; and the mother let them look as much as they chose, for green is good for the eyes.

"How wide the world is!" said the young ones, for they certainly had much more room now than when they were in the eggs.

"Do you think this is all the world?" asked the mother. "That extends far across the other side of the garden, quite

into the parson's field, but I have never been there yet. I hope you are all together," she continued, and stood up. "No, I have not all. The largest egg still lies there. How long is that to last? I am really tired of it." And she sat down again.

"Well, how goes it?" asked an old Duck who had come to pay her a visit.

"It lasts a long time with that one egg," said the Duck who sat there. "It will not burst. Now, only look at the others; are they not the prettiest ducks one could possibly see? They are all like their father: the bad fellow never comes to see me."

"Let me see the egg which will not burst," said the old visitor. "Believe me, it is a turkey's egg. I was once cheated in that way, and had much anxiety and trouble with the young ones, for they are afraid of the water. I could not get them to venture in. I quacked and clucked, but it was no use. Let me see the egg. Yes, that's a turkey's egg! Let it lie there, and teach the other children to swim."

"I think I will sit on it a little longer," said the Duck. "I've sat so long now that I can sit a few days more."

"Just as you please," said the old Duck; and she went away.

At last the great egg burst. "Piep! piep!" said the little one, and crept forth. It was very large and very ugly. The Duck looked at it.

"It's a very large duckling," said she; "none of the others look like that: can it really be a turkey chick? Now we shall soon find it out. It must go into the water, even if I have to thrust it in myself."

The next day the weather was splendidly bright, and the sun shone on all the green trees. The Mother Duck went down to the water with all her little ones. Splash she jumped into the water. "Quack! quack!" she said, and one duckling after another plunged in. The water closed over their heads, but they came up in an instant, and swam capitally; their legs went of themselves, and there they were all in the water. The ugly gray Duckling swam with them.

"No, it's not a turkey," said she; "look how well it can use its legs, and how upright it holds itself. It is my own child! On the whole it's quite pretty, if one looks at it rightly. Quack! quack! come with me, and I'll lead you out into the

great world, and present you in the poultry yard; but keep close to me, so that no one may tread on you, and take care of the cats!"

And so they came into the poultry yard. There was a terrible riot going on in there, for two families were quarrelling about an eel's head, and the cat got it after all.

"See, that's how it goes in the world!" said the Mother Duck; and she whetted her beak, for she, too, wanted the eel's head. "Only use your legs," she said. "See that you can bustle about, and bow your heads before the old duck yonder. She's the grandest of all here; she's of Spanish blood—that's why she's so fat; and do you see, she has a red rag around her leg; that's something particularly fine, and the greatest distinction a duck can enjoy: it signifies that one does not want to lose her, and that she's to be recognized by

man and beast. Shake yourselves—don't turn in your toes; a well brought up duck turns its toes quite out, just like father and mother, so! Now bend your necks and say 'Rap!' "

And they did so; but the other ducks round about looked at them, and said quite boldly:

"Look there! Now we're to have these hanging on as if there were not enough of us already! And—fie!—how that Duckling yonder looks; we won't stand that!" And one duck flew up immediately, and bit it in the neck.

"Let it alone," said the mother; "it does no harm to any one."

"Yes, but it's too large and peculiar," said the Duck who had bitten it; "and therefore it must be buffeted."

"Those are pretty children that the mother has there," said the old Duck with the rag round her leg. "They're all

206

pretty but that one; that was a failure. I wish she could alter it."

"That cannot be done, my lady," replied the Mother Duck. "It is not pretty, but it has a really good disposition, and swims as well as any other; I may even say it swims better. I think it will grow up pretty, and become smaller in time; it has lain too long in the egg, and therefore is not properly shaped." And then she pinched it in the neck, and smoothed its feathers. "Moreover, it is a drake," she said, "and therefore it is not so much consequence. I think he will be very strong: he makes his way already."

"The other ducklings are graceful enough," said the old Duck. "Make yourself at home; and if you find an eel's head, you may bring it to me."

And now they were at home. But the poor Duckling which had crept last out of the egg, and looked so ugly, was bitten and pushed and jeered, as much by the ducks as by chickens.

"It is too big!" they all said. And the turkey cock, who had been born with spurs, and therefore thought himself an emperor, blew himself up like a ship in full sail, and bore straight down upon it; then he gobbled, and grew quite red in the face. The poor Duckling did not know where it should stand or walk; it was quite melancholy because it looked ugly, and was scoffed at by the whole yard.

So it went on the first day; and afterward it became worse and worse. The poor Duckling was hunted about by every one; even its brothers and sisters were quite angry with it, and said, "If the cat would only catch you, you ugly crea-

ture!" And the mother said, "If you were only far away!" And the ducks bit it, and the chickens beat it, and the girl who had to feed the poultry kicked at it with her foot.

Then it ran and flew over the fence, and the little birds in the bushes flew up in fear.

"That is because I am so ugly!" thought the Duckling; and it shut its eyes, but flew on farther; thus it came out into the great moor, where the wild ducks lived. Here it lay the whole night long; and it was weary and downcast.

Toward morning the wild ducks flew up, and looked at their new companion.

"What sort of a one are you?" they asked; and the Duckling turned in every direction, and bowed as well as it could. "You are remarkably ugly!" said the Wild Ducks. "But that is very indifferent to us, so long as you do not marry into our family."

Poor thing! It certainly did not think of marrying, and only hoped to obtain leave to lie among the reeds and drink some of the swamp water.

Thus it lay two whole days; then came thither two wild geese, or, properly speaking, two wild ganders. It was not long since each had crept out of an egg, and that's why they were so saucy.

"Listen, comrade," said one of them. "You're so ugly that I like you. Will you go with us, and become a bird of passage? Near here, in another moor, there are a few sweet lovely wild geese, all un-

married, and all able to say 'Rap!' You've a chance of making your fortune, ugly as you are!"

"Piff! paff!" resounded through the air; and the two ganders fell down dead in the swamp, and the water became blood-red. "Piff! paff!" it sounded again, and whole flocks of wild geese rose up from the reeds. And then there was another report. A great hunt was going on. The hunters were lying in wait all round the moor, and some were even sitting up in the branches of the trees, which spread far over the reeds. The blue smoke rose up like clouds among the dark trees, and was wafted far away across the water; and the hunting dogs came — splash, splash!—into the swamp, and the rushes and the reeds bent down on every side. That was a fright for the poor Duckling! It turned its head, and put it under its wing; but at that moment a frightful great dog stood close by the Duckling. His tongue hung far out of his mouth and his eyes gleamed horrible and ugly; he thrust out his nose close against the Duckling, showed his sharp teeth, and—splash, splash!—on he went, without seizing it.

"Oh, Heaven be thanked!" sighed the Duckling. "I am so ugly that even the dog does not like to bite me!"

And so it lay quiet, while the shots rattled through the reeds and gun after gun was fired. At last, late in the day, silence was restored; but the poor Duckling did not dare to rise up; it waited several hours before it looked round, and then hastened away out of the moor as fast as it could. It ran on over field and meadow; there was such a storm raging that it was difficult to get from one place to another.

Toward evening the Duckling came to a little miserable peasant's hut. This hut was so dilapidated that it did not know on which side it should fall; and that's why it remained standing. The storm whistled round the Duckling in such a way that the poor creature was obliged to sit down, to stand against it; and the tempest grew worse and worse. Then the Duckling noticed that one of the hinges of the door had given way, and the door hung so slanting that the Duckling could slip through the crack into the room.

Here lived a woman, with her Tom Cat and her Hen. And the Tom Cat, whom she called Sonnie, could arch his back and purr, he could even give out sparks; but for that one had to stroke his fur the wrong way. The Hen had quite little short legs, and therefore she was called Chickabiddy-shortshanks; she laid good eggs, and the woman loved her as her own child.

In the morning the strange Duckling was at once noticed, and the Tom Cat began to purr, and the Hen to cluck.

"What's this?" said the woman, and looked all round; but she could not see well, and therefore she thought the

Duckling was a fat duck that had strayed. "This is a rare prize!" she said. "Now I shall have duck's eggs. I hope it is not a drake. We must try that."

And so the Duckling was admitted on trial for three weeks; but no eggs came. And the Tom Cat was master of the house, and the Hen was the lady, and always said, "We and the world!" for she thought they were half the world, and by far the better half. The Duckling thought one might have a different opinion, but the Hen would not allow it.

"Can you lay eggs?" she asked.

"No."

"Then you'll have the goodness to hold your tongue."

And the Tom Cat said, "Can you curve your back, and purr, and give out sparks?"

"No."

"Then you cannot have any opinion of your own when sensible people are speaking."

And the Duckling sat in a corner and was melancholy; then the fresh air and the sunshine streamed in; and it was seized with such a strange longing to swim on the water, that it could not help telling the Hen of it.

"What are you thinking of?" cried the Hen. "You have nothing to do, that's why you have these fancies. Purr or lay eggs, and they will pass over."

"But it is so charming to swim on the water!" said the Duckling, "so refreshing to let it close above one's head, and to dive down to the bottom."

"Yes, that must be a mighty pleasure truly," quoth the Hen. "I fancy you must have gone crazy. Ask the Cat about it—he's the cleverest animal I know—ask him

if he likes to swim on the water, or to dive down: I won't speak about myself. Ask our mistress, the old woman; no one in the world is cleverer than she. Do you think she has any desire to swim, and to let the water close above her head?"

"You don't understand me," said the Duckling.

"We don't understand you? Then pray who is to understand you? You surely don't pretend to be cleverer than the Tom Cat and the woman—I won't say anything of myself. Don't be conceited, child, and be grateful for all the kindness you have received. Did you not get into a warm room, and have you not fallen into company from which you may learn something? But you are a chatterer, and it is not pleasant to associate with you. You may believe me, I speak for your good. I tell you disagreeable things, and by that one may always know one's true

friends! Only take care that you learn to lay eggs, or to purr and give out sparks!"

"I think I will go out into the wide world," said the Duckling.

"Yes, do go," replied the Hen.

And the Duckling went away. It swam on the water, and dived, but it was slighted by every creature because of its ugliness.

Now came the autumn. The leaves in the forest turned yellow and brown; the wind caught them so that they danced about, and up in the air it was very cold. The clouds hung low, heavy with hail and snowflakes, and on the fence stood the raven, crying, "Croak! croak!" for mere cold; yes, it was enough to make one feel cold to think of this. The poor little Duckling certainly had not a good time. One evening—the sun was just setting in his beauty—there came a whole flock of great handsome birds out of the bushes; they were dazzlingly white, with long flexible necks; they were swans. They uttered a very peculiar cry, spread forth their glorious great wings, and flew away from that cold region to warmer lands, to fair open lakes. They mounted so high, so high! and the ugly little Duckling felt quite strangely as it watched them. It turned round and round in the water like a wheel, stretched out its neck toward them, and uttered such a strange loud cry as frightened itself. Oh! it could not forget those beautiful, happy birds; and so soon as it could see them no longer, it dived down to the very bottom, and when it came up again, it was quite beside itself. It knew not the name of those birds, and knew not whither they were flying; but it loved them more than it had ever loved any one. It was not at all envious of them. How could it think of wishing to possess such loveliness as they had? It would have been glad if only the ducks would have endured its company—the poor ugly creature!

And the winter grew cold, very cold! The Duckling was forced to swim about in the water, to prevent the surface from freezing entirely; but every night the hole in which it swam about became smaller and smaller. It froze so hard that the icy covering crackled again; and the Duckling was obliged to use its legs continually to prevent the hole from freezing up. At last it became exhausted, and lay quite still, and thus froze fast into the ice.

Early in the morning a peasant came by, and when he saw what had happened, he took his wooden shoe, broke the ice crust to pieces, and carried the Duckling home to his wife. Then it came to itself again. The children wanted to play with it; but the Duckling thought they would do it an injury, and in its terror fluttered up into the milk pan, so that the milk spurted down into the room. The woman clapped her hands, at which the Duckling flew down into the butter tub, and then into the meal barrel and out again. How it looked then! The woman screamed, and struck at it with the fire tongs; the children tumbled over one another in their efforts to catch the Duckling; and they laughed and screamed finely! Happily the door stood open, and the poor creature was able to slip out between the shrubs into the newly fallen snow; and there it lay quite exhausted.

But it would be too melancholy if I were to tell all the misery and care which the Duckling had to endure in the hard winter. It lay out on the moor among the reeds, when the sun began to shine again and the larks to sing: it was a beautiful spring.

Then all at once the Duckling could flap its wings: they beat the air more strongly than before, and bore it strongly away; and before it well knew how all this happened, it found itself in a great garden, where the elder-trees smelt sweet, and bent their long green branches down to the canal that wound through the region. Oh, here it was so beautiful, such a gladness of spring! and from the thicket came three glorious white swans; they rustled their wings, and swam lightly on the water. The Duckling knew the splendid creatures, and felt oppressed by a peculiar sadness.

"I will fly away to them, to the royal birds! and they will kill me, because I, that am so ugly, dare to approach them. But it is of no consequence! Better to be killed by them than to be pursued by ducks, and beaten by fowls, and pushed about by the girl who takes care of the poultry yard, and to suffer hunger in winter!" And it flew out into the water, and swam toward the beautiful swans: these looked at it, and came sailing down upon it with outspread wings. "Kill me!" said the poor creature, and bent its head down upon the water, expecting nothing but death. But what was this that it saw in the clear water? It beheld its own image; and, lo! it was no longer a clumsy dark gray bird, ugly and hateful to look at, but—a swan!

It matters nothing if one is born in a duck-yard, if one has only lain in a swan's egg.

It felt quite glad at all the need and

misfortune it had suffered; now it realized its happiness in all the splendor that surrounded it. And the great swans swam round it, and stroked it with their beaks.

Into the garden came little children, who threw bread and corn into the water; and the youngest cried, "There is a new one!" and the other children shouted joyously, "Yes, a new one has arrived!" And they clapped their hands and danced about, and ran to their father and mother; and bread and cake were thrown into the water; and they all said, "The new one is the most beautiful of all! so young and handsome!" and the old swans bowed their heads before him.

Then he felt quite ashamed, and hid his head under his wings, for he did not know what to do; he was so happy, and yet not at all proud. He thought how he had been persecuted and despised; and now he heard them saying that he was the most beautiful of all birds. Even the elder-tree bent its branches straight down into the water before him, and the sun shone warm and mild. Then his wings rustled, he lifted his slender neck, and cried rejoicingly from the depths of his heart:

"I never dreamed of so much happiness when I was still the ugly Duckling!"

Although The Emperor's New Clothes *is usually grouped
with fairy tales, it is not a tale of enchantment at all.
It is a comic story about a vain and foolish king.
We smile at the king's folly, but even as we laugh,
we learn something.*

The Emperor's New Clothes

BY HANS CHRISTIAN ANDERSEN
Illustrated by GRACE DALLES CLARKE

MANY years ago there lived an Emperor, who cared so enormously for new clothes that he spent all his money upon them, that he might be very fine. He did not care about his soldiers, nor about the theatre, and only liked to drive out and show his new clothes. He had a coat for every hour of the day; and just as they say of a king, "He is in council," one always said of him, "The Emperor is in the wardrobe."

In the great city in which he lived it was always very merry; every day a number of strangers arrived there. One day two cheats came: they gave themselves out as weavers, and declared that they could weave the finest stuff any one could imagine. Not only were their colors and patterns, they said, uncommonly beautiful, but the clothes made of the stuff possessed the wonderful quality that they became invisible to any one who was unfit for the office he held, or was incorrigibly stupid.

"Those would be capital clothes!" thought the Emperor. "If I wore those, I should be able to find out what men in my empire are not fit for the places they have; I could distinguish the clever from the stupid. Yes, the stuff must be woven for me directly!"

And he gave the two cheats a great deal of cash in hand, that they might begin their work at once. As for them, they put up two looms, and pretended to be working; but they had nothing at all on their looms. They at once demanded the finest silk and the costliest gold; this they put into their own pockets, and worked at the empty looms till late into the night.

"I should like to know how far they have got on with the stuff," thought the Emperor. But he felt quite uncomfortable when he thought that those who were not fit for their offices could not see it. He believed, indeed, that he had nothing to

fear for himself, but yet he preferred first to send someone else to see how matters stood. All the people in the whole city knew what peculiar power the stuff possessed, and all were anxious to see how bad or how stupid their neighbors were.

"I will send my honest old Minister to the weavers," thought the Emperor. "He can judge best how the stuff looks, for he has sense, and no one understands his office better than he."

Now the good old Minister went out into the hall where the two cheats sat working at the empty looms.

"Mercy preserve us!" thought the old Minister, and he opened his eyes wide. "I cannot see anything at all!" But he did not say this.

Both the cheats begged him to be kind enough to come nearer, and asked if he

did not approve of the colors and the pattern. Then they pointed to the empty loom, and the poor old Minister went on opening his eyes; but he could see nothing, for there was nothing to see.

"Mercy!" thought he, "can I indeed be so stupid? I never thought that, not a soul must know it. Am I not fit for my office?—No, it will never do for me to tell that I could not see the stuff."

"Do you say nothing to it?" said one of the weavers.

"Oh, it is charming—quite charming!" answered the old Minister, as he peered through his spectacles. "What a fine pattern, and what colors! Yes, I shall tell the Emperor that I am very much pleased with it."

"Well, we are glad of that," said both the weavers; and then they named the colors, and explained the strange pattern. The old Minister listened attentively, that he might be able to repeat it when the Emperor came. And he did so.

Now the cheats asked for more money, and more silk and gold, which they declared they wanted for weaving. They put all into their own pockets, and not a thread was put upon the loom; but they continued to work at the empty frames as before.

The Emperor soon sent again, dispatching another honest statesman, to see how the weaving was going on, and if the stuff would soon be ready. He fared just like the first: he looked and looked, but, as there was nothing to be seen but the empty looms, he could see nothing.

"Is not that a pretty piece of stuff?" asked the two cheats, and they displayed and explained the handsome pattern which was not there at all.

"I am not stupid!" thought the man; "it must be my good office, for which I am not fit. It is odd enough, but I must not let it be noticed." And so he praised the stuff which he did not see, and expressed his pleasure at the beautiful colors and the charming pattern. "Yes, it is enchanting," he said to the Emperor.

All the people in the town were talking of the gorgeous stuff. The Emperor wished to see it himself while it was still upon the loom. With a whole crowd of chosen men, among whom were also the two honest statesmen who had already been there, he went to the two cunning cheats, who were now weaving with might and main without fibre or thread.

"Is that not splendid?" said the two old statesmen, who had already been there once. "Does not your Majesty remark the pattern and the colors?" And then they pointed to the empty loom, for they thought that others could see the stuff.

"What's this?" thought the Emperor. "I can see nothing at all! That is terrible. Am I stupid? Am I not fit to be Emperor? That would be the most dreadful thing that could happen to me.—Oh, it is *very* pretty!" he said aloud. "It has our exalted approbation." And he nodded in a contented way, and gazed at the empty loom, for he would not say that he saw nothing. The whole suite whom he had with him looked and looked, and saw nothing, any more than the rest; but, like the Emperor, they said, "That *is* pretty!" and counselled him to wear these splendid new clothes for the first time at the great procession that was presently to take place. "It is splendid, tasteful, excellent!" went from mouth to mouth. On all sides there seemed to be general rejoicing, and the

Emperor gave the cheats the title of Imperial Court Weavers.

The whole night before the morning on which the procession was to take place the cheats were up, and had lighted more than sixteen candles. The people could see that they were hard at work, completing the Emperor's new clothes. They pretended to take the stuff down from the loom; they made cuts in the air with great scissors; they sewed with needles without thread; and at last they said, "Now the clothes are ready!"

The Emperor came himself with his noblest cavaliers; and the two cheats lifted up one arm as if they were holding something, and said, "See, here are the trousers! Here is the coat! Here is the cloak!" and so on. "It is as light as a spider's web: one would think one had nothing on; but that is just the beauty of it."

"Yes," said all the cavaliers; but they could not see anything, for nothing was there.

"Does your Imperial Majesty please to condescend to undress?" said the cheats; "then we will put on you the new clothes here in front of the great mirror."

The Emperor took off his clothes, and the cheats pretended to put on him each new garment as it was ready; and the Emperor turned round and round before the mirror.

"Oh, how well they look! How capitally they fit!" said all. "What a pattern! What

colors! That *is* a splendid dress!"

"They are standing outside with the canopy which is to be borne above your Majesty in the procession!" announced the head master of the ceremonies.

"Well, I am ready," replied the Emperor. "Does it not suit me well?" And then he turned again to the mirror, for he wanted it to appear as if he contemplated his adornment with great interest.

The chamberlains, who were to carry the train, stooped down with their hands toward the floor, just as if they were picking up the mantle; then they pretended to be holding something up in the air. They did not dare to let it be noticed that they saw nothing.

So the Emperor went in procession under the rich canopy, and every one in the streets said, "How incomparable are

the Emperor's new clothes! What a train he has to his mantle! How it fits him!" No one would it let be perceived that he could see nothing, for that would have shown that he was not fit for his office, or was very stupid. No clothes of the Emperor's had ever had such a success as these.

"But he has nothing on!" a little child cried out at last.

"Just hear what that innocent says!" said the father; and one whispered to another what the child had said.

"But he has nothing on!" said the whole people at length. That touched the Emperor, for it seemed to him that they were right; but he thought within himself, "I must go through with the procession." And the chamberlains held on tighter than ever, and carried the train which did not exist at all.

When the African Negroes came to America
they brought many of their stories with them.
Some of them were retold by a Southern writer,
in Uncle Remus, His Songs and Sayings.
Uncle Remus is an old Negro who speaks in the odd
and humorous dialect of a hundred years ago.
His audience consists of one: a little boy
living on the plantation where Uncle Remus works.
Many of the phrases are so quaint and the spellings so queer
that it has been necessary to simplify some of them.
However, when read aloud.
the original fun and flavor come through.

The Wonderful Tar-Baby Story

From Uncle Remus, His Songs and Sayings

BY JOEL CHANDLER HARRIS

Illustrated by A. B. FROST

"DIDN'T THE fox *never* catch the rabbit, Uncle Remus?" the little boy asked the old man one evening.

"He come mighty nigh it, honey, sure as you're born. One day after Brer Rabbit had fooled him so many times, Brer Fox went to work an' got him some tar, an' then he mixed it with some turpentine an' fixed up a contraption that he called a Tar-Baby. He took this here Tar-Baby an' set him down right smack in the big road an' then lay down in the bushes an' watched for to see what was goin' to happen.

"Brer Fox didn't have to wait long either. Pretty soon Brer Rabbit come prancin' down the road lippity-clippity, clippity-lippity, just as sassy as a jay-bird. Brer Fox, he lay low. Brer Rabbit come prancin' right along 'til he spied the Tar-Baby settin' there, an' then he fetched up on his hind legs lookin' mighty astonished. The Tar-Baby just set there doin' nothin', an' Brer Fox, he kept on layin' low.

" 'Mornin'!' says Brer Rabbit. 'Nice weather this mornin', says he.

"Tar-Baby ain't sayin' nothin', an' Brer Fox, he lay low.

" 'How is the state of your health at

present?' says Brer Rabbit to Tar-Baby.

"Brer Fox, he wing his eye slow, an' lay low, an' Tar-Baby she ain't sayin' nothin'.

"'How you gettin' along?' says Brer Rabbit. An' when there ain't no answer, he says, 'Is you deaf?' he says, 'Because if you is, I can holler louder.'

"Tar-Baby just kept on settin' there, an' Brer Fox he lay low.

"'You're mighty stuck up, that's what you is,' says Brer Rabbit. 'An' I'm goin' to cure you, that's what I'm goin' to do,' he says.

"Brer Fox, he sorta chuckle in his stomach, he did, but Tar-Baby ain't sayin' nothin'.

"'I'm going to learn you how to talk to respectable folk if it's the last thing I do,' says Brer Rabbit. 'If you don't take off that old hat an' say howdy-do to me, I'm going to bust you wide open,' says he.

"Tar-Baby stay still, an' Brer Fox lay low.

"Brer Rabbit kept on askin' him to say

howdy-do, an' Tar-Baby kept on sayin' nothin' at all, 'til finally Brer Rabbit draw back his fist and—*blip*—he hit Tar-Baby right smack on the side of the head. Right there's where Brer Rabbit made his big mistake. His fist stuck fast, an' he couldn't pull loose. The tar held him tight. But Tar-Baby just set still. And Brer Fox, he lay low.

"'If you don't let me loose, I'll knock you again,' says Brer Rabbit, an' with that he fetched Tar-Baby a swipe with the other hand. An' *that* stuck. Tar-Baby, she ain't sayin' nothin', and Brer Fox, he lay low.

"'Turn me loose,' hollers Brer Rabbit. 'Turn me loose before I kick the natural stuffin' out of you,' he says. But Tar-Baby ain't sayin' nothin'—just keeps on holdin' fast. Then Brer Rabbit he commenced to kick, an' the next thing he know his feet are stuck fast too. Brer Rabbit squall out that if Tar-Baby didn't turn him loose, he'd butt with his head. Brer Rabbit butted, an' then he got his head stuck, too.

"Then Brer Fox, he sauntered out of the bushes, lookin' just as innocent as a mockin' bird.

"'Howdy, Brer Rabbit,' says Brer Fox, says he. 'You look sort of stuck up this mornin',' he says, an' then he rolled on the ground and he laughed and laughed 'til he couldn't laugh no more. 'I reckon you're goin' to have dinner with me this time, Brer Rabbit,' he says. 'I've laid in a heap o' nice vegetables an' things, an' I ain't goin' to take no excuse,' says Brer Fox."

Here Uncle Remus paused and raked a huge sweet potato out of the ashes on the hearth.

"Did the fox eat the rabbit, Uncle Remus?" asked the little boy.

"Well, now, that's as far as the tale goes," replied the old man. "Maybe he did—an' then again, maybe he didn't. Some people say that Judge B'ar come along an' turned him loose. And some say he didn't. . . . But ain't that Miss Sally I hear callin' you? You better run along now."

How Brer Rabbit Was Too Sharp For Brer Fox

"Uncle Remus," said the little boy one evening when he found the old man with little or nothing to do, "Uncle Remus, *did* the fox kill and eat the rabbit when he caught him with the Tar-Baby?"

"Law, honey, ain't I tell you about that?" replied the old man, chuckling slyly. "I declare to gracious, I ought to told you that. But old man Nod was ridin' on my eyelids till a little more and I'd a disremembered my own name. And on top o' that, just then your mammy come callin' you.

"What was it I tell you when I first begin? I tole you that Brer Rabbit was a monstrous clever creature—leastways, that's what I laid out for to tell you.

Well, then, honey, don't you go and make no other calculations. 'Cause in them days when anything was goin' on, Brer Rabbit and his family was right at the head of the gang when anything was on hand, and there they stayed. Before you sheds any tears about Brer Rabbit, you just wait and see whereabouts Brer Rabbit ends up.

"When old Brer Fox find Brer Rabbit all mixed up with that Tar-Baby, he feel mighty good. He just roll on the ground and laugh. By and by he up and says, says he:

"'Well, I 'spect I got you this time, Brer Rabbit,' says he. 'Maybe I ain't, but I reckon I has. You been runnin' round here sassin' me a mighty long time. But

now I 'spect you done come to the end of the row. You been cuttin' up your capers and bouncin' round in this neighborhood 'til you come to believe that you're the boss of the whole gang.'

" 'And besides that, you're always gettin' in somewheres where you don't have no business,' says Brer Fox, says he. 'Who asked you to come and strike up an acquaintance with this here Tar-Baby? And who got you all stuck up there the way you is? Nobody in the whole round world but yourself. You just took and jam yourself on that Tar-Baby without waitin' for any invite,' says Brer Fox.

" 'Well, there you is,' says Brer Fox, 'and there you'll stay 'til I fixes up a brush-pile and fires her up,' he says, " 'cause I'm goin' to barbecue you this day, sure,' says Brer Fox, says he.

"Then Brer Rabbit he begin to talk mighty humble.

" 'I don't care what you do with me, Brer Fox,' says he, 'just so you don't fling me in that brier patch. Roast me, Brer Fox,' says he, 'but don't fling me in that brier patch.'

"It's so much trouble for to kindle a fire,' says Brer Fox, says he, 'that I 'spect maybe I'll have to hang you instead,' he says.

" 'Hang me just as high as you please, Brer Fox,' says Brer Rabbit, 'but for the Lord's sake don't fling me in that brier patch,' says he.

" 'I ain't got no string,' says Brer Fox. 'I 'spect I'll just have to drown you,' says he.

" 'Drown me just as deep as you please, Brer Fox,' says Brer Rabbit, says he, 'but don't fling me in that there brier patch,' he says.

" 'There ain't no water nigh here,' says Brer Fox, 'so I 'spect maybe I'll just have to skin you instead,' he says.

" 'Skin me, Brer Fox,' says Brer Rabbit, says he, 'snatch out my eyeballs, tear out my ears by the roots, and cut off my legs,' he says, 'but please, Brer Fox, please don't fling me in that brier patch,' says he.

"Brer Fox he want to hurt Brer Rabbit just as bad as he can, of course, so he catch him by the hind legs and he slung him right in the middle of the brier patch. There was a considerable flutter when Brer Rabbit struck the bushes, and Brer Fox he sorta hang 'round for to see what goin' to happen. By and by he hear somebody call him, and he look and 'way up on the hill he see Brer Rabbit settin' cross-legged on a log, combin' the tar out of his hair with a chip. Then Brer Fox know he been tricked mighty bad. And Brer Rabbit he couldn't help but fling back some of his sass, and he holler out from the hill:

" 'Why, I was bred and born in a brier patch, Brer Fox—bred and born in a brier patch!'

"And with that he skip out o' there just as lively as a cricket in the embers."

Brer Rabbit Grossly Deceives Brer Fox

ONE EVENING WHEN the little boy, whose nights with Uncle Remus were as entertaining as those Arabian Nights of blessed memory, had finished supper and hurried out to sit with his venerable patron, he found the old man in great glee. Indeed, Uncle Remus was talking and laughing to himself at such a rate that the little boy was afraid that he had company. The truth is, Uncle Remus had heard that child coming and, when the rosy-cheeked little chap put his head in at the door, was engaged in a monologue, the burden of which seemed to be:

> *"Ole Molly Har'*
> *W'at you doin' dar*
> *Settin' in de cornder*
> *Smokin' yo' seegar?"*

Whatever this meant, it somehow reminded the little boy that the wicked Fox was still in pursuit of the Rabbit, and his curiosity immediately took the shape of a question.

"Uncle Remus, did the Rabbit have to go clean away when he got loose from the Tar-Baby?"

"Bless gracious honey, that he didn't. Who? Him? You don't know nothin' at all about Brer Rabbit if that's the way you puttin' him down. What he goin' 'way for? He maybe stayed sorta close 'til the tar rub off his hair some. But it wasn't many days before he was lopin' up and down the neighborhood the same as ever—and I don't know if he wasn't more sassier than before.

"Seems like the tale about how he got mixed up with the Tar-Baby got 'round amongst the neighbors. Leastways, Miss Meadows and the gals got wind of it, and the next time Brer Rabbit paid them a visit Miss Meadows tackled him 'bout it. The gals set up a monstrous gigglement, but Brer Rabbit he set up just as cool as a cucumber, he did, and let 'em run on."

"Who was Miss Meadows, Uncle Remus?" inquired the little boy.

"Well, don't ask me honey. They was just in the tale, Miss Meadows and the gals was, and I tell the tale to you just the way it was give to me. . . . Well, then, Brer Rabbit just set there sorta like a lamb, he did, and then by and by he cross his legs, and he lean back and wink his eye slow. Then he up and say, says he:

"'Ladies, Brer Fox was my daddy's ridin' horse for thirty year—maybe more, but thirty year that I knows about,' says he. Then he paid the ladies his respects, and he tip his hat, he did. And off he march, just as stiff and stuck up as a stick.

"Next day, Brer Fox he come a'callin' on the ladies, and when he begin to laugh about Brer Rabbit, Miss Meadows and the gals they ups and tells him about what Brer Rabbit say. Well, Brer Fox he grit his teeth, sure enough, he did, and he look mighty grumpy. But when he stood up for to go, he up and he say, says he:

"'Ladies, I ain't disputin' what you say—but I tell you this: I'll make Brer Rabbit chew up his words and spit 'em right here where you can see 'em,' says

he. And with that, off went Brer Fox.

"As soon as he got to the bit road, Brer Fox shook the dew off his tail and made a straight shoot for Brer Rabbit's house. Brer Rabbit was expectin' him, of course, and when he got there, the door was shut fast. Brer Fox knock. Nobody ain't answer. Brer Fox knock again. Nobody answer. Brer Fox keep on knockin'— blam, blam! And then Brer Rabbit holler out, but mighty weak.

"'Is that you, Brer Fox? I want you to run and fetch the doctor. Somethin' I et this mornin' is killin' me. Please Brer Fox, run quick, quick,' says Brer Rabbit. says he.

"'I just come to get you, Brer Rabbit,' says Brer Fox. 'There's going to be a party up at Miss Meadows's' says he. 'All the gals goin' to be there, and I promise that I'd fetch you. The gals they all said that it wouldn't be no party exceptin' I fetch you,' says Brer Fox, says he.

"Brer Rabbit say he was to sick to go. Brer Fox say he wasn't—and then they had it up and down, disputin' and contendin'. Brer Rabbit say he can't walk. Brer Fox say he carry him. Brer Rabbit

say how? Brer Fox say in his arms. Brer Rabbit say he 'fraid he drop him. Brer Fox promise he won't.

"By and by Brer Rabbit say he go if Brer Fox tote him on his back. Brer Fox say he do that. But Brer Rabbit say he can't ride without a saddle. Brer Fox say he get a saddle. Brer Rabbit say he can't set in the saddle unless he have a bridle for to hold on to. Brer Fox say he get the bridle. But Brer Rabbit say he can't ride without blinders on the bridle, 'cause maybe Brer Fox shy at stumps along the way and fling him off. Brer Fox he say he get a blind bridle.

"Then Brer Rabbit say he go. And Brer Fox say he ride Brer Rabbit most up to Miss Meadows's, but then he let him get down and walk the rest of the way. Brer Rabbit agree and Brer Fox hustle off after the saddle and the bridle.

"Of course, all along Brer Rabbit know the game that Brer Fox was fixin' for to play, and he determine to outdo him. Well, by the time he comb his hair, and twist his mustache, and sorta spruce himself up, here come Brer Fox with the saddle and bridle on, lookin' as pert as a circus pony. He trot right up to the door and stand there pawin' the ground and chompin' the bit like a sure enough horse. Brer Rabbit he mount, he did, and they amble off.

"Brer Fox he can't see behind because of the blind bridle he wearin', but by and by he feel Brer Rabbit raise one of his feet.

" 'What you doin', Brer Rabbit?' says he.

" 'Shortenin' the left stirrup, Brer Fox,' says he.

"By and by Brer Rabbit raise up the other foot.

" 'What you doin' now, Brer Rabbit?' says he.

" 'Pullin' down my pants, Brer Fox,' says he.

"All this time, gracious honey, Brer Rabbit was puttin' on his spurs. When they got close to Miss Meadows's where Brer Rabbit was to git off, Brer Fox made a motion for to stop. Then Brer Rabbit he slap the spurs into Brer Fox' flanks—and you better believe that Brer Fox begin to cover the ground. When they got to the house, Miss Meadows and all the gals was settin' on the piazza. Instead of stoppin' at the gate, Brer Rabbit rode right on by, he did, and then came gallopin' back down the road and up to the horse-rack, which he hitch Brer Fox at, and then he sauntered into the house, he did, and shake hands with the gals, and set there smokin' his seegar same as a town man. By and by he draw in a long puff and let it out in a cloud. Then he square himself back and holler out, he did:

" 'Ladies, ain't I done tell you Brer Fox was the ridin' horse for our family? He sorta losin' his gait now, but I reckon I can fetch him 'round in a month or so,' says he.

"Then Brer Rabbit sorta grin, he did, and the gals giggle, and Miss Meadows, she praise up the pony. And there was Brer Fox hitched fast to the rack, and couldn't help himself."

"Is that all, Uncle Remus?" asked the little boy as the old man paused.

"Well, that ain't exactly all, honey—but it wouldn't do to give out too much cloth for to make one pair of pants," replied the old man sententiously.

Pinocchio is an Italian story,
which has been loved by millions of children in every land
ever since it was written almost one hundred years ago.
The first three chapters, which follow,
tell how Pinocchio came to life...
and, even before his first breath,
was naughty.

Illustrated by GORDON LAITE

From Pinocchio *by Carlo Collodi*

A Stick of Wood That Talked

ONCE UPON a time there was—

"A king!" my little readers will say at once.

No, my dears, you are wrong. Once upon a time there was a stick of wood. It was not a fine stick, either, but just such another as you would put in the fireplace to heat the room.

I do not know how it came about, but one fine day this stick of wood was found in the carpenter shop of an old man named Antonio. Everybody called him Master Cherry, however, because of the color of his nose which was red and shiny like a ripe cherry.

As soon as Master Cherry saw the stick of wood he was delighted. He rubbed his hands together and mumbled to himself: "The very thing! This stick will make a fine table leg."

Saying this, he picked up a sharp axe to begin to smooth off the bark; but just as he was about to strike he stopped with arm in air, for he thought he heard a thin sharp voice cry out: "Do not strike me too hard!"

Imagine good old Master Cherry's surprise! He rolled his eyes around in every corner of the room to see whence came the voice, but could discover no one. He looked under the workbench; nobody. He looked into the tightly-shut cupboard; nobody. He looked into the chip basket and shavings; nobody. He opened

229

the door and looked up and down the street; but still nobody. What then?

"Ah, I see!" he laughed to himself and scratched his wig. "I only dreamed that I heard a voice. Let's begin again."

He took up the axe again and hit the stick of wood a lively blow.

"Ouch! You have hurt me!" cried the little voice in pain.

This time Master Cherry stood as if turned to stone, his eyes fairly sticking out of his head, his tongue hanging out of his mouth for all the world like a gorgon head on a fountain. As soon as he found his voice he said, trembling and stammering:

"Who was it that cried out? There is not a living soul here. Is it possible that this stick can cry like a baby? I can't believe it. It's just like any other piece of wood that you put on the fire to boil a pot of beans. What then? Can somebody be hidden inside? If so, so much the worse for him. I'll fix him!"

So saying he laid hold of the poor stick of wood and began to pound it against the wall. Then he paused to listen if any one should cry out. He listened for two minutes — nothing; for five minutes — nothing; for ten minutes, and still nothing.

"Ah, I see!" he tried to laugh again and scratch his wig; "this little voice that called 'Ouch!' was only my imagination. Let's begin again."

And because he had really begun to be frightened, he tried to hum a tune to keep up his courage. At the same time he laid his axe aside and took up a plane, in order to smooth and polish the wood; but he had no sooner begun to push it back and forth, when he heard the same sharp little voice say with a laugh: "Stop, you are tickling me!"

This time, poor Master Cherry fell down as if thunderstricken. When he opened his eyes he found himself seated upon the ground. His face was blank with amazement, and the end of his nose had changed from red to blue because of his great alarm.

Master Cherry Gives the Stick to Gepetto

At this moment a knock was heard on the door.

"Come in," said the carpenter, who did not have strength enough to get up.

A little old man whose name was Gepetto entered. He was often called Polendina by the bad boys who wished to tease him, on account of his yellow wig which looked like a bag of yellow meal. You must know, that is what "polendina" means in Italy, and it always made him angry to be called this.

"Good morning, Antonio," said Gepetto, "what are you doing on the ground?"

"I am teaching the ants to read."

"May it do you good!"

"What has brought you here, friend Gepetto?" asked the other in his turn.

"My legs. But I would like to ask a favor of you."

"At your service," replied the carpenter, beginning to rise.

"This morning an idea popped into my head."

"Let's have it."

"I thought to myself that I would carve out a clever marionette of wood; and with this marionette, which I can teach to dance and do tricks, I can wander about over the world and earn my living. What do you think?"

"Bravo, Polendina!" cried a sharp little voice.

On hearing this nickname, Gepetto grew as red as a pepper, and turned upon the carpenter saying harshly, "What do you mean by insulting me?"

"I never insulted you!"

"You called me Polendina."

"Indeed I did not."

"Don't you think I can believe my ears? I heard you."

"No!"

"Yes!"

"No!"

"Yes!"

From words they soon came to blows, and scuffled about until each had seized the other by the wig.

"Give me back my wig!" cried Antonio.

"Then give me mine, and let us make peace," said Gepetto.

So the two foolish old fellows ex-changed wigs, shook hands again, and promised to be good friends for the rest of their lives.

"And now, friend Gepetto," said the carpenter, "what is the favor you desire of me?"

"I need a piece of wood, from which to carve my marionette. Can you give me one?"

Master Antonio was glad enough to go after the stick of wood which had already given him so much alarm. But when he tried to hand it over to his friend, the wood gave a kick and sliding out of his hands landed violently upon the shins of poor Gepetto.

"Ah, you are not very polite when you give presents, Master Antonio," he groaned. "You have nearly lamed me."

"Upon my word, I didn't do it!"

"Then I suppose *I* must have!"

"The fault is all in that wood."

"Oh, I know the wood hit me—but you threw it at my legs."

"No, I did not throw it."

"Scoundrel!"

"Gepetto, don't insult me, or I shall call you Polendina."

"Donkey!"

"Polendina!"

"Monkey!"

"Polendina!"

"Ugly ape!"

"Polendina!"

Gepetto now thoroughly angry threw himself upon the carpenter and they fought it out to a finish. Antonio got his nose scratched, and Gepetto lost two buttons off his coat. Having thus squared accounts they shook hands solemnly and promised again to be good friends for the rest of their lives. Then Gepetto picked

up the stick of wood, thanked Antonio, and limped back home.

How Pinocchio Was Made

GEPETTO's home was one small room on a ground floor under a staircase. Its furniture could not have been simpler: there was a tumble-down chair, a poor bed, and a rickety table. There seemed to be a fireplace at the back, but it was only a picture, and so was the fire and the pot above it, which appeared to give out clouds of steam.

As soon as he reached home, Gepetto took up his tools and fell to work carving out his marionette.

"What name shall I give him?" he asked himself. "I think it shall be Pinocchio; that's a name which will bring him good luck. I once knew a whole family called Pinocchio, and all did well. The richest of the lot knew how to beg."

Now that he had found a name for his marionette, Gepetto fell hard to work and soon had carved the hair, then the top of the head, and then the eyes. No sooner had he made the eyes than—much to his surprise—the marionette moved them and began to stare at him!

Gepetto did not like this and said sharply: "Why do you stare at me, wooden eyes?"

No reply.

Next he made the nose, but no sooner was it made than it began to grow. It grew and grew and grew as though it never would stop. Poor Gepetto tried to cut it short, but the more he chipped the longer that impudent nose became. So he let it alone and began on the mouth. But the mouth was not half done before it began to laugh and mock him.

"Stop your laughing!" scolded Gepetto; but it was like talking to the wall.

"Stop your laughing, I tell you!" he called loudly.

The mouth ceased its grinning, but began to make faces at him. Gepetto pretended not to see this, and went on with his work. After the mouth he made the chin, then the neck, the shoulders, the body, the arms and the hands.

No sooner had he made the hands than they grabbed the wig from Gepetto's head. He turned quickly.

"Pinocchio," he called, "put back my wig at once!"

But instead of doing so, Pinocchio put it upon his own head, making himself look half smothered.

At this piece of insolence, Gepetto grew sad and thoughtful—something he had never been before in his life.

"You naughty little scamp!" he said; "you are not all made yet, and already you begin to lack respect for your father. Bad, bad boy!"

And he wiped away a tear.

There were still legs and feet to be carved. The moment Gepetto finished making them, he felt a kick on the end of his nose.

"It's all my fault," he said to himself. "I ought to have thought of this at first. Now it is too late."

He took the marionette by the arms and stood him up on the floor, in order to teach him to walk. But Pinocchio's joints were stiff so that he could hardly move them, and Gepetto had to lead him about by the hand. Pretty soon his legs grew more limber, and Pinocchio began to run by himself around the room. Finally, as the door was open, he jumped through it and started at full speed down the street.

Poor Gepetto went after him as hard as he could but could not catch him, because the little rascal ran by leaps and bounds like a rabbit, striking his wooden feet on the pavement with a lively clatter.

"Stop him! stop him!" yelled Gepetto; but the passers-by, seeing a wooden marionette charging down the street like a Barbary horse, only stared and then

laughed and laughed in a way you could hardly imagine.

At last by good luck a policeman came along who, hearing all the racket, thought that some colt was running away from his owner; and planting himself bravely in the middle of the street he decided to stop the runaway at all hazards. When Pinocchio saw him in the way he tried to get past by dodging between the officer's legs, but failed. The policeman without budging caught him by the nose —which was long enough for a handle— and turned him over to the panting Gepetto. The latter wanted to punish him by boxing his ears; but fancy his disappointment, when, after searching vainly he could find no ears to box! He had forgotten to make any!

So he contented himself with seizing the marionette by the nape of the neck, and led him back saying with an ominous shake of the head, "Just wait till I get you home! I'll give you a good one—never doubt it!"

When Pinocchio heard this he threw himself flat on the ground and would not stir another step. At once a group of idlers and curious people gathered around them—one saying one thing, another saying another.

"Poor Marionette!" quoth one. "He is right in not wanting to go home. Who knows how hard that Gepetto might beat him!"

Another added: "This Gepetto seems to be a good sort, but he is harsh with boys. If he gets this poor marionette into his hands, he might smash it to pieces."

Indeed, they all said so much that the policeman finally gave Pinocchio his liberty, and marched the unlucky Gepetto to jail. All the way there he wept and cried so that he wasn't able to plead his innocence. He could only wail: "Wicked son! To think that I took so much pains to make a *good* marionette! But it serves me right! I ought to have thought of this at first!"

*

What happened afterward is a very strange story. Pinocchio kept on being naughty. If there was any mischief brewing within miles, Pinocchio was sure to get into it. There were times when he was sorry for what he had done and promised himself to be a good son to Gepetto. But he could not resist temptation and adventures. He started off for school, but sold his books and, with the money, went to a marionette show. Wandering in places where he should not have been, he fell in with thieves who stole his money and tried to kill him. He was saved by the Fairy with the Blue Hair, who put a spell upon him so that every time he told a lie, his nose grew longer. Pinocchio arrived in Playland, where the lazy boys never did any work and frolicked all day; like them, he was punished by being turned into a donkey. By a kind of miracle, he was turned back into a marionette again only to be swallowed by a monster Dog-Fish. In the Dog-Fish, he found Gepetto who, looking for his strayed son, had been lost at sea. He saved Gepetto's life and, as a reward, the Fairy turned him into a living "bright intelligent boy with brown hair, blue eyes, and fresh glowing complexion." So the story ends happily as Pinocchio says, "How funny I was when I was a marionette. And how glad I am to be a real boy at last."

For some people, night is not a happy time.
They hate to see the end of day
and the coming of dark.
The boy in this story was one of those people.
He had to learn about the delight,
the play, and the wonders of
the great world of darkness.

Switch on the Night

BY RAY BRADBURY   *Illustrated by* HILARY KNIGHT

ONCE there was a little boy who didn't like the Night.

He liked lanterns and lamps and torches and tapers and beacons and bonfires and flashlights and flares. But he didn't like the Night.

You saw him in parlors and pantries and cellars and cupboards and attics and alcoves and hollering in halls. But you never saw him outside . . . in the Night.

He didn't like light-switches at all. Because light-switches turned off the yellow lamps, the green lamps, the white lamps, the hall lights, the house lights, the lights in all the rooms. He wouldn't touch a light-switch.

And he wouldn't go out to play after dark.

He was very lonely. And unhappy.

For he saw, from his window, the other children playing on the summer-night lawns. In and out of the dark and lamplight ran the children . . . happily.

But where was our little boy?

Up in his room. With his lanterns and lamps and flashlights and candles and chandeliers. All by himself.

He liked only the sun. The yellow sun. He didn't like the Night.

When it was time for his mother and father to walk around switching off all the lights. . . .

One by one.
One by one.
The porch lights
the parlor lights
the pale lights
the pink lights
the pantry lights
and stair lights . . .

Then the little boy hid in his bed.

Late at night his was the only room with a light in all the town.

Then one night, with his father away on a trip and his mother gone to bed early, the little boy wandered alone. All alone through the house.

My, how he had the lights blazing!

The parlor lights
the porch lights
the pantry lights
the pale lights
the pink lights
the hall lights
the kitchen lights
even the attic *lights!*

The house looked like it was on fire!

But still the little boy was alone. While the other children played on the night lawns . . . Laughing . . . far away.

All of a sudden he heard a rap at a window!

Something dark was there.

A knock at the screen door.

Something dark was there.

A tap at the back porch.

Something dark was there!

And all of a sudden someone said "Hello!"

And a little girl stood there in the middle of

the white lights, the bright lights,
the hall lights, the small lights,
the yellow lights, the mellow lights.

HILARY
KNIGHT

236

"My name is Dark," she said.

And she had dark hair, and dark eyes, and wore a dark dress, and dark shoes.

But her face was as white as the moon. And the light in her eyes shone like white stars.

"You're lonely," she said.

"I want to run with the children outside," said the little boy. "But I don't like the Night."

"I'll introduce you to the Night," said Dark. "And you'll be friends."

She put out a porch light.

"You see," she said. "It's not switching off the light. No, not at all! It's simply switching *on* the Night. You can turn the Night off and on, just like you can turn a light off and on. With the same switch!" she said.

"I never thought of that," the little boy said.

"And when you switch on the Night," said Dark, "why, you switch on the crickets!"

"And you switch on the frogs!"

"And you switch on the stars!"
The light stars
the bright stars
the true stars
the blue stars!
Heaven is a house
with porch lights
and parlor lights
pink lights and pantry lights
red lights
green lights
blue lights
yellow lights
flashlights
candle lights
and hall lights!

"Who can hear the crickets with the lights on?"

Nobody.

"Who can hear the frogs with the lights on?"

Nobody.

"Who can see the stars with the lights on?"

Nobody.

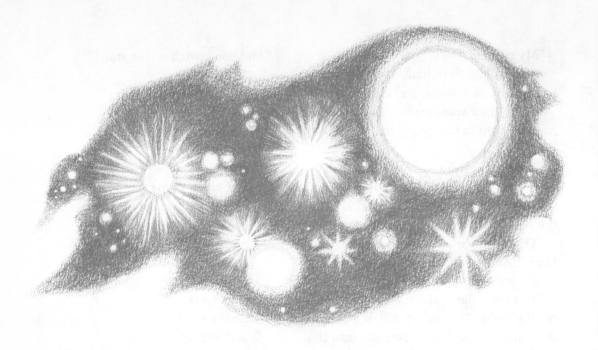

"Who can see the moon with the lights on?"

Nobody.

"Think what you're missing! Have you ever thought of
switching on the crickets,
switching on the frogs,
switching on the stars,
and the great big white moon?"

"No," said the little boy.

"Well, try it," said Dark.

And they did.

They climbed up and down stairs, switching on the Night. Switching on the dark. Letting the Night live in every room.

> *Like a frog.*
> *Or a cricket.*
> *Or a star.*
> *Or a moon.*

And they switched on the crickets.

And they switched on the frogs.

And they switched on the white, ice-cream moon.

"Oh, I like this!" said the little boy. "Can I switch on the Night always?"

"Of course!" said Dark, the little girl.

And then she vanished.

And now the little boy is very happy. He likes the Night.

Now he has a Night-switch instead of a light-switch!

He likes switches now.

He threw away his candles and flashlights and lamplights.

And any night in summer that you wish you can see him
switching on the white moon,
switching on the red stars,
switching on the blue stars,
the green stars, the light stars,
the white stars,
switching on the frogs, the crickets,
and Night.

And running in the dark, on the lawns, with the happy children . . .

Laughing.

238

Most giants, it is true, are disagreeable,
and since everything about them is big—
their thundering voices, their huge appetites,
their mountainous tread—when they are bad
they are enormously bad.
Occasionally, however, along comes an agreeable giant—
a giant with a heart as large as he is.

The Amiable Giant

BY LOUIS SLOBODKIN
Illustrated by GRACE DALLES CLARKE

THERE was once an amiable Giant who lived, as most giants do, in a big, black, granite castle on the top of a tremendous mountain. And since he was an amiable (really friendly) Giant and he was lonesome living all alone in his big castle, sometimes he came down from his mountain top to visit the little people who lived in the pretty village in the valley.

But the villagers did not understand the purpose of his visit. They would slam their doors in the face of the amiable Giant and shutter their windows.

"Take anything you want. Take our cattle. Take our grain. Take anything but leave us be," shouted the terror-stricken villagers from behind their locked doors.

When the Giant tried to explain that he did not want their cattle (since he was a vegetarian) and he did not need their grain (since he raised all the grain he wanted on the mountain top) . . . all he wanted was to visit and talk friendly talk . . . the villagers, who always clamped their hands to their ears, did not hear a word! That was because the Giant's voice was like the rumble and crash of thunder even when he spoke very softly.

239

Now there was one person in the village who could hear the Giant. He was a wicked man who spent most of his time cooking up strange poisonous brews which he said could work wonders. This man pretended that he was a wizard and he was almost completely deaf. Therefore, when the Giant came down the mountain and said to the villagers, "Good morning, I just came down to pass the time of day," the wicked wizard did not clamp his hands over his ears. And although he was almost deaf he could hear the great voice of the Giant!

"That ugly Giant wants more grain," he told the villagers after the Giant went back home. "Yes, that ugly Giant wants two hundred and ten ... no, two hundred and nineteen ... I wrote down the exact number in this notebook ... Yes, two hundred and nineteen bushels of corn, all the watermelon you've raised in your garden and two dozen of your best milk cows ... and he wants you to bring all that halfway up the mountain by next Tuesday morning."

And that's just what the frightened villagers did.

It so happened that on Tuesdays the amiable Giant was very busy and he never put his nose out of his castle on that day and he never saw the frightened villagers dragging the grain and other things halfway up the mountain. The wicked Wizard knew that. He knew that the amiable Giant always did his laundry on Monday and he always spent all day Tuesday ironing his gigantic sheets and shirts as big as tents ... because he was a bachelor and he lived by himself.

On Tuesday nights, when everyone was fast asleep, the wicked Wizard with the help of his servants (all of them ex-robbers, ex-pirates, and ex-bandits) would cart away the things the villagers had brought up the mountain to a big secret cave. There they stored the grain and other things.

And so it went for many years. The Wizard became richer, the villagers became poorer and the innocent amiable Giant became lonesomer and lonesomer. Things might have gone on that way ... the Wizard getting richer and the villagers getting poorer and the amiable Giant becoming sadder and sadder because of his lonesomeness if it had not been for a little girl named Gwendolyn.

Gwendolyn was the village cobbler's granddaughter. She, like everyone else, trembled and cowered behind locked doors with her hands clamped over her ears when the Giant visited the village. But it happened that one morning Gwendolyn was playing with her doll Marguerite on the wooden cover of a dried-up well in the village square. The well had run dry so long ago there was only one man who remembered the time when it held water. That man was Gwendolyn's grandfather, the oldest man in the village.

He always said when he talked of times past, "Yes, that was just a few summers *before* the well dried up," or "Yep, that happened just three winters *after* the well dried up." Some years after the well dried up a wooden cover had been made to fit the top of it.

So much time was spent dragging children out of the dried-up well that the busy villagers took time off from their many tasks and built the wooden well cover as a time saver. Since then the children played ring-round-rosie around the well . . . follow the leader over the well . . . and constables and bandits all over the well . . . but no children fell into the well.

The old wooden cover had been jumped on by so many sturdy little feet it was well-worn and a few of the old wooden boards were rather loose.

On this particular morning Gwendolyn had sat herself and her doll Marguerite on the old well cover as she sang a lullaby. The other village children had gone to pick the first flowers of May up on the mountainside. Unfortunately, flowers made Gwendolyn sneeze and even though she loved them dearly she just loved them from a distance and never picked them.

Just as Gwendolyn was singing the fourteenth verse of a song that she had made up, the children rushed down the mountainside, helter-skelter, dropping their flowers as they ran.

"The Giant's coming!" they screamed. "Oh, dear, the Giant's coming down the mountain."

All the villagers promptly dropped whatever they were doing and ran for home and bolted their windows and doors!

Everyone but Gwendolyn! She was so startled she stumbled and fell backward on the old well cover and right down through a loose board, down into the dried-up well!

Fortunately, people had used the old well like a big wastebasket. They had thrown their old mattresses and such rubbish into the well before it had been covered over. And grass and weeds had

blown into it, too, so Gwendolyn was not hurt when she landed on the bottom of the well. In fact, she even bounced once or twice.

Gwendolyn was not frightened when she found herself at the bottom of the dry well. She knew she would be found after the Giant went home again. And she knew, too, that the Giant was too big to squeeze himself into the old well. And even though his gigantic arms were long, they were not long enough to reach her at the bottom of the well. Then she thought of something that made her tremble. What if he were to see her sitting down in the well . . . and what if he were to poke at her with a stick?

She trembled so her teeth chattered at that thought and she hugged her doll Marguerite to her bosom. Fearfully she listened to the earth-shaking steps of the Giant as he walked along the village street. The sound of his steps came closer and closer and they sounded like the approach of a great storm.

Suddenly the sound of his steps stopped. The Giant had knelt down and tapped gently at some village door as he always did when he visited the village.

Gwendolyn hugged Marguerite tighter during that sudden silence. And she forgot to cover her ears as she always had done when the Giant spoke. Now, for the first time, she heard his loud booming voice. Down there at the bottom of the well his voice sounded like the mumbling roar of distant thunder.

"Anybody home?" asked the amiable Giant.

No one answered him.

"Nice weather we're having," he went on.

The frightened villagers behind their bolted doors kept their hands clamped to their ears and they all pretended they were not at home.

"I guess we could stand a little rain. . . ."

The villagers still remained silent.

"I saw the village children picking wildflowers up on the mountain," said the Giant after another moment of silence. "I have some especially fine pansies growing in one of my window boxes . . . I could bring some down for you . . . if you want them. I have very pretty purple ones."

The Giant waited a moment for someone to say something. Then he tapped on one of the shutters of the house.

"Do you hear me?" asked the Giant, raising his voice a little.

The frightened villagers gave up pretending they were not at home.

"Please go away," shouted one villager. Then the others joined in and from behind their locked doors and windows they wailed. "Please leave us alone . . . We can't give you any grain . . . Our crops have been bad."

"I guess you don't hear very well . . . I don't want your grain or anything you have," said the Giant, sadly. "I'll come again next week and I'll bring my purple pansies."

Then the Giant stood up and slowly walked back to his lonesome black granite castle on the top of the mountain.

When at last the sound of the Giant's great steps was lost in the distance, the villagers unlocked their doors and cautiously looked up and down the village street. Then when they saw that the Giant was really gone, they ran out of

their houses and gathered in the village square.

"Oh dear, oh dear . . . What shall we do?" they all cried as they wrung their hands. "Won't that Giant ever leave us alone?"

The wicked Wizard also came bustling out of his big house. He carried the black notebook in which he said he always wrote down what the Giant had ordered. He climbed up on the cover of the old well and raised his hand above his head.

"Listen to me! Listen to me, everybody!" screamed the old Wizard. "Here's what the ugly old Giant ordered."

"One minute, please," interrupted the cobbler, Gwendolyn's grandfather.

"Silence, cobbler," commanded the wicked Wizard, haughtily, "I must report to the village what the Giant has ordered . . ."

"But please . . . I must speak," insisted the cobbler. "Has anyone seen my granddaughter, Gwendolyn? She did not come in when the Giant came."

"Oh! Oh! Oh, the poor dear child," cried some of the village ladies. "The poor, poor dear, the Giant must have taken her up to his castle!"

And for the moment all the villagers forgot to worry about the Giant and everyone worried about little Gwendolyn.

Almost everyone had some idea what should be done to rescue little Gwendolyn from the Giant. Some said they ought to drag the village cannon up the mountain and bombard the Giant. Others suggested dynamiting his big black granite castle. Suddenly everybody had become brave as they all planned to rescue Gwendolyn from the Giant.

Gwendolyn's grandfather, the village

cobbler, moved away from the loud-talking villagers and sat mournfully on the stone wall of the old dry well.

"Oh, Gwendolyn, my poor little granddaughter," he moaned. "Will I ever see my poor lost Gwendolyn again?"

And from deep down in the dry well a little voice called . . .

"Grandfather . . . I am *not* lost! I'm not lost a bit. I'm down here at the bottom of the well with Marguerite. Look down. You can see me right now."

Her grandfather quickly hopped off the wall and looked down at the smiling face of Gwendolyn.

"She's here! Gwendolyn is found," he shouted, joyfully.

The villagers crowded around the well and looked down at Gwendolyn. Then some people ran off to get the long ladder that was always used to climb down into the well to carry out the children who fell into it. In a few minutes, Gwendolyn, still hugging Marguerite, was in her grandfather's arms.

Then the villagers, having forgotten all about the Giant, all returned to their homes.

"Here! Here!" screamed the wicked old Wizard. "You'd better wait up until I read the orders the ugly Giant gave. You know what will happen if you do not carry out his orders."

The villagers stood still in their tracks. Some of them trembled. No one had ever thought what the Giant would do if they did not carry out his orders, but they all were sure it would be something terrible . . . very terrible.

"Now then," began the wicked Wizard, as he adjusted his spectacles and opened his black notebook. "First he wants one hundred and seventy-four bushels of wheat . . . full bushels, mind you . . ."

"But we have no wheat," cried the miller. "My mill has not ground any new wheat for two weeks . . ."

The wicked Wizard went on reading as if nothing had been said.

". . . And he wants one hundred and ninety-eight bushels of barley . . . and two hundred and eighty-five . . . no, that's a three . . . yes, three hundred and eighty-five bushels of corn."

"We have no more barley and we have no more corn," protested the village farmers. "We haven't had any rain and we have no new crops . . ."

But the Wizard paid no attention to their protests and went on reading until he had completed the list of things he said the Giant had ordered.

". . . And you had better get them all delivered by noon next Tuesday . . . or else!" and with that the wicked Wizard snapped his black notebook shut, slowly climbed down from the top of the dry well, and stalked across the village square to his big house.

For a moment after the Wizard left them the villagers were speechless . . . What did he mean by ". . . or else!"

The village blacksmith who was also the mayor of the village stepped forward and made a short speech.

"My friends," he said, "this looks like a very serious situation. As mayor of this village, I am herewith officially calling a meeting of all the able-bodied men of this village to consider this matter. We will meet this very night in my black-smith shop at 8 o'clock. Please be on time."

Little Gwendolyn held on tight to her grandfather's hand and listened quietly to everything that was said both by the wicked Wizard and the village black-smith. And she did not say a word until she and her grandfather had walked all the way home and had begun to prepare supper.

"Grandfather," she said, as the old cobbler lit the fire under the soup kettle, "did you not once tell me that the Wizard is a little deaf?"

"A little deaf, did you say?" repeated the old cobbler. "Why, yes, I did say that. He never seems to hear me when I first tell him how much it will cost to mend his pointed shoes. And he can only hear me after I've shouted the cost at least three times . . . Even then he never pays as much as I ask. Yes, I would say he is a little hard of hearing."

"Grandfather," said Gwendolyn, slow-ly, "I think he is not hard of hearing. I think he is absolutely stone deaf!"

"Stone deaf, child! What makes you think that?"

"Yes, I'm sure he is stone deaf. Because he could not have heard a word that the Giant said. Marguerite and I heard every-thing the Giant said as we sat on the bot-tom of the well. He did not say one word about wanting all that wheat and all that barley and corn. In fact, he did not want the villagers to give him any wheat or

anything else. Indeed, he said he wanted to give us something."

"What did he say he'd give us?"

"Purple pansies . . . that's what."

"PURPLE PANSIES!" exclaimed the old cobbler.

"Yes, Grandfather . . . Beautiful purple pansies and he said he'd bring them next week. Didn't he say that, Marguerite?"

"H-m-m," said the old cobbler, thought-fully. "Are you sure you heard him say that, child?"

"Yes, Grandfather, I am sure," said Gwendolyn.

"Very well. Let us have our supper at once. Then I must go on to the meeting at the blacksmith shop. I must get there early for a private word with the mayor."

The minute the supper dishes were washed and put away the old cobbler hurried over to the blacksmith shop as fast as his old legs could carry him. None of the other villagers had arrived yet and

244

he was able to have his private word with the blacksmith, the mayor of the village.

He quickly told the blacksmith mayor what Gwendolyn had told him.

"And your granddaughter told you the Giant says he wants us to give him nothing, but that he wants to give us something?" asked the blacksmith mayor with his eyebrows high.

"Yes," said the old cobbler.

"And what does he want to give us?" asked the blacksmith mayor.

"Purple pansies," said the cobbler.

"PURPLE PANSIES!" roared the blacksmith mayor and he collapsed in a fit of laughter, and sat down on his anvil. "Purple pansies! Ho, Ho, Ho. . . ." and he laughed and laughed until tears rolled down his cheeks.

The old cobbler stood there nervously for a moment or two and then he became very angry.

"Yes! Purple pansies *is* what the Giant

said!" he said, angrily. "That's what Gwendolyn said he said and my granddaughter never tells an untruth. True, she is an imaginative child but she never never tells an untruth!"

The blacksmith mayor suppressed his fit of laughter, but still smiling, he patted the old cobbler on the shoulder.

"Now don't get angry, my old friend," he said. "This has been such an unfortunate day . . . and this is the first good laugh I have had. Now let us be serious. Gwendolyn said . . ."

But before he could go on the old cobbler repeated again, word for word, exactly what Gwendolyn had said.

"Now I'm not saying your granddaughter told an untruth," said the blacksmith mayor, "but as you have often said, Gwendolyn *is* an imaginative child . . . and she did tumble into the dry well. Have you thought that she might have bumped her head a little as she went tumbling down to the bottom of that well . . . And maybe that affected her hearing or her power of remembering?"

The old cobbler stroked his chin. He had not thought of that!

"Well . . . maybe there is something in what you say," he said slowly. "She may have bumped her head a little . . . h-m-m . . . Well, I can't stay for the meeting. I must put my granddaughter to bed. I would . . . h-m-m . . . I would be very obliged to you if you would not mention anything of this talk at the meeting tonight."

"Not mention a word," said the blacksmith mayor, cheerfully.

The meeting in the blacksmith shop was short, quick and to the point, mainly because the village blacksmith mayor was so cheerful that night. He opened the meeting and told the frightened villagers that he already had a plan how they could fulfill the Giant's orders . . . or what the Wizard had reported were the Giant's orders.

They would borrow the wheat, barley, corn and all the other things the Giant had ordered from the friendly villagers in the neighboring valley. The blacksmith mayor, the miller and a few other good men and true, would drive their big wagons to their friendly neighbors the very next day.

And that's what they did. But their neighbors had also had a bad year with small crops so the blacksmith mayor and the others drove to more distant villages. At last, after four long hot days, they returned with their big wagons only half full. All the villagers they had visited had had a bad year with poor crops. They had been able to borrow only about half of what the Wizard said the Giant had ordered.

The next few days dragged by as the downcast villagers waited for the fateful Tuesday morning when they must deliver the grain and other things halfway up the mountain. And they trembled as they drove their wagons up the mountain and unloaded the scant bushels of grain and other things. Then they drove back to their village and sat sadly in their darkened homes as they waited for the terrible things to happen which they all were sure would happen after the Giant found out they had not obeyed his orders. Some frightened villagers were sure he would tear off the roofs of their houses. Others were just as sure he would kick in their walls with one flick of his boots.

Tuesday passed! Wednesday passed! Thursday passed! And still nothing happened!

But that Friday noon just as the children were coming home for lunch, they heard in the distance the great steps of the Giant as he walked down the mountainside.

"The Giant's coming! The Giant's coming!" they screamed. And all the villagers ran for home as fast as they could. And they shuttered their windows, bolted their doors, clamped their hands to their ears and sat trembling in their dark houses as they awaited the coming of the Giant.

Everybody in the village did that except two people. One was the wicked Wizard. And the other was little Gwendolyn.

Gwendolyn had run up to her bedroom under the eaves of her grandfather's house and she threw her shutters wide open! And she did not clamp her hands tight to her ears. She wanted to hear the Giant talk. But she did protect her ears a little from the Giant's great roaring voice by wrapping a big muffler around her head and over her ears.

Closer and closer came the great earth-shaking steps of the Giant. When he reached the old cobbler's house, his face lit up with a gigantic smile. For there he saw Gwendolyn's unshuttered friendly-looking little window.

And looking out through her friendly window were the smiling rosy faces of Gwendolyn and her doll Marguerite.

"Hello, Giant!" shouted Gwendolyn in the loudest voice she could manage.

"Hello," said the Giant in the softest voice he could manage. "You need not shout. I can hear little things."

"It is a nice day," said Gwendolyn in her natural voice.

"It is a very fine day," said the Giant. "A little too hot. We do need some rain."

"Yes, indeed," said Gwendolyn. "We do indeed need rain."

Then there was a moment of silence as Gwendolyn wondered what one should say to a Giant after one says hello and talks about the weather. And the Giant wondered what one talks about to a little girl. Then he noticed the muffler wrapped around her head.

"Do you have mumps?" he asked, nodding at the muffler.

"Oh, no," said Gwendolyn. "It's just to protect my ears. You do have a strong voice, you know."

"Oh," said the Giant, sadly.

"Giant," said Gwendolyn, "I just thought of something."

"What?" asked the Giant as he knelt down.

"I believe if you raised a big thick beard like the miller's, people could listen to your big voice without hurting their ears . . . Are you old enough to raise a beard?"

"I am old," said the Giant . . . "Yes, I guess I am old enough to raise a beard . . . And how old are you, girl?"

"Oh, I am seven going on eight," said Gwendolyn. "I have been seven going on eight for the longest time. I will be eight on Hallowe'en, October 31st."

And there was another moment of silence.

"Do you like flowers?" asked the Giant.

"I love flowers," said Gwendolyn. "But they do make me sneeze."

"Not my flowers," said the Giant. "It's the pollen that makes one sneeze and I always shake them well when I pick flowers."

The Giant opened one of his huge hands and showed Gwendolyn the flowers he carried. They were the biggest, most beautiful, purple pansies anyone had ever seen!

"How beautiful!" exclaimed Gwendolyn.

"You can have them," said the Giant, and he shoved the flowers into the little window.

"Oh, thank you, Giant," said Gwendolyn. "Wait till I put them on my bed."

With some difficulty she carried the big pansies to her bed. They covered the bed from head to foot like a big purple comforter. In a moment she was back at the window again.

"Well, goodbye," said the Giant.

"Goodbye, Giant," said Gwendolyn, "come again."

And the Giant walked back to his big black granite castle on the top of the tremendous mountain with a happy, springy step that shook all the little village houses like a series of earthquakes.

As soon as the Giant left her window Gwendolyn ran to the door of her room and called her grandfather. The old cobbler stumbled up the stairs as fast as he could, not knowing what to expect.

"Look, Grandfather," she cried, "look, he brought them and gave them all to me."

"Who brought what?" asked her grandfather.

"The Giant brought the purple pansies as he said he would . . . Here, you can have two."

By this time the old cobbler saw the big purple pansies spread out on Gwendolyn's bed.

"So he did . . . so he did," was all he could say. Then as he looked at the two pansies Gwendolyn had laid in his hands he said, "I never saw such pansies . . ."

Gwendolyn chattered on and on telling about the Giant's visit and what they had talked about. Her grandfather listened carefully. Then he sat down deep in thought.

As usual, right after a visit from the Giant the wicked Wizard read his report on what he said the Giant had ordered. This time he told the villagers the Giant was very angry and he again read off a list of orders that the unhappy villagers knew they never could fulfill. And as usual everything must be delivered halfway up the mountain by Tuesday noon . . . no later.

Gwendolyn and her grandfather stood at the edge of the crowd and listened to the wicked Wizard's report but they said not a word to anyone.

That evening right after supper the old cobbler put some things in a sack, threw the sack over his shoulder and again he hurried over to the blacksmith shop before the regular meeting of the villagers.

The blacksmith mayor let him in the door. He was very distressed.

"Please, my old friend, not tonight," he said. "Please do not tell me of the bright fantastic things your granddaughter said. I know . . . I know she is a very remarkable, very imaginative child. But please, not tonight, there are so many serious . . ."

"I did not come to tell you anything," interrupted the old cobbler, "I came to show you something."

Then the old cobbler reached into the sack he had carried on his shoulder and he pulled out two big shoes.

"Here are your shoes," he said. "I mended them and I am delivering them."

"Shoes! . . . Shoes!" roared the blacksmith. "Here we are faced with the worst catastrophe this village has ever known . . . and you come showing me shoes."

"They are your shoes," said the old cobbler.

The blacksmith picked up his mended shoes and looked at the soles with an impatient frown. Then he looked into them.

"What's this?" he cried. "What's this purple lining you've put in my shoes . . . What do you mean . . ."

"*That* is not a purple lining," said the cobbler. "Look again."

The blacksmith looked and then he reached his hand into one of his shoes and picked out a large purple pansy. He reached into the other and pulled out another purple pansy.

"Purple pansies!" he gasped.

"Yes, purple pansies," said the cobbler. "And pansies this big do not grow any place in this valley . . . Do you want to know where they came from? I'll tell you!"

In a few minutes the old cobbler told the blacksmith everything Gwendolyn had told him about the Giant's visit.

That evening the regular meeting of the villagers at the blacksmith shop was over even quicker than the last meeting. The blacksmith mayor said he knew of a large secret store of grain and all of the other things the Giant wanted. All he would need was a number of good strong silent men to help and he would guarantee everything would be taken care of by Tuesday. Then he chose the biggest, strongest men in the village. Everyone knew these men never gossiped and never told any secrets. He arranged to hold a special secret meeting. The Wizard was not invited.

The following Tuesday, promptly at noon, the blacksmith and the strong, silent men he had chosen drove halfway up the mountain and they unloaded hundreds of baskets of what looked like good grain and other things, exactly as the Wizard had said the Giant had ordered.

But those baskets were not full of good grain . . . Oh, no. They were just full of twigs and pebbles. And each basket was covered with a cloth sprinkled with just a handful of grain. Late that night when the wicked Wizard and his servants loaded the baskets on their own wagons and carted them away to the secret cave where they had hidden all the other things the Giant was supposed to have ordered, the blacksmith and his chosen men followed them as silent as panthers.

There, armed with great homemade clubs, the villagers quickly subdued the wicked Wizard and his villainous servants. And all the grain and cattle and sheep that had been stolen from the villagers and hidden in the secret cave were returned to their rightful owners.

Naturally, the wicked Wizard and his

servants (all of them ex-robbers, ex-pirates, and ex-bandits) were driven from that peaceful little valley and were never seen again.

The villagers settled back again to a peaceful, prosperous, carefree life. Now that they knew that the Giant was really a gentle, amiable fellow (because Gwendolyn had said so and her grandfather had told everyone else) the villagers looked forward to the next visit of their gigantic neighbor.

And they went to some trouble to show the Giant he was welcome in their village. They decorated the fronts of their houses with colored streamers and flags. And Gwendolyn and the other children lettered a big sign that was stretched across the village street. The sign read, "Welcome Giant."

And when all that was done, they sat back and waited. And they waited...and they waited...and they waited! But weeks went by, months went by and still there was no visit from the Giant. The decorations became tattered, the flags were limp and the big sign the children had printed looked washed out and shaggy. And just as the villagers were beginning to think that perhaps they had hurt his feelings and that he might never visit them again, along came the Giant!

It was on a fine, warm Indian summer day. Just as the children were coming home from school they heard his great steps as he walked down from his tremendous mountain. Some of the villagers thought it was the sound of a late summer thunderstorm. But the children knew better. They danced through the street shouting, "The Giant's coming!"

And everyone ran for home. This time not to bolt their doors and windows as they had formerly done, but to throw them wide open to show the Giant he was welcome. And no one clamped his hands to his ears. They all wrapped their heads in mufflers (as Gwendolyn said they should do) to muffle the sound of the Giant's great voice so that they could hear what he said.

At last along came the Giant.

He was very pleasantly surprised to find all the village doors and windows open wide and to see all the villagers and the children looking out and smiling as they nodded him a good-day. He stepped over the sign that the children had printed and stopped again at the old cobbler's house. There he knelt and looked into Gwendolyn's window.

If it were not for the size of him and his kindly twinkling eyes, Gwendolyn would have hardly recognized her Giant friend. For the rest of the Giant's great face was almost all covered with a gigantic red beard and a tremendous moustache!

"Hello," said the Giant. His voice now coming through his great beard and moustache was so deep and mellow Gwendolyn could hardly hear him.

She quickly unwrapped the muffler she had tied around her head to protect her ears and she did the same for her doll Marguerite.

"Hello, Giant," said Gwendolyn, "I missed you...Have you been sick?"

"No," said the Giant, with a sheepish grin, "I have been raising this beard."

"It is a beautiful beard," said Gwendolyn.

The Giant blushed at her compliment and for a moment there was a silence between them.

"Nice day we're having," said the Giant at last.

"It is a beautiful day indeed," said Gwendolyn.

Then after another pause the Giant said: "Did you not tell me that October 31st was your birthday?"

"How nice of you to remember," said Gwendolyn with a surprised look on her face. "Yes, October 31st, tomorrow, is my birthday. I'll be eight."

"Well," said the Giant, slowly. "I'd like to have you and all the children come halfway up the mountain tomorrow . . . I'm making a birthday party for you . . . I baked a cake."

"Oh, how kind and thoughtful you are, Giant," said Gwendolyn, joyfully. "I'd love a birthday party up on the mountain."

And so it happened on the very next day when Gwendolyn, who had been seven going on eight for the longest time, finally became eight years old on October 31st (Hallowe'en), the Giant spread a great cloth halfway up on the mountain-side and on it he laid great platters. These platters held more goose-berry tarts, more cookies, more sugarplums and candies than anyone had ever seen. And right in the center of the cloth was the cake the Giant had baked *himself!* It was the biggest homemade, pink-frosted birthday cake in the world with eight candles and one to grow on, stuck in the center of it.

The village children came to the party all dressed up in Hallowe'en costumes. Some boys came dressed as girls and some girls came dressed as boys. And some chil-

dren were goblins and others were witches and there were those who pretended to be black cats and even pumpkins. But *no one* came dressed as a *Wizard*.

And they all ate as much as they could hold and they played games and sang, "Happy Birthday, dear Gwendolyn," over and over again. And that was the song they sang as they walked down the mountain when the sun set and it was time to go home to bed.

Everyone said that the birthday party the amiable Giant gave for Gwendolyn when she became eight years old was the best party that ever was.

And that still holds true to this day!

If anyone has any doubts about that, all he need do is to go visit that little village in the valley at the foot of the tremendous mountain. He is sure to meet some very old people sitting around in the sunny village square. And they will tell him that it is true, because their great-great-great grandfathers and great-great-grandmothers had been guests at that gigantic birthday party for Gwendolyn, the cobbler's granddaughter. And these very old people when they tell this story will point to the exact spot in the village square where there once was an old dried-up well into which Gwendolyn tumbled. And then, they will point with their canes to the tremendous mountain, now crowned with great, billowy, white clouds where the amiable Giant lived in his big black, granite castle a long, long, long time ago.

The Wizard of Oz *begins with a cyclone.*
The big wind rushes through the country and
sweeps a little girl named Dorothy and her dog, Toto,
from their home in Kansas to a place
that is not found on any map.
She learns that the country is called Oz,
that it is ruled by a wizard,
and that part of it is in the power of a wicked witch.
No one but the Wizard of Oz himself
can tell Dorothy how to get back home.
The Wizard lives in the Emerald City.
Dorothy and Toto set out to see him,
and on the way they make three odd but good friends:
the Scarecrow, the Tin Woodman, and the Cowardly Lion.
When they all arrive at the entrance
to the Emerald City, the Guardian of the Gate
fits them with green spectacles,
so that they won't be blinded by what they see.
Then he ushers them into the city.

Dorothy Meets the Wizard

From The Wizard of Oz

BY L. FRANK BAUM
Illustrated by W. W. DENSLOW

Even with eyes protected by the green spectacles, Dorothy and her friends were at first dazzled by the brilliancy of the wonderful City. The streets were lined with beautiful houses, all built of green marble and studded everywhere with sparkling emeralds. They walked over a pavement of the same green marble, and where the blocks were joined together were rows of emeralds, set closely, and glittering in the brightness of the sun. The windowpanes were of green glass; even the sky above the City had a green tint, and the rays of the sun were green.

There were many people, men, women and children, walking about, and these were all dressed in green clothes and had greenish skins. They looked at Dorothy and her strangely assorted company with wondering eyes, and the children all ran away and hid behind their mothers when they saw the Lion; but no one spoke to them. Many shops stood in the street, and Dorothy saw that everything in them was green. Green candy and green popcorn were offered for sale, as well as green shoes, green hats and green clothes of all sorts. At one place a man was selling green lemonade, and when the children bought it Dorothy could see that they paid for it with green pennies.

There seemed to be no horses nor animals of any kind; the men carried things around in little green carts, which they pushed before them. Everyone seemed happy and contented and prosperous.

The Guardian of the Gates led them through the streets until they came to a big building, exactly in the middle of the City, which was the Palace of Oz, the Great Wizard. There was a soldier before the door, dressed in a green uniform and wearing a long green beard.

"Here are strangers," said the Guardian of the Gates to him, "and they demand to see the Great Oz."

"Step inside," answered the soldier, "and I will carry your message to him."

So they passed through the palace gates and were led into a big room with a green carpet and lovely green furniture set with emeralds. The soldier made them all wipe their feet upon a green mat before entering this room, and when they were seated he said politely,

"Please make yourselves comfortable while I go to

the door of the Throne Room and tell Oz you are here."

They had to wait a long time before the soldier returned. When, at last, he came back, Dorothy asked,

"Have you seen Oz?"

"Oh, no," returned the soldier; "I have never seen him. But I spoke to him as he sat behind his screen and gave him your message. He says he will grant you an audience, if you so desire; but each one of you must enter his presence alone, and he will admit but one each day. Therefore, as you must remain in the Palace for several days, I will have you shown to rooms where you may rest in comfort after your journey."

"Thank you," replied the girl; "that is very kind of Oz."

The soldier now blew upon a green whistle, and at once a young girl, dressed in a pretty green silk gown, entered the room. She had lovely green hair and green eyes, and she bowed low before Dorothy as she said,

"Follow me and I will show you your room."

So Dorothy said good-bye to all her friends except Toto, and, taking the dog in her arms, followed the green girl through seven passages and up three flights of stairs until they came to a room at the front of the Palace. It was the sweetest little room in the world, with a soft, comfortable bed that had sheets of green silk and a green velvet counterpane. There was a tiny fountain in the middle of the room, that shot a spray of green perfume into the air, to fall back into a beautifully carved green marble basin. Beautiful green flowers stood in the windows, and there was a shelf with a row of little green books. When Dorothy had time to open these books she found them full of queer green pictures that made her laugh, they were so funny.

In a wardrobe were many green dresses, made of silk and satin and velvet; and all of them fitted Dorothy exactly.

"Make yourself perfectly at home," said the green girl, "and if you wish for anything ring the bell. Oz will send for you tomorrow morning."

She left Dorothy alone and went back to the others. These she also led to rooms, and each one of them found himself lodged in a very pleasant part of the Palace. Of course this politeness was wasted on the Scarecrow; for when he found himself alone in his room he stood stupidly in one spot, just within the doorway, to wait till morning. It would not rest him to lie down, and he could not close his eyes; so he remained all night staring at a little spider which was weaving its web in a corner of the room, just as if it were not one of the most wonderful rooms in the world. The Tin Woodman lay down on his bed from force of habit, for he remembered when he was made of flesh; but not being able to sleep he passed the night moving his joints up and down to make sure they kept in good working order. The Lion would have preferred a bed of dried leaves in the forest, and did not like being shut up in a room; but he had too much sense to let this worry him, so he sprang upon the bed and rolled himself up like a cat and purred himself asleep in a minute.

The next morning, after breakfast, the green maiden came to fetch Dorothy, and she dressed her in one of the prettiest gowns made of green brocaded satin. Dorothy put on a green silk apron and tied a green ribbon around Toto's neck, and they started for the Throne Room of the Great Oz.

First they came to a great hall in which were many
ladies and gentlemen of the court, all dressed in rich costumes. These people had nothing to do but talk to each
other, but they always came to wait outside the Throne
Room every morning, although they were never permitted
to see Oz. As Dorothy entered they looked at her curiously,
and one of them whispered,

"Are you really going to look upon the face of Oz the
Terrible?"

"Of course," answered the girl, "if he will see me."

"Oh, he will see you," said the soldier who had taken
her message to the Wizard, "although he does not like to
have people ask to see him. Indeed, at first he was angry,
and said I should send you back where you came from.
Then he asked me what you looked like, and when I mentioned your silver shoes he was very much interested. At
last I told him about the mark upon your forehead, and he
decided he would admit you to his presence."

Just then a bell rang, and the green girl said to Dorothy, "This is the signal. You must go into the Throne Room alone."

She opened a little door and Dorothy walked boldly through and found herself in a wonderful place. It was a big, round room with a high arched roof, and the walls and ceiling and floor were covered with large emeralds set closely together. In the center of the ceiling was a great light, as bright as the sun, which made the emeralds sparkle in a wonderful manner.

But what interested Dorothy most was the big throne of green marble that stood in the middle of the room. It was shaped like a chair and sparkled with gems, as did everything else. In the center of the chair was an enormous Head, without body to support it or any arms or legs whatever. There was no hair upon this head, but it had eyes and nose and mouth, and was bigger than the head of the biggest giant.

As Dorothy gazed upon this in wonder and fear the eyes turned slowly and looked at her sharply and steadily. Then the mouth moved, and Dorothy heard a voice say:

"I am Oz, the Great and Terrible. Who are you, and why do you seek me?"

It was not such an awful voice as she had expected to come from the big Head; so she took courage and answered,

"I am Dorothy, the Small and Meek. I have come to you for help."

The eyes looked at her thoughtfully for a full minute. Then said the voice:

"Where did you get the silver shoes?"

"I got them from the Wicked Witch of the East, when my house fell on her and killed her," she replied.

"Where did you get the mark upon your forehead?" continued the voice.

"That is where the good Witch of the North kissed me when she bade me good-bye and sent me to you," said the girl.

Again the eyes looked at her sharply, and they saw she was telling the truth. Then Oz asked,

"What do you wish me to do?"

"Send me back to Kansas, where my Aunt Em and Uncle Henry are," she answered earnestly. "I don't like your country, although it is so beautiful. And I am sure Aunt Em will be worried over my being away so long."

The eyes winked three times, and then they turned up to the ceiling and down to the floor and rolled around so queerly that they seemed to see every part of the room. And at last they looked at Dorothy again.

"Why should I do this for you?" asked Oz.

"Because you are strong and I am weak; because you are a Great Wizard and I am only a helpless little girl," she answered.

"But you were strong enough to kill the wicked Witch of the East," said Oz.

"That just happened," returned Dorothy simply; "I could not help it."

"Well," said the Head, "I will give you my answer. You have no right to expect me to send you back to Kansas unless you do something for me in return. In this country everyone must pay for everything he gets. If you wish me to use my magic power to send you home again you must do something for me first. Help me and I will help you."

"What must I do?" asked the girl.

"Kill the wicked Witch of the West," answered Oz.

"But I cannot!" exclaimed Dorothy, greatly surprised.

"You killed the Witch of the East and you wear the silver shoes, which bear a powerful charm. There is now but one Wicked Witch left in all this land, and when you can tell me she is dead I will send you back to Kansas—but not before."

The little girl began to weep, she was so disappointed; the eyes winked again and looked at her anxiously, as if the Great Oz felt that she could help him if she would.

"I never killed anything willingly," she sobbed; "and even if I wanted to, how could I kill the Wicked Witch? If you, who are Great and Terrible, cannot kill her yourself, how do you expect me to do it?"

"I do not know," said the Head; "but that is my answer, and until the Wicked Witch dies you will not see your Uncle and Aunt again. Remember that the Witch is Wicked—tremendously Wicked—and ought to be killed. Now go, and do not ask to see me again until you have done your task."

Sorrowfully Dorothy left the Throne Room and went back where the Lion and the Scarecrow and the Tin Woodman were waiting to hear what Oz had said to her.

"There is no hope for me," she said sadly, "for Oz will not send me home until I have killed the Wicked Witch of the West; and that I can never do."

Her friends were sorry, but could do nothing to help her; so she went to her own room and lay down on the bed and cried herself to sleep.

The next morning the soldier with the green whiskers came to the Scarecrow and said,

"Come with me, for Oz has sent for you."

So the Scarecrow followed him and was admitted into the great Throne Room, where he saw, sitting in the emerald throne, a most lovely lady. She was dressed in green silk gauze and wore upon her flowing green locks a crown of jewels. Growing from her shoulders were wings, gorgeous in color and so light that they fluttered if the slightest breath of air reached them.

When the Scarecrow had bowed, as prettily as his straw stuffing would let him, before this beautiful creature, she looked upon him sweetly, and said,

"I am Oz, the Great and Terrible. Who are you, and why do you seek me?"

Now the Scarecrow, who had expected to see the great Head Dorothy had told him of, was much astonished; but he answered her bravely.

"I am only a Scarecrow, stuffed with straw. Therefore I have no brains, and I come to you praying that you will put brains in my head instead of straw, so that I may become as much a man as any other in your dominions."

"Why should I do this for you?" asked the lady.

"Because you are wise and powerful, and no one else can help me," answered the Scarecrow.

"I never grant favors without some return," said Oz; "but this much I will promise. If you will kill for me the Wicked Witch of the West I will bestow upon you a great many brains, and such good brains that you will be the wisest man in all the Land of Oz."

"I thought you asked Dorothy to kill the Witch," said the Scarecrow, in surprise.

"So I did. I don't care who kills her. But until she is dead I will not grant your wish. Now go, and do not seek me again until you have earned the brains you so greatly desire."

The Scarecrow went sorrowfully back to his friends and told them what Oz had said; and Dorothy was surprised to find that the great Wizard was not a Head, as she had seen him, but a lovely lady.

"All the same," said the Scarecrow, "she needs a heart as much as the Tin Woodman."

On the next morning the soldier with the green whiskers came to the Tin Woodman and said,

"Oz has sent for you. Follow me."

So the Tin Woodman followed him and came to the great Throne Room. He did not know whether he would find Oz a lovely lady or a Head, but he hoped it would be the lovely lady. "For," he said to himself, "if it is the Head,

I am sure I shall not be given a heart, since a head has no heart of its own and therefore cannot feel for me. But if it is the lovely lady I shall beg hard for a heart, for all ladies are themselves said to be kindly hearted."

But when the Woodman entered the great Throne Room he saw neither the Head nor the Lady, for Oz had taken the shape of a most terrible Beast. It was nearly as big as an elephant, and the green throne seemed hardly strong enough to hold its weight. The Beast had a head like that of a rhinoceros, only there were five eyes in its face. There were five long arms growing out of its body and it also had five long, slim legs. Thick, woolly hair covered every part of it, and a more dreadful-looking monster could not be imagined. It was fortunate the Tin Woodman had no heart at that moment, for it would have beat loud and fast from terror. But being only tin, the Woodman was not at all afraid, although he was much disappointed.

"I am Oz, the Great and Terrible," spake the Beast, in a voice that was one great roar. "Who are you, and why do you seek me?"

"I am a Woodman, and made of tin. Therefore I have no heart, and cannot love. I pray you to give me a heart that I may be as other men are."

"Why should I do this?" demanded the Beast.

"Because I ask it, and you alone can grant my request," answered the Woodman.

Oz gave a low growl at this, but said gruffly,

"If you indeed desire a heart, you must earn it."

"How?" asked the Woodman.

"Help Dorothy to kill the Wicked Witch of the West," replied the Beast. "When the Witch is dead, come to me, and I will then give you the biggest and kindest and most loving heart in all the Land of Oz."

So the Tin Woodman was forced to return sorrowfully to his friends and tell them of the terrible Beast he had seen. They all wondered greatly at the many forms the great Wizard could take upon himself, and the Lion said, "If he is a beast when I go to see him, I shall roar my loudest, and so frighten him that he will grant all I ask. And if he is the lovely lady, I shall pretend to spring upon her, and so compel her to do my bidding. And if he is the great Head, he will be at my mercy; for I will roll this head all about the room until he promises to give us what we desire. So cheer up my friends, for all will yet be well."

The next morning the soldier with the green whiskers led the Lion to the great Throne Room and bade him enter the presence of Oz.

The Lion at once passed through the door, and glancing around saw, to his surprise, that before the throne was a Ball of Fire, so fierce and glowing he could scarcely bear to gaze upon it. His first thought was that Oz had by accident caught on fire and was burning up; but, when he tried to go nearer, the heat was so intense that it singed his whiskers, and he crept back tremblingly to a spot nearer the door.

Then a low, quiet voice came from the Ball of Fire, and these were the words it spoke:

"I am Oz, the Great and Terrible. Who are you, and why do you seek me?" And the Lion answered,

"I am a Cowardly Lion, afraid of everything. I come to you to beg that you give me courage, so that in reality I may become the King of Beasts, as men call me."

"Why should I give you courage?" demanded Oz.

"Because of all Wizards you are the greatest, and alone have power to grant my request," answered the Lion.

The Ball of Fire burned fiercely for a time, and the voice said,

"Bring me proof that the Wicked Witch is dead, and that moment I will give you courage. But so long as the Witch lives you must remain a coward."

The Lion was angry at this speech, but could say nothing in reply, and while he stood silently gazing at the Ball of Fire it became so furiously hot that he turned tail and rushed from the room. He was glad to find his friends waiting for him, and told them of his terrible interview with the Wizard.

"What shall we do now?" asked Dorothy sadly.

"There is only one thing we can do," returned the Lion, "and that is to go to the land of the Winkies, seek out the Wicked Witch, and destroy her."

"But suppose we cannot?" said the girl.

"Then I shall never have courage," declared the Lion.

"And I shall never have brains," added the Scarecrow.

"And I shall never have a heart," spoke the Tin Woodman.

"And I shall never see Aunt Em and Uncle Henry," said Dorothy, beginning to cry.

"Be careful!" cried the green girl; "the tears will fall on your green silk gown, and spot it."

So Dorothy dried her eyes and said,

"I suppose we must try it; but I am sure I do not want to kill anybody, even to see Aunt Em again."

"I will go with you; but I'm too much of a coward to kill the Witch," said the Lion.

"I will go too," declared the Scarecrow; "but I shall not be of much help to you, I am such a fool."

"I haven't the heart to harm even a Witch," remarked the Tin Woodman; "but if you go I certainly shall go with you."

Therefore it was decided to start upon their journey the next morning, and the Woodman sharpened his axe on a green grindstone and had all his joints properly oiled. The Scarecrow stuffed himself with fresh straw and Dorothy put new paint on his eyes that he might see better. The green girl, who was very kind to them, filled Dorothy's basket with good things to eat, and fastened a little bell around Toto's neck with a green ribbon.

They went to bed quite early and slept soundly until daylight, when they were awakened by the crowing of a green cock that lived in the back yard of the palace, and the cackling of a hen that had laid a green egg.

In the rest of the story,
all of which is in The Wizard of Oz,
Dorothy and Toto, and
their three companions, travel through dangerous
country, escape from the Winged Monkeys, find a Golden
Cap, are aided by the Queen of the Mice,
and finally succeed in destroying the Wicked Witch.
When they get back to the Emerald City,
they discover that the Wizard of Oz really is
just a little man who used to be a magician in Omaha.
But his powers are so great that the Scarecrow
gets the brains he always wanted,
the Tin Woodman gets the longed-for heart,
and the Cowardly Lion gets back his courage.
Dorothy's silver slippers turn out,
much to her surprise, to be magical.
And it is the slippers that finally transport her
and Toto back to their home in Kansas.

This is the first story in the first of
ten books about Dr. Dolittle.
The full title of the book is The Story of Doctor Dolittle,
Being the Story of His Peculiar Life at Home
and Astonishing Adventures in Foreign Parts.

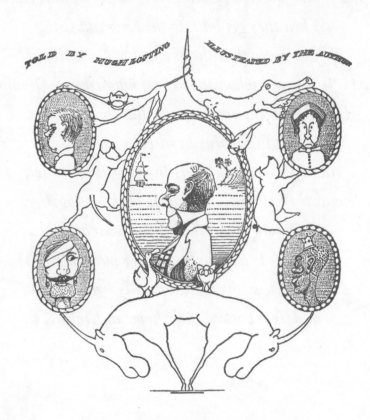

The opening episode, which follows,
explains how the Doctor gave up all his human patients
to devote himself to animals.

"A little town called Puddleby-on-the-Marsh"

Doctor Dolittle Learns Animal Language

From The Story of Doctor Dolittle

BY HUGH LOFTING

Illustrated by HUGH LOFTING

ONCE UPON a time, many years ago, when our grandfathers were little children, there was a doctor; and his name was Dolittle—John Dolittle, M. D. *M. D.* means that he was a proper doctor and knew a whole lot. He lived in a little town called Puddleby-on-the-Marsh. His sister, Sarah Dolittle, was housekeeper for him.

The Doctor was very fond of animals and kept many kinds of pets. Besides the goldfish in the pond at the bottom of his garden, he had rabbits in the pantry, white mice in his piano, a squirrel in the linen closet, and a hedgehog in the cellar. He had a cow with a calf, too, and an old lame horse—twenty-five years of age—and chickens, and pigeons, and two lambs, and many other animals. But his favorite pets were Dab-Dab the duck, Jip the dog, Gub-Gub the baby pig, Polynesia the parrot, and the owl Too-Too. One day when an old lady with rheumatism came to see the Doctor, she sat on the hedgehog who was sleeping on the sofa and never came to see him any more.

Then his sister, Sarah Dolittle, came to him and said, "John, how can you expect sick people to come and see you when you keep all these animals in the house?"

"But I like the animals better than the 'sick people,'" said the Doctor.

"You are ridiculous," said his sister, and walked out of the room.

273

"And she never came to see him any more"

So, as time went on, the Doctor got more and more animals, and the people who came to see him got less and less. And the money he had saved up grew littler and littler...

It happened one day that the Doctor was sitting in his kitchen talking with the Cat's-meat Man who had come to see him with a stomach-ache.

"Why don't you give up being a people's doctor, and be an animal doctor?" asked the Cat's-meat Man.

The parrot, Polynesia, was sitting in the window looking out at the rain and singing a sailor song to herself. She stopped singing and started to listen.

"You see, Doctor," the Cat's-meat Man went on, "you know all about animals, much more than what these here vets do. That book you wrote about cats, why, it's wonderful! I can't read or write myself, or maybe I'd write some books. But my wife, Theodosia, she's a scholar, she is. And she read your book to me. Well, it's wonderful. You might have been a cat yourself. You know the way they think. And listen! You can make a lot of money doctoring animals. I'd send all the old women who had sick cats or dogs to you. And if they didn't get sick fast enough, I could put something in the meat I sell 'em to make 'em sick, see?"

"Oh, no," said the Doctor quickly. "That wouldn't be right."

"Oh, I didn't mean real sick," answered the Cat's-meat Man. "But as you say, maybe it ain't quite fair on the animals. But they'll get sick anyway, because the old women always give 'em too much to eat. And look, all the farmers round about who had lame horses and weak lambs—they'd come. Be an animal doctor."

When the Cat's-meat Man had gone, the parrot flew off the window on to the Doctor's table and said: "That man's got sense. Give the silly people up—if they haven't brains enough to see you're the best doctor in the world. Take care of animals instead. They'll soon find it out. Be an animal doctor."

274

"Oh, there are plenty of animal doctors," said John Dolittle, putting the flowerpots outside on the window sill to get the rain.

"Yes, there are plenty," said Polynesia. "But none of them are any good at all. Now listen, Doctor, and I'll tell you something. Did you know that animals can talk?"

"I knew that parrots can talk," said the Doctor.

"Oh, we parrots can talk in two languages—people's language and bird language," said Polynesia proudly. "If I say, 'Polly wants a cracker,' you understand me. But hear this: *Ka-ka oi-ee, fee-fee?*"

"Good gracious!" cried the Doctor. "What does that mean?"

"That means, 'Is the porridge hot yet?' in bird language."

"My! You don't say so!" said the Doctor. "You never talked that way to me before."

"What would have been the good?" said Polynesia, dusting some cracker crumbs off her left wing. "You wouldn't have understood me if I had."

"Tell me some more," said the Doctor, all excited. He rushed over to the dresser drawer and came back with the butcher's book and a pencil. "Now don't go too fast, and I'll write it down. This is interesting, very interesting, something quite new. Give me the Birds' ABC first, slowly now."

So that was the way the Doctor came to know that animals had a language of their own and could talk to one another. And all that afternoon, while it was raining, Polynesia sat on the kitchen table giving him bird words to put down in the book.

At teatime, when the dog, Jip, came in, the parrot said to the Doctor, "See, *he's* talking to you."

"Looks to me as though he were scratching his ear," said the Doctor.

"But animals don't always speak with their mouths," said the parrot, raising her eyebrows. "They talk with their ears, with their feet, with their tails—with everything. Sometimes they don't *want* to make a noise. Do you see now the way he's twitching up one side of his nose?"

"What's that mean?" asked the Doctor.

"That means, 'Can't you see that it has stopped raining?'" Polynesia answered. "He is asking you a question. Dogs nearly always use their noses for asking questions."

After a while, with the parrot's help, the Doctor got to learn the language of the animals so well that he could talk to them himself and understand everything they said. Then he gave up being a people's doctor altogether.

As soon as the Cat's-meat Man had told everyone that John Dolittle was going to become an animal doctor, old ladies began to bring him their pet pugs and poodles who had eaten too much cake, and farmers came many miles to show him sick cows and sheep.

One day a plow horse was brought to him; and the poor thing was terribly glad to find a man who could talk in horse language.

"You know, Doctor," said the horse, "that vet over the hill knows nothing at all. He has been treating me six weeks now, for spavins. What I need is *spectacles*. I am going blind in one eye. There's no reason why horses shouldn't wear glasses, the same as people. But that

275

stupid man over the hill never even looked at my eyes. He kept on giving me big pills. I tried to tell him; but he couldn't understand a word of horse language. What I need is spectacles."

"Of course, of course," said the Doctor. "I'll get you some at once."

"I would like a pair like yours," said the horse, "only green. They'll keep the sun out of my eyes while I'm plowing the Fifty-Acre Field."

"Certainly," said the Doctor. "Green ones you shall have."

"You know, the trouble is, Sir," said the plow horse as the Doctor opened the front door to let him out, "the trouble is that *anybody* thinks he can doctor animals, just because the animals don't complain. As a matter of fact, it takes a much cleverer man to be a really good animal doctor than it does to be a good people's doctor. My farmer's boy thinks he knows all about horses, and he has got as much brain as a potato bug. He tried to put a mustard plaster on me last week."

"Where did he put it?" asked the Doctor.

"Oh, he didn't put it anywhere—on me," said the horse. "He only tried to. I kicked him into the duck pond."

"Well, well!" said the Doctor.

"I'm a pretty quiet creature as a rule," said the horse, "very patient with people, don't make much fuss. But it was bad enough to have that vet giving me the wrong medicine. And when that booby started to monkey with me, I just couldn't bear it any more."

"Did you hurt the boy much?" asked the Doctor.

"Oh, no," said the horse. "I kicked him in the right place. The vet's looking after

him now. When will my glasses be ready?"

"I'll have them for you next week," said the Doctor. "Come in again Tuesday."

Then John Dolittle got a fine, big pair of green spectacles; and the plow horse stopped going blind in one eye and could see as well as ever. Soon it became a common sight to see farm animals wearing glasses in the country round Puddleby, and a blind horse was a thing unknown.

"He could see as well as ever"

And so it was with all the other animals that were brought to him. As soon as they found that he could talk their language, they told him where the pain was and how they felt, and of course it was easy for him to cure them.

Now all these animals went back and told their brothers and friends that there was a doctor in the little house with the big garden who really *was* a doctor. And whenever any creatures got sick—not only horses and cows and dogs, but all the little things of the fields, like harvest mice and water voles, badgers and bats—they came at once to his house on the edge of the town. His big garden was nearly always crowded with animals trying to get in to see him.

There were so many that came that he

had to have special doors made for the different kinds. He wrote *Horses* over the front door, *Cows* over the side door, and *Sheep* on the kitchen door. Each kind of animal had a separate door. Even the mice had a tiny tunnel made for them into the cellar, where they waited patiently in rows for the Doctor to come round to them.

And so, in a few years' time, every living thing for miles and miles got to know about John Dolittle, M. D. And the birds who flew to other countries in the winter told the animals in foreign lands of the wonderful doctor of Puddleby-on-the-Marsh, who could understand their talk and help them in their troubles. In this way he became famous among the animals, all over the world, better known even than he had been among the folks of the West Country. And he was happy and liked his life very much.

When people are angry,
it is said they "fight like cats and dogs."
But cats and dogs don't always fight each other,
especially if they are brought up together.
"The Kitten Who Barked" is a true story,
about five cats and a dog who lived in the home of the author.

The Kitten Who Barked

BY LOUIS UNTERMEYER
Illustrated by LILIAN OBLIGADO

HIS name was Puck. In a dog's fairy-land he would have been the shortest, the shaggiest, and the most mischievous of four-legged sprites. He was not quite a foot long, and he would never grow more than another inch or two. In Yorkshire, England, where he was born, he was known as a Yorkie or a Toy Terrier. Sometimes he really looked like a toy, bouncing about on springs that never gave out.

At other times, especially when he raised his little round ragged head, he looked like a chrysanthemum with eyes.

He was just two months old when he was brought across the ocean to a country home in Connecticut. It was a home with two people, surrounded by five cats. The people were ordinary people, like most other people, and like each other. But the cats were like nothing except themselves.

The oldest was a large, calico-colored cat, red, white, and black. Her name was Missy Potato. No one knew how she got her name, but it was said she had been found sleeping in a bushel basket of potatoes at the grocery store. She looked hurt whenever she heard one of the people explain it to a visitor, for she was a proud cat. "My great-great-great-great-grandmother came from Egypt," she told each new cat as soon as it came into the house. "We were gods in Egypt, and we were *treated* like gods. We sat on a throne at the right hand of the king or, when we wanted to, in the lap of the queen. When we wished to be by ourselves—and even a god sometimes wants privacy—we had nine cushions to choose from: cushions of velvet, silk, satin, plush, swansdown, sweet-smelling flax, gold-threaded cloth, spun linen from the north, and fine-combed cotton from the Nile. We never would dream of chasing a mouse," she sniffed haughtily. "Our food was brought to us on golden dishes—every day a new dainty—and when we were thirsty, we were given ivory bowls of pure cream which had been blessed by the priests. "But," she sighed, "things happen, kings and queens die, and you learn to take your food wherever you find it. You're lucky," she said to Puck, "that you will find it here waiting for you every morning—if you behave yourself."

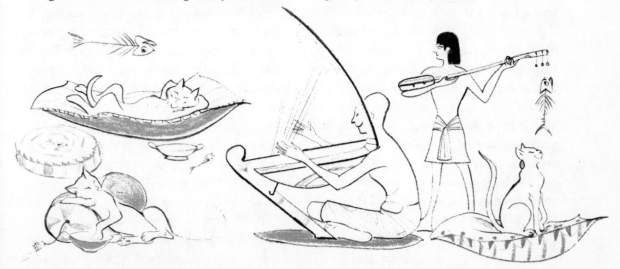

The second cat was called Bobo. He could not make up his mind whether he was a black cat with queer white markings or a white cat with funny looking black spots. He was very mischievous, and his full name was Bobo the Clown. But as he grew up he took himself and his work very seriously, and he would let no one ever say he looked clownish. His work consisted of taking care of the property. He thought of himself as a watch-cat, and he guarded every one of the nine acres as fiercely as if he owned them all. Right after breakfast, he would go out and drive the frogs off the lawn, keep the woodchucks out of the garden, and worry the moles who were trying to build tunnels under the house. Once when the neighbor's tomcat walked over to pay a social call, Bobo, who was something of a bully, snarled, made such a savage face, and called the visitor such ugly names that he never came back. "I am monarch of all I survey," he would yowl as he sat on his favorite rock. "My right there is none to dispute," he would sing, for he picked up scraps of poetry (which the people read to each other) as easily as he picked up scraps of meat.

Plush and Flash were twins, but they did not look or act alike. They were as different as hot and cold, good and bad,

light and dark, sweet and sour, work and play, right and wrong, in and out, up and down, here and there. They were not only completely unlike each other, they were not even like their own names.

Plush was a girl cat. She looked like a little ball of gray fur, something made to do nothing but lie on a soft bed or curl up in front of the fireplace and make a warm bed of her own. But that was something that Plush never did, for Plush was a mighty hunter. Underneath the velvet coat, she was all fire and fury. Her velvet paws sheathed twenty little daggers; there was quicksilver in her veins and lightning in her bones. Other cats prowled; she pounced. Other cats pretended to be asleep until some unsuspecting field-mouse came within easy reach; but Plush gave fair warning. She refused to hide; waving her tail like a flag, and, sounding her battle-cry, she would take after her game. She was always the last one to come home, and, after gulping down her dinner, would dash back to the fields, her blood singing with the joy of the chase. She never ate her prey outside, but brought whatever she caught into the house. Then she would display it proudly to the other cats, carry it from room to room, and win a gasp from the admiring people.

Flash was a boy cat, and he looked as if he were made to fit his name. Lean and limber as a lynx, black as the blackest panther, all rippling muscle, a threat like a thunderbolt, ready to strike . . . But he never moved. He was always looking for a lap—anyone's lap—or a bed—anybody's bed. Other cats could not wait for the night so they could howl; but Flash was afraid of the dark and cried when he was left outside. He had been the baby of the litter, and a baby he intended to remain. He never stopped talking; he had to tell everyone, especially the people, how helpless this poor, fourteen-pound house-cat was. Huge, heavy, and always hungry, he was sorry for himself. No one, he felt, absolutely no one, ever gave him enough love.

Cleo was named for Cleopatra, Queen of the Nile. Actually, her ancestors had been proud Persians, but she was too modest to mention the fact. Modesty and Beauty might have been her other names, for she never talked about herself—she rarely spoke at all—and she was almost too beautiful to be real. Her lovely body moved like music. Her hair was long and silky, the color of polished ebony, except under her neck, where she wore a wide silver ruff. At night her eyes were pure gold; in sunlight they sparkled like Spanish topazes. But her greatest beauty shone out of her face, for it had the gentlest, sweetest, and kindest expression a cat ever wore. There was a little loneliness in it, too, for Cleo had been a good young mother, and her kittens had been given away to other people. She needed to be needed.

That was the way things were when Puck arrived and found himself in the midst of five cats. Each cat reacted differently. Missy Potato was much too grand to talk or even to associate with him. She did not like his looks or his walk or his smell or anything he did. When he whined a question, she refused to answer; when he whimpered, she walked away. She put him in his place by just ignoring his presence.

Bobo cared—in the worst way; he showed he did not want Puck around. Bobo had a built-in dislike of dogs; he hissed and spat and arched his back in a fighting pose whenever Puck came near. As time passed, he permitted Puck to stay in the same room—after all, he was twice as big as the tiny bundle of dog—but he warned him to keep his distance.

Plush was inclined to be friendly. She allowed Puck to sniff her and she sniffed in return; but, once the sniffing was over, she did not encourage further intimacies. At first she talked quite a bit to him about things in general and hunting in particular; but when she saw he did not understand, she gave it up.

Flash was frankly jealous. He felt he never got enough attention as it was, and now here was someone—or something—else who would be patted and petted by the people.

Cleo was the only one who liked Puck at once. As soon as she saw him she decided to adopt him. She knew he needed someone who would not only care *for* him but would take care *of* him. He had lost his mother; she had lost her kittens. She treated him like one of her lost children, and it was not long before she believed he really *was* a kitten, a clumsy backward kitten who needed a lot of training.

"Teaching him is hard," she would say

to Missy Potato, who had to listen but was not really interested. "He is quite bright about some things and very stupid about others. No matter how often I've shown him, he doesn't seem to know how to wash himself behind the ears. He walks awkwardly; he can't curl himself up properly. He doesn't understand about mice—I must have brought in a dozen from the meadow—but I can't interest him in running after them, playing with them, catching, throwing them in the air, and finally eating them. He gives them a puzzled stare, looks at them, sniffs, and turns away in disgust. That's no way for a kitten to act. I don't know what I'm going to do with him. Children are *so* difficult."

Nevertheless, Puck learned. Cleo was as patient as she was kind; she gave him lessons twenty times a day, and Puck was

so fond of her that he began to imitate her. First she taught him Attack and Defense. He was very good at this. She would lie on her back, growl, and dare him to attack her; he would return her growl, make little dashes at her body, snap at her tail, and bite her ears. When he bit too hard, she would give him a cuff, and he would yelp and run away—which is what he was supposed to do. Then she would come at him, springing from a sofa or a table, and he would run under a chair and make little noises that said "Never touched me!" and "Dare you to try it again!" Round and round the rooms they would go, running up the stairs—it took a long time before she could coax him to run *down* the stairs—skidding around the furniture, tumbling over each other, until exhausted, they stopped. Then they would sleep. They had separate beds, but, once in a while, when he looked particularly appealing, she let him sleep in hers. Sometimes she believed she heard him purr.

Gradually she got him used to the sport of the outdoors. She began with little things—ants, and grasshoppers, and crickets—and he learned to pounce on them as though they were his natural prey. Next came objects to seize, balls to chase, twigs to carry; and she was delighted when he did these things better than she. Then there were rocks and stone walls to get over, and again she was happy when she saw how swift and sure-footed he had become.

The other cats began to accept him. They ate their meals together—he was just as eager as they for the Sunday treat of cooked liver—and they showed him what holes and crannies in the walls had

the most interesting smells. Cleo was pleased, and *so* proud of him.

Then came the unhappy day when they organized a family chase. The game was to see who could chase who how many times around the orchard. It was a combination of obstacle race and hide-and-seek with big rocks, tall grasses, barrels, and a wheel-barrow to jump in, around, across, and over. It was going splendidly until Plush and Flash sprang into an apple tree. Puck ran to the foot of the tree and suddenly stopped. "Go on!" cried Cleo, "go on up!" But Puck stayed where he was and whined. "Don't be a baby," said Cleo. "Look—try the low branch first—it's easy—one good jump will do it. Then just claw your way up." But Puck could not make a move. He whimpered. Then, as Plush and Flash sprang from bough to bough, he began to cry hard. He kept on crying until the others felt sorry for him and took him home.

Again and again Cleo tried to teach him to take that first leap. She picked out trees that had boughs close to the ground —heavy quince trees, low dogwoods, wide-spreading willows — but nothing happened. "What kind of a kitten will you ever be if you don't learn to climb! Climbing is nature's first law. Trees were made for us. They are our best means of escape, an easy refuge, a cat's heaven. What's to become of you if you always stay on the ground!"

When she talked like this, Puck felt miserable. Everything in him wanted to please Cleo, yet something in him knew he could never do it. His body would not obey him; his muscles refused to do what he wanted. Puck did not know why this was so, but he knew he had failed her. "A kitten who can't climb doesn't deserve to be a kitten," he told himself bitterly. Cleo walked sadly away, and Puck was heartbroken.

Puck's unhappiness lasted for weeks. He stopped playing. He moped; he looked sick; he crouched in corners; he sighed himself to sleep. Even when he came for his food, he did not bound into the kitchen with the others as he had always done; he crept in by himself. His stump of a tail stopped wagging; his pointed ears drooped; his whole body slumped. Cleo watched him painfully. She longed to help, but there was nothing she could do.

Then the unexpected happened. Puck was sitting half asleep under a maple tree—Cleo was lying a few feet away— when a monster, huge and hairy, leaped over the wall and came straight at them. "Look out," cried Cleo, as she sprang up the branches. "It's a dog—a vicious dog! If you can't climb, run! Run!"

But something in Puck refused to let him run away. Something forced him to dash at the intruder, making sounds he had never made before. His throat rumbled; his chest shook; his short hairs bristled; his whole body became a roar of anger. He barked . . . and *barked* . . . and BARKED!

Stiff with fury he plunged after the invader. The big beast, ten times Puck's size, was so taken by surprise that he did not stay to fight. He put his tail between his legs and vanished. Then Puck set up a howl, a great, long shout of triumph. "Now I know what I am!" he told the world. "Now I know why I couldn't climb trees! I'm not a kitten learning to be a cat. I'm a dog! That's what I've always been—" he could not help boasting a little—"a fearless, furious, frightening DOG!"

Cleo sprang down from the tree, purring with praise, and licked his shining face. The other cats, all of whom had seen what had happened, looked at Puck with respect. "Maybe we were wrong about him," said Missy Potato. "He certainly knows how to take care of himself," admitted Bobo. "I always said he would amount to something," said Plush, "if he'd only learn to hunt." "You can't help admiring him," admitted Flash, "and I'm really not going to be jealous." They all waited for Cleo to speak. She purred for a moment, and all she said was "That's my boy." Then, quietly but very proudly, she walked off with Puck at her side.

And after that the little dog and the five big cats were one rollicking family. They never stopped enjoying each other. Puck barked and they miaowed; he stole their food and they stole his; he chased them and they chased him. They had a wild and wonderful time. And Cleo, with her golden eyes on Puck, had the best time of all.

Raoul the Owl

BY JAY WILLIAMS
Illustrated by LILIAN OBLIGADO

IN AN OLD hollow tree near the edge of a thick wood lived a family of owls.

In the first limb lived Mother and Father. They were a comfortable pair, and they liked everything to be just so. For many generations, their family had lived in this particular tree, and Father Owl, who was very respectable and upright, often said, "Owls will always live here, and life will always go on as it has before." He was convinced that the world had been arranged for his particular benefit: the nights dark and pleasant for hunting on wide, silent wings, and the long warm days for sleeping.

In the second limb lived the three eldest sons: Randolph, Reginald, and Rudyard. They were blustery, hail-owl-well-

met fellows, fond of roistering and good times.

In the third limb lived the three middle sons: Roderick, Rufus, and Russell. They were sober and studious. Roderick had written a book on flying techniques.

In the topmost limb lived the smallest and youngest son. Father had named him Raoul, after a distant cousin who was said to have migrated from France in a shipment of Lombardy poplar trees. Raoul was modest and good-tempered, polite and cheerful, but he had one serious prob-

lem, for an owl. He couldn't see in the dark.

Nobody was quite sure why this was so. Father said that it came from a vitamin deficiency of some sort, and Mother said that none of her relatives had ever had night-blindness and that while she didn't want to mention any names she recalled a certain uncle of Father's who had flown into a brick wall one evening before sunset, and Father said that was enough of that and they'd just have to make the best of a bad bargain.

So they did.

Poor Raoul! Every evening the family woke up, yawned, stretched, said good morning to each other and started out. Raoul would blink and peer and strain his eyes, but all remained dark. He could dimly see the shapes of trees, and when the moon was up he could make out where he was, but he had to fly very slowly and close to the ground, and since it was impossible for him to hunt he had to go home early and wait to be fed. His six brothers took it in turn to bring him some dinner, and he wasn't sure which he disliked most, the lectures he got on the feeding habits of owls from Roderick, Rufus, and Russell, or the jolly slaps on the back and loud hoots of laughter from Randolph, Reginald and Rudyard.

At last, Raoul could stand it no longer. "This won't do," he said, firmly, to himself. "I," he said, grimly, "am neither fish, nor flesh, nor good horned owl. I will simply have to change my habits," he said. And then and there he made up his mind to a tremendous and daring thing.

He decided to sleep all night and get up in the morning.

When they heard this decision, Mother and Father were terribly upset.

"Whooo ever heard of such a thing?" Mother cried.

"Disgraceful!" said Father. "None of our family has ever done such a thing. In fact, I don't believe any owl has ever remained awake during the daytime."

"On the contrary," Roderick put in. "A considerable number of Arctic owls may be found hunting diurnally, that is, during the long daylight hours."

Rufus nodded, and Russell went to get the encyclopedia.

"We are not and never have been Arctic owls," said his father, coldly.

Randolph, Reginald, and Rudyard laughed raucously. "Hoo, hoo, hoo! Maybe he isn't even an owl."

"He is your brother," Father said, "and I'll thank you to leave him alone." He turned to Raoul, and said more gently, "If you persist in this course, my boy, I won't stop you. But I hope that you will behave as an owl and a gentleman during the daylight."

Mother dried her eyes, and Father patted her wing, and whispered, "Don't worry, my dear. He'll soon change his mind."

The following night, while the rest of the family were out flying, Raoul went to sleep, to refresh and prepare himself for his great adventure. The next morning, when the family was going to bed, he got up. He yawned, stretched, and stepped outside. He sidled out on the branch, looked about, blinked, and took an enormous breath.

"Gowly!" he said.

He could see *everything*. And there was so much to see, and the colors were so bright and fresh, and the rustling morning was so lovely, that he hardly knew where to look first.

There was a bright, hot, yellow thing in the sky. The other parts of the sky were a pale melting blue. On one side of him was the forest, brown and green, mossy and dim with the shadows of many trees. And on the other side was a wide meadow starred with flowering grasses, with dandelions and devil's-paint-brush, buttercups and asters.

Raoul spread his wings and flew out

over the meadow. He glided on his soft owl wings and settled down beside some of the flowers. He had never seen anything like these in his whole life. He looked at them from one side and then from the other, and then he peeped into the yellow heart of a buttercup. There was a striped brown and yellow thing in the middle of it. Raoul touched it gently.

"Ow!" he exclaimed. "I beg your pardon."

"Humm," said the bee, crawling out and dusting itself off. It flew proudly away.

After that, Raoul was more cautious. You never knew what might come out of a flower, he told himself.

He flew on, and then he saw some large spotted things in the meadow. Some were tan and some were black and white, and some were a lovely grey with black speckles. He thought they were another kind of flower. He made sure there were no bees on them, and then sat down on one to rest.

"Mooo!" said the flower in a deep voice, tossing its horns.

Raoul flung himself into the air.

The cow went away and found another spot to sleep in, mumbling something about *too many birds* . . . drat . . . etc.

Raoul was learning things all the time. Flowers that mooed and flowers that stung you, and that hot thing in the sky, and all the many birds that sang loudly in the morning. . . . He was quite giddy with excitement.

For a long while, he flew about inspecting things. He smelled the fresh sweetness of the summer grass. He talked to birds who had always been asleep before, when he was awake. He felt so good he flew upside down, and did barrel-rolls and loop-the-loops, and floated on his back. And finally, worn out but contented, he perched in a tree and took a brief nap.

When he awoke it was noon and he was hungry. He rubbed his eyes and began to search for dinner.

Near a rickety red barn, with a big white house behind it, he spied a small mouse. With a quick swoop he darted down and caught it.

Now Raoul had never really seen a mouse before, although he had eaten lots of them. (You may wonder how he knew what it was, so that he could catch it, if he had never seen one before. This is what is called "instinct.") He looked at it closely and with surprise. It had a sad, whiskery little face, and it held its sad little hands together, and squeaked, "Oh, please, Mr. Hawk, let me go."

Raoul's heart was touched. Slowly he opened his claws and let the mouse go free.

"But why do you call me a hawk?" he asked.

The mouse was holding its heart and panting with fright, but now it looked up at him. "Good heavens," it said. "You're *not* a hawk, you're a NOWL!"

"Well . . ." said Raoul, "really, an *owl.*"

"What on earth are you doing flying around in the daytime?" the mouse demanded. "Are you crazy?"

Raoul shuffled his feet uncomfortably. "I—I don't think you ought to be so rude," he said. "After all, I might have eaten you."

"I'm sorry," said the mouse. "Please forgive me. But you must admit, it is rather strange to find an owl flying about in the sun."

Raoul hung his head. "I can't see in the dark," he explained. "I had to do something. I couldn't spend my life just sitting in that old tree. So I decided to try the daylight."

"Well," said the mouse, sitting up straight. "I think that's the bravest thing I ever heard of."

Raoul felt very much cheered up. "Thanks," he said.

"And not eating me was the nicest thing I ever heard of," the mouse added. "You're a very exceptional owl, for an owl. Let me introduce myself," he said. "My name is Bertram."

"Mine's Raoul," said Raoul. "Oh, dear, I just happened to think. If I don't eat you, what *shall* I eat?"

Bertram thought for a while. "Have you ever tried cheese?"

Raoul shook his head. "I don't even know what it is," he said humbly. "Is it a flower?"

"You just wait here," said Bertram. He scampered into the barn and soon returned with a large piece of yellow cheese.

Raoul pecked at it doubtfully. "Mg-mmf," he said, and cleared his beak. "Too sticky."

"Hmm," said Bertram. "What about some nice corn?"

He hurried off again, and came back with an armful of kernels from his winter store. Raoul tried one.

"Owp!" he said. "Too hard."

Bertram rubbed his ears to help him think. "Aha!" he cried. "I have it. You're a bird, aren't you. What about some bird seed?"

He darted into a hole that led to the big house beyond the barn. Raoul waited patiently, and after a bit Bertram returned with a small box of bird seed. Raoul took a beakful. Then he took another, and another.

"Delicious!" he cried.

He ate a good lunch, and then, with his new friend, explored a little more. He took Bertram for a ride on his back, and the mouse explained to him about cows and bees as well as all the many wonderful things there were to see. By the middle of the afternoon Raoul was quite worn out, and he went home early after promising to meet Bertram again next day.

Early the following morning, Raoul got up as his family was coming home.

"My poor boy," said Mother, embracing him. "You must have had a terrible time."

"No," said Raoul, cheerfully, "it was fun."

Mother shook her head sadly. "You must be starving," she said. "We've brought you a lovely mouse for dinner."

"Mouse!" cried Raoul. "Oh, no, I can't eat mice. Why, it would be awful. My

best friend is a mouse."

Mother clasped her wings. "Oh, Ralph," she said, to Father. "The daylight has turned my child's brain. Did you hear what he said?"

Randolph, Reginald, and Rudyard said, "Look here, old chap, you'd better pull yourself together."

Roderick, Rufus, and Russel said, "Not all owls eat rodents. Several species are known to prey upon lizards, crickets, and even fish."

"Fish!" Mother uttered a screech, and fainted.

When they had revived her, Father drew himself up and said, "Raoul, I don't wish to hear such talk, especially in front of your mother. If you don't intend to eat mice, please tell me just what you do intend to eat."

"Bird seed," said Raoul, showing his box.

Father turned pale. Then he said, sternly, "If you insist on this nonsense, my boy, I won't stop you. But I warn you, it won't work. When you are ready to give it up, your parents will be glad to receive you back again."

Meantime, Randolph, who was the eldest, had eaten the mouse.

The family went to bed, and Raoul flew off into the sunrise. The grass was shiny with dew, and the sweet smell of clover filled the air. He met Bertram at the barn and together they played and raced, romped and explored. Bertram showed him some sheep and a dangerous cat, and they met a family of robins and Raoul had a race with the father robin and won.

But about noon, he began to have a headache. The sun was very bright, and he found he couldn't see very well. And pretty soon he had to stop what he was doing and sit down.

"Oh, dear," he said, "perhaps Father and Mother were right. Perhaps it's wrong for owls to fly in the daytime. Maybe I'll have to give up, Bertram."

Bertram squinted at him. "Now, don't be hasty," he said. "You've been doing very well. I think it's just that you aren't used to the sunlight, yet. Even the people who live in the big house and own the barn are dazzled by too much bright sun."

"They are?" asked Raoul. "What do they do about it?"

Bertram snapped his fingers. "I know," he said. "Wait here."

He ran off through one of his tunnels to the big house, and when he came back he was dragging something behind him. It was a small but lovely pair of green sun-glasses with black frames.

Raoul was a little nervous about them. First he put them on like a hat. "They don't seem to do much good," he said.

Bertram showed him how to wear them, and even though his beak was rather small he was able to keep them on by tying the ear-pieces together with grass.

"Why, this is wonderful," he exclaimed, when he could see through them. "Everything is green, now. It's very soothing and beautiful. And the sun doesn't hurt my eyes a bit."

He kept them on, and he and Bertram played for an hour or so. Then Bertram had to go home and sort his corn kernels and cheese, and Raoul went off to the forest. He flew about for a while in the shade, and met many new friends. He got home at evening just as the family was getting up.

Mother took one look at him in his new green sun-glasses, and fainted again. Father fanned her with one wing, and said, "Take those horrible things off at once, sir!"

Raoul took them off, and said, "Why, Father? What's the matter?"

"Matter?" said Randolph, Reginald, and Ruydard. "You look like a green-eyed Glop!"

"It is certainly rare and unusual to see an owl wearing what we recognize as spectacles," said Roderick, Rufus, and Russell.

"Spectacles!" snorted Father. "You're a spectacle, all right. Wear them in the daytime, Raoul, if you must, but take them off in this tree."

"Oh, Ralph," said Mother, who had just opened her eyes. "Surely our son must see that it isn't fit for him to fly in the daytime. Not if he must eat bird-seed and wear those awful things over his eyes."

"No," said Raoul, stubbornly. "It's fun."

"Very well," said Father. "If you insist on this nonsense, my boy, I won't stop you. But I warn you, one of these days you will go too far."

The next morning, Raoul started out as the rim of the sun turned the sky red over the forest. He met Bertram at the barn, and they frolicked and skipped and played tag, and then Bertram took him down to the brook.

It was the first time Raoul had seen a brook, and he was fascinated by the bubbling brown water. "It seems to be

293

talking, almost in owl language," he said. "It says, 'Kewick. Hoop. Gloogle. Bloop.'"

"I thought owls just hooted," said Bertram.

"Oh, no," Raoul answered. "Owls make all sorts of calls and gurgles. Some go, 'Tu-whit! Tu-whoo!' Some go 'Kek, kek, kek.' And some make a soft, sweet laughing sound just like the water going over those pebbles."

They had a picnic on the sunny banks, and when they had eaten lunch Raoul lay down in the grass and listened to the voices of the stream. Before he knew it, he had fallen fast asleep, and Bertram,

smiling, nestled close to his friend and went to sleep, too.

When they awoke, the sun was very low and Raoul felt very strange. His neck feathers itched. His back ached. His stomach burned. His claws were stiff, and his beak was blistered.

"What's happened?" he said, in alarm. "What's the matter with me? Is it measles?"

Bertram looked him over carefully. Then he said, "Worse. You're *sunburned*."

Raoul began to cry. "Oh, my," he sniffled. "What shall I do? Mother and Father were right, after all. Owls haven't

room at the top of the tree, and had to climb the rest of the way. His family was awakened by the noise, and they all came out and stared at him.

"Whoo is it?" said Mother. "Is it Raoul?"

"Whoever he is," said Father, "he is a most peculiar color."

"It is Raoul," said Rufus. "I recognize him by the wart on his right leg."

"Oh, my poor baby, what have they done to you?" cried Mother. She tried to hug him, but when she touched him Raoul yelped with pain.

"He's frazzled," remarked Randolph. "To a crisp."

Father put his wings behind his back, and said in a kindly tone, "My dear boy, now you see what comes of doing what you weren't intended to do. Owls have always lived in this tree in the same way, and they always will. You can't change owl nature. Get some sleep, and perhaps you'll feel better in the morning."

And holding Mother, who was thinking about fainting again, he flew solemnly off, followed by Randolph, Reginald, Rudyard, Roderick, Rufus, and Russell.

Raoul crept sadly into his bed, and even there he was far from happy. He couldn't find a comfortable spot to lie in, for no matter which way he turned, he pressed his poor scorched feathers. At last, he stood up in a corner, rested his head against the wall and slept for a little while that way.

When the miserable night was over, the family came home, and Mother and Father looked in on him. They comforted him as best they could, and went to bed. The sun rose, the dew dried on

any business flying in the day."

Bertram shook his head. "It certainly is serious," he said. "You aren't quite used to the sun, yet. And sleeping in it all afternoon — well, we should have been more careful."

"But isn't there any cure?" said Raoul, wringing his wings.

"I don't know," Bertram replied. "I've never seen anything like it before. After all, you're the first owl I've ever known socially."

Slowly and painfully, Raoul got up and started for home. He could barely fly, and he gave out halfway to his own

the grass, and Raoul said, "Maybe I was wrong after all."

But then he plucked up his courage, for owls have never been quitters or cowards. "It's no use sitting in this hole and moping," he said. "I may as well go outside. Maybe the air will cool my feathers."

He hopped out on his limb and stretched cautiously. "Oohooo!" he groaned.

He began to fly, very carefully. He had learned a lot so far, and he knew it was cooler in the shade. He limped along in the air, and after a while he came to a mossy spot where the stream began. It chuckled up between two large stones, and the mud lay dark and smooth, and there were thick shadows under the bushes. It looked so inviting that he headed down to it.

But his sunburn hurt and his wings weren't working as they should. He slipped in the air. Down he came with a *whoosh!* and plop! he went, headfirst in the mud.

The breath was knocked out of him

and he lay still for a moment. Then—he rolled over and lay still some more. The cool wet mud felt *so* good on his sunburn.

"Oho!" said Raoul to himself. "So this is how it's done."

He realized that you learn something new every day.

First, he made some mud packs so he could keep the mud over his sunburn. He put mud on his back and on each wing, and covered it with large laurel leaves.

Then he looked at the trees, and at the shade under them. He picked some leaves and fastened them together with thorns, and stuck a branch through the middle of them and made a kind of little tree so he could carry his own shade around with him. He called it an "under-ella" because he stood under it.

Then he flew off to find Bertram. He was feeling much better.

When the mouse saw him coming down out of the sky, he turned perfectly white to the tips of his long, trembly whiskers. He started to run, but Raoul called out, "It's me, Bertram. Don't you recognize me?"

"Frankly, no," said Bertram. "You look like something from a flying saucer."

"Well, I'm not," Raoul said proudly. "I'm me. And I'm comfortable, whatever I look like."

He explained to his friend how he had solved the problem of sunburn. And Bertram said, "How perfectly intelligent of you! But Raoul," he added, "suppose some other problem comes up?"

Raoul considered for a moment. "I expect it will," he said. "But if it does, we'll think of a way to get over it. Won't we?"

"Yes," said Bertram. "We will."

They had a fine day together, racing and playing games, and exploring (with Bertram on Raoul's back) and picnicking beside the stream.

That evening, when Raoul got home, his family was perfectly speechless. Even Roderick couldn't think of anything to say, although he made a lot of notes.

But after a few days, they began to take it for granted that he would sleep all night and stay out all day. After a while, he got nice and brown and didn't mind the sun. His family got used to his odd things, and once, when it was rather cloudy and he was going to leave his sunglasses behind, his mother said, "Hadn't you better take them, dear, just in case? They look so distinguished on you."

And when Father chatted with other owls, he usually always managed to bring the conversation around to flying, and then to daylight, and then he would say, clearing his throat, "Of course, my son Raoul, you know, flies in the sunlight. First owl to do it, you know. Real Yankee ingenuity, that's what that youngster has." And with a smile, he would add, "Nothing like progress. You can't keep a good owl down."

And as for Raoul, every night he slept. And every day, before the dew dried on the grass or the sun rose, he got up. He generally put on his sun-glasses and took his underella, and he packed a box of bird-seed for lunch. Then he would go out to meet Bertram, for in spite of the fact that he soon got to know many of the other daytime birds and animals, Bertram remained his best and closest friend.

And in time, Raoul grew up and got married and became a father. All his children and his grandchildren flew in the daytime. And Raoul would look fondly at them, and when he was quite old he would say, "Owls have always lived here, and they've always flown in the daytime and they always will."

You know, he absolutely believed it.

Ting-a-ling is a particularly small fairy,
even smaller than Thumbelina.
He rides on the backs of butterflies;
he walks through keyholes with plenty of room to spare.
But his best friend is a giant.
There is a whole book, Ting-a-Ling Tales,
about the little fairy and his adventures with dwarfs,
magicians, and other strange people.

Ting-a-Ling and the Five Magicians

From Ting-a-Ling Tales

BY FRANK R. STOCKTON
Illustrated by JEAN WINSLOW

TING-A-LING, for some weeks after the death of his young companion, Ling-a-ting, seemed quite sad and dejected. He spent nearly all his time lying in a half-opened rose-bud, and thinking of the dear little creature who was gone. But one morning, the bud having become a full-blown rose, its petals fell apart, and dropped little Ting-a-ling out on the grass. The sudden fall did not hurt him, but it roused him to exertion, and he said, "O ho! This will never do. I will go up to the palace, and see if there is anything going on." So off he went to the great palace; and sure enough something was going on. He had scarcely reached

that not one word of it could Ting-a-ling hear. The King himself was by his throne, putting on the bulky boots, which he only wore when he went to battle, and which made him look so terrible that a person could hardly see him without trembling. The last time that he had worn those boots, as Ting-a-ling very well knew, he had made war on a neighboring country, and had defeated all the armies, killed all the people, torn down all the towns and cities, and every house and cottage, and ploughed up the whole country, and sowed it with thistles, so that it could never be used as a country any more. So Ting-a-ling thought that as the King was putting on his war boots, something very great was surely about to happen. Hearing a fizzing noise behind him, he turned around, and there was the Prince in the court-yard, grinding his sword on a grindstone, which was turned by two slaves, who were working away so hard and fast that they were nearly ready to drop. Then he *knew* that wonderful things were surely coming to pass, for in ordinary times the Prince never lifted his finger to do anything for himself.

Just then, a little page, who had been sent for the King's spurs, and couldn't find them, and who was therefore afraid to go back, stopped to rest himself for a minute against the window where Ting-a-ling was standing. As his head just reached a little above the window-seat, Ting-a-ling went close to his ear and shouted to him, to please tell him what was the matter. The page started at first, but, seeing it was only a little fairy, he told him that the Princess was lost, and that the whole army was going out to

the courtyard, when the bells began to ring, the horns to blow, the drums to beat, and crowds of people to shout and run in every direction, and there was never such a noise and hubbub before.

Ting-a-ling slipped along close to the wall, so that he would not be stepped on by anybody; and having reached the palace, he climbed up a long trailing vine, into one of the lower windows. There he saw the vast audience-chamber filled with people, shouting, and calling, and talking, all at once. The grand vizier was on the wide platform of the throne, making a speech, but the uproar was so great find her. Before he could say anything more, the King was heard to roar for his spurs, and away ran the little page, whether to look again for the spurs, or to hide himself, is not known at the present day. Ting-a-ling now became very much excited. The Princess Aufalia, who had been married to the Prince but a month ago, was very dear to him, and he felt that he must do something for her. But while he was thinking what this something might possibly be, he heard the clear and distinct sound of a tiny bell, which, however, no one but a fairy could possibly have heard above all that noise. He knew it was the bell of the fairy Queen, summoning her subjects to her presence; and in a moment he slid down the vine, and scampered away to the gardens. There, although the sun was shining brightly, and the fairies seldom assembled but by night, there were great crowds of them, all listening to the Queen, and keeping much better order than the people in the King's palace. The Queen addressed them in soul-stirring strains, and urged every one to do their best to find the missing Princess. In the night she had been taken away, while the Prince and everybody were asleep. "And now," said the Queen, untying her scarf, and holding it up, "away with you, every one! Search every house, garden, mountain, and plain, in the land, and the first one who comes to me with news of the Princess Aufalia, shall wear my scarf!" And, as this was a mark of high distinction, and conveyed privileges of which there is no time now to tell, the fairies gave a great cheer (which would have sounded to you, had you heard it, like a puff of wind through a thicket of reeds), and they all rushed away in every direction. Now, though the fairies of this tribe could go almost anywhere, through small cracks and key-holes, under doors, and into places where no one else could possibly penetrate, they did not fly, or float in the air, or anything of that sort. When they wished to travel fast or far, they would mount on butterflies, and all sorts of insects; but they seldom needed such assistance, as they were not in the habit of going far from their homes in the palace gardens. Ting-a-ling ran, as fast as he could, to where a friend of his, whom we have mentioned before, kept grasshoppers and butterflies to hire; but he found he was too late,—every one of them was taken by the fairies who had got there before him. "Never mind," said Ting-a-ling to himself, "I'll catch a wild one"; and, borrowing a bridle, he went out into the meadows, to catch a grasshopper for himself. He soon perceived one, quietly feeding under a clover-blossom. Ting-a-ling slipped up softly behind him; but the grasshopper heard him, and rolled his big eyes backward, drawing in his hind-legs in the way which all boys know so well. "What's the good of his seeing all around him?" thought Ting-a-ling; but there is no doubt that the grasshopper thought there was a great deal of good in it, for, just as Ting-a-ling made a rush at him, he let fly with one of his hind-legs, and kicked our little friend so high into the air, that he thought he was never coming down again. He landed, however, harmlessly on the grass on the other side of a fence. Nothing discouraged, he jumped up, with his bridle still in his hand, and looked around for the grasshopper. There he was, with his eyes

still rolled back, and his leg ready for another kick, should Ting-a-ling approach him again. But the little fellow had had enough of those strong legs, and so he slipped along the fence, and, getting through it, stole around in front of the grasshopper; and, while he was still looking backward with all his eyes, Ting-a-ling stepped quietly up before him, and slipped the bridle over his head! It was of no use for the grasshopper to struggle and pull back, for Ting-a-ling was astraddle of him in a moment, kicking him with his heels, and shouting "Hi! Hi!"

Away sprang the grasshopper like a bird, and he sped on and on, faster than he had ever gone before in his life, and Ting-a-ling waved his little sword over his head, and shouted, "Hi! Hi!"

So on they went for a long time; and in the afternoon the grasshopper began to get very tired, and did not make anything like such long jumps as he had done at first. They were going down a grassy hill, and had just reached the bottom, when Ting-a-ling heard someone calling him. Looking around him in astonishment, he saw that it was a little fairy of his acquaintance, younger than himself, named Parsley, who was sitting in the shade of a wide-spreading dandelion.

"Hello, Parsley!" cried Ting-a-ling, reining up. "What are you doing there?"

"Why you see, Ting-a-ling," said the other, "I came out to look for the Princess—"

"You!" cried Ting-a-ling; "a little fellow like you!"

"Yes, *I!*" said Parsley; "and Sourgrass and I rode the same butterfly; but by the time we had come this far, we got too

heavy, and Sourgrass made me get off."

"And what ever are you going to do now?" asked Ting-a-ling.

"O, I'm all right!" replied Parsley. "I shall have a butterfly of my own soon."

"How's that?" asked Ting-a-ling, quite curious to know.

"Come here!" said Parsley; and so Ting-a-ling got off his grasshopper, and led it up close to his friend. "See what I've found!" said Parsley, showing a cocoon that lay beside him. "I'm going to wait till this butterfly's hatched, and I shall have him the minute he comes out."

The idea of waiting for the butterfly to be hatched seemed so funny to Ting-a-ling, that he burst out laughing, and Parsley laughed too, and so did the grasshopper, for he took this opportunity to slip his head out of the bridle, and away he went!

Ting-a-ling turned and gazed in amazement at the grasshopper skipping up the hill; and Parsley, when he had done laughing, advised him to hunt around for another cocoon, and follow his example.

Ting-a-ling did not reply to this advice, but throwing his bridle to Parsley, said, "There, you would better take that. You may want it when your butterfly's hatched. I shall push on."

"What! walk?" cried Parsley.

"Yes, walk," said Ting-a-ling. "Good-by."

So Ting-a-ling travelled on by himself for the rest of the day, and it was nearly evening when he came to a wide brook with beautiful green banks, and overhanging trees. Here he sat down to rest himself; and while he was wondering if it would be a good thing for him to try to get across, he amused himself by watching the sports and antics of various insects and fishes that were enjoying themselves that fine summer evening. Plenty of butterflies and dragon-flies were there, but Ting-a-ling knew that he could never catch one of them, for they were nearly all the time over the surface of the water; and many a big fish was watching them from below, hoping that in their giddy flights, some of them would come near enough to be snapped down for supper. There were spiders, who shot over the surface of the brook as if they had been skating; and all sorts of beautiful bugs and flies were there,—green, yellow, emerald, gold, and black. At a short distance, Ting-a-ling saw a crowd of little minnows, who had caught a young tadpole, and, having tied a bluebell to his tail, were now chasing the affrighted creature about. But after a while the tadpole's mother came out, and then the minnows caught it!

While watching all these lively creatures. Ting-a-ling fell asleep, and when he awoke, it was dark night. He jumped up, and looked about him. The butterflies and dragon-flies had all gone to bed, and now the great night-bugs and buzzing beetles were out; the katydids were chirping in the trees, and the frogs were croaking among the long reeds. Not far off, on the same side of the brook, Ting-a-ling saw the light of a fire, and so he walked over to see what it meant. On his way, he came across some wild honeysuckles, and, pulling one of the blossoms, he sucked out the sweet juice for his supper, as he walked along. When he reached the fire, he saw sitting around it five men, with turbans and great black beards. Ting-a-ling instantly perceived

that they were magicians, and, putting the honeysuckle to his lips, he blew a little tune upon it, which the magicians hearing, they said to one another, "There is a fairy near us." Then Ting-a-ling came into the midst of them, and, climbing up on a pile of cloaks and shawls, conversed with them; and he soon heard that they knew, by means of their magical arts, that the Princess had been stolen the night before, by the slaves of a wicked dwarf, and that she was now locked up in his castle, which was on top of a high mountain, not far from where they then were.

"I shall go there right off," said Ting-a-ling.

"And what will you do when you get there?" said the youngest magician, whose name was Zamcar. "This dwarf is a terrible little fellow, and the same one who twisted poor Nerralina's head, which circumstance of course you remember. He has numbers of fierce slaves, and a great castle. You are a good little fellow, but I don't think you could do much for the Princess, if you did go to her."

Ting-a-ling reflected a moment, and then said that he would go to his friend, the Giant Tur-il-i-ra; but Zamcar told him that that tremendous individual had gone to the uttermost limits of China, to launch a ship. It was such a big one, and so heavy, that it had sunk down into the earth as tight as if it had grown there, and all the men and horses in the country could not move it. So there was nothing to do but to send for Tur-il-i-ra. When Ting-a-ling heard this, he was disheartened, and hung his little head. "The best thing to do," remarked Alcahazar, the oldest of the magicians, "would be to inform the King and his army of the place where the Princess is confined, and let them go and take her out."

"O no!" cried Ting-a-ling, who, if his body was no larger than a very small pea-pod, had a soul as big as a water-melon. "If the King knows it, up he will come with all his drums and horns, and the dwarf will hear him a mile off, and either kill the Princess, or hide her away. If we were all to go to the castle, I should think we could do something ourselves." This was the longest speech that Ting-a-ling had ever made; and when he was through, the youngest magician said to the others that he thought it was growing cooler, and the others agreed that it was. After some conversation among themselves in an exceedingly foreign tongue, these kind magicians agreed to go up to the castle, and see what they could do. So Zamcar put Ting-a-ling in the folds of his turban, and the whole party started off for the dwarf's castle. They looked like a company of travelling merchants, each one having a package on his back and a great staff in his hand.

When they reached the outer gate of the castle, Alcahazar, the oldest, knocked at it with his stick, and it was opened at once by a shiny black slave, who, coming out, shut it behind him, and inquired what the travellers wanted.

"Is your master within?" asked Alcahazar.

"I don't know," said the slave.

"Can't you find out?" asked the magician.

"Well, good merchant, perhaps I might; but I don't particularly want to know," said the slave, as he leaned back against the gate, leisurely striking with his long sword at the night-bugs and beetles that were buzzing about.

"My friend," said Alcahazar, "don't you think that is rather a careless way of using a sword? You might cut somebody."

"That's true," said the slave. "I didn't think of it before"; but he kept on striking away, all the same.

"Then stop it!" said Alcahazar, the oldest magician, striking the sword from his hand with one blow of his staff. Upon this, up stepped Ormanduz, the next oldest, and whacked the slave over his head; and then Mahalla, the next oldest, struck him over the shoulders; and Akbeck, the next oldest, cracked him on the shins; and Zamcar, the youngest, punched him in the stomach; and the slave sat down, and begged the noble merchants to please stop. So they stopped, and he humbly informed them that his master was in.

"We would see him," said Alcahazar.

"But, sirs," said the slave, "he is having a grand feast."

"Well," said the magician, "we're invited."

"O noble merchants!" cried the slave,

"why did you not tell me that before?" and he opened wide the gate, and let them in. After they had passed the outer gate, which was of wood, they went through another of iron, and another of brass, and another of copper, and then walked through the court-yard, filled with armed slaves, and up the great castle steps; at the top of which stood the butler, dressed in gorgeous array.

"Whom have you here, base slave?" cried the gorgeous butler.

"Five noble merchants, invited to my lord's feast," said the slave, bowing to the ground.

"But they cannot enter the banqueting hall in such garbs," said the butler. "They cannot be noble merchants, if they come not nobly dressed to my lord's feast."

"O sir!" said Alcahazar, "may your delicate and far-reaching understanding be written in books, and taught to youth in foreign lands, and may your profound judgment ever overawe your country! But allow us now to tell you that we have gorgeous dresses in these our packs. Would we soil them with the dust of travel, ere we entered the halls of my lord the dwarf?"

The butler bowed low at this address, and caused the five magicians to be conducted to five magnificent chambers, where were slaves, and lights, and baths, and soap, and towels, and wash-rags, and tooth-brushes; and each magician took a gorgeous dress from his pack, and put it on, and then they were all conducted (with Ting-a-ling still in Zamcar's turban) to the grand hall, where the feast was being held. Here they found the dwarf and his guests, numbering a hundred, having a truly jolly time. The dwarf, who was dressed in white (to make him look larger), was seated on a high red velvet cushion at the end of the hall, and the company sat cross-legged on rugs, in a great circle before him. He was drinking out of a huge bottle nearly as big as himself, and eating little birds; and judging by the bones that were left, he must have eaten nearly a whole flock of them. When he saw the five magicians entering, he stopped eating, and opened his eyes in amazement, and then shouted to his servants to tell him who these people were, who came without permission to his feast; but as no one knew, nobody answered. The guests, seeing the stately demeanor and magnificent dresses of the visitors, thought that they were at least five great monarchs.

"My lord the dwarf," said Alcahazar, advancing toward him, "I am the king of a far country; and passing your castle, and hearing of your feast, I have made bold to come and offer you some of the sweet-tasting birds of my kingdom." So saying, he lifted up his richly embroidered cloak, and took from under it a great silver dish containing about two hundred dozen hot, smoking, delicately cooked, fat little birds. Under the dish were fastened lamps of perfumed oil, all lighted, and keeping the savory food nice and hot. Making a low bow, the magician placed the dish before the dwarf, who tasted one of the birds, and immediately clapped his hands with joy. "Great King!" he cried, "welcome to my feast! Slaves, quick! make room for the great king!" As there was no vacant place, the slaves took hold of one of the guests, and gave him what the boys would call a "hist," right through the window, and Alcahazar took his place.

Then stepped forward Ormanduz, and said, "My lord the dwarf, I am also the king of a far country, and I have made bold to offer you some of the wine of my kingdom." So saying, he lifted his gold-lined cloak, and took from beneath it a crystal decanter, covered with gold and ruby ornaments, with one hundred and one beautifully carved silver goblets hanging from its neck, and which contained about eleven gallons of the most delicious wine. He placed it before the dwarf, who, having tasted the wine, gave a great cheer, and shouted to his slaves to make room for this mighty king. So the slaves took another guest by the neck and heels, and sent him, slam-bang, through the window, and Ormanduz took his place. Then stepped forward Mahallah, and said, "My lord the dwarf, I am also the king of a far country, and I bring you a sample of the venison of my kingdom." So saying, he raised his velvet cloak, trimmed with diamonds, and took from under it a whole deer, already cooked, and stuffed with oysters, anchovies, buttered toast, olives, tamarind seeds, sweet-marjoram, sage and many other herbs and spices, and all piping hot, and smelling deliciously. This he put down before the dwarf, who, when he had tasted it, waved his goblet over his head, and cried out to the slaves to make room for this mighty king. So the slaves seized another guest, and out of the window, like a shot, he went, and Mahallah took his place. Then Akbeck stepped up, and said, "My lord the dwarf, I am also the king of a far country, and I bring you some of the confections of my dominions." So saying, he took from under his cloak of gold cloth, a great basket of silver filagree work, in which were cream-chocolates, and burnt almonds, and sponge-cake, and lady's fingers, and mixtures, and gingernuts, and hoar hound candy, and gumdrops, and fruit-cake, and cream candy, and mint-stick, and pound-cake, and rock candy, and butter taffy, and many other confections, amounting in all to about two hundred and twenty pounds. He placed the basket before the dwarf, who tasted some of these good things, and found them so delicious, that he lay on his back and kicked up his heels in delight, shouting to his slaves to make room for this great king. As the next guest was a big, fat man, too

heavy to throw far, he was seized by four slaves, who walked him Spanish right out of the door, and Akbeck took his place. Then Zamcar stepped forward and said, "My lord the dwarf, I also am king of a far country, and I bring you some of the fruit of my dominions." And so saying, he took from beneath his gold and purple cloak, a great basket filled with currants as big as grapes, and grapes as big as plums, and plums as big as peaches, and peaches as big as cantaloupes, and cantaloupes as big as water-melons, and watermelons as big as barrels. There were about nineteen bushels of them altogether, and he put them before the dwarf, who, having tasted some of them, clapped his hands, and shouted to his slaves to make room for this mighty king; but as the next guest had very sensibly got up and gone out, Zamcar took his seat without any delay. Then Ting-a-ling, who was very much excited by all these wonderful performances, slipped down out of Zamcar's turban, and, running up towards the dwarf, cried out, "My lord the dwarf, I am also the king of a far country, and I bring you"—and he lifted up his little cloak; but as there was nothing there, he said no more, but clambered up into Zamcar's turban again. As nobody noticed or heard him, so great was the bustle and noise of the festivity, his speech made no difference one way or the other. After everybody had eaten and drunk until they could eat and drink no more, the dwarf jumped up and called to the chief butler, to know how many beds were prepared for the guests; to which the butler answered that there were thirty beds prepared. "Then," said the dwarf, "give these five noble kings each one of the best

rooms, with a down bed, and a silken comfortable; and give the other beds to the twenty-five biggest guests. As to the rest, turn them out!" So the dwarf went to bed, and each of the magicians had a splendid room, and twenty-five of the biggest guests had beds, and the rest were all turned out. As it was pouring down rain, and freezing, and cold, and wet, and slippery (for the weather was very unsettled on this mountain), and all these guests, who now found themselves outside of the castle gates, lived many miles away, and as none of them had any hats, or knew the way home, they were very miserable indeed.

Alcahazar did not go to bed, but sat in his room and reflected. He saw that the dwarf had given this feast on account of his joy at having captured the Princess, and thus caused grief to the King and Prince, and all the people; but it was also evident that he was very sly, and had not mentioned the matter to any of the company. The other magicians did not go to bed either, but sat in their rooms, and thought the same thing; and Ting-a-ling, in Zamcar's turban, was of exactly the same opinion. So, in about an hour, when all was still, the magicians got up, and went softly over the castle. One went down into the lower rooms, and there were all the slaves, fast asleep; and another into one wing of the castle, and there were half the guests, fast asleep; and another into the other wing, and there were the rest of the guests, fast asleep; and Alcahazar went into the dwarf's room, in the centre of the castle, and there was he, fast asleep, with one of his fists shut tight. The magician touched his fist with his magic staff, and it immediately

opened, and there was a key! So Alcahaz-ar took the key, and shut up the dwarf's hand again. Zamcar went up to the floor, near the top of the house, and entered a large room, which was empty, but the walls were hung with curtains made of snakes' skins, beautifully woven together. Ting-a-ling slipped down to the floor, and, peeping behind these curtains, saw the hinge of a door; and without saying a word, he got behind the curtain; and, sure enough, there was a door! and there was a keyhole! and in a minute, there was Ting-a-ling right through it! and there was the Princess in a chair in the middle of a great room, crying as if her heart would break! By the light of the moon, which had now broken through the clouds, Ting-a-ling saw that she was tied fast to the chair. So he climbed up on her shoulder, and called her by name; and when the Princess heard him and knew him, she took him into her lovely hands, and kissed him, and cried over him, and laughed over him so much, that her joy had like to have been the death of him. When she got over her excitement, she told him how she had been stolen away; how she had heard her favorite cat squeak in the middle of the night, and how she had got up quickly to go to it, supposing it had been squeezed in some door, and how the wicked dwarf, who had been im-itating the cat, was just outside the door with his slaves; and how they had seized her, and bound her, and carried her off to this castle, without waking up any of the King's household. Then Ting-a-ling told her that his five friends were there, and that they were going to see what they could do; and the Princess was very glad to hear that, you may be sure. Then Ting-

a-ling slipped down to the floor, and through the keyhole; and as he entered the room where he had left Zamcar, in came Alcahazar with the key, and the other magicians with news that every-body was asleep. When Ting-a-ling had told about the Princess, Alcahazar pushed aside the curtains, unlocked the door with the key, and they all entered the next room.

There, sure enough, was the Princess Aufalia; but, right in front of her, on the floor, squatted the dwarf, who had missed his key, and had slipped up by a back way! The magicians started back on see-ing him; the Princess was crying bitterly, and Ting-a-ling ran past the dwarf (who was laughing too horribly to notice him), and climbing upon the Princess's shoul-der, sat there among her curls, and did his best to comfort her.

"Anyway," said he, "*I* shall not leave you again," and he drew his little sword, and felt as big as a house. The magicians now advanced towards the dwarf; but he, it seems, was a bit of a magician himself, for he waved a little wand, and instantly a strong partition of iron wire rose up out of the floor, and reaching from one wall to the other, separated him completely from the five men. The magicians no soon-er saw this, than they cried out, "O ho! Mr. Dwarf, is that your game?"

"Yes," said the little wretch, chuckling; "can you play at it?"

"A little," said they; and each one pulled from under his cloak a long file; and filing the partition from the wall on each side, which only needed a few strokes from their sharp files, they pulled it entirely down. But before the magicians could reach him, the dwarf again waved his wand, and a great chasm opened in the floor before them, which was too wide to jump over, and so deep that the bottom could not be seen.

"O ho!" cried the magicians; "another game, eh!"

"Yes indeed," cried the dwarf. "Just let me see you play at *that*."

Each of the magicians then took from under his magic cloak a long board, and, putting them over the chasm, they began to walk across them. But the dwarf jumped up and waved his wand, and water commenced to fall on the boards, where it immediately froze; and they were so slippery, that the magicians could hardly keep their feet, and could not make one step forward. Even standing still, they came very near falling off into the chasm below. "I suppose you can play at that," said the dwarf; and the magicians replied, "O yes!" and each one took from under his cloak a pan of ashes, and sprinkled the boards, and walked right over. But before they reached the other edge, the dwarf pushed the chair, which was on rollers, up against the wall behind him, which opened; and instantly the Princess, Ting-a-ling, and the dwarf disappeared, and the wall closed up. Without saying a word, the magicians each drew from beneath his cloak a pickaxe, and they cut a hole in the wall in a few minutes. There was a large room on the other side, but it was entirely empty. So they sat down, and got out their magical calculators, and soon discovered that the Princess was in the lowest part of the castle; but the magical calculators being a little out of order, they could not show exactly her place of confinement. Then the five hurried downstairs, where they found the slaves still

asleep; but one poor little boy, whose business it was to get up early every morning and split kindling wood, having had none of the feast, was not very sleepy, and woke up when he heard footsteps near him. The magicians asked him if he could show them to the lowest part of the castle. "All right," said he; "this way"; and he led them to where there was a great black hole, with a windlass over it. "Get in the bucket," said he, "and I will lower you down."

"Bucket!" cried Alcahazar. "Is that a well?"

"To be sure it is," said the boy, who had

nothing on but the baby-clothes he had worn ever since he was born; and which, as he was now about ten years old, had split a good deal in the back and arms, but in length they were very suitable.

"But there can be no one down there," said the magician. "I see deep water."

"Of course there is nobody there," replied the boy. "Were you told to go down there to meet anybody? Because, if you were, you had better take some tubs down with you, to sit in. But all I know about it is, that it's the lowest part of this old hole of a castle."

"Boy," said Alcahazar, "there is a young lady shut up down here somewhere. Do you know where she is?"

"How old is she?" asked the boy.

"About seventeen," said the magician.

"O then! if she is not older than that, I should think she'd be in the preserve-closet, if she knew where it was," and the boy pointed to a great door, barred and locked, where the dwarf, who had a very sweet tooth, kept all his preserves locked up tight and fast. Zamcar stooped and looked through the key-hole of this door, and there, sure enough, was the Princess! So the boy proved to be smarter than all the magicians. Each of our five friends

now took from under his cloak a crowbar, and in a minute they had forced open the great door. But they had scarcely entered, when the dwarf, springing on the arm of the chair to which the Princess was still tied, drew his sword, and clapped it to her throat, crying out, that if the magicians came one step nearer, he would slice her head off.

"O ho!" cried they, "is that your game?"

"Yes indeed," said the chuckling dwarf; "can you play at it?"

The magicians did not appear to think that they could; but Ting-a-ling, who was still on the Princess's shoulder, though unseen by the dwarf, suddenly shouted, "I can play!" and in an instant he had driven his little sword into the dwarf's eye, who immediately sprang from the chair with a howl of anguish. While he was yelling and skipping about, with his

hands to his eyes, the poor boy, who hated him worse than pills, clapped a great jar of preserves over him, and sat down on the bottom of the jar! The magicians then untied the Princess; and as she looked weak and faint, Zamcar, the youngest, took from under his cloak a little table, set with everything hot and nice for supper; and when the Princess had eaten something and taken a cup of tea, she felt a great deal better. Alcahazar lifted up the jar from the dwarf, and there was the little rascal, so covered up with the sticky jam, that he could not speak and could hardly move. So, taking an oil-cloth bag from under his cloak, Alcahazar dropped the dwarf into it, and tied it up, and hung it to his girdle. The two youngest magicians made a sort of chair out of a shawl, and they carried the Princess on it between them, very comfortably; and as

Ting-a-ling still remained on her shoulder, she began to feel that things were beginning to look brighter. They then asked the poor boy what he would like best as a reward for what he had done; and he said that if they would shut him up in that room, and lock the door tight, and lose the key, he would be happy all the days of his life. So they left the boy (who knew what was good, and was already sucking away at a jar of preserved green-gages) in the room, and they shut the door and locked it tight, and lost the key; and he lived there for ninety-one years, eating preserves; and when they were all gone, he died. All that time he never had any clothes but his baby-clothes, and they got pretty sticky before his death. Then our party left the castle; and as they passed the slaves still fast asleep, the three oldest magicians took from under their cloaks watering-pots, filled with water that makes men sleep, and they watered the slaves with it, until they were wet enough to sleep a week. When they went through the gates of copper, brass, iron, and wood, they left them all open behind them. They had not gone far before they saw seventy-five men, all sitting in a row at the side of the road, and looking woefully indeed. They had been wet to the skin, and were now frozen stiff, not one of them being able to move anything but his eyelids, and they were all crying as if their hearts would break. So the magicians stopped, and the three oldest each took from under his cloak a pair of bellows, and they blew hot air on the poor creatures until they were all thawed. Then Alcahazar told them to go up to the castle, and take it for their own, and live there all the rest of their lives. He informed them that the

dwarf was his prisoner, and that the slaves would sleep for a week.

When the seventy-five guests (for those who had been taken from the feast, had joined their comrades) heard this, they all started up, and ran like deer for the castle; and when they reached it, they woke up their comrades, and took possession, and lived there all their lives. The man who had been first thrown through the window, and who had broken the way through the glass for the others, was elected their chief, because he had suffered the most; and excepting the trouble of doing their own work for a week, until the slaves awoke, these people were very happy ever afterwards.

It was just daylight when our party left the dwarf's castle, and by the next evening they had reached the palace. The army had not got back, and there was no

one there but the ladies of the Princess. When these saw their dear mistress, there was never before such a kissing, and hugging, and crying, and laughing. Ting-a-ling came in for a good share of praise and caressing; and if he had not slipped away to tell his tale to the fairy Queen, there is no knowing what would have become of him. The magicians sat down outside of the Princess's apartments, to guard her until the army should return; and the ladies would have kissed and hugged them, in their gratitude and joy, if they had not been such dignified and grave personages.

Now, the King, the Prince, and the great army, had gone miles and miles away in the opposite direction to the dwarf's castle, and the Princess and her ladies could not think how to let them know what had happened. As for ringing the great bell, they knew that that would be useless, for they would never hear it at the distance they were, and so they wished that they had some fireworks to set off. Therefore Zamcar, the youngest magician, offered to go up to the top of the palace and set off some. So, when he got up to the roof, he lifted up his cloak, and took out some fireworks, and set them

lively air of

"Cream cakes for supper,
Heigh O! Heigh O!
O! Cream cakes for supper,
Heigh O! Heigh O!"—

so as to keep up the spirits of the tired men. When they approached the palace, which was all lighted up, there was the Princess standing at the great door, in her Sunday clothes, and looking as lovely as a full-blown rose. The King jumped from his high-mettled racer, and went up the steps, two at a time; but the Prince, springing from his fiery steed, bounded up three steps at once, and got there first. When he and the King had got through hugging and kissing the Princess, her Sunday clothes looked as if they had been worn a week.

"Now then for supper," said the King, "and I hope it's ready." But the Princess said never a word, for she had forgotten all about supper; and all the ladies hung their heads, and were afraid to speak. But when they reached the great hall, they found that the magicians had been at work, and had cooked a grand supper. There it was, on ever so many long tables, all smoking hot, and smelling delightfully. So they all sat down, for there was room enough for every man, and nobody said a word until he was as tight as a drum.

When they had all had enough, and were just about to begin to talk, there were heard strains of the most delightful soft music; and directly, in at a window came the Queen of the fairies, attended by her court, all mounted on beautiful golden moths and dragon-flies. When they reached the velvet table in front of

off; and the light shone for miles and miles, and the King and all his army saw it. The King had just begun to feel tired, and to think that he would pitch his tent, and rest for the night by the side of a pleasant stream they had reached, when he saw the light from the palace, and instantly knew that there had been tidings of the Princess,—kings are so smart, you know. So, when his slaves came to ask him where they should pitch his tent, he shouted, "Pitch it in the river! 'Tention, army! Right about face, for home, — MARCH!" and away the whole army marched for home, the band playing the

315

the throne, where the King had been eating, with his plate in his lap, they arranged themselves in a circle on the table, and the Queen spoke out in a clear little voice, that could have been heard almost anywhere, and announced to the King that the little Ting-a-ling, who now wore her royal scarf, was the preserver of her daughter.

"O ho!" said the King; "and what can I do for such a mite as you, my fine fellow?"

Then Ting-a-ling, who wanted nothing for himself, and only thought of the good of his people, made a low bow to the King, and shouted at the top of his voice,

"Your royal gardeners are going to make asparagus beds all over our fairy pleasure grounds. If you can prevent that, I have nothing more to ask."

"Blow, Horner, blow!" cried the King, "and hear, all men! If any man, woman, or child, from this time hence forward forever, shall dare to set foot in the garden now occupied by the fairies, he shall be put to death, he and all his family, and his relations, as far as they can be traced. Take notice of that, every one of you!"

Ting-a-ling then bowed his thanks, and all the people made up their minds to take very particular notice of what the King had said.

toes, and eleven pounds of bran crackers, and to drink a gallon of cambric tea, all of which things he despised from the bottom of his miserable little heart.

"Now," cried the King, "all is settled, and let everybody go to bed. There is room enough in the palace for all to sleep to-night. Form in line, and to bed,—MARCH!" So they all formed in line, and began to march to bed, to the music of the band; and the fairies, their little horns blowing, and with Ting-a-ling at the post of honor by the Queen, took up their line of march, out of the window to the garden, which was to be, henceforward forever, their own. Just as they were all filing out, in flew little Parsley on the back of his butterfly, which had been hatched out at last.

"Hello!" cried he. "Is it all over?"

"Pretty nearly," said Ting-a-ling. "It's just letting out. How come you to be so late?"

"Easy enough," said poor little Parsley. "Of all the mean things that ever was the pokiest long time in unwrapping its wings, this butterfly's the meanest."

Then the magicians were ordered to come forward and name their reward; but they bowed their heads, and simply besought the King that he would grant them seven rye straws, the peeling from a red apple, and the heel from one of his old slippers. What in the name of common sense they wanted with these, no one but themselves knew; but magicians are such strange creatures! When these valuable gifts had been bestowed upon them, the five good magicians departed, leaving the dwarf for the King to do what he pleased with. This little wretch was shut up in an iron cage, and every day was obliged to eat three codfish, a bushel of Irish pota-

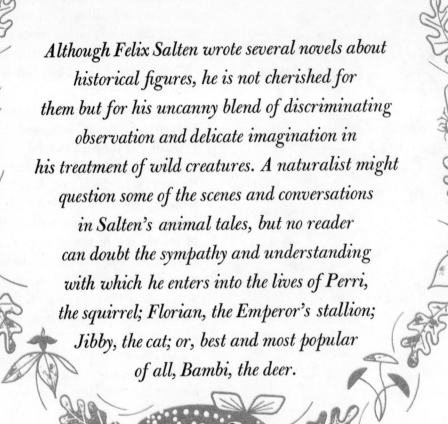

*Although Felix Salten wrote several novels about
historical figures, he is not cherished for
them but for his uncanny blend of discriminating
observation and delicate imagination in
his treatment of wild creatures. A naturalist might
question some of the scenes and conversations
in Salten's animal tales, but no reader
can doubt the sympathy and understanding
with which he enters into the lives of Perri,
the squirrel; Florian, the Emperor's stallion;
Jibby, the cat; or, best and most popular
of all, Bambi, the deer.*

Bambi Finds the Meadow

From Bambi

BY FELIX SALTEN
Illustrated by CHARLES HARPER

IN EARLY SUMMER the trees stood still under the blue sky, held their limbs outstretched and received the direct rays of the sun. On the shrubs and bushes in the undergrowth, the flowers unfolded their red, white and yellow stars. On some the seed pods had begun to appear again. They perched innumerable on the fine tips of the branches, tender and firm and resolute, and seemed like small, clenched fists. Out of the earth came whole troops of flowers, like motley stars, so that the soil of the twilit forest floor shone with a silent, ardent, colorful gladness. Everything smelled of fresh leaves, of blossoms, of moist clods and green wood. When morning broke, or when the sun went down, the whole woods resounded with a thousand voices, and from morning till night, the bees hummed, the wasps droned, and filled the fragrant stillness with their murmur.

These were the earliest days of Bambi's life. He walked behind his mother on a narrow track that ran through the midst of the bushes. How pleasant it was to walk there. The thick foliage stroked his flanks softly and bent supplely aside. The track appeared to be barred and obstructed in a dozen places and yet they advanced with the greatest ease. There were tracks like this everywhere, running criss-cross through the whole woods. His mother knew them all, and if Bambi sometimes stopped before a bush as if it were an impenetrable green wall, she always found where the path went through, without hesitation or searching.

Bambi questioned her. He loved to ask his mother questions. It was the pleasantest thing for him to ask a question and then to hear what answer his mother would give. Bambi was never surprised that question after question should come into his mind continually and without effort. He found it perfectly natural, and it delighted him very much. It was very delightful, too, to wait expectantly till the answer came. If it turned out the way he wanted, he was satisfied. Sometimes, of course, he did not understand, but that was pleasant also because he was kept busy picturing what he had not understood, in his own way. Sometimes he felt very sure that his mother was not giving him a complete answer, was intentionally not telling him all she knew. And, at first, that was very pleasant, too. For then there

would remain in him such a lively curiosity, such suspicion, mysteriously and joyously flashing through him, such anticipation, that he would become anxious and happy at the same time, and grow silent.

Once he asked, "Whom does this trail belong to, Mother?"

His mother answered, "To us."

Bambi asked again, "To you and me?"

"Yes."

"To us two?"

"Yes."

"Only to us two?"

"No," said his mother, "to us deer."

"What are deer?" Bambi asked, and laughed.

His mother looked at him from head to foot and laughed too. "You are a deer and I am a deer. We're both deer," she said. "Do you understand?"

Bambi sprang into the air for joy. "Yes, I understand," he said. "I'm a little deer and you're a big deer, aren't you?"

His mother nodded and said, "Now you see."

But Bambi grew serious again. "Are there other deer besides you and me?" he asked.

"Certainly," his mother said. "Many of them."

"Where are they?" cried Bambi.

"Here, everywhere."

"But I don't see them."

"You will soon," she said.

"When?" Bambi stood still, wild with curiosity.

"Soon." The mother walked on quietly. Bambi followed her. He kept silent for he was wondering what "soon" might mean. He came to the conclusion that "soon" was certainly not "now." But he wasn't sure at what time "soon" stopped being "soon" and began to be a "long while." Suddenly he asked, "Who made this trail?"

"We," his mother answered.

Bambi was astonished. "We? You and I?"

The mother said, "We, we . . . we deer."

Bambi asked, "Which deer?"

"All of us," his mother said sharply.

They walked on. Bambi was in high spirits and felt like leaping off the path, but he stayed close to his mother. Some-thing rustled in front of them, close to the ground. The fern fronds and wood-lettuce concealed something that advanced in violent motion. A threadlike, little cry shrilled out piteously; then all was still. Only the leaves and the blades of grass shivered back into place. A ferret had caught a mouse. He came slinking by, slid sideways, and prepared to enjoy his meal.

"What was that?" asked Bambi excitedly.

"Nothing," his mother soothed him.

"But," Bambi trembled, "but I saw it."

"Yes, yes," said his mother. "Don't be frightened. The ferret has killed a mouse." But Bambi was dreadfully frightened. A vast, unknown horror clutched at his heart. It was long before he could speak again. Then he asked, "Why did he kill the mouse?"

"Because," his mother hesitated. "Let us walk faster," she said as though something had just occurred to her and as though she had forgotten the question. She began to hurry. Bambi sprang after her.

A long pause ensued. They walked on quietly again. Finally Bambi asked anxiously, "Shall we kill a mouse, too, sometime?"

"No," replied his mother.

"Never?" asked Bambi.

"Never," came the answer.

"Why not?" asked Bambi, relieved.

"Because we never kill anything," said his mother simply.

Bambi grew happy again.

Loud cries were coming from a young ash tree which stood near their path. The mother went along without noticing them, but Bambi stopped inquisitively. Overhead two jays were quarreling about a nest they had plundered.

"Get away, you murderer!" cried one.

"Keep cool, you fool," the other answered, "I'm not afraid of you."

"Look for your own nests," the first one shouted, "or I'll break your head for you." He was beside himself with rage. "What vulgarity!" he chattered, "what vulgarity!"

The other jay had spied Bambi and fluttered down a few branches to shout at him. "What are you gawking at, you freak?" he screamed.

Bambi sprang away terrified. He reached his mother and walked behind her again, frightened and obedient, thinking she had not noticed his absence.

After a pause he asked, "Mother, what is vulgarity?"

"I don't know," said his mother.

Bambi thought a while; then he began again. "Why were they both so angry with each other, Mother?" he asked.

"They were fighting over food," his mother answered.

"Will we fight over food, too, sometime?" Bambi asked.

"No," said his mother.

Bambi asked, "Why not?"

"Because there is enough for all of us," his mother replied.

Bambi wanted to know something else. "Mother," he began.

"What is it?"

"Will we be angry with each other sometime?" he asked.

"No, child," said his mother, "we don't do such things."

They walked along again. Presently it grew light ahead of them. It grew very bright. The trail ended with the tangle of vines and bushes. A few steps more and they would be in the bright open space that spread out before them. Bambi wanted to bound forward, but his mother had stopped.

"What is it?" he asked impatiently, already delighted.

"It's the meadow," his mother answered.

"What is a meadow?" asked Bambi insistently.

His mother cut him short. "You'll soon find out for yourself," she said. She had become very serious and watchful. She stood motionless, holding her head high and listening intently. She sucked in deep breathfuls of air and looked very severe.

"It's all right," she said at last, "we can go out."

Bambi leaped forward, but his mother barred the way.

"Wait till I call you," she said. Bambi obeyed at once and stood still. "That's right," said his mother, to encourage him, "and now listen to what I am saying to you." Bambi heard how seriously his mother spoke and felt terribly excited.

"Walking on the meadow is not so simple," his mother went on. "It's a difficult and dangerous business. Don't ask me why. You'll find that out later on. Now do exactly as I tell you to. Will you?"

"Yes," Bambi promised.

"Good," said his mother, "I'm going out alone first. Stay here and wait. And don't take your eyes off me for a minute. If you see me run back here, then turn round and run as fast as you can. I'll catch up with you soon." She grew silent and seemed to be thinking. Then she went on

earnestly, "Run anyway as fast as your legs will carry you. Run even if something should happen . . . even if you should see me fall to the ground. . . . Don't think of me, do you understand? No matter what you see or hear, start running right away and just as fast as you possibly can. Do you promise me to do that?"

"Yes," said Bambi softly. His mother spoke so seriously.

She went on speaking. "Out there if I should call you," she said, "there must be no looking around and no questions, but you must get behind me instantly. Understand that. Run without pausing or stopping to think. If I begin to run, that means for you to run too, and no stopping until we are back here again. You won't forget, will you?"

"No," said Bambi in a troubled voice.

"Now I'm going ahead," said his mother, and seemed to become calmer.

She walked out. Bambi, who never took his eyes off her, saw how she moved forward with slow, cautious steps. He stood there full of expectancy, full of fear and curiosity. He saw how his mother listened in all directions, saw her shrink together, and shrank together himself, ready to leap back into the thickets. Then his mother grew calm again. She stretched herself. Then she looked around satisfied and called, "Come!"

Bambi bounded out. Joy seized him with such tremendous force that he forgot his worries in a flash. Through the thicket he could see only the green tree-tops overhead. Once in a while he caught a glimpse of the blue sky.

Now he saw the whole heaven stretching far and wide and he rejoiced without knowing why. In the forest he had seen only a stray sunbeam now and then, or the tender, dappled light that played through the branches. Suddenly he was standing in the blinding hot sunlight whose boundless power was beaming upon him. He stood in the splendid warmth that made him shut his eyes but which opened his heart.

Bambi was as though bewitched. He was completely beside himself with pleasure. He was simply wild. He leaped into the air three, four, five times. He had to do it. He felt a terrible desire to leap and jump. He stretched his young limbs joyfully. His breath came deeply and easily. He drank in the air. The sweet smell of the meadow made him so wildly happy that he had to leap into the air.

Bambi was a child. If he had been a human child he would have shouted. But he was a young deer, and deer cannot shout, at least not the way human children do. So he rejoiced with his legs and with his whole body as he flung himself into the air. His mother stood by and was glad. She saw that Bambi was wild. She watched how he bounded into the air and fell again awkwardly, in one spot. She saw how he stared around him, dazed and bewildered, only to leap up over and over again. She understood that Bambi knew only the narrow deer tracks in the forest

and how his brief life was used to the limits of the thicket. He did not move from one place because he did not understand how to run freely around the open meadow.

So she stretched out her forefeet and bent laughingly towards Bambi for a moment. Then she was off with one bound, racing around in a circle so that the tall grass stems swished.

Bambi was frightened and stood motionless. Was that a sign for him to run back to the thicket? His mother had said to him, "Don't worry about me no matter what you see or hear. Just run as fast as you can." He was going to turn around and run as she had commanded him to, but his mother came galloping up suddenly. She came up with a wonderful swishing sound and stopped two steps from him. She bent towards him, laughing as she had at first and cried, "Catch me." And in a flash she was gone.

Bambi was puzzled. What did she mean? Then she came back again running so fast that it made him giddy. She pushed his flank with her nose and said quickly, "Try to catch me," and fled away.

Bambi started after her. He took a few steps. Then his steps became short bounds. He felt as if he were flying without any effort on his part. There was a space under his hoofs, space under his bounding feet, space and still more space. Bambi was beside himself with joy.

The swishing grass sounded wonderful to his ears. It was marvelously soft and as fine as silk where it brushed against him. He ran round in a circle. He turned and flew off in a new circle, turned around again and kept running.

His mother was standing still, getting her breath again. She kept following Bambi with her eyes. He was wild.

Suddenly the race was over. He stopped and came up to his mother, lifting his hoofs elegantly. He looked joyfully at her. Then they strolled contentedly side by side.

Since he had been in the open, Bambi had felt the sky and the sun and the green meadow with his whole body. He took one blinding, giddy glance at the sun, and he felt its rays as they lay warmly on his back.

Presently he began to enjoy the meadow with his eyes also. Its wonders amazed him at every step he took. You could not see the tiniest speck of earth the way you could in the forest. Blade after blade of grass covered every inch of the ground. It tossed and waved luxuriantly. It bent softly aside under every footstep, only to rise up unharmed again. The broad green meadow was starred with white daisies, with the thick, round red and purple clover blossoms and bright, golden dandelion heads.

"Look, look, Mother!" Bambi exclaimed. "There's a flower flying."

"That's not a flower," said his mother, "that's a butterfly."

Bambi stared at the butterfly, entranced. It had darted lightly from a

as if they really had settled somewhere, yet always flying up again, a little way at first, then higher and higher, and always searching farther and farther because all the good places have already been taken.

Bambi gazed at them all. He would have loved to see one close by. He wanted to see one face to face but he was not able to. They sailed in and out continually. The air was aflutter with them.

When he looked down at the ground again he was delighted with the thousands of living things he saw stirring under his hoofs. They ran and jumped in all directions. He would see a wild swarm of them, and the next moment they had disappeared in the grass again.

"Who are they, Mother?" he asked.

"Those are ants," his mother answered.

"Look," cried Bambi, "see that piece of grass jumping. Look how high it can jump!"

"That's not grass," his mother explained, "that's a nice grasshopper."

"Why does he jump that way?" asked Bambi.

"Because we're walking here," his mother answered, "he's afraid we'll step on him."

"O," said Bambi, turning to the grasshopper who was sitting on a daisy; "O," he said again politely, "you don't have to be afraid; we won't hurt you."

"I'm not afraid," the grasshopper replied in a quavering voice; "I was only frightened for a moment when I was talking to my wife."

"Excuse us for disturbing you," said Bambi shyly.

"Not at all," the grasshopper quavered. "Since it's you, it's perfectly all right. But

blade of grass and was fluttering about in its giddy way. Then Bambi saw that there were many butterflies flying in the air above the meadow. They seemed to be in a hurry and yet moved slowly, fluttering up and down in a sort of game that delighted him. They really did look like gay flying flowers that would not stay on their stems but had unfastened themselves in order to dance a little. They looked, too, like flowers that come to rest at sundown but have no fixed places and have to hunt for them, dropping down and vanishing

you never know who's coming and you have to be careful."

"This is the first time in my life that I've ever been on the meadow," Bambi explained; "my mother brought me...."

The grasshopper was sitting with his head lowered as though he were going to butt. He put on a serious face and murmured, "That doesn't interest me at all. I haven't time to stand here gossiping with you. I have to be looking for my wife. Hopp!" And he gave a jump.

"Hopp!" said Bambi in surprise at the high jump with which the grasshopper vanished.

Bambi ran to his mother. "Mother, I spoke to him," he cried.

"To whom?" his mother asked.

"To the grasshopper," Bambi said, "I spoke to him. He was very nice to me. And I like him so much. He's so wonderful and green and you can see through his sides. They look like leaves, but you can't see through a leaf."

"Those are his wings," said his mother.

"O," Bambi went on, "and his face is so serious and wise. But he was very nice to me anyhow. And how he can jump! 'Hopp!' he said, and he jumped so high I couldn't see him any more."

They walked on. The conversation with the grasshopper had excited Bambi and tired him a little, for it was the first time he had ever spoken to a stranger. He felt hungry and pressed close to his mother to be nursed.

Then he stood quietly and gazed dreamily into space for a little while with a sort of joyous ecstasy that came over him every time he was nursed by his mother. He noticed a bright flower moving in the tangled grasses. Bambi looked

more closely at it. No, it wasn't a flower, but a butterfly. Bambi crept closer.

The butterfly hung heavily to a grass stem and fanned its wings slowly.

"Please sit still," Bambi said.

"Why should I sit still? I'm a butterfly," the insect answered in astonishment.

"O, please sit still, just for a minute," Bambi pleaded, "I've wanted so much to see you close to. Please."

"Well," said the butterfly, "for your sake I will, but not for long."

Bambi stood in front of him. "How beautiful you are!" he cried fascinated; "how wonderfully beautiful, like a flower!"

"What?" cried the butterfly, fanning

his wings, "did you say like a flower? In my circle it's generally supposed that we're handsomer than flowers."

Bambi was embarrassed. "O, yes," he stammered, "much handsomer, excuse me, I only meant . . ."

"Whatever you meant is all one to me," the butterfly replied. He arched his thin body affectedly and played with his delicate feelers.

Bambi looked at him enchanted. "How elegant you are!" he said. "How elegant and fine! And how splendid and white your wings are!"

The butterfly spread his wings wide apart, then raised them till they folded together like an upright sail.

"O," cried Bambi, "I know that you are handsomer than the flowers. Besides, you can fly and the flowers can't because they grow on stems, that's why."

The butterfly spread his wings. "It's enough," he said, "that I can fly." He soared so lightly that Bambi could hardly see him or follow his flight. His wings moved gently and gracefully. Then he fluttered into the sunny air.

"I only sat still that long on your account," he said balancing in the air in front of Bambi. "Now I'm going."

That was how Bambi found the meadow.

The next story was written by the greatest art critic
of the nineteenth century, John Ruskin,
an enormously rich man who gave his
wealth away to help others.
Besides being an art lover and a lover of mankind,
Ruskin was also a moralist.
In "The King of the Golden River" he
not only composed a fairy tale,
but also made it teach a lesson.
The lesson, however, is only implied—
but it should add to your pleasure in following the fortunes
of young and tender-hearted Gluck,
(a name which, translated from German, means Luck),
in meeting the wind disguised as a crusty old man
who exposes Gluck's greedy brothers,
and in the flow of the story itself.
We always like to see good triumph over evil—
and here it emphatically does.

The King of the Golden River

BY JOHN RUSKIN

Illustrated by MAE GERHARD

IN A SECLUDED and mountainous part of Stiria, there was, in old time, a valley of the most surprising and luxuriant fertility. It was surrounded, on all sides, by steep and rocky mountains, rising into peaks, which were always covered with snow, and from which a number of torrents descended in constant cataracts. One of these fell westward, over the face of a crag so high, that, when the sun had set to everything else, and all below was darkness, his beams still shone full upon this waterfall, so that it looked like a shower of gold. It was, therefore, called by the people of the neighborhood the Golden River. It was strange that none of these streams fell into the valley itself. They all descended on the other side of the mountains, and wound away through broad plains and by populous cities. But the clouds were drawn so constantly to the snowy hills, and rested so softly in the circular hollow, that, in time of drought and heat, when all the country was burnt up, there was still rain in the little valley; and its crops were so heavy, and its hay so high, and its apples so red, and its grapes so blue, and its wine so rich, and its honey so sweet, that it was a marvel to everyone who beheld it, and was commonly called the Treasure Valley.

The whole of this little valley belonged to three brothers, called Schwartz, Hans, and Gluck. Schwartz and Hans, the two older brothers, were very ugly men, with overhanging eyebrows and small, dull eyes, which were always half shut, so that you couldn't see into *them,* and always fancied they saw very far into *you.* They lived by farming the Treasure Valley, and very good farmers they were. They killed everything that did not pay for its eating. They shot the blackbirds, because they pecked the fruit; and killed the hedgehogs, lest they should suck the cows; they poisoned the crickets for eating the crumbs in the kitchen; and smothered the cicadas, which used to sing all summer in the lime trees. They worked their servants without any wages, till they would not work any more, and then quarreled with them, and turned them out-of-doors without paying them. It would have been very odd, if, with such a farm, and such a system of farming, they hadn't got very rich; and very rich they *did* get. They generally contrived to keep their corn by them till it was very dear, and then sell it for twice its value; they had heaps of gold lying about on their floors, yet it was never known that they had given so much as a penny or a crust in charity; they never went to Mass; grumbled perpetually at paying tithes; and were, in a word, of so cruel and grinding a temper as to receive from all those with whom they had any dealings the nickname of the "Black Brothers."

The youngest brother, Gluck, was as completely opposed, in both appearance and character, to his seniors as could possibly be imagined or desired. He was not above twelve years old, fair, blue-eyed, and kind in temper to every living thing.

He did not, of course, agree particularly well with his brothers, or rather, they did not agree with *him*. He was usually appointed to the honorable office of turnspit, when there was anything to roast, which was not often; for, to do the brothers justice, they were hardly less sparing upon themselves than upon other people. At other times he used to clean the shoes, floors, and sometimes the plates, occasionally getting what was left on them, by way of encouragement, and a wholesome quantity of dry blows, by way of education.

Things went on in this manner for a long time. At last came a very wet summer, and everything went wrong in the country round. The hay had hardly been got in, when the haystacks were floated bodily down to the sea by an inundation; the vines were cut to pieces with the hail; the corn was all killed by a black blight; only in the Treasure Valley, as usual, all was safe. As it had rain when there was rain nowhere else, so it had sun when there was sun nowhere else. Everybody came to buy corn at the farm, and went away pouring maledictions on the Black Brothers. They asked what they liked, and got it, except from poor people, who could only beg, and several of whom were starved at their very door, without the slightest regard or notice.

It was drawing towards winter, and very cold weather, when one day the two elder brothers had gone out, with their usual warning to little Gluck, who was left to mind the roast, that he was to let nobody in, and give nothing out. Gluck sat down quite close to the fire, for it was raining very hard, and the kitchen walls were by no means dry or comfortable-looking. He turned and turned, and the roast got nice and brown. "What a pity," thought Gluck, "my brothers never ask anybody to dinner. I'm sure, when they've got such a nice piece of mutton as this, and nobody else has got so much as a piece of dry bread, it would do their hearts good to have somebody to eat it with them."

Just as he spoke, there came a double knock at the house door, yet heavy and dull, as though the knocker had been tied up—more like a puff than a knock.

"It must be the wind," said Gluck; "nobody else would venture to knock double knocks at our door."

No; it wasn't the wind; there it came again very hard, and what was particularly astounding, the knocker seemed to be in a hurry, and not to be in the least afraid of the consequences. Gluck went to the window, opened it, and put his head out to see who it was.

It was the most extraordinary-looking little gentleman that he had ever seen in his life. He had a very large nose, slightly brass-colored; his cheeks were very round, and very red, and might have warranted a supposition that he had been blowing a refractory fire for the last eight-and-forty hours; his eyes twinkled merrily through long silky eyelashes, his moustaches curled twice round like a corkscrew on each side of his mouth, and his hair, of a curious mixed pepper-and-salt color, descended far over his shoulders. He was about four feet six in height, and wore a conical-pointed cap of nearly the same altitude, decorated with a black feather some three feet long. His doublet was prolonged behind into something resembling a violent exaggeration of what is now

termed a "swallow-tail," but was much obscured by the swelling folds of an enormous black, glossy-looking cloak, which must have been very much too long in calm weather, as the wind, whistling round the old house, carried it clear out from the wearer's shoulders to about four times his own length.

Gluck was so perfectly paralyzed by the singular appearance of his visitor, that he remained fixed without uttering a word, until the old gentleman, having performed another, and a more energetic concerto on the knocker, turned round to look after his fly-away cloak. In so doing he caught sight of Gluck's little yellow head jammed in the window, with his mouth and eyes very wide open indeed.

"Hollo!" said the little gentleman, "that's not the way to answer the door; I'm wet; let me in."

To do the little gentleman justice, he *was* wet. His feather hung down between his legs like a beaten puppy's tail, dripping like an umbrella; and from the ends of his moustaches the water was running into his waistcoat pockets, and out again like a mill stream.

"I beg pardon, sir," said Gluck, "I'm very sorry, but I really can't."

"Can't what?" said the old gentleman.

"I can't let you in, sir—I can't indeed; my brothers would beat me to death, sir, if I thought of such a thing. What do you want, sir?"

"Want?" said the old gentleman petulantly, "I want fire and shelter; and there's your great fire there blazing, crackling, and dancing on the wall, with nobody to feel it. Let me in, I say; I only want to warm myself."

Gluck had had his head, by this time, so long out of the window that he began to feel it was really unpleasantly cold; and when he turned, and saw the beautiful fire rustling and roaring, and throwing

long bright tongues up the chimney, as if it were licking its chops at the savory smell of the leg of mutton, his heart melted within him that it should be burning away for nothing. "He does look *very* wet," said little Gluck; "I'll just let him in for a quarter of an hour." Round he went to the door and opened it; and as the little gentleman walked in there came a gust of wind through the house that made the old chimneys totter.

"That's a good boy," said the little gentleman. "Never mind your brothers. I'll talk to them."

"Pray, sir, don't do any such thing," said Gluck. "I can't let you stay till they come; they'd be the death of me."

"Dear me," said the old gentleman, "I'm very sorry to hear that. How long may I stay?"

"Only till the mutton's done, sir," replied Gluck, "and it's very brown."

Then the old gentleman walked into

the kitchen and sat himself down on the hob, with the top of his cap accommodated up the chimney, for it was a great deal too high for the roof.

"You'll soon dry there, sir," said Gluck, and sat down again to turn the mutton. But the old gentleman did *not* dry there, but went on drip, drip, dripping among the cinders, and the fire fizzed, and sputtered, and began to look very black and uncomfortable; never was such a cloak; every fold in it ran like a gutter.

"I beg pardon, sir," said Gluck at length, after watching the water spreading in long, quicksilver-like streams over the floor for a quarter of an hour; "mayn't I take your cloak?"

"No, thank you," said the old gentleman.

"Your cap, sir?"

"I am all right, thank you," said the old gentleman rather gruffly.

"But—sir—I'm very sorry," said Gluck, hesitatingly; "but—really, sir—you're putting the fire out."

"It'll take longer to do the mutton then," replied his visitor dryly.

Gluck was very much puzzled by the behavior of his guest; it was such a strange mixture of coolness and humility. He turned away at the string meditatively for another five minutes.

"That mutton looks very nice," said the old gentleman at length. "Can't you give me a little bit?"

"Impossible, sir," said Gluck.

"I'm very hungry," continued the old gentleman; "I've had nothing to eat yesterday, nor today. They surely couldn't miss a bit from the knuckle!"

He spoke in so very melancholy a tone, that it quite melted Gluck's heart. "They

promised me one slice today, sir," said he; "I can give you that, but not a bit more."

"That's a good boy," said the old gentleman again.

Then Gluck warmed a plate, and sharpened a knife. "I don't care if I do get beaten for it," thought he. Just as he had cut a large slice out of the mutton, there came a tremendous rap at the door. The old gentleman jumped off the hob, as if it had suddenly become inconveniently warm. Gluck fitted the slice into the mutton again, with desperate efforts at exactitude, and ran to open the door.

"What did you keep us waiting in the rain for?" said Schwartz, as he walked in, throwing his umbrella in Gluck's face. "Ay! what for, indeed, you little vagabond?" said Hans, administering an educational box on the ear, as he followed his brother into the kitchen.

"Bless my soul!" said Schwartz when he opened the door.

"Amen!" said the little gentleman, who had taken his cap off, and was standing in the middle of the kitchen, bowing with the utmost possible velocity.

"Who's that?" said Schwartz, catching up a rolling pin, and turning to Gluck with a fierce frown.

"I don't know, indeed, brother," said Gluck in great terror.

"How did he get in?" roared Schwartz.

"My dear brother," said Gluck, deprecatingly, "he was so *very* wet!"

The rolling pin was descending on Gluck's head; but, at the instant, the old gentleman interposed his conical cap, on which it crashed with a shock that shook the water out of it all over the room. What was very odd, the rolling pin no sooner touched the cap, than it flew out of Schwartz's hand, spinning like a straw in a high wind, and fell into the corner at the farther end of the room.

"Who are you, sir?" demanded Schwartz, turning upon him.

"What's your business?" snarled Hans.

"I'm a poor old man, sir," the little gentleman began very modestly, "and I saw your fire through the window, and begged shelter for a quarter of an hour."

"Have the goodness to walk out again, then," said Schwartz. "We've quite enough water in our kitchen, without making it a drying house."

"It is a cold day to turn an old man out, sir; look at my gray hairs." They hung down to his shoulders, as I told you before.

"Ay!" said Hans, "there are enough of them to keep you warm. Walk!"

"I'm very, very hungry, sir; couldn't you spare me a bit of bread before I go?"

"Bread, indeed!" said Schwartz; "do you suppose we've nothing to do with our bread but to give it to such red-nosed fellows as you?"

"Why don't you sell your feather?" said Hans, sneeringly. "Out with you!"

"A little bit," said the old gentleman.

"Be off!" said Schwartz.

"Pray, gentlemen."

"Off, and be hanged!" cried Hans, seizing him by the collar. But he had no sooner touched the old gentleman's collar, than away he went after the rolling pin, spinning round and round, till he fell into the corner on top of it. Then Schwartz was very angry, and ran at the old gentleman to turn him out; but he also had hardly touched him, when away he went after Hans and the rolling pin, and hit his head against the wall as he tumbled into the corner. And so there they lay, all three.

Then the old gentleman spun himself round with velocity in the opposite direction; continued to spin until his long cloak was all wound neatly about him; clapped his cap on his head, very much on one side (for it could not stand upright without going through the ceiling); gave an additional twist to his corkscrew moustaches; and replied with perfect coolness: "Gentlemen, I wish you a very good morning. At twelve o'clock tonight, I'll call again; after such a refusal of hospitality as I have just experienced, you will not be surprised if that visit is the last I ever pay you."

"If ever I catch you here again," muttered Schwartz, coming, half frightened, out of his corner—but, before he could finish his sentence, the old gentleman had shut the house door behind him with a great bang; and there drove past the window, at the same instant, a wreath of ragged cloud, that whirled and rolled away down the valley in all manner of shapes; turning over and over in the air; and melting away at last in a gush of rain.

"A very pretty business, indeed, Mr. Gluck!" said Schwartz. "Dish the mutton, sir. If ever I catch you at such a trick again—bless me, why the mutton's been cut!"

"You promised me one slice, brother, you know," said Gluck.

"Oh! and you were cutting it hot, I suppose, and going to catch all the gravy. It'll be long before I promise you such a thing again. Leave the room, sir; and have the kindness to wait in the coal-cellar till I call you."

Gluck left the room melancholy enough. The brothers ate as much mutton as they could, locked the rest in the cupboard, and proceeded to get very drunk after dinner.

Such a night as it was! Howling wind, and rushing rain, without intermission. The brothers had just sense enough left to put up all the shutters, and double bar the door, before they went to bed. They usually slept in the same room. As the clock struck twelve, they were both awakened by a tremendous crash. Their door burst open with a violence that shook the house from top to bottom.

"What's that?" cried Schwartz, starting up in his bed.

"Only I," said the little gentleman.

The two brothers sat up on their bolster, and stared into the darkness. The room was full of water, and by a misty moonbeam, which found its way through a hole in the shutter, they could see, in the midst of it, an enormous foam globe, spinning round, and bobbing up and down like a cork, on which, as on a most luxurious cushion, reclined the little old gentleman, cap and all. There was plenty of room for it now, for the roof was off.

"Sorry to incommode you," said their visitor, ironically. "I'm afraid your beds are dampish; perhaps you had better go to your brother's room; I've left the ceiling on there."

They required no second admonition, but rushed into Gluck's room, wet through, and in an agony of terror.

"You'll find my card on the kitchen table," the old gentleman called after them. "Remember the *last* visit."

"Pray Heaven it may!" said Schwartz, shuddering. And the foam globe disappeared.

Dawn came at last, and the two brothers looked out of Gluck's little window in the morning. The Treasure Valley was one mass of ruin and desolation. The inundation had swept away trees, crops, and cattle, and left, in their stead, a waste of red sand and gray mud. The two brothers crept, shivering and horror-struck, into the kitchen. The water had gutted the whole first floor; corn, money, almost every movable thing had been swept away, and there was left only a small white card on the kitchen table. On it, in large, breezy, long-legged letters were engraved the words:

South-West Wind Esq.

Chapter II

SOUTH-WEST WIND, ESQUIRE, was as good as his word. After the momentous visit above related, he entered the Treasure Valley no more; and, what was worse, he had so much influence with his relations, the West Winds in general, and used it so effectually, that they all adopted a similar line of conduct. So no rain fell in the valley from one year's end to another. Though everything remained green and flourishing in the plains below, the inheritance of the three brothers was a desert. What had once been the richest soil in the kingdom became a shifting heap of red sand; and the brothers, unable longer to contend with the adverse skies, abandoned their valueless patrimony in despair, to seek some means of gaining a livelihood among the cities and people of the plains. All their money was gone, and they had nothing left but some curious, old-fashioned pieces of gold plate, the last remnants of their ill-gotten wealth.

"Suppose we turn goldsmiths?" said Schwartz to Hans, as they entered the large city. "It is a good knave's trade; we can put a great deal of copper into the gold, without anyone's finding it out."

The thought was agreed to be a very good one; they hired a furnace, and turned goldsmiths. But two slight circumstances affected their trade: the first, that people did not approve of the coppered gold; the second, that the two elder brothers, whenever they had sold anything, used to leave little Gluck to mind the furnace, and go and drink out the money in the ale-house next door. So they melted all their gold, without making money enough to buy more, and were at last reduced to one large drinking-mug, which an uncle of his had given to little Gluck, and which he was very fond of, and would not have parted with for the world; though he never drank anything out of it but milk and water. The mug was a very odd mug to look at. The handle was formed of two wreaths of flowing golden hair, so finely spun that it looked more like silk than metal, and these wreaths descended into, and mixed with, a beard and whiskers, of the same exquisite workmanship, which surrounded and decorated a very fierce little face, of the reddest gold imaginable, right in the front of the mug, with a pair of eyes in it which seemed to command its whole circumference. It was impossible to drink out of the mug without being subjected to an intense gaze out of the side of these eyes; and Schwartz positively averred that once, after emptying it full of Rhenish seven-

teen times, he had seen them wink! When it came to the mug's turn to be made into spoons, it half broke poor little Gluck's heart; but the brothers only laughed at him, tossed the mug into the melting-pot, and staggered out to the ale-house; leaving him, as usual, to pour the gold into bars, when it was all ready.

When they were gone, Gluck took a farewell look at his old friend in the melting-pot. The flowing hair was all gone; nothing remained but the red nose, and the sparkling eyes, which looked more malicious than ever. "And no wonder," thought Gluck, "after being treated in that way." He sauntered disconsolately to the window, and sat himself down to catch the fresh evening air, and escape the hot breath of the furnace. Now this window commanded a direct view of the range of mountains, which, as I told you before, overhung the Treasure Valley, and more especially of the peak from which fell the Golden River. It was just at the close of the day, and, when Gluck sat down at the window, he saw the rocks of the mountain tops, all crimson and purple with the sunset; and there were bright tongues of fiery cloud burning and quivering about them; and the river, brighter than all, fell, in a waving column of pure gold, from precipice to precipice, with the double arch of a broad purple rainbow stretched across it, flushing and fading alternately in the wreaths of spray.

"Ah!" said Gluck aloud, after he had looked at it for a little while, "if that river were really all gold, what a nice thing it would be."

"No it wouldn't, Gluck," said a clear metallic voice, close at his ear.

"Bless me! what's that?" exclaimed

337

Gluck, jumping up. There was nobody there. He looked round the room, and under the table, and a great many times behind him, but there was certainly nobody there, and he sat down again at the window. This time he didn't speak, but he couldn't help thinking again that it would be very convenient if the river were really all gold.

"Not at all, my boy," said the same voice, louder than before.

"Bless me!" said Gluck again, "what *is* that?" He looked again into all the corners and cupboards, and then began turning round and round, as fast as he could, in the middle of the room, thinking there was somebody behind him, when the same voice struck again on his ear. It was singing now very merrily "Lala-lira-la"; no words, only a soft running effervescent melody, something like that of a kettle on the boil. Gluck looked out of the window. No, it was certainly in the house. Upstairs, and downstairs. No, it was certainly in that very room, coming in quicker time, and clearer notes, every moment: "Lala-lira-la." All at once it struck Gluck that it sounded louder near the furnace. He ran to the opening, and looked in; yes, he saw right, it seemed to be coming, not only out of the furnace, but out of the pot. He uncovered it, and ran back in a great fright, for the pot was certainly singing. He stood in the farthest corner of the room, with his hands up, and his mouth open, for a minute or two, when the singing stopped, and the voice became clear, and pronunciative.

"Hollo!" said the voice.

Gluck made no answer.

"Hollo! Gluck, my boy," said the pot again.

Gluck summoned all his energies, walked straight up to the crucible, drew it out of the furnace, and looked in. The gold was all melted, and its surface as smooth and polished as a river; but instead of reflecting little Gluck's head, as he looked in, he saw meeting his glance, from beneath the gold, the red nose and sharp eyes of his old friend of the mug, a thousand times redder and sharper than ever he had seen them in his life.

"Come, Gluck, my boy," said the voice out of the pot again, "I'm all right; pour me out."

But Gluck was too much astonished to do anything of the kind.

"Pour me out, I say," said the voice, rather gruffly. Still Gluck couldn't move

"*Will* you pour me out?" said the voice, passionately; "I'm too hot."

By a violent effort, Gluck recovered the use of his limbs, took hold of the crucible, and sloped it, so as to pour out the gold. But instead of a liquid stream, there came out, first, a pair of pretty little yellow legs, then some coat tails, then a pair of arms stuck akimbo, and, finally, the well-known head of his friend of the mug; all which articles, uniting as they rolled out, stood up energetically on the floor, in the shape of a little golden dwarf, about a foot and a half high.

"That's right!" said the dwarf, stretching out first his legs, and then his arms, and then shaking his head up and down, and as far round as it would go, for five minutes, without stopping; apparently with the view of ascertaining if he were quite correctly put together, while Gluck stood contemplating him in speechless amazement. He was dressed in a slashed doublet of spun gold, so fine in its texture that the prismatic colors gleamed over it, as if on a surface of mother-of-pearl; and, over this brilliant doublet, his hair and beard fell full half-way to the ground, in

waving curls, so exquisitely delicate that Gluck could hardly tell where they ended; they seemed to melt into air. The features of the face, however, were by no means finished with the same delicacy; they were rather coarse, slightly inclining to coppery in complexion, and indicative, in expression, of a very pertinacious and intractable disposition in their small proprietor. When the dwarf had finished his self-examination, he turned his small sharp eyes full on Gluck, and stared at him deliberately for a minute or two. "No, it wouldn't, Gluck, my boy," said the little man.

This was certainly rather an abrupt and unconnected mode of commencing conversation. It might indeed be supposed to refer to the course of Gluck's thoughts, which had first produced the dwarf's observations out of the pot; but whatever it referred to, Gluck had no inclination to dispute the dictum.

"Wouldn't it, sir?" said Gluck, very mildly and submissively indeed.

"No," said the dwarf, conclusively. "No, it wouldn't." And with that the dwarf pulled his cap hard over his brows, and took two turns of three feet long, up and down the room, lifting his legs up very high, and setting them down very hard. This pause gave time for Gluck to collect his thoughts a little, and, seeing no great reason to view his diminutive visitor with dread, and feeling his curiosity overcome his amazement, he ventured on a question of peculiar delicacy.

"Pray, sir," said Gluck, rather hesitatingly, "were you my mug?"

On which the little man turned sharp round, walked straight up to Gluck, and drew himself up to his full height. "I," said the little man, "am the King of the Golden River." Whereupon he turned about again, and took two more turns, some six feet long, in order to allow time for the consternation which this announcement produced in his auditor to evaporate. After which he again walked up to Gluck, and stood still, as if expecting some comment on his communication.

Gluck determined to say something at all events. "I hope Your Majesty is very well," said Gluck.

"Listen!" said the little man, deigning no reply to this polite inquiry. "I am the King of what you mortals call the Golden River. The shape you saw me in was owing to the malice of a stronger king, from whose enchantments you have this instant freed me. What I have seen of you, and your conduct to your wicked brothers, renders me willing to serve you; therefore attend to what I tell you. Whoever shall climb to the top of that mountain from which you see the Golden River issue, and shall cast into the stream at its source three drops of holy water, for him, and for him only, the river shall turn to gold. But no one failing in his first, can succeed in a second, attempt; and if anyone shall cast unholy water into the river, it will overwhelm him, and he will become a black stone." So saying, the King of the Golden River turned away, and deliberately walked into the center of the hottest flame of the furnace. His figure became red, white, transparent, dazzling —a blaze of intense light—rose, trembled and disappeared. The King of the Golden River had evaporated.

"Oh!" cried poor Gluck, running to look up the chimney after him; "oh, dear, dear, dear me! My mug! my mug! my mug!"

Chapter III

THE KING of the Golden River had hardly made the extraordinary exit related in the last chapter, before Hans and Schwartz came roaring into the house very savagely drunk. The discovery of the total loss of their last piece of plate had the effect of sobering them just enough to enable them to stand over Gluck, beating him very steadily for a quarter of an hour; at the expiration of which period they dropped into a couple of chairs, and requested to know what he had to say for himself. Gluck told them his story, of which of course they did not believe a word. They beat him again, till their arms were tired, and staggered to bed. In the morning, however, the steadiness with which he adhered to his story obtained him some degree of credence; the immediate consequence of which was, that the two brothers, after wrangling a long time on the knotty question, which of them should try his fortune first, drew their swords, and began fighting. The noise of the fray alarmed the neighbors, who, finding they could not pacify the combatants, sent for the constable.

Hans, on hearing this, contrived to escape, and hid himself; but Schwartz was taken before the magistrate, fined for breaking the peace, and, having drunk out his last penny the evening before, was thrown into prison till he should pay.

When Hans heard this, he was much delighted, and determined to set out immediately for the Golden River. How to get the holy water was the question. He went to the priest, but the priest could not give any holy water to so abandoned a character. So Hans went to vespers in the evening for the first time in his life, and, under pretense of crossing himself, stole a cupful, and returned home in triumph.

Next morning he got up before the sun rose, put the holy water into a strong flask, and two bottles of wine and some meat in a basket, slung them over his back, took his alpine staff in his hand, and set off for the mountains.

On his way out of the town he had to pass the prison, and as he looked in at the windows, whom should he see but Schwartz himself peeping out of the bars, and looking very disconsolate.

"Good morning, brother," said Hans; "have you any message for the King of the Golden River?"

Schwartz only gnashed his teeth with rage, and shook the bars with all his strength; but Hans only laughed at him, and advised him to make himself comfortable till he came back again, shouldered his basket, shook the bottle of holy water in Schwartz's face till it frothed again, and marched off in the highest spirits in the world.

It was, indeed, a morning that might have made anyone happy, even with no Golden River to seek for. Level lines of dewy mist lay stretched along the valley, out of which rose the massy mountains—their lower cliffs in pale gray shadow, hardly distinguishable from the floating vapor, but gradually ascending till they caught the sunlight, which ran in sharp touches of ruddy color along the angular crags, and pierced, in long level rays, through their fringes of spear-like pine. Far above shot up red splintered masses of castellated rock, jagged and shivered into myriads of fantastic forms, with here and there a streak of sunlit snow, traced down their chasms like a line of forked lightning; and, far beyond, and far above all these, fainter than the morning cloud, but purer and changeless, slept, in the blue sky, the utmost peaks of the eternal snow.

The Golden River, which sprang from one of the lower and snowless elevations, was now nearly in shadow; all but the uppermost jets of spray, which rose like slow smoke above the undulating line of the cataract, and floated away in feeble wreaths upon the morning wind.

On this object, and on this alone, Hans' eyes and thought were fixed; forgetting the distance he had to traverse, he set off at an imprudent rate of walking, which greatly exhausted him before he had scaled the first range of the green and low hills. He was, moreover, surprised, on surmounting them, to find that a large glacier, of whose existence, notwithstanding his previous knowledge of the mountains, he had been absolutely ignorant, lay between him and the source of the Golden River. He entered on it with the boldness of a practiced mountaineer; yet he thought he had never traversed so strange or so dangerous a glacier in his life. The ice was excessively slippery, and out of all its chasms came wild sounds of gushing water; not monotonous or low, but changeful and loud, rising occasionally into drifting passages of wild melody, then breaking off into short melancholy tones, or sudden shrieks, resembling those of human voices in distress or pain. The ice was broken into thousands of confused shapes, but none, Hans thought, like the ordinary forms of splintered ice. There seemed a curious *expression* about all

341

their outlines — a perpetual resemblance to living features, distorted and scornful. Myriads of deceitful shadows and lurid lights played and floated about and through the pale blue pinnacles, dazzling and confusing the sight of the traveler; while his ears grew dull and his head giddy with the constant gush and roar of the concealed waters. These painful circumstances increased upon him as he advanced; the ice crashed and yawned into fresh chasms at his feet, tottering spires nodded around him, and fell thundering across his path; and though he had repeatedly faced these dangers on the most terrific glaciers, and in the wildest weather, it was with a new and oppressive feeling of panic terror that he leaped the last chasm, and flung himself, exhausted and shuddering, on the firm turf of the mountain.

He had been compelled to abandon his basket of food, which became a perilous incumbrance on the glacier, and had no means of refreshing himself but by breaking off and eating some of the pieces of ice. This, however, relieved his thirst; an hour's repose recruited his hardy frame, and with the indomitable spirit of avarice he resumed his laborious journey.

His way now lay straight up a ridge of bare red rocks, without a blade of grass to ease the foot, or a projecting angle to afford an inch of shade from the south sun. It was past noon, and the rays beat intensely upon the steep path, while the whole atmosphere was motionless, and penetrated with heat. Intense thirst was soon added to the bodily fatigue with which Hans was now afflicted; glance after glance he cast on the flask of water which hung at his belt. "Three drops are

enough," at last thought he; "I may, at least, cool my lips with it."

He opened the flask, and was raising it to his lips when his eyes fell on an object lying on the rock beside him; he thought it moved. It was a small dog, apparently in the last agony of death from thirst. Its tongue was out, its jaws dry, its limbs extended lifelessly, and a swarm of black ants were crawling about its lips and throat. Its eye moved to the bottle which Hans held in his hand. He raised it, drank, spurned the animal with his foot, and passed on. And he did not know how it was, but he thought that a strange shadow had suddenly come across the blue sky.

The path became steeper and more rugged every moment; and the high hill air, instead of refreshing him, seemed to throw his blood into a fever. The noise of the hill cataracts sounded like mockery in his ears; they were all distant, and his thirst increased every moment. Another hour passed, and he again looked down to the flask at his side; it was half empty, but there was much more than three drops in it. He stopped to open it, and again, as he did so, something moved in the path above him. It was a fair child, stretched nearly lifeless on the rock, its breast heaving with thirst, its eyes closed, and its lips parched and burning. Hans eyed it deliberately, drank, and passed on. And a dark gray cloud came over the sun, and long, snake-like shadows crept up along the mountain sides. Hans struggled on. The sun was sinking, but its descent seemed to bring no coolness; the leaden weight of the dead air pressed upon his brow and heart, but the goal was near. He saw the cataract of the Golden River springing from the hill-side, scarcely five hundred feet above him. He paused for a moment to breathe, and sprang on to complete his task.

At this instant a faint cry fell on his ear. He turned, and saw a gray-haired old man extended on the rocks. His eyes were sunk, his features deadly pale, and gathered into an expression of despair. "Water!" he stretched his arms to Hans and cried, feebly: "Water! I am dying."

"I have none," replied Hans; "thou hast had thy share of life." He strode over the prostrate body, and darted on. And a flash of blue lightning rose out of the east, shaped like a sword; it shook thrice over the whole heaven, and left it dark with one heavy, impenetrable shade. The sun was setting; it plunged towards the horizon like a red-hot ball.

The roar of the Golden River rose on Hans' ear. He stood at the brink of the chasm through which it ran. Its waves were filled with the red glory of the sunset; they shook their crests like tongues of fire, and flashes of bloody light gleamed along their foam. Their sound came mightier and mightier on his senses; his brain grew giddy with the prolonged thunder. Shuddering, he drew the flask from his girdle and hurled it into the center of the torrent. As he did so, an icy chill shot through his limbs; he staggered, shrieked, and fell. The waters closed over his cry. And the moaning of the river rose wildly into the night, as it gushed over THE BLACK STONE.

Chapter IV

POOR LITTLE GLUCK waited very anxiously alone in the house for Hans' return. Finding he did not come back, he was terribly frightened, and went and told Schwartz in the prison all that had happened. Then Schwartz was very much pleased, and said that Hans must certainly have been turned into a black stone, and he should have all the gold to himself. But Gluck was very sorry, and cried all night. When he got up in the morning, there was no bread in the house, nor any money; so Gluck went and hired himself to another goldsmith, and he worked so hard, and so neatly, and so long every day, that he soon got money enough together to pay his brother's fine, and he went, and gave it all to Schwartz, and Schwartz got out of prison. Then Schwartz was quite pleased, and said he should have some of the gold of the river. But Gluck only begged he would go and see what had become of Hans.

Now when Schwartz had heard that Hans had stolen the holy water, he thought to himself that such a proceeding might not be considered altogether correct by the King of the Golden River, and determined to manage matters better. So he took some more of Gluck's money, and went to a bad priest, who gave him some holy water very readily for it. Then Schwartz was sure it was all quite right. So Schwartz got up early in the morning before the sun rose, and took some bread and wine, in a basket, and put his holy water in a flask, and set off for the mountains. Like his brother, he was much surprised at the sight of the glacier, and had great difficulty in crossing it, even after leaving his basket behind him. The day was cloudless, but not bright; there was a heavy purple haze hanging over the sky, and the hills looked lowering and gloomy. And as Schwartz climbed the steep rock path, the thirst came upon him, as it had upon his brother, until he lifted his flask to his lips to drink. Then he saw the fair child lying near him on the rocks, and it cried to him, and moaned for water.

"Water, indeed," said Schwartz; "I haven't half enough for myself," and passed on. And as he went he thought the sunbeams grew more dim, and he saw a low bank of black cloud rising out of the west; and, when he had climbed for another hour, the thirst overcame him again, and he would have drunk. Then he saw the old man lying before him on the path, and heard him cry out for water. "Water, indeed," said Schwartz, "I haven't half enough for myself," and on he went.

Then again the light seemed to fade from before his eyes, and he looked up, and, behold, a mist, of the color of blood, had come over the sun; and the bank of black cloud had risen very high, and its edges were tossing and tumbling like the waves of an angry sea. And they cast long shadows, which flickered over Schwartz's path.

Then Schwartz climbed for another hour, and again his thirst returned; and as he lifted his flask to his lips, he thought he saw his brother Hans lying exhausted on the path before him, and, as he gazed, the figure stretched its arms to him, and cried for water. "Ha, ha," laughed Schwartz, "are you there? Remember the prison bars, my boy. Water, indeed! do you suppose I carried it all the way up here for *you?*" And he strode over the figure; yet, as he passed, he thought he saw a strange expression of mockery about its lips. And, when he had gone a few yards farther, he looked back; but the figure was not there.

And a sudden horror came over Schwartz, he knew not why; but the thirst for gold prevailed over his fear, and he rushed on. And the bank of black cloud rose to the zenith, and out of it came bursts of spiry lightning, and waves of darkness seemed to heave and float between their flashes over the whole heavens. And the sky where the sun was setting was all level, and like a lake of blood; and a strong wind came out of that sky, tearing its crimson clouds into fragments, and scattering them far into the darkness. And when Schwartz stood by the brink of the Golden River, its waves were black, like thunder-clouds, but their foam was like fire; and the roar of the waters below and the thunder above met, as he cast the flask into the stream. And, as he did so, the lightning glared in his eyes, and the earth gave way beneath him, and the waters closed over his cry. And the moaning of the river rose wildly into the night, as it gushed over the

TWO BLACK STONES.

Chapter V

WHEN GLUCK found that Schwartz did not come back, he was very sorry, and did not know what to do. He had no money, and was obliged to go and hire himself again to the goldsmith, who worked him very hard, and gave him very little money. So, after a month or two, Gluck grew tired and made up his mind to go and try his fortune with the Golden River. "The little king looked very kind," thought he. "I don't think he will turn me into a black stone." So he went to the priest, and the priest gave him some holy water as soon as he asked for it. Then

Gluck took some bread in his basket, and the bottle of water, and set off very early for the mountains.

If the glacier had occasioned a great deal of fatigue to his brothers, it was twenty times worse for him, who was neither so strong nor so practiced on the mountains. He had several very bad falls, lost his basket and bread, and was very much frightened at the strange noises under the ice. He lay a long time to rest on the grass, after he had got over, and began to climb the hill just in the hottest part of the day. When he had climbed for an hour he got dreadfully thirsty, and was going to drink, like his brothers, when he saw an old man coming down the path above him, looking very feeble, and leaning on a staff. "My son," said the old man, "I am faint with thirst, give me some of that water." Then Gluck looked at him, and when he saw that he was pale and weary, he gave him the water. "Only pray don't drink it all," said Gluck. But the old man drank a great deal, and gave him back the bottle two-thirds empty. Then he bade him good speed, and Gluck went on again merrily. And the path became easier to his feet, and two or three blades of grass appeared upon it, and some grasshoppers began singing on the bank beside it; and Gluck thought he had never heard such merry singing.

Then he went on for another hour, and the thirst increased on him so that he thought he should be forced to drink. But, as he raised the flask, he saw a little child lying panting by the road-side, and it cried out piteously for water. Then Gluck struggled with himself, and determined to bear the thirst a little longer; and he put the bottle to the child's lips, and it drank all but a few drops. Then it smiled on him, and got up, and ran down the hill; and Gluck looked after it, till it became as small as a little star, and then turned, and began climbing again. And then there were all kinds of sweet flowers growing on the rocks, bright green moss, with pale-pink starry flowers, and soft belled gentians, more blue than the sky at its deepest, and pure white transparent lilies. And crimson and purple butterflies darted hither and thither, and the sky sent down such pure light that Gluck had never felt so happy in his life.

Yet, when he had climbed for another hour, his thirst became intolerable again; and when he looked at his bottle he saw that there were only five or six drops left in it, and he could not venture to drink. As he was hanging the flask to his belt again, he saw a little dog lying on the rocks, gasping for breath — just as Hans had seen it on the day of his ascent. And Gluck stopped and looked at it, and then at the Golden River, not five hundred yards above him; and he thought of the dwarf's words, "that no one could succeed, except in his first attempt"; and he tried to pass the dog, but it whined piteously, and Gluck stopped again. "Poor beastie," said Gluck, "it'll be dead when I come down again if I don't help it." Then he looked closer and closer at it, and its eye turned on him so mournfully that he could not stand it. "Confound the King and his gold too," said Gluck; and he opened the flask and poured all the water into the dog's mouth.

The dog sprang up and stood on its hind legs. Its tail disappeared, its ears became long, longer, silky, golden; its nose became very red; its eyes became

very twinkling; in three seconds the dog
was gone, and before Gluck stood his old
acquaintance, the King of the Golden
River.

"Thank you," said the monarch; "but
don't be frightened, it's all right;" for
Gluck showed manifest symptoms of consternation at this unlooked-for reply to
his last observation. "Why didn't you
come before," continued the dwarf, "instead of sending me those rascally brothers of yours, for me to have the trouble
of turning into stones? Very hard stones
they make too."

"Oh, dear me!" said Gluck, "have you
really been so cruel?"

"Cruel!" said the dwarf. "They poured
unholy water into my stream; do you suppose I'm going to allow that?"

"Why," said Gluck, "I am sure, sir—
Your Majesty, I mean—they got the water
out of the church font."

"Very probably," replied the dwarf;
"but," and his countenance grew stern as
he spoke, "the water which has been refused to the cry of the weary and dying
is unholy, though it had been blessed by
every saint in heaven; and the water
which is found in the vessel of mercy is
holy, though it had been defiled with
corpses."

So saying, the dwarf stooped and
plucked a lily that grew at his feet. On
its white leaves there hung three drops
of clear dew. And the dwarf shook them
into the flask which Gluck held in his
hand. "Cast these into the river," he said,
"and descend on the other side of the
mountains into the Treasure Valley. And
so good speed."

As he spoke, the figure of the dwarf
became indistinct. The playing colors of
his robe formed themselves into a prismatic mist of dewy light; he stood for an
instant veiled with them as with the belt
of a broad rainbow. The colors grew faint,
the mist rose into the air; the monarch
had evaporated.

And Gluck climbed to the brink of the
Golden River, and its waves were as clear

as crystal, and as brilliant as the sun. And when he cast the three drops of dew into the stream, there opened where they fell a small circular whirlpool, into which the waters descended with a musical noise.

Gluck stood watching it for some time, very much disappointed, because not only the river was not turned into gold, but its waters seemed much diminished in quantity. Yet he obeyed his friend the dwarf, and descended the other side of the mountains, toward the Treasure Valley; and, as he went, he thought he heard the noise of water working its way under the ground. And, when he came in sight of the Treasure Valley, behold, a river like the Golden River was springing from a new cleft of the rocks above it, and was flowing in innumerable streams among the dry heaps of red sand.

And as Gluck gazed, fresh grass sprang beside the new streams, and creeping plants grew and climbed among the moistening soil. Young flowers opened suddenly along the river sides, as stars leap out when twilight is deepening, and thickets of myrtle and tendrils of vine cast lengthening shadows over the valley as they grew. And thus the Treasure Valley became a garden again, and the inheritance, which had been lost by cruelty, was regained by love.

And Gluck went and dwelt in the valley, and the poor were never driven from his door; so that his barns became full of corn, and his house of treasure. And, for him, the river had, according to the dwarf's promise, become a River of Gold.

And, to this day, the inhabitants of the valley point out the place where the three drops of holy dew were cast into the stream, and trace the course of the Golden River under the ground until it emerges in the Treasure Valley. And at the top of the cataract of the Golden River are still to be seen TWO BLACK STONES, round which the waters howl mournfully every day at sunset; and these stones are still called by the people of the valley THE BLACK BROTHERS.

In his famous novels, Charles Dickens created characters
humorous and humane, like
Oliver Twist and David Copperfield,
who are as familiar to us as any characters in literature.
Dickens was devoted to simple people
and was a champion of the poor and oppressed.
Even in so light a fairy tale as "The Magic Fishbone,"
he pictured a family with many children and
too little means to support them.
The ironical story is a curious combination of
real life drudgery and fairy tale elements
that might well be in the daydreams of a girl like Alicia.
In her imagination Alicia is a true Princess,
her humble family is a royal one—
and, of course, she has a fairy godmother.

The Magic Fishbone

BY CHARLES DICKENS
Illustrated by W. T. MARS

THERE was once a king, and he had a queen. They had nineteen children and were always having more. Seventeen of the children took care of the baby; and Alicia, the eldest, took care of them all. Their ages varied from seven years to seven months.

One day the king was going to the office, when he stopped at Mr. Pickle's, the fishmonger's, to buy a pound and a half of salmon not too near the tail.

The king then went on towards the office in a melancholy mood, for payday was such a long way off, and his children were growing out of their clothes.

Just then a rich-looking old lady came trotting up.

"King Watkins the First, I believe?" said the old lady.

"Watkins," replied the king, "is my name."

"Listen. You are going to the office," said the old lady.

It instantly flashed upon the king that she must be a fairy, or how could she know that?

"You are right," said the old lady, answering his thoughts. "I am the good Fairy Grandmarina. Listen! When you return home to dinner, politely invite the Princess Alicia to have some of the salmon you bought just now. Then she will leave a fishbone on her plate. Tell her to dry it, and to rub it, and to polish it, till it shines like mother-of-pearl, and to take care of it as a present from me.

"Tell the Princess Alicia," said the fairy, "that the fishbone is a magic present which can only be used once; but that it will bring her, just once, whatever she wishes for, provided she wishes for it at the right time."

With those words, Grandmarina vanished, and the king went on and on, till he came to the office. There he wrote and wrote and wrote, till it was time to go home.

Then he invited the Princess Alicia, as the fairy had directed him, to eat some salmon. And when she had enjoyed it very much, he saw the fishbone on her plate, and he delivered the fairy's message, and the Princess Alicia took care to dry the bone, and to rub it, and to polish it, till it shone like mother-of-pearl.

And so, when the queen was going to get up in the morning, she said, "Oh, dear me, dear me, my head, my head!" and then she fainted away.

The Princess Alicia was very much alarmed when she saw her royal mamma in this state, and she rang the bell for Peggy, which was the name of the lord chamberlain. But remembering where the smelling-bottle was, she climbed on a chair and got it; and after that she climbed on another chair by the bedside, and held the smelling-bottle to the queen's nose; and after that she got some water and wet the queen's forehead; and, in short, when the lord chamberlain came in, that dear old woman said to the little princess, "I couldn't have done it better myself!"

But that was not the worst of the good queen's illness. Oh, no! She was very ill indeed, for a long time. The Princess Alicia kept the seventeen young princes and princesses quiet, and dressed and undressed the baby, and made the kettle boil, and heated the soup, and swept the hearth, and poured out the medicine, and nursed the queen. For there were not many servants at that palace for three reasons: because the king was short of money, because a raise in his salary never seemed to come, and because payday was far off.

But on the morning when the queen fainted away, where was the magic fishbone? Why, there it was in the Princess Alicia's pocket! She had almost taken it out to bring the queen to life again, when she put it back, and looked for the smelling-bottle.

After the queen had come out of her swoon, the Princess Alicia hurried upstairs to tell a secret to her friend the duchess. People thought she was a doll, but Alicia knew she was really a duchess.

"Alicia," said the king, one evening, when she wished him good night.

"Yes, Papa."

"What is become of the magic fishbone?"

"In my pocket, Papa."

"I thought you had lost it?"

"Oh, no, Papa!"

"Or forgotten it?"

"No, indeed, Papa."

And so another time the little snapping dog, next door, made a rush at one of the young princes, and he put his hand through a pane of glass, and bled, bled, bled. Then the sixteen other young princes and princesses saw him and screamed themselves black in their sixteen faces all at once.

But the Princess Alicia put her hands over all their sixteen mouths, one after another, and persuaded them to be quiet because of the sick queen. And then she put the wounded prince's hand in a basin of cold water.

Then she said to two chubby-legged princes, "Bring me in the royal rag-bag: I must snip and stitch and cut and contrive." So these two young princes tugged at the royal rag-bag, and she made a bandage, and it fitted beautifully; and so when it was all done, she saw the king, her papa, looking on by the door.

"Alicia."

"Yes, Papa."

"Where is the magic fishbone?"

"In my pocket, Papa."

"I thought you had lost it?"

"Oh, no, Papa!"

"Or forgotten it?"

"No, indeed, Papa."

After that, she ran upstairs to the duchess, and told her what had happened, and told her the secret over again; and the duchess shook her flaxen curls and laughed with her rosy lips.

Well! and so another time the baby fell under the grate, and it gave him a swelled face and a black eye.

The way the poor little darling came to tumble was that he was out of the Princess Alicia's lap just as she was beginning to peel the turnips for the broth for dinner; and the way she came to be doing that was, that the king's cook had run away that morning with her own true love, who was a very tall but very tipsy soldier.

Then the seventeen young princes and princesses, who cried at everything that happened, cried and roared. But the Princess Alicia (who couldn't help crying a little herself) said, "Hold your tongues, you wicked little monkeys, every one of you, while I examine the baby."

Then she examined the baby, and found that he hadn't broken anything, and she held a cold cloth to his poor dear eye, and he presently fell asleep in her arms.

Then she said to the seventeen princes and princesses, "I am afraid to let him down yet, lest he should wake and feel pain; be good and you shall all be cooks."

They jumped for joy when they heard that, and began making themselves cooks' caps out of old newspapers. So to one she gave the salt-box, and to one she gave the barley, and to one she gave the herbs, and to one she gave the turnips, and to one she gave the carrots, and to one she gave the onions, and to one she gave the spice-box, till they were all cooks, and all running about at work, she sitting in the middle smothered in the great coarse apron, nursing baby.

By and by the broth was done; and the baby woke up, smiling like an angel, and was trusted to the sedatest princess to hold.

When the broth came tumbling out, steaming beautifully, and smelling like a nosegay good to eat, they clapped their hands. That made the baby clap his hands; and that, and his looking as if he

had a comic toothache, made all the princes and princesses laugh.

So the Princess Alicia said, "Laugh and be good; and after dinner we will make him a nest on the floor in a corner, and he shall sit in his nest and see a dance of eighteen cooks." That delighted the young princes and princesses, and they ate up all the broth, and washed up all the plates and dishes, and cleared away, and pushed the table into a corner; and then they in their cooks' caps and the Princess Alicia in her apron danced a dance of eighteen cooks before the angelic baby.

And so then, once more the Princess Alicia saw King Watkins the First, her father, standing in the doorway looking on, and he said, "Where is the magic fishbone, Alicia?"

"In my pocket, Papa."

"I thought you had lost it?"

"Oh, no, Papa!"

"Or forgotten it?"

"No, indeed, Papa."

The king then sighed so heavily, and seemed so low-spirited, that the seventeen princes and princesses crept softly out of the kitchen, and left him alone with the Princess Alicia and the angelic baby.

"What is the matter, Papa?"

"I am dreadfully poor, my child."

"Have you no money at all, Papa?"

"None, my child."

"Is there no way of getting any, Papa?"

"No way," said the king.

"Papa," said she, "when we have tried very hard, and tried all ways, we must have done our very, very best. And when we have done our very, very best, Papa, and that is not enough, then I think the

right time must have come for asking help of others."

This was the very secret connected with the magic fishbone, which she had found out for herself from the good Fairy Grandmarina's words, and which she had so often whispered to her beautiful and fashionable doll, the duchess.

So she took out of her pocket the magic fishbone that had been dried and rubbed and polished till it shone like mother-of-pearl; and she gave it one little kiss and wished it was payday. And immediately it was payday; and the king's salary came rattling down the chimney, and bounced into the middle of the floor.

Immediately afterwards the good Fairy Grandmarina came riding in, in a carriage and four (peacocks), with Mr. Pickle's boy up behind, dressed in silver and gold, with a cocked hat, powdered hair, pink silk stockings, a jewelled cane, and a nosegay.

The Princess Alicia embraced her; and then Grandmarina turned to the king, and said rather sharply, "Are you good?"

The king said he hoped so.

"I suppose you know the reason now why my goddaughter here," kissing the princess again, "did not apply to the fishbone sooner?" said the fairy.

The king made a shy bow.

"Ah! but you didn't then?" said the fairy.

The king made a shyer bow.

"Any more questions to ask?" said the fairy.

The king said no, and he was very sorry.

"Be good, then," said the fairy, "and live happy ever afterwards."

Then Grandmarina waved her fan, and the queen came in most splendidly dressed; and the seventeen young princes and princesses came in, newly fitted out from top to toe, with tucks in everything to admit of its being let out.

After that, the fairy tapped the Princess Alicia with her fan.The smothering coarse apron flew away, and she appeared exquisitely dressed, like a little bride, with a wreath of orange blossoms and a silver veil.

After that, the kitchen dresser changed of itself into a wardrobe, made of beautiful woods and gold and looking glass, which was full of dresses of all sorts, all for her and all exactly fitting her. After that, the angelic baby came in running alone, with his face and eye not a bit worse, but much the better.

A little whispering took place between the fairy and the duchess; and then the fairy said out loud, "Yes, I thought she would have told you." Grandmarina then turned to the king and queen, and said, "We are going in search of Prince Certainpersonio. The pleasure of your company is requested at church in half an hour precisely."

So she and the Princess Alicia got into the carriage; and Mr. Pickle's boy handed in the duchess, who sat by herself on the opposite seat; and then Mr. Pickle's boy put up the steps and got up behind, and peacocks flew away with their tails behind.

Prince Certainpersonio was sitting by himself, eating barley-sugar, and waiting to be ninety. When he saw the peacocks, followed by the carriage, coming in at the window he knew something unusual was going to happen.

"Prince," said Grandmarina, "I bring you your bride."

The moment the fairy said those words, Prince Certainpersonio's face left off being sticky, and his jacket and corduroys changed into peach-bloom velvet, and his hair curled, and a cap and feather flew in like a bird and settled on his head. He got into the carriage by the fairy's invitation and smiled at the duchess, whom he had seen before.

The marriage in the church was ever so beautiful! The duchess was bridesmaid and looked on at the ceremony from the pulpit, where she was propped up by the cushion of the desk.

Grandmarina gave a magnificent wedding-feast afterwards. The wedding-cake was delicately ornamented with white satin ribbons, frosted silver, and white lilies, and was forty-two yards round.

When Grandmarina had drunk a toast to the young people, and Prince Certainpersonio had made a speech, and everybody had cried, "Hip, hip, hip, hurrah!" Grandmarina announced to the king and the queen that in the future there would be eight paydays every year, except in leap year, when there would be ten.

She then turned to Certainpersonio and Alicia, and said, "My dears, you will have thirty-five children, and they will all be good and beautiful. Seventeen of your children will be boys, and eighteen will be girls. They will never have the measles and will have recovered from the whooping cough before being born."

"It only remains," said Grandmarina in conclusion, "to make an end of the fish-bone."

So she took it from the hand of the Princess Alicia, and it instantly vanished, before it could possibly be snapped up by the little pugdog next door.

The stories known as **The Arabian Nights**
are supposed to have been told by a queen named Scheherazade
in order to save her life. Her husband, the king,
had been deceived by his first wife and had vowed
to marry another woman every night and have her killed
the very next morning. On her wedding night,
Scheherazade began to tell the king a story,
but did not finish it.
The king was so eager to hear
the end of it that he postponed her execution.
The second night, Scheherazade finished the story
and began a second one, which she also left uncompleted.
This she cleverly continued to do for one thousand and one nights
—the collection is sometimes called
"The Book of the Thousand Nights and One Night"
—at the end of which time the king
was so delighted with her that he never
again referred to his fatal vow.
"The Story of the Enchanted Horse"
is one of the least known but most
marvelous of these stories.

355

The Story of the Enchanted Horse

From The Arabian Nights

Illustrated by ROBERT J. LEE

ON THE FESTIVAL of the Nooroze, which is the first day of the year and of spring, the Sultan of Shiraz was just concluding his public audience, when a Hindu appeared at the foot of the throne with an artificial horse, so spiritedly modeled that at first sight he was taken for a living animal.

The Hindu prostrated himself before the throne, and pointing to the horse, said to the Sultan, "This horse is a great wonder; if I wish to be transported to the most distant parts of the earth, I have only to mount him. I offer to show your Majesty this wonder if you command me."

The Sultan, who was very fond of everything that was curious, and who had never beheld or heard anything quite so strange as this, told the Hindu that he would like to see him perform what he had promised.

The Hindu at once put his foot into the stirrup, swung himself into the saddle, and asked the Sultan whither he wished him to go.

"Do you see yonder mountain?" said the Sultan, pointing to it. "Ride your horse there, and bring me a branch from the palm tree that grows at the foot of the hill."

No sooner had the Sultan spoken than the Hindu turned a peg, which was in the hollow of the horse's neck, just by the pommel of the saddle. Instantly the horse rose from the ground, and bore his rider into the air with the speed of lightning, to the amazement of the Sultan and all the spectators. Within less than a quarter of an hour they saw him returning with the palm branch in his hand. Alighting amidst the acclamations of the people, he dismounted and, approaching the throne, laid the palm branch at the Sultan's feet.

The Sultan, still marveling at this unheard-of sight, was filled with a great desire to possess the horse, and said to the Hindu, "I will buy him of you, if he is for sale."

"Sire," replied the Hindu, "there is only one condition on which I will part with my horse, namely, the hand of the Princess, your daugher, as my wife."

The courtiers surrounding the Sultan's throne could not restrain their laughter at the Hindu's extravagant proposal. But Prince Feroze Shah, the Sultan's eldest son, was very indignant. "Sire," said he, "I hope that you will at once refuse this impudent demand, and not allow this miserable juggler to flatter himself for a moment with the hope of a marriage with one of the most powerful houses in the world. Think what you owe to yourself and to your noble blood!"

"My son," replied the Sultan, "I will not grant him what he asks. But putting my daughter the Princess out of the question, I may make a different bargain with him. First, however, I wish you to examine the horse; try him yourself, and tell me what you think of him."

On hearing this the Hindu eagerly ran forward to help the Prince mount, and show him how to guide and manage the horse. But without waiting for the Hindu's assistance, the Prince mounted and turned the peg as he had seen the other do. Instantly the horse darted into the air, swift as an arrow shot from a bow; and in a few moments neither horse nor Prince could be seen. The Hindu, alarmed at what had happened, threw himself before the throne and begged the Sultan not to be angry.

"Your Majesty," he said, "saw as well as I with what speed the horse flew away. The surprise took away my power of speech. But even if I could have spoken to advise him, he was already too far away to hear me. There is still room to hope, however, that the Prince will discover that there is another peg, and as soon as he turns that, the horse will cease to rise, and will descend gently to the ground."

Notwithstanding these arguments the Sultan was much alarmed at his son's evident danger, and said to the Hindu, "Your head shall answer for my son's life, unless he returns safe in three months' time, or unless I hear that he is alive." He then ordered his officers to secure the Hindu and keep him a close prisoner; after which he retired to his palace, sorrowing that the Festival of Nooroze had ended so unluckily.

Meanwhile, the Prince was carried through the air with fearful rapidity. In less than an hour he had mounted so high that the mountains and plains below him all seemed to melt together. Then for the first time he began to think of returning, and to this end he began turning the peg, first one way and then the other, at the same time pulling upon the bridle. But when he found that the horse continued to ascend he was greatly alarmed, and deeply repented of his folly in not learning to guide the horse before he mounted. He now began to examine the horse's head and neck very carefully, and discovered behind the right ear a second peg, smaller than the first. He turned this peg and presently felt that he was descending in the same oblique manner as he had mounted, but not so swiftly.

Night was already approaching when the Prince discovered and turned the small peg; and as the horse descended he gradually lost sight of the sun's last setting rays, until presently it was quite dark. He was obliged to let the bridle hang loose, and wait patiently for the horse to choose his own landing place, whether it might be in the desert, in the river or in the sea.

At last, about midnight, the horse stopped upon solid ground, and the Prince dismounted, faint with hunger, for he had eaten nothing since the morning. He found himself on the terrace of a magnificent palace; and groping about, he presently reached a staircase which led down into an apartment, the door of which was half open.

The Prince stopped and listened at the door, then advanced cautiously into the room, and by the light of a lamp saw a number of black slaves, sleeping with their naked swords beside them. This was evidently the guard chamber of some Sultan or Princess. Advancing on tiptoe, he drew aside the curtain and saw a magnificent chamber, containing many beds, one of which was placed higher than the others on a raised dais—evidently the

beds of the Princess and her women. He crept softly toward the dais, and beheld a beauty so extraordinary that he was charmed at the first sight. He fell on his knees and gently twitched the sleeve of the Princess, who opened her eyes and was greatly surprised to see a handsome young man bending over her, yet showed no sign of fear. The Prince rose to his feet, and, bowing to the ground, said:

"Beautiful Princess, through a most extraordinary adventure you see at your feet a suppliant Prince, son of the Sultan of Persia, who prays for your assistance and protection."

In answer to this appeal of Prince Feroze Shah, the beautiful Princess said:

"Prince, you are not in a barbarous country, but in the kingdom of the Rajah of Bengal. This is his country estate, and I am his eldest daughter. I grant you the protection that you ask, and you may depend upon my word."

The Prince of Persia would have thanked the Princess, but she would not let him speak. "Impatient though I am," said she, "to know by what miracle you have come here from the capital of Persia, and by what enchantment you escaped the watchfulness of my guards, yet I will restrain my curiosity until later, after you have rested from your fatigue."

The Princess' women were much surprised to see a Prince in her bedchamber, but they at once prepared to obey her command, and conducted him into a handsome apartment. Here, while some prepared the bed, others brought and served a welcome and bountiful supper.

The next day the Princess prepared to receive the Prince, and took more pains in dressing and adorning herself than she ever had done before. She decked her neck, head and arms with the finest diamonds she possessed, and clothed herself in the richest fabric of the Indies, of a most beautiful color, and made only for Kings, Princes and Princesses. After once more consulting her glass, she sent word to the Prince of Persia that she would receive him.

The Prince, who had just finished dressing when he received the Princess' message, hastened to avail himself of the honor conferred on him. He told her of the wonders of the Enchanted Horse, of his wonderful journey through the air, and of the means by which he had gained entrance to her chamber. Then, after thanking her for her kind reception, he expressed a wish to return home and relieve the anxiety of the Sultan his father. The Princess replied, "I cannot approve, Prince, of your leaving so soon. Grant me the favor of a somewhat longer visit, so that you may take back to the court of Persia a better account of what you have seen in the Kingdom of Bengal."

The Prince could not well refuse the Princess this favor, after the kindness she had shown him; and she busied herself with plans for hunting parties, concerts and magnificent feasts to render his stay agreeable.

For two whole months the Prince of Persia abandoned himself entirely to the will of the Princess, who seemed to think that he had nothing to do but pass his whole life with her. But at last he declared that he could stay no longer, and begged leave to return to his father.

"And, Princess," he added, "if I were not afraid of giving offense, I would ask the favor of taking you along with me."

The Princess made no answer to this address of the Prince of Persia; but her silence and downcast eyes told him plainly that she had no reluctance to accompany him. Her only fear, she confessed, was that the Prince might not know well enough how to govern the horse. But the Prince soon removed her fear by assuring her that after the experience he had had, he defied the Hindu himself to manage the horse better. Accordingly they gave all their thoughts to

planning how to get away secretly from the palace, without anyone having a suspicion of their design.

The next morning, a little before daybreak, when all the attendants were still asleep, they made their way to the terrace of the palace. The Prince turned the horse toward Persia, and as soon as the Princess had mounted behind him and was well settled with her arms about his waist, he turned the peg, whereupon the horse mounted into the air with his accustomed speed, and in two hours' time they came in sight of the Persian capital.

Instead of alighting at the palace, the Prince directed his course to a kiosk a little distance outside the city. He led the Princess into a handsome apartment, ordered the attendants to provide her with whatever she needed, and told her that he would return immediately after in-

forming his father of their arrival. Thereupon he ordered a horse to be brought and set out for the palace.

The Sultan received his son with tears of joy, and listened eagerly while the Prince related his adventures during his flight through the air, his kind reception at the palace of the Princess of Bengal, and his long stay there due to their mutual affection. He added that, having promised to marry her, he had persuaded her to accompany him to Persia. "I brought her with me on the Enchanted Horse," he concluded, "and left her in your summer palace till I could return and assure her of your consent."

Upon hearing these words, the Sultan embraced his son a second time, and said to him, "My son, I not only consent to your marriage with the Princess of Bengal, but will myself go and bring her to

the palace, and your wedding shall be celebrated this very day."

The Sultan now ordered that the Hindu should be released from prison and brought before him. When this was done, the Sultan said, "I held you prisoner that your life might answer for that of the Prince my son. Thanks be to God, he has returned in safety. Go, take your horse, and never let me see your face again."

The Hindu had learned of those who brought him from prison, all about the Princess whom Prince Feroze Shah had brought with him and left at the kiosk, and at once he began to think of revenge. He mounted his horse and flew directly to the kiosk, where he told the Captain of the Guard that he came with orders to conduct the Princess of Bengal through the air to the Sultan, who awaited her in

the great square of his palace.

The Captain of the Guard, seeing that the Hindu had been released from prison, believed his story. And the Princess at once consented to do what the Prince, as she thought, desired of her.

The Hindu, overjoyed at the ease with which his wicked plan was succeeding, mounted his horse, took the Princess up behind him, turned the peg, and instantly the horse mounted into the air.

Meanwhile, the Sultan of Persia, attended by his court, was on the road to the kiosk where the Princess of Bengal had been left, while the Prince himself had hurried on ahead to prepare the Princess to receive his father. Suddenly the Hindu, to brave them both, and avenge himself for the ill-treatment he had received, appeared over their heads with his prize.

When the Sultan saw the Hindu, his surprise and anger were all the more keen because it was out of his power to punish his outrageous act. He could only stand and hurl a thousand maledictions at him, as did also the courtiers who had witnessed this unequaled piece of insolence. But the grief of Prince Feroze Shah was indescribable, when he beheld the Hindu bearing away the Princess who he loved so passionately. He made his way, melancholy and brokenhearted, to the kiosk where he had last taken leave of the Princess. Here, the Captain of the Guard, who had already learned of the Hindu's treachery, threw himself at the Prince's feet, and condemned himself to die by his own hand, because of his fatal credulity.

"Rise," said the Prince, "I blame, not you, but my own want of precaution, for the loss of my Princess. But lose no time, bring me a dervish's robe, and take care that you give no hint that it is for me."

When the Captain of the Guard had procured the dervish's robe, the Prince at once disguised himself in it, and taking with him a box of jewels, left the palace, resolved not to return until he had found his Princess or perish in the attempt.

Meanwhile, the Hindu, mounted on his Enchanted Horse, with the Princess behind him, arrived at the capital of the Kingdom of Cashmere. He did not enter the city, but alighted in a wood, and left the Princess on a grassy spot close to a rivulet of fresh water, while he went to seek food. On his return, and after he and the Princess had partaken of refreshment, he began to maltreat the Princess, because she refused to become his wife.

Now it happened that the Sultan of Cashmere and his court were passing through the wood on their return from hunting, and hearing a woman's voice calling for help, went to her rescue. The Hindu with great impudence asked what business anyone had to interfere, since the lady was his wife! Whereupon the Princess cried out:

"My Lord, whoever you are whom Heaven has sent to my assistance, have compassion on me! I am a Princess. This Hindu is a wicked magician who has forced me away from the Prince of Persia, whom I was to marry, and has brought me hither on the Enchanted Horse that you see there."

The Princess' beauty, majestic air, and tears all declared that she spoke the truth. Justly enraged at the Hindu's insolence, the Sultan of Cashmere ordered his guards to seize him and strike off his head, which sentence was immediately carried out.

The Princess' joy was unbounded at finding herself rescued from the wicked Hindu. She supposed that the Sultan of Cashmere would at once restore her to the Prince of Persia, but she was much deceived in these hopes. For her rescuer had resolved to marry her himself the next day, and issued a proclamation commanding the general rejoicing of the inhabitants.

The Princess of Bengal was awakened at break of day by drums and trumpets and sounds of joy throughout the palace, but was far from guessing the true cause. When the Sultan came to wait upon her, he explained that these rejoicings were in honor of their marriage, and begged her to consent to the union. On hearing this the Princess fainted away.

The serving-women who were present ran to her assistance, but it was long before they could bring her back to consciousness. When at last she recovered, she resolved that sooner than be forced to marry the Sultan of Cashmere she would pretend that she had gone mad. Accordingly she began to talk wildly, and show other signs of a disordered mind, even springing from her seat as if to attack the Sultan, so that he became greatly alarmed and sent for all the court physicians to ask if they could cure her of her disease.

When he found that his court physicians could not cure her, he sent for the most famous doctors in his kingdom, who had no better success. Next, he sent word to the courts of neighboring Sultans with promises of generous reward to anyone who could cure her malady. Physicians arrived from all parts, and tried their skill, but none could boast of success.

Meanwhile, Prince Feroze Shah, disguised as a dervish, traveled through many provinces and towns, everywhere inquiring about his lost Princess. At last in a certain city of Hindustan he learned of a Princess of Bengal who had gone mad on the day of her intended marriage with the Sultan of Cashmere. Convinced that there could be but one Princess of Bengal, he hastened to the capital of Cashmere and upon arriving was told the story of the Princess, and the fate of the Hindu magician. The Prince was now convinced that he had at last found the beloved object of his long search.

Providing himself with the distinctive dress of a physician, he went boldly to the palace and announced his wish to be allowed to attempt the cure of the Princess. Since it was now some time since any physician had offered himself, the Sultan had begun to lose hope of ever seeing the Princess cured, though he still wished to marry her. So he at once ordered the new physician to be brought before him; and upon the Prince being admitted, told him that the Princess could not bear the sight of a physician without falling into the most violent paroxysms. Accordingly he conducted the Prince to a closet from which he might see her through a lattice without himself being seen. There Feroze Shah beheld his lovely Princess sitting in hopeless sorrow, the tears flowing from her beautiful eyes, while she sang a plaintive air deploring her unhappy fate. Upon leaving the closet, the Prince told the Sultan that he had assured himself that the Princess' complaint was not incurable, but that if he was to aid her he must speak with her in private and alone.

The Sultan ordered the Princess' chamber door to be opened, and Feroze Shah went in. Immediately the Princess resorted to her old practice of meeting physicians with threats, and indications of attacking them. But Feroze Shah came close to her and said in so low a voice that only she could hear, "Princess, I am not a physician, but Feroze Shah, and have come to obtain your liberty."

The Princess, who knew the sound of his voice, and recognized him, notwithstanding he had let his beard grow so long, grew calm at once, and was filled with secret joy at the unexpected sight of the Prince she loved. After they had briefly informed each other of all that had happened since their separation, the Prince asked if she knew what had become of the horse after the death of the Hindu magician. She replied that she did not know, but supposed that he was carefully guarded as a curiosity. Feroze Shah then told the Princess that he intended to obtain and use the horse to convey them both back to Persia; and they planned together, as the first step to this end, that the Princess the next day should receive the Sultan.

On the following day the Sultan was overjoyed to find that the Princess' cure was apparently far advanced, and regarded the Prince as the greatest physician in the world. The Prince of Persia, who accompanied the Sultan on his visit to the Princess, inquired of him how she had come into the Kingdom of Cashmere from her far-distant country.

The Sultan then repeated the story of the Hindu magician, adding that the Enchanted Horse was kept safely in his treasury as a great curiosity, though he knew not how to use it.

"Sire," replied the pretended physician, "this information affords me a means of curing the Princess. When she was brought hither on the Enchanted Horse, she contracted part of the enchantment, which can be dispelled only by a certain incense of which I have knowledge. Let the horse be brought tomorrow into the great square before the palace, and leave the rest to me. I promise to show you and all your assembled people, in a few moments' time, the Princess of Bengal completely restored in body and mind. But to assure the success of what I propose, the Princess must be dressed as magnificently as possible and adorned with the most valuable jewels in your treasury."

All this the Sultan eagerly promised, for he would have undertaken far more difficult things to assure his marriage

The next day the Enchanted Horse was taken from the treasury and brought to the great square before the palace. The rumor of something extraordinary having spread through the town, crowds of people flocked thither from all sides. The Sultan of Cashmere, surrounded by his nobles and ministers of state, occupied a gallery erected for the purpose. The Princess of Bengal, attended by her ladies in waiting, went up to the Enchanted Horse, and the women helped her to mount. The pretended physician then placed around the horse many vessels full of burning charcoal, into which he cast handfuls of incense. After which, he ran three times about the horse, pretending to utter certain magic words. The pots sent forth a dark cloud of smoke that surrounded the Princess, so that neither she nor the horse could be seen. The Prince mounted nimbly behind her and turned the peg; and as the horse rose with them into the air, the Sultan distinctly heard these words, "Sultan of Cashmere, when you would marry Princesses who implore your protection, learn first to obtain their consent!"

Thus the Prince delivered the Princess of Bengal, and carried her that same day to the capital of Persia where the Sultan his father made immediate preparation for the solemnization of their marriage with all fitting pomp and magnificence. After the days appointed for rejoicing were over, the Sultan named and appointed an ambassador to go to the Rajah of Bengal, to ask his approval of the alliance contracted by this marriage; which the Rajah of Bengal took as an honor, and granted with great pleasure.

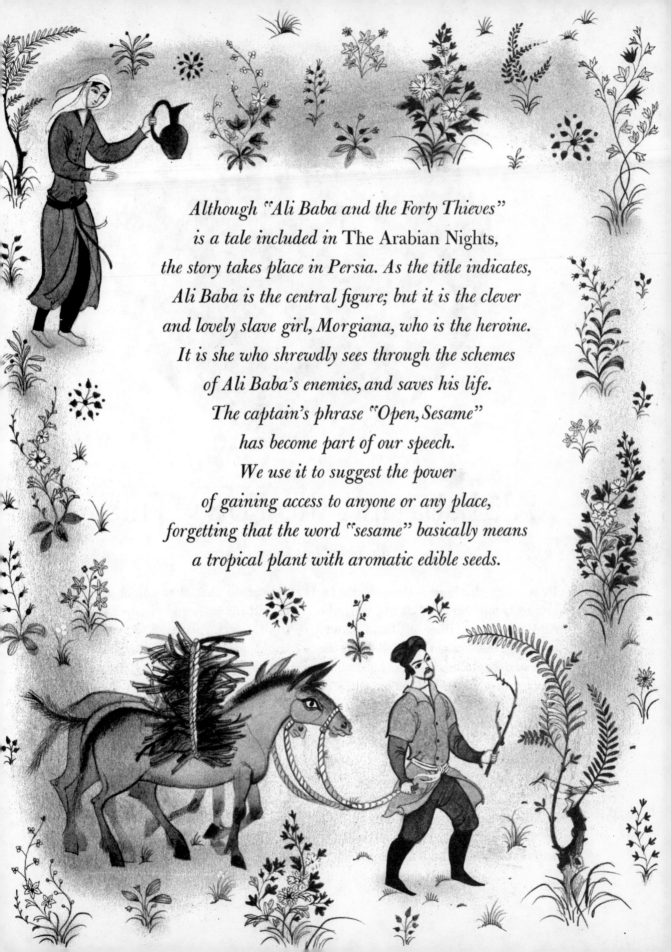

Although "Ali Baba and the Forty Thieves"
is a tale included in The Arabian Nights,
the story takes place in Persia. As the title indicates,
Ali Baba is the central figure; but it is the clever
and lovely slave girl, Morgiana, who is the heroine.
It is she who shrewdly sees through the schemes
of Ali Baba's enemies, and saves his life.
The captain's phrase "Open, Sesame"
has become part of our speech.
We use it to suggest the power
of gaining access to anyone or any place,
forgetting that the word "sesame" basically means
a tropical plant with aromatic edible seeds.

Ali Baba and the Forty Thieves

Illustrated by GORDON LAITE

IN A TOWN in Persia, there lived two brothers, one named Cassim, the other Ali Baba. Their father left them scarcely anything; but Cassim married a wealthy wife and prospered in life, becoming a famous merchant. Ali Baba, on the other hand, married a woman as poor as himself, and lived by cutting wood, and bringing it upon three asses into the town to sell.

One day, when Ali Baba was in the forest, he saw at a distance a great cloud of dust, which seemed to be approaching. He observed it very attentively, and distinguished a body of horsemen.

Fearing that they might be robbers, he left his asses and climbed into a tree, from which place of concealment he could watch all that passed in safety.

The troop consisted of forty men, all well mounted, who, when they arrived, dismounted and tied up their horses and fed them. They then removed their saddlebags, which seemed heavy, and followed the captain, who approached a rock that stood near Ali Baba's hiding place. When he was come to it, he said, in a loud voice, "Open, Sesame!" As soon as the captain had uttered these words, a door opened in the rock; and after he

366

had made all his troop enter before him, he followed them, after which the door shut again of itself.

Although the robbers remained some time in the rock, Ali Baba did not dare to move until after they had filed out again, and were out of sight. Then, when he thought that all was safe, he descended, and going up to the door, said, "Open, Sesame!" as the captain had done, and instantly the door flew open.

Ali Baba, who expected a dark dismal cavern, was surprised to see it well lighted and spacious, receiving light from an opening at the top of the rock. He saw all sorts of provisions, rich bales of silk, brocades, and valuable carpeting, piled upon one another; gold and silver ingots in great heaps, and money in bags. The sight of all these riches made him suppose that this cave must have been occupied for ages by robbers, who had succeeded one another.

Ali Baba loaded his asses with gold coin, and then covering the bags with sticks he returned home. Having secured the door of his house, he emptied out the gold before his wife, who was dazzled by its brightness, and told her all, urging upon her the necessity of keeping the secret.

The wife rejoiced at their good fortune, and wished to count all the gold, piece by piece. "Wife," said Ali Baba, "you do not know what you undertake, when you pretend to count the money. You will never have done. I will dig a hole, and bury it. There is no time to be lost."

"You are right, husband," replied she; "but let us know, as nigh as possible, how much we have. I will borrow a small measure and measure it, while you dig the hole."

Away the wife ran to her brother-in-law Cassim, who lived just by, and addressing herself to his wife, desired her to lend her a measure for a little while. The sister-in-law did so, but as she knew Ali Baba's poverty, she was curious to know what sort of grain his wife wanted to measure, and artfully putting some suet at the bottom of the measure, brought it to her with an excuse, that she was sorry that she had made her stay so long, but that she could not find it sooner.

Ali Baba's wife went home and continued to fill the measure from the heap of gold and empty it till she had done: when she was very well satisfied to find the number of measures amounted to as many as they did, and went to tell her husband, who had almost finished digging the hole. While Ali Baba was burying the gold, his wife, to show her exactness and diligence to her sister-in-law, carried the measure back again, but without taking notice that a piece of gold had stuck to the bottom. "Sister," said she, giving it to her again, "you see that I have not kept your measure long. I am obliged to you for it, and return it with thanks."

As soon as Ali Baba's wife was gone, Cassim's wife looked at the bottom of the measure and was greatly surprised to find a piece of gold stuck to it. Envy immediately possessed her breast. "What!" said she, "has Ali Baba gold so plentiful that he has to measure it?" When Cassim came home, his wife said to him, "I know you think yourself rich, but you are much mistaken. Ali Baba is infinitely richer than you. He does not count his

367

money, but measures it." Cassim desired her to explain the riddle, which she did, by telling him the stratagem she had used to make the discovery, and showed him the piece of money, which was so old that they could not tell in what prince's reign it was coined.

Cassim was also envious when he heard this, and slept so badly that he rose early and went to his brother.

"Ali Baba," said he, "you pretend to be miserably poor, and yet you measure gold. My wife found this at the bottom of the measure you borrowed yesterday."

Ali Baba perceived that Cassim and his wife, through his own wife's folly, knew what they had so much reason to conceal. However, what was done could not be recalled. Therefore, without showing the least surprise or trouble, he confessed all, and offered him part of his treasure to keep the secret. "I expected as much," replied Cassim haughtily. "But I must know exactly where this treasure is, and how I may visit it myself when I choose. Otherwise I will go and inform against you, and then you will not only get no more, but will lose all you have, and I shall have a share for my information."

Ali Baba told him all he desired, and even the very words he was to use to gain admission into the cave.

Cassim rose the next morning, long before the sun, and set out for the forest with ten mules bearing great chests, which he planned to fill. He was not long before he reached the rock, and found out the place by the tree and other marks which his brother had given him. When he reached the entrance of the cavern, he pronounced the words, "Open, Sesame!" The door immediately opened, and when he was in, closed upon him. He quickly entered, and laid as many bags of gold as he could carry at the door of the cavern, but his thoughts were so full of the great riches he should possess, that he could not think of the necessary word to make it open. Instead of Sesame, he said, "Open, Barley!" and was much amazed to find that the door remained fast shut. He named several sorts of grain, but still the door would not open.

Cassim had never expected such an incident, and was so alarmed at the danger he was in that the more he endeavored to remember the word "Sesame," the more his memory was confounded, and he had as much forgotten it as if he had never heard it mentioned. He threw down the bags he had loaded himself with, and walked distractedly up and down the cave, without having the least regard for the riches about him.

About noon the robbers chanced to visit their cave, and at some distance from it saw Cassim's mules straggling about the rock, with great chests on their backs. Alarmed at this, they galloped full speed to the cave. Cassim, who heard the noise of the horses' feet from the middle of the cave, never doubted of the arrival of the robbers, and resolved to make one effort to escape from them. To this end he rushed to the door, and no sooner saw it open, than he ran out and struck down the leader, but could not escape the other robbers, who with their sabers soon made an end of him.

The first care of the robbers after this was to examine the cave. They found all the bags which Cassim had brought to the door, to be ready to load his mules, and carried them again to their places,

without missing what Ali Baba had taken away the previous day. Then holding a council, they agreed to cut Cassim's body into four quarters, to hang two on one side and two on the other, within the door of the cave, to terrify any person who should attempt the same thing. This done, they mounted their horses, went to beat the roads again, and to attack any caravans they might meet.

In the meantime, Cassim's wife was very uneasy when night came and her husband had not returned. She ran to Ali Baba in alarm, and said, "I believe, brother-in-law, that you know Cassim your brother is gone to the forest, and upon what account. It is now night and he is not returned. I am afraid some misfortune has happened to him." Ali Baba told her that she need not frighten herself, for that certainly Cassim would not think it proper to come into the town till late at night.

Cassim's wife passed a miserable night, and bitterly repented of her curiosity. As soon as daylight appeared, she went to Ali Baba, weeping profusely.

Ali Baba departed immediately with his three asses to seek for Cassim, begging of her first to cease her lamentations. He went to the forest, and when he came near the rock, having seen neither his brother nor the mules on his way, was seriously alarmed at finding some blood spilt near the door, which he took for an ill omen. But when he had pronounced the password, and the door had opened, he was struck with horror at the dismal sight of his brother's remains. He loaded one of his asses with them, and covered them over with wood. The other two asses he loaded with bags of gold, covering them with wood also as before; and then bidding the door shut, came away. But he took care to stop some time at the edge of the forest, so that he might not reach the town before night. When he came home, he drove the two asses loaded with gold into his little yard, and left the care of unloading them to his wife, while he led the other to his sister-in-law's house.

Ali Baba knocked at the door, which was opened by Morgiana, an intelligent slave, whose tact was to be relied upon. When he came into the court, he unloaded the ass, and taking Morgiana aside, said to her, "Mention what I say to no one. Your master's body is contained in these two bundles, and our business is to bury him as if he had died a natural death. I can trust you to manage this for me."

Ali Baba consoled the widow as best he could, and having deposited the body in the house returned home.

Morgiana went out at the same time to an apothecary, and asked for a sort of lozenge very efficacious in the most dangerous disorders. The apothecary inquired who was ill. She replied with a sigh, "My good master Cassim himself. He can neither eat nor speak." After these words Morgiana carried the lozenges home with her, and the next morning went to the same apothecary's again, and with tears in her eyes, asked for an essence which they used to give to sick people only when at the last extremity. "Alas!" said she, "I am afraid that this remedy will have no better effect than the lozenges; and that I shall lose my good master."

On the other hand, as Ali Baba and his wife were often seen to go between Cassim's and their own house all that day, and to seem melancholy, nobody was surprised in the evening to hear the lamentable shrieks and cries of Cassim's wife and Morgiana, who gave out everywhere that her master was dead. The next morning Morgiana betook herself early to the stall of a cobbler named Mustapha, and bidding him good morrow, put a piece of gold into his hand, saying, "Baba Mustapha, you must take your sewing tackle, and come with me. But I must tell you, I shall have to blindfold you when you come to the place."

Baba Mustapha hesitated a little at these words. "Oh! oh!" replied he, "you would have me do something against my conscience, or against my honor?"

"God forbid!" said Morgiana, putting another piece of gold into his hand, "that I should ask anything that is contrary to your honor. Only come along with me, and fear nothing."

Baba Mustapha went with Morgiana, who, after she had bound his eyes with a handkerchief, conveyed him to her deceased master's house, and never unloosed his eyes till he had entered the room, where she had put the corpse together. "Baba Mustapha," said she, "you must make haste and sew these quarters together. And when you have done, I will give you another piece of gold."

After Baba Mustapha had finished his task, she once more blindfolded him, gave him the third piece of gold as she had promised, and recommending secrecy to him, conducted him back again to the place where she had first bound his eyes, pulled off the bandage, and let him go home, but watched him that he returned toward his shop, till he was quite out of sight, for fear that he should have the curiosity to return and follow her. She then went home.

The ceremony of washing and dressing the body was hastily performed by Morgiana and Ali Baba, after which it was sewed up ready to be placed in the mausoleum. While Ali Baba and the other members of the household followed the body, the women of the neighborhood came, according to custom, and joined their mourning with that of the widow, so that the whole quarter was filled with the sound of their weeping. Thus was Cassim's horrible death successfully concealed.

Three or four days after the funeral, Ali Baba removed his goods openly to the widow's house. But the money he had taken from the robbers he conveyed thither by night. When at length the robbers came again to their retreat in the forest, great was their surprise to find Cassim's body taken away, with some of their bags of gold. "We are certainly discovered," said the captain, "and if we do not find and kill the man who knows our secret, we shall gradually lose all the riches."

The robbers unanimously approved of the captain's speech.

"The only way in which this can be discovered," said the captain, "is by spying on the town. And, lest any treachery may be practiced, I suggest that whoever undertakes the task shall pay dearly if he fails—even with his life."

One of the robbers immediately started up, and said, "I submit to this condition, and think it an honor to expose my life to serve the troop."

The robber's courage was highly commended by the captain and his comrades, and when he had disguised himself so that nobody would know him, he went into the town and walked up and down, till accidentally he came to Baba Mustapha's shop.

Baba Mustapha was seated, with an awl beside him, on the bench, just starting to work. The robber saluted him and, perceiving that he was old, said, "Honest man, you begin to work very early. How is it possible that one of your age can see so well? I question, even if it were somewhat lighter, whether you could see to stitch."

"Why," replied Baba Mustapha, "I sewed a dead body together in a place where I had not so much light as I have now."

"A dead body!" cried the robber, with affected amazement.

"It is so," replied Baba Mustapha. "But I will tell you no more."

"Indeed," answered the robber, "I do not want to learn your secret, but I would fain to see the house in which this strange thing was done." To impress the cobbler he gave him a piece of gold.

"If I were disposed to do you that favor," replied Baba Mustapha, "I assure you I cannot, for I was led both to and from the house blindfolded."

"Well," replied the robber, "you may, however, remember a little of the way that you were led blindfolded. Come, let me bind your eyes at the same place. We will walk together; and as everybody ought to be paid for his trouble, there is another piece of gold for you. Gratify me in what I ask you."

The two pieces of gold were too great a temptation for Baba Mustapha, who said, "I am not sure that I remember the way exactly. But since you desire, I will see what I can do." At these words Baba Mustapha rose up, and led the robber to the place where Morgiana had bound his eyes. "It was here," said Baba Mustapha, "I was blindfolded; and I turned as you see me."

The robber, who had his handkerchief ready, tied it over his eyes, walked by him till he stopped, partly leading, and

partly guided by him. "I think," said Baba Mustapha, "I went no farther." He had now stopped directly at Cassim's house, where Ali Baba then lived. The thief, before he pulled off the band, marked the door with a piece of chalk which he had already in his hand. Then he asked him if he knew whose house that was, to which Baba Mustapha replied, that, as he did not live in that neighborhood, he could not tell.

The robber, finding he could discover no more from Baba Mustapha, thanked him for the trouble he had taken, and left him to go back to his shop, while he, himself, returned to the forest, persuaded that he should be very well received.

Shortly after the robber and Baba Mustapha had parted, Morgiana went out of Ali Baba's house upon some errand, and upon her return, she saw the mark the robber had made and stopped to observe it. "What can be the meaning of this mark?" said she to herself. "Somebody intends my master no good. However, with whatever intention it was done, it is advisable to guard against the worst." Accordingly, she fetched a piece of chalk, and marked two or three doors on each side, in the same manner.

When the robber reached the camp, he reported the success of his expedition. It was at once decided that they should very quietly enter the city and watch for an opportunity of slaying their enemy. To the utter confusion of the guide, several of the neighboring doors were found to be marked in a similar manner. "Come," said the captain, "this will not do. We must return, and you must die." They returned to the camp, and the false guide was promptly slain.

Then another volunteer came forward, and he in like manner was led by Baba Mustapha to the spot. He cautiously marked the door with red chalk, in a place not likely to be seen. But the quick eye of Morgiana detected this likewise, and she repeated her previous action, with equal effectiveness, for when the robbers came they could not distinguish the house. Then the captain, in great anger, led his men back to the forest, where the second offender was immediately put to death.

The captain, dissatisfied by this waste of time and loss of men, decided to undertake the task himself. And so having been led to the spot by Baba Mustapha, he walked up and down before the house until it was impressed upon his mind. He then returned to the forest. When he came into the cave, where the troop waited for him, he said, "Now, comrades, nothing can prevent our full revenge." He then told them his contrivance. When they approved of it, he ordered them to go into the villages about, and buy nineteen mules, with thirty-eight large leather jars, one full of oil, and the others empty.

In two days all preparations were made, and the nineteen mules were loaded with thirty-seven robbers in jars, and the jar of oil. The captain, as their driver, set out with them, and reached the town by the dusk of the evening, as he had intended. He led them through the streets till he came to Ali Baba's, at whose door he planned to have knocked; but was prevented, as Ali Baba was sitting there after supper to take a little fresh air. He stopped his mules, and said, "I have brought some oil a great way, to sell at tomorrow's market, but it is now so late that I do not know where to lodge. Will you allow me to pass the night with you, and I shall be very much obliged for your hospitality."

Ali Baba, not recognizing the robber, bade him welcome, and gave directions for his entertainment, and after they had eaten he retired to rest.

The captain, pretending that he wished to see how his jars stood, slipped into the garden, and passing from one to the other he raised the lids of the jars and spoke: "As soon as I throw some stones out of my window, do not fail to come out, and I will immediately join you." After this he retired to his chamber; and to avoid any suspicion, put the light out soon after, and laid himself down in his clothes, that he might be the more ready to rise.

While Morgiana was preparing the food for breakfast, the lamp went out, and there was no more oil in the house, nor were there any candles. What to do she did not know, for the broth must be made. Abdalla, seeing her very uneasy, said, "Do not fret, but go into the yard, and take some oil out of one of the jars."

Morgiana thanked Abdalla for his advice, took the oil pot, and went into the yard. As she came nigh the first jar, the robber within said softly, "Is it time?"

Morgiana naturally was much surprised

at finding a man in a jar instead of the oil she wanted, but she at once made up her mind that no time was to be lost, if a great danger was to be averted, so she passed from jar to jar, answering at each, "Not yet, but presently."

At last she came to the oil jar, and made what haste she could to fill her oil pot, and returned into her kitchen. Here, as soon as she had lighted her lamp, she took a great kettle, went again to the oil jar, filled the kettle, set it on a large wood fire, and as soon as it boiled went and poured enough into every jar to stifle and destroy the robber within.

When this action, worthy of the courage of Morgiana, was executed without any noise, as she had planned, she returned to the kitchen with the empty kettle. She then put out the great fire which she had made to boil the oil. Leaving just enough to make the broth, she put out the lamp also, and remained silent; resolving not to go to rest till she had observed what might follow through a window of the kitchen, which opened into the yard.

She had not waited long before the captain gave his signal, by throwing the stones. Receiving no response, he repeated it several times, until becoming alarmed he descended into the yard and discovered that all the gang were dead. And by the oil he missed out of the last jar he guessed the means and manner of their death. Enraged to despair at having failed in his design, he forced the lock of a door that led from the yard to the garden, and climbing over the walls, made his escape.

Morgiana then went to bed, happy at the success of her plan.

Ali Baba rose before day, and followed by his slave, went to the baths, entirely ignorant of the important events which had taken place at home. When he returned from the baths, the sun had risen. He was very much surprised to see the oil jars, and that the merchant had not gone with the mules. He asked Morgiana, who opened the door, the reason of it. "My good master," answered she, "God preserve you and all your family. You will be better informed of what you wish to know when you have seen what I have to show you, if you will but give yourself the trouble to follow me."

Ali Baba following her, she requested him to look into the first jar and see if there was any oil. Ali Baba did so, and seeing a man, started back in alarm, and cried out. "Do not be afraid," said Morgiana, "the man you see there can neither do you nor anybody else any harm. He is dead."

"Ah, Morgiana!" said Ali Baba, "what is it you show me? Explain yourself."

"I will," replied Morgiana. "Moderate your astonishment, and do not excite the curiosity of your neighbors. Look into all the jars."

Ali Baba examined all the other jars, one after another. And when he came to that which had been filled with oil, he found it almost empty. He stood for some time motionless, sometimes looking at the jars, and sometimes at Morgiana, without saying a word, so great was his surprise. At last, when he had recovered himself, he said, "And what is become of the merchant?"

"Merchant!" answered she, "he is as much a merchant as I am. I will tell you who he is, and what has become of him."

She then told the whole story from beginning to end; from the marking of the house to the destruction of the robbers.

Ali Baba was overcome by this account, and he cried, "You have saved my life, and in return I give you your liberty —but this shall not be all."

Ali Baba and his slave Abdalla then dug a long deep trench at the farther end of the garden, in which the robbers were buried. Afterward the jars and weapons were hidden, and by degrees Ali Baba managed to sell the mules for which he had no use.

Meanwhile the captain, who had returned to the forest, found life very miserable. The cavern became too frightful to be endured. But, resolved to be revenged upon Ali Baba, he laid new plans, and having taken a shop which happened to be opposite Cassim's, where Ali Baba's son now lived, he transported many rich stuffs thither. And, disguised as a silk mercer, he set up in business, under the name of Cogia Houssain.

Having by chance discovered whose son his opposite neighbor was, he often made him presents and invited him to dinner, and did everything to win his good opinion.

Ali Baba's son, who did not like to be indebted to any man, told his father that he desired to ask him to dinner in return, and requested him to do so. Ali Baba readily complied with his wishes, and it was arranged that on the following day he should bring Cogia Houssain with him to dinner.

At the appointed time Ali Baba's son conducted Cogia Houssain to his father's house. And strange to say, when the robber found himself at the door, he would have liked to withdraw, though he had now gained access to the very man he wanted to kill. But at that moment Ali Baba came forward to receive him and thank him for his goodness to his son. "And now," said Ali Baba, "you will do me the honor of dining with me."

"Sir," replied Cogia Houssain, "I would gladly, but that I have vowed to abstain from salt, and I scarcely like to sit at your table under such conditions."

"Trouble not yourself about that," answered Ali Baba, "I will go and bid the cook put no salt in the food."

When Ali Baba went to the kitchen to give this order, Morgiana was much surprised, and desired to see this strange man. Therefore she helped Abdalla to carry up the dishes, and directly she saw Cogia Houssain, she recognized him as the captain of the robbers.

Morgiana at once decided to rescue

Ali Baba from this fresh danger, and resolved upon a very daring plan to frustrate the robber's designs; for she guessed that he intended no good. In order to carry out her plan she went to her room and put on the garments of a dancer, hid her face under a mask and fastened a handsome girdle around her waist, from which hung a dagger. Then she said to Abdalla, "Fetch your tabor, that we may divert our master and his guest."

Ali Baba bade her dance, and she commenced to move gracefully about, while Abdalla played on his tabor. Cogia Houssain watched, but feared that he would have no opportunity of executing his fell purpose.

After Morgiana had danced for some time, she seized the dagger in her right hand and danced wildly, pretending to stab herself the while. As she swept round, she buried the dagger deep in Cogia Houssain's breast and killed him.

Ali Baba and his son, shocked at this action, cried out aloud, "Unhappy wretch! what have you done to ruin me and my family?"

"It was to preserve, not to ruin you," answered Morgiana. "For see here," continued she, opening the pretended Cogia Houssain's garment, and showing the dagger, "what an enemy you had entertained! Look well at him, and you will find him to be both the fictitious oil merchant and the captain of a gang of forty robbers. Remember, too, that he would eat no salt with you. And what would you have more to persuade you of his wicked design?"

Ali Baba, who immediately felt the new obligation he had to Morgiana for saving his life a second time, embraced her. "Morgiana," said he, "I gave you your liberty, and then promised you that my gratitude should not stop there, but that I would soon give you higher proofs of its sincerity, which I now do by making you my daughter-in-law." Then addressing himself to his son, he said, "I believe, son, that you will not refuse Morgiana for your wife. You see that Cogia Houssain sought your friendship with a treacherous design to take away my life. And, if he had succeeded, there is no doubt but he would have sacrificed you also to his revenge. Consider, that by marrying Morgiana you marry the preserver of my family and your own."

The son, far from showing any reluctance, readily consented to the marriage. And a few days afterward, Ali Baba celebrated the nuptials of his son and Morgiana with great solemnity, with a sumptuous feast, and the usual dancing and spectacles.

Ali Baba, fearing that the other two robbers might be alive still, did not visit the cave for a whole year. Finding, however, that they did not seek to disturb him, he then went to the cave, and, having pronounced the words, "Open, Sesame," entered and saw that no one had been there recently. He then knew that he alone in the world knew the secret of the cave; and he rejoiced to think of his good fortune. When he returned to the city he took as much gold as his horse could carry from his inexhaustible storehouse.

Afterward Ali Baba took his son to the cave, taught him the secret, which they handed down to their posterity, who, using their good fortune with moderation, lived in great honor and splendor.

Most people believe that "Aladdin and the Wonderful Lamp"
belongs to The Arabian Nights.
Actually, it is not to be found in the original assembly.
When a French translator of the tales made a selection,
he filled out his volume with a few stories
in the same Oriental vein.
One of these was the tale of Aladdin.
No one knows where the Frenchman got the plot of the story;
scholars have been unable to learn whether he found it
in some obscure manuscript,
or heard it somewhere, or made it up himself.

Aladdin and the Wonderful Lamp

EDITED BY ANDREW LANG
Illustrated by LOWELL HESS

THERE once lived a poor tailor who had a son called Aladdin, a careless, idle boy who would do nothing but play ball all day long in the streets with little idle boys like himself. This so grieved the father that he died; yet, in spite of his mother's tears and prayers, Aladdin did not mend his ways.

One day, when he was playing in the streets as usual, a stranger asked him his age, and if he was not the son of Mustapha the tailor. "I am, sir," replied Aladdin; "but he died a long while ago." On this the stranger, who was a famous African magician, fell on his neck and kissed him, saying, "I am your uncle, and knew

you from your likeness to my brother. Go to your mother and tell her I am coming." Aladdin ran home and told his mother of his newly found uncle. "Indeed, child," she said, "your father had a brother, but I always thought he was dead." However, she prepared supper, and bade Aladdin seek his uncle, who came laden with wine and fruit. He presently fell down and kissed the place where Mustapha used to sit, bidding Aladdin's mother not to be surprised at not having seen him before, as he had been forty years out of the country. He then turned to Aladdin, and asked him his trade, at which the boy hung his head, while his mother burst into tears. On learning that Aladdin was idle and would learn no trade, he offered to take a shop for him and stock it with merchandise. Next day he bought Aladdin a fine suit of clothes and took him all over the city, showing him the sights, and brought him home at nightfall to his mother, who was overjoyed to see her son so fine.

The next day the magician led Aladdin into some beautiful gardens a long way outside the city gates. They sat down by a fountain and the magician pulled a cake from his girdle, which he divided between them. They then journeyed onward till they almost reached the mountains. Aladdin was so tired that he begged to go back, but the magician beguiled him with pleasant stories, and led him on in spite of himself. At last they came to two mountains divided by a narrow valley. "We will go no farther," said the false uncle. "I will show you something wonderful; only do you gather up sticks while I kindle a fire." When it was lit the magician threw on it a powder he had about him, at the same time saying some magical words. The earth trembled a little and opened in front of them, disclosing a square flat stone with a brass ring in the middle to raise it by. Aladdin tried to run away, but the magician caught him and gave him a blow that knocked him down. "What have I done, Uncle?" he said piteously; whereupon the magician said more kindly: "Fear nothing, but obey me. Beneath this stone lies a treasure which is to be yours, and no one else may touch it, so you must do exactly as I tell you." At the word treasure Aladdin forgot his fears, and grasped the ring as he was told, saying the names

of his father and grandfather. The stone came up quite easily, and some steps appeared. "Go down," said the magician; "at the foot of those steps you will find an open door leading into three large halls. Tuck up your gown and go through them without touching anything, or you will die instantly. These halls lead into a garden of fine fruit trees. Walk on until you come to a niche in a terrace where stands a lighted lamp. Pour out the oil it contains, and bring it to me." He drew a ring from his finger and gave it to Aladdin, bidding him prosper.

Aladdin found everything as the magician had said, gathered some fruit off the trees, and having got the lamp, arrived at the mouth of the cave. The magician cried out in a great hurry: "Make haste and give me the lamp." This Aladdin refused to do until he was out of the cave. The magician flew into a terrible passion and, throwing some more powder on to the fire, he said something, and the stone rolled back into its place.

The magician left China forever, which plainly showed that he was no uncle of Aladdin's, but a cunning magician, who had read in his magic books of a wonderful lamp which would make him the most powerful man in the world. Though he alone knew where to find it, he could only receive it from the hand of another. He had picked out the foolish Aladdin for this purpose, intending to get the lamp and kill him afterward.

For two days Aladdin remained in the dark, crying and lamenting. At last he clasped his hands in prayer, and in so doing rubbed the ring, which the magician had forgotten to take from him. Immediately an enormous and frightful genie rose out of the earth, saying: "What wouldst thou with me? I am the Slave of the Ring, and will obey thee in all things." Aladdin fearlessly replied: "Deliver me from this place!" whereupon the earth opened, and he found himself outside. As soon as his eyes could bear the light he went home, but fainted on the threshold. When he came to himself he told his mother what had passed, and showed her the lamp and the fruits he had gathered in the garden, which were, in reality, precious stones. He then asked for some food. "Alas, child!" she said. "I have nothing in the house, but I have spun a little cotton and will go and sell it." Aladdin bade her keep her cotton, for he would sell the lamp instead. As it was very dirty she began to rub it, that it might fetch a higher price. Instantly a hideous genie appeared, and asked what she would have. She fainted away, but Aladdin, snatching the lamp, said boldly: "Fetch me something to eat!" The genie returned with a silver bowl, twelve silver plates containing rich meats, two silver cups, and two bottles of wine. Aladdin's mother, when she came to herself, said: "Whence comes this splendid feast?" "Ask not, but eat," replied Aladdin. So they sat at breakfast till it was dinnertime, and Aladdin told his mother about the lamp. She begged him to sell it, and have nothing to do with devils. "No," said Aladdin, "since chance hath made us aware of its virtues, we will use it, and the ring likewise, which I shall always wear on my finger." When they had eaten all the genie had brought, Aladdin sold one of the silver plates, and so on until none were left. He then had recourse to the genie, who gave him another set of plates, and thus they lived

for many years.

One day Aladdin heard an order from the Sultan proclaiming that everyone was to stay at home and close his shutters while the Princess, his daughter, went to and from the bath. Aladdin was seized by a desire to see her face, which was very difficult as she always went veiled. He hid himself behind the door of the bath, and peeped through a chink. The Princess lifted her veil as she went in, and looked so beautiful that Aladdin fell in love with her at first sight. He went home so changed that his mother was frightened. He told her he loved the Princess so deeply that he could not live without her, and meant to ask her hand in marriage of her father. His mother, on hearing this, burst out laughing, but Aladdin at last prevailed upon her to go before the Sultan and carry his request. She fetched a napkin and laid in it the magic fruits from the enchanted garden, which sparkled and shone like the most beautiful jewels. She took these with her to please the Sultan, and set out, trusting in the lamp. The Grand Vizier and the lords of council had just gone in as she entered the hall and placed herself in front of the Sultan. He, however, took no notice of her. She went every day for a week, and stood in the same place. When the council broke up on the sixth day the Sultan said to his Vizier: "I see a certain woman in the audience chamber every day carrying something in a napkin. Call her next time, that I may find out what she wants." Next day, at a sign from the Vizier, she went up to the foot of the throne and remained kneeling till the Sultan said to her: "Rise, good woman, and tell me what you want." She hesitated, so the Sultan sent away all but the Vizier, and bade her speak frankly, promising to forgive her beforehand for anything she might say. She then told him of her son's violent love for the Princess. "I prayed him to forget her," she said, "but in vain; he threatened to do some desperate deed if I refused to go and ask Your Majesty for the hand of the Princess. Now I pray you to forgive not me alone, but my son Aladdin." The Sultan asked her kindly what she had in the napkin, whereupon she unfolded the jewels and presented them. He was thunderstruck, and turning to the Vizier said: "What sayest thou? Ought I not to bestow the Princess on one who values her at such a price?" The Vizier, who wanted her for his own son, begged the Sultan to withhold her for three months, in the course of which he hoped his son would contrive to make him a richer present. The Sultan granted this, and told Aladdin's mother that, though he consented to the marriage, she must not appear before him again for three months.

Aladdin waited patiently for nearly three months, but after two had elapsed, his mother, going into the city to buy oil, found everyone rejoicing, and asked what was going on. "Do you not know," was the answer, "that the son of the Grand Vizier is to marry the Sultan's daughter tonight?" Breathless, she ran and told Aladdin, who was overwhelmed at first, but presently bethought him of the lamp. He rubbed it, and the genie appeared, saying, "What is thy will?" Aladdin replied: "The Sultan, as thou knowest, has broken his promise to me, and the Vizier's son is to have the Princess. My command is that tonight you bring hither the bride and bridegroom." "Master, I obey," said

the genie. Aladdin then went to his chamber, where, sure enough, at midnight the genie transported the bed containing the Vizier's son and the Princess. "Take this new-married man," he said, "and put him outside in the cold, and return at daybreak." Whereupon the genie took the Vizier's son out of bed, leaving Aladdin with the Princess. "Fear nothing," Aladdin said to her; "you are my wife, promised to me by your unjust father, and no harm shall come to you." The Princess was too frightened to speak, and passed the most miserable night of her life, while Aladdin lay down beside her and slept soundly. At the appointed hour the genie fetched in the shivering bridegroom, laid him in his place, and transported the bed back to the palace.

Presently the Sultan came to wish his daughter good morning. The unhappy Vizier's son jumped up and hid himself, while the Princess would not say a word, and was very sorrowful. The Sultan sent her mother to her, who said: "How comes it, child, that you will not speak to your father? What has happened?" The Princess sighed deeply, and at last told her mother how, during the night, the bed had been carried into some strange house, and what had passed there. Her mother did not believe her in the least, but bade her rise and consider it an idle dream.

The following night exactly the same thing happened, and next morning, on the Princess's refusal to speak, the Sultan threatened to cut off her head. She then confessed all, bidding him to ask the Vizier's son if it were not so. The Sultan told the Vizier to ask his son, who owned the truth, adding that, dearly as he loved the Princess, he had rather die than go through another such fearful night, and wished to be separated from her. His wish was granted, and there was an end to feasting and rejoicing.

When the three months were over, Aladdin sent his mother to remind the Sultan of his promise. She stood in the same place as before, and the Sultan, who had forgotten Aladdin, at once remembered him, and sent for her. On seeing her poverty the Sultan felt less inclined than ever to keep his word, and asked his Vizier's advice, who counseled him to set so high a value on the Princess that no man living could come up to it. The Sultan then turned to Aladdin's mother, saying: "Good woman, a sultan must remember his promises, and I will remember mine, but your son must first send me forty basins of gold brimful of jewels, carried by forty black slaves, led by as many white ones, splendidly dressed. Tell him that I await his answer." The mother of Aladdin bowed low and went home, thinking all was lost. She gave Aladdin the message, adding: "He may wait long enough for your answer!" "Not so long, Mother, as you think," her son replied. "I would do a great deal more than that for the Princess." He summoned the genie, and in a few moments the eighty slaves arrived, and filled up the small house and garden. Aladdin made them set out to the palace, two and two, followed by his mother. They were so richly dressed, with such splendid jewels in their girdles, that everyone crowded to see them and the basins of gold they carried on their heads. They entered the palace, and after kneeling before the Sultan, stood in a half circle round the throne with their arms crossed, while Aladdin's mother presented them

to the Sultan. He hesitated no longer, but said: "Good woman, return and tell your son that I wait for him with open arms." She lost no time in telling Aladdin, bidding him make haste. But Aladdin first called the genie. "I want a scented bath," he said, "a richly embroidered habit, a horse surpassing the Sultan's, and twenty slaves to attend me. Besides this, six slaves, beautifully dressed, to wait on my mother; and lastly, ten thousand pieces of gold in ten purses." No sooner said than done. Aladdin mounted his horse and passed through the streets, the slaves strewing gold as they went. Those who had played with him in his childhood knew him not, he had grown so handsome. When the Sultan saw him he came down from his throne, embraced him, and led him into a hall where a feast was spread, intending to marry him to the Princess that very day. But Aladdin refused, saying, "I must build a palace fit for her," and took his leave. Once home, he said to the genie: "Build me a palace of the finest marble, set with jasper, agate, and other precious stones. In the middle you shall build me a large hall with a dome, its four walls of massy gold and silver, each having six windows, whose lattices, all except one which is to be left unfinished, must be set with diamonds and rubies. There must be stables and horses and grooms and slaves; go and see about it!"

The palace was finished by the next day, and the genie carried him there and showed him all his orders faithfully carried out, even to the laying of a velvet carpet from Aladdin's palace to the Sultan's. Aladdin's mother then dressed herself carefully, and walked to the palace with her slaves, while he followed her on horseback. The Sultan sent musicians with trumpets and cymbals to meet them, so that the air resounded with music and cheers. She was taken to the Princess, who saluted her and treated her with great honor. At night the Princess said good-by to her father and set out on the carpet for Aladdin's palace, with his mother at her side, and followed by the hundred slaves. She was charmed at the sight of Aladdin, who ran to receive her. "Princess," he said, "blame your beauty for my boldness if I have displeased you." She told him that, having seen him, she willingly obeyed her father in this matter. After the wedding had taken place Aladdin led her into the hall, where a feast was spread, and she supped with him, after which they danced till midnight.

Next day Aladdin invited the Sultan to see the palace. On entering the hall with the four-and-twenty windows, with their rubies, diamonds, and emeralds, he cried: "It is a world's wonder! There is only one thing that surprises me. Was it by accident that one window was left unfinished?" "No, sir, by design," returned Aladdin. "I wished Your Majesty to have the glory of finishing this palace." The Sultan was pleased, and sent for the best jewelers in the city. He showed them the unfinished window, and bade them fit it up like the others. "Sir," replied their spokesman, "we cannot find jewels enough." The Sultan had his own fetched, which they soon used, but to no purpose, for in a month's time the work was not half done. Aladdin, knowing that their task was vain, bade them undo their work and carry the jewels back, and the genie finished the window at his command. The

Sultan was surprised to receive his jewels again, and visited Aladdin, who showed him the window finished. The Sultan embraced him, the envious Vizier meanwhile hinting that it was the work of enchantment.

Aladdin had won the hearts of the people by his gentle bearing. He was made captain of the Sultan's armies, and won several battles for him, but remained modest and courteous as before, and lived thus in peace and content for several years.

But far away in Africa the magician remembered Aladdin, and by his magic arts discovered that Aladdin, instead of perishing miserably in the cave, had escaped, and had married a princess, with whom he was living in great honor and wealth. He knew that the poor tailor's son could only have accomplished this by means of the lamp, and traveled night and day until he reached the capital of China, bent on Aladdin's ruin. As he passed through the town he heard people talking everywhere about a marvelous palace. "Forgive my ignorance," he said, "what is this palace you speak of?" "Have you not heard of Prince Aladdin's palace," was the reply, "the greatest wonder of the world? I will direct you if you have a mind to see it." The magician thanked him who spoke, and, having seen the palace, knew that it had been raised by the Genie of the Lamp, and became half mad with rage. He determined to get hold of the lamp, and again plunge Aladdin into the deepest poverty.

Unluckily, Aladdin had gone a-hunting for eight days, which gave the magician plenty of time. He bought a dozen copper lamps, put them into a basket, and went

to the palace, crying: "New lamps for old!" followed by a jeering crowd. The Princess, sitting in the hall of four-and-twenty windows, sent a slave to find out what the noise was about, who came back laughing, so that the Princess scolded her. "Madam," replied the slave, "who can help laughing to see an old fool offering to exchange fine new lamps for old ones?" Another slave, hearing this, said: "There is an old one on the cornice there which he can have." Now this was the magic lamp, which Aladdin had left there, as he could not take it out hunting with him. The Princess, not knowing its value, laughingly bade the slave take it and make the exchange. She went and said to the magician: "Give me a new lamp for this." He snatched it and bade the slave

take her choice, amid the jeers of the crowd. Little he cared, but left off crying his lamps, and went out of the city gates to a lonely place, where he remained till nightfall, when he pulled out the lamp and rubbed it. The genie appeared, and at the magician's command carried him, together with the palace and the Princess in it, to a lonely place in Africa.

Next morning the Sultan looked out of the window toward Aladdin's palace and rubbed his eyes, for it was gone. He sent for the Vizier and asked what had become of the palace. The Vizier looked out too, and was lost in astonishment. He again put it down to enchantment, and this time the Sultan believed him, and sent thirty men on horseback to fetch Aladdin in chains. They met him riding home, bound him, and forced him to go with them on foot. The people, however, who loved him, followed, armed, to see that he came to no harm. He was carried before the Sultan, who ordered the executioner to cut off his head. The executioner made Aladdin kneel down, bandaged his eyes, and raised his scimitar to strike. At that instant the Vizier, who saw that the crowd had forced their way into the courtyard and were scaling the walls to rescue Aladdin, called to the executioner to stay his hand. The people, indeed, looked so threatening that the Sultan gave way and ordered Aladdin to be unbound, and pardoned him in the sight of the crowd. Aladdin now begged to know what he had done. "False wretch!" said the Sultan, "come hither," and showed him from the window the place where his palace had stood. Aladdin was so amazed that he could not say a word. "Where is my palace and my daughter?" demanded the Sultan. "For the first I am not so deeply concerned, but my daughter I must have, and you must find her or lose your head." Aladdin begged for forty days in which to find her, promising, if he failed, to return and suffer death at the Sultan's pleasure. His prayer was granted, and he went forth sadly from the Sultan's presence. For three days he wandered about like a madman, asking everyone what had become of his palace, but they only laughed and pitied him. He came to the banks of a river, and knelt down to say his prayers before throwing himself in. In so doing he rubbed the magic ring he still wore. The genie he had seen in the cave appeared, and asked his will. "Save my life, genie," said Aladdin, "bring my palace back." "That is not in my power," said

the genie; "I am only the Slave of the Ring; you must ask him of the lamp." "Even so," said Aladdin, "but thou canst take me to the palace, and set me down under my dear wife's window." He at once found himself in Africa, under the window of the Princess, and fell asleep out of sheer weariness.

He was awakened by the singing of the birds, and his heart was lighter. He saw plainly that all his misfortunes were owing to the loss of the lamp, and vainly wondered who had robbed him of it.

That morning the Princess rose earlier than she had done since she had been carried into Africa by the magician, whose company she was forced to endure once a day. She, however, treated him so harshly that he dared not live there altogether. As she was dressing, one of her women looked out and saw Aladdin. The Princess ran and opened the window, and at the noise she made Aladdin looked up. She called to him to come to her, and great was the joy of these lovers at seeing each other again. After he had kissed her Aladdin said: "I beg of you, Princess, in God's name, before we speak of anything else, for your own sake and mine, tell me what has become of an old lamp I left on the cornice in the hall of four-and-twenty windows, when I went a-hunting." "Alas!" she said. "I am the innocent cause of our sorrows," and told him of the exchange of the lamp. "Now I know," cried Aladdin, "that we have to thank the African magician for this! Where is the lamp?" "He carries it about with him," said the Princess. "I know, for he pulled it out of his breast to show me. He wishes me to break my faith with you and marry him, saying that you were beheaded by my

father's command. He is forever speaking ill of you, but I only reply by my tears. If I persist, I doubt not but he will use violence." Aladdin comforted her, and left her for a while. He changed clothes with the first person he met in the town, and having bought a certain powder, returned to the Princess, who let him in by a little side door. "Put on your most beautiful dress," he said to her, "and receive the magician with smiles, leading him to believe that you have forgotten me. Invite him to sup with you, and say you wish to taste the wine of his country. He will go for some and while he is gone I will tell you what to do." She listened carefully to Aladdin and when he left she arrayed herself gaily for the first time since she had left China. She put on a girdle and headdress of diamonds, and, seeing in a glass that she was more beautiful than ever, received the magician, saying, to his great amazement: "I have made up my mind that Aladdin is dead, and that all my tears will not bring him back to me, so I am resolved to mourn no more, and have therefore invited you to sup with me; but I am tired of the wines of China, and would fain taste those of Africa." The magician flew to his cellar, and the Princess put the powder Aladdin had given her in her cup. When he returned she asked him to drink her health in the wine of Africa, handing him her cup in exchange for his, as a sign she was reconciled to him. Before drinking, the magician made her a speech in praise of her beauty, but the Princess cut him short, saying: "Let us drink first, and you shall say what you will afterward." She set her cup to her lips and kept it there, while the magician drained his to the dregs and fell back lifeless. The Princess then opened the door to Aladdin, and flung her arms round his neck; but Aladdin put her away, bidding her leave him, as he had more to do. He then went to the dead magician, took the lamp out of his vest, and bade

the genie carry the palace and all in it back to China. This was done, and the Princess in her chamber only felt two little shocks, and little thought she was at home again.

The Sultan, who was sitting in his chamber, mourning for his lost daughter, happened to look up, and rubbed his eyes, for there stood the palace as before! He hastened thither, and Aladdin received him in the hall of the four-and-twenty windows, with the Princess at his side. Aladdin told him what had happened, and showed him the dead body of the magician, that he might believe. A ten-day feast was proclaimed, and it seemed

as if Aladdin might now live the rest of his life in peace; but it was not to be.

The African magician had a younger brother, who was, if possible, more wicked and more cunning than he. He traveled to China to avenge his brother's death, and went to visit a pious woman called Fatima, thinking she might be of use to him. He entered her cell and clapped a dagger to her breast, telling her to rise and do his bidding on pain of death. He changed clothes with her, colored his face like hers, put on her veil, and murdered her, that she might tell no tales. Then he went toward the palace of Aladdin, and all the people, thinking he was the holy woman, gathered round him, kissing his hands and begging his blessing. When he got to the palace there was such a noise going on round him that the Princess bade her slave look out of the window and ask what was the matter. The slave said it was the holy woman, curing people by her touch of their ailments, whereupon the Princess, who had long desired to see Fatima, sent for her. On coming to the Princess the magician offered up a prayer for her health and prosperity. When he had done, the Princess made him sit by her, and begged him to stay with her always. The false Fatima, who wished for nothing better, consented, but kept his veil down for fear of discovery. The Princess showed him the hall, and asked him what he thought of it. "It is truly beautiful," said the false Fatima. "It wants but one thing." "And what is that?" said the Princess. "If only a roc's egg," replied he, "were hung up from the middle of this dome, it would be the wonder of the world."

After this the Princess could think of nothing but the roc's egg, and when Aladdin returned from hunting he found her in a very ill humor. He begged to know what was amiss, and she told him that all her pleasure in the hall was spoiled for the want of a roc's egg hanging from the dome. "If that is all," replied Aladdin, "you shall soon be happy." He left her and rubbed the lamp, and when the genie appeared commanded him to bring a roc's egg. The genie gave such a loud and terrible shriek that the hall shook. "Wretch!" he cried, "is it not enough that I have done everything for you, but you must command me to bring my master and hang him up in the midst of this dome? You and your wife and your palace deserve to be burned to ashes, but that this request does not come from you, but from the brother of the African magician whom you destroyed. He is now in your palace disguised as the holy woman—whom he murdered. He it was who put that wish into your wife's head. Take care of yourself, for he means to kill you." So saying, the genie disappeared.

Aladdin went back to the Princess, saying his head ached, and requesting that the holy Fatima should be fetched to lay her hands on it. But when the Magician came near, Aladdin, seizing his dagger, pierced him to the heart. "What have you done?" cried the Princess. "You have killed the holy woman!" "Not so," replied Aladdin, "but a wicked magician," and told her of how she had been deceived.

After this Aladdin and his wife lived in peace. He succeeded the Sultan when he died, and reigned for many years, leaving behind him a long line of kings.

Favorite Fables of
Aesop

RETOLD BY LOUIS UNTERMEYER

Illustrated by A. AND M. PROVENSEN

Aesop was born a slave more than
two thousand five hundred years ago.
It is thought that Aesop means Aethiop (or Ethiopian),
that he came from Africa and was probably black.
His Greek owner was so impressed with his intelligence
and the way he applied it that he gave Aesop his freedom.
Under the fabulously rich King Croesus
the former slave acted as a kind of ambassador
and visited the provinces, telling stories
to emphasize his points. Since he was a diplomat
and did not want to offend his listeners
by referring to their human faults, he took the ideas
in the minds of men and put them in the
mouths of animals. All of his stories, or fables,
concealed lessons for listeners to think over.
Some of Aesop's translators made each lesson plain
by concluding every fable with a Moral—a custom that
the editors have followed. If, however, you feel that
the stories show the Morals by themselves,
you can ignore the added lines.

Δὲν
φέρθηκε
καλά.

The Fox and the Crow

A Crow had stolen a good-sized piece of cheese from a cottage window and had flown with it into a tall tree. A Fox, who had seen this happen, said to himself, "If I am smart, I will have cheese for supper tonight." He thought for a moment, and then decided on his plan.

"Good afternoon, Miss Crow," he said. "How really beautiful you look today. I've never seen your feathers so glistening. Your neck is as graceful as a swan's and your wings are mightier than an eagle's. I am sure that if you had a voice, you would sing as sweetly as a nightingale."

The Crow, pleased with such praise, wanted to prove that she could sing. As soon as she opened her mouth to caw, the cheese fell to the ground and the Fox snapped it up.

As he trotted off he made things worse by calling back to the Crow, "I may have talked much about your beauty, but I said nothing about your brains."

"Don't be fooled by flattery."

The Grasshopper and the Ant

ONE clear winter's day an Ant dragged out some grains of food to dry in the sun. A hungry Grasshopper passing by asked the Ant to let him have some of the food.

"Why do you come to me to be fed?" asked the Ant. "What were you doing during the summer?"

"Oh," replied the Grasshopper, "I spent the summer singing."

"Well, then," said the Ant, "you sang all summer, you can dance all winter."

The Great and Little Fishes

"WE ARE the terrors of the deep," said the Great Fishes. "Everything is afraid of us; we fear nothing. You, Little Fishes, do not count. You cannot fight; you are easily captured."

At that moment, a fisherman lowered a strong new net. The Great Fishes were quickly caught and hauled into the ship, while the Little Fishes escaped through the wide meshes.

Ἔχω πονοκέφαλο

"Clothes do not make the man. Your talk gives you away."

The Ass in the Lion's Skin

AN Ass once found the skin of a dead Lion. Putting it on, he frightened all the animals by strutting about without a sound. Only the clever Fox was suspicious. In an attempt to frighten him, the Ass tried to roar. As soon as he heard the familiar bray, the Fox laughed and said, "I, too, might have been alarmed if you had kept your mouth shut."

393

Μετα.θα πᾶμε ὅλοι στη ταβέρνα γιὰ ποτό

The Cat and the Mice

THE MICE were much bothered by a Cat. They decided to hold a council to see what could be done about the matter. During the meeting a young mouse there said, "If the Cat had a little bell tied to her neck, it would tinkle every time she made a step. This would warn us, and we would have plenty of time to reach our homes in safety."

All the Mice applauded this clever scheme until one of them spoke up and said, "It's a fine plan. But which one of us is going to put the bell on the Cat?"

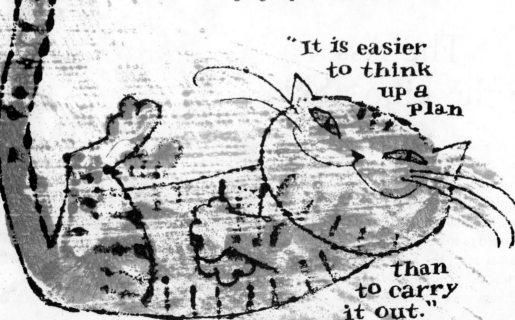

"It is easier to think up a plan than to carry it out."

Στείλετε
γιὰ
τὸν
γιατρόν

The Goose and the Golden Eggs

A MAN had the great good fortune to own a marvelous Goose—every day it laid a golden egg. The Man was growing rich, but the more he got, the more he wanted. Making up his mind to have the whole treasure at once, he killed the Goose. But when he killed her and cut her open, instead of finding a horde of golden eggs, he found that she was just like any other Goose.

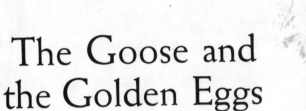

"Beware of being greedy. It doesn't pay to be impatient."

395

"There is comfort in pretending that what we can't get isn't worth having."

The Fox and the Grapes

THE Fox had gone without breakfast as well as without dinner, so when he found himself in a vineyard his mouth began to water. There was one particularly juicy-looking bunch of grapes hanging on a trellis. The Fox leaped to pull it down, but it was just beyond his reach. He went back a few steps, took a running start, and jumped again. Again he missed. Once more he tried, and once more he failed to get the tempting prize. Finally, weary and worn out, he left the vineyard. "I really wasn't very hungry," he said to console himself. "Besides, I'm sure those grapes are sour."

Τί εἶναι;
Τί εἴπατε;
Τί θὰ γίνη;
Τί θέλετε;

Μην τὸ λάβετε ὑπόψη.

"A liar will not be believed even when he speaks the truth."

The Boy and the Wolf

A Boy who was employed to tend sheep was often bored with the task. To create a little excitement he would rush toward the village crying "Wolf! Wolf!" When the villagers came with clubs and pitchforks to help him, they found nothing. This seemed such good sport that a few days later the Boy cried out again, and once more the people ran to help him.

One day a Wolf actually did come out of the forest. But this time when the Boy cried "Wolf, Wolf," the villagers thought he was playing his tricks again, and refused to stir. Meanwhile, the sheep were at the mercy of the Wolf, who enjoyed a hearty meal.

397

"He who tries to please everybody pleases nobody."

The Miller,
the Son,
and
the Donkey

ONE DAY a Miller and his Son were driving their Donkey to market. They had not gone far when some girls saw them and broke out laughing. "Look!" cried one. "Look at those fools! How silly they are to be trudging along on foot when the Donkey might be carrying one of them on his back."

398

Τί κρίμα!..

Βεβαίως όχι.

πρέπει υτρέπεται.

Ποίος είπεν έτζι;

This seemed to make sense, so the Father lifted his Son on the Donkey and walked along contentedly by his side. They trod on for a while until they met an old Man who spoke to the Son scornfully. "You should be ashamed of yourself, you lazy rascal. What do you mean by riding when your poor old Father has to walk. It shows that no one respects age any more. The least you can do is get down and let your Father rest his old bones."

Red with shame, the Son dismounted and made his Father get on the Donkey's back.

They had gone only a little further when they met a group of young fellows who mocked them. "What a cruel old Man!" jeered one of the fellows. "There he sits, selfish and comfortable, while the poor Boy has to stumble along the dusty road to keep up with him." So the Father lifted the Son up, and the two of them rode along.

However, before they reached the market place, a townsman stopped them. "Have you no feeling for dumb creatures!" he shouted. "The way that you load that little animal is a crime. You two men are better able to carry the poor little beast than he you!"

Wanting to do the right thing the Miller and his Son got off the Donkey, tied his legs together, slung him on a pole, and carried him on their shoulders. When the crowd saw this spectacle the people laughed so loudly that the Donkey was frightened, kicked through the cords that bound him and, falling off the pole, fell into the river and was drowned.

399

"Don't belittle little things. A friend in need is a friend indeed, no matter how small he may be."

The Lion and the Mouse

ONE DAY a Mouse happened to run over the paws of a sleeping Lion. Angrily the mighty beast woke and seized the offender. He was about to crush the little animal when the Mouse cried out, "Please, mighty monarch, spare me. I would be only a tiny mouthful, and you would not relish me. Besides, I might be able to help you some day. You never can tell."

The idea that this insignificant creature could ever help him amused the Lion so much that he let his little prisoner go.

Some time after this the Lion, roaming the forest for food, was caught in a hunter's net. The more he struggled the more he became entangled; his roar of rage echoed through the forest. Hearing the sound, the Mouse ran to the trap and began to gnaw the ropes that bound the Lion. It was not long before he had severed the last cord with his little teeth and set the huge beast free.

Τι ὥρα εἶναι;

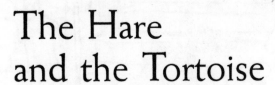

Εἶνα νωρίτερα ἀπὸ ὅτι νόμιζα...

The Hare and the Tortoise

Aesop

"The race is not always to the swift; slow and steady is sure to win."

A HARE was always boasting about his speed and sneering at a Tortoise because he was so slow. One day the Tortoise said, "You may laugh at me, but if we ever had a race I know I could beat you." "Ridiculous!" said the Hare. "Is it?" said the Tortoise. "We shall see. Are you ready?"

They started up at once and, of course, the Hare quickly outran the Tortoise who merely crawled along. The Hare, in fact, was so far ahead that he treated the whole matter as a joke and lay down. "I'll take a little nap here in the grass," he said to himself, "and when I wake up I'll finish the race far ahead."

Nevertheless, the Hare overslept himself and when he arrived at the finish line, the Tortoise, who had plodded steadily along, was there ahead of him.

401

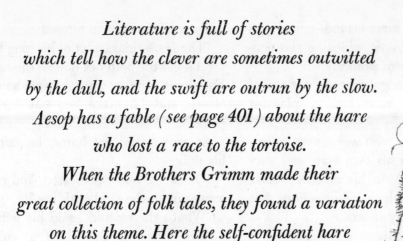

Literature is full of stories
which tell how the clever are sometimes outwitted
by the dull, and the swift are outrun by the slow.
Aesop has a fable (see page 401) about the hare
who lost a race to the tortoise.
When the Brothers Grimm made their
great collection of folk tales, they found a variation
on this theme. Here the self-confident hare
is tricked by the plodding hedgehog.

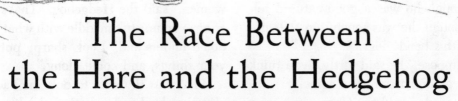

The Race Between the Hare and the Hedgehog

BY JAKOB AND WILHELM GRIMM
Illustrated by JEAN WINSLOW

IT WAS once upon a time on a Saturday morning in autumn, while the barley fields were still in bloom.

The sun was shining, the morning wind was blowing over the stubble, the larks were singing high in the air, the bees were buzzing in the barley blossoms, and the people were going blithely about their day's work. In short, all the world was happy, and the Hedgehog, too.

The Hedgehog stood in front of his door with folded arms, looked at the weather, and hummed a tune such as only a hedgehog can hum on a Saturday morning.

Now, as he stood there humming, he thought to himself all at once that, while his wife was washing and dressing the children, he might as well go for a little walk in the fields and see how his turnips were getting on.

The turnips grew near his house, and as he and his family ate as many of them as ever they wanted, he looked upon them quite naturally as his own property.

Well, the Hedgehog slammed his door and started for the turnip field. He hadn't got very far, and was just sauntering round the brier bush that stood outside the field, when he met the Hare, who was out on the same errand—namely, to look at the cabbages, which he also considered as his own property.

When the Hedgehog caught sight of the Hare, he gave him a pleasant "Good morning."

But the Hare, who was a very aristocratic person in his own way, and very high and mighty in his manner, didn't answer the Hedgehog's greeting, but said, with a nasty sneer:

"What are you running about the fields for so early in the morning?"

"I'm just walking," said the Hedgehog.

"Walking?" grinned the Hare. "I don't think your legs are very suited for walking!"

This remark annoyed the Hedgehog, for, though he was a good-natured fellow enough, he was touchy on the subject of his bandy legs.

"I suppose," he said tartly, "you think your legs are better than mine?"

"That I do," said the Hare.

"It remains to be seen," said the Hedgehog. "I bet you that if we two were to run a race I should beat you."

"What a joke!" cried the Hare. "You with your bandy legs! But if you're so anxious to try, I've no objection. What will you bet?"

"A golden guinea," said the Hedgehog.

"Agreed!" said the Hare. "We'll start right away!"

"Oh, don't be in such a hurry," said the Hedgehog. "I haven't had my breakfast yet. I must go home first and get something to eat. I'll come back here in an hour."

So away he trotted, for the Hare made no objection.

Then he thought to himself:

"The Hare thinks a lot of his long legs, but I'll get the better of him all the same. For all his haughty ways, he's not so very clever, and I'll make him pay for his pride."

As soon as he got home, he said to his wife:

"Quick! go and get dressed. You must come out to the field with me."

"What's the matter?" said his wife.

"I've wagered the Hare a golden guinea that I will beat him in a race, and I want you to be there."

"Good gracious me!" cried the Hedgehog's wife. "Have you lost your senses? How can you think of racing the Hare?"

"Don't be so quick with your words, woman," said the Hedgehog. "That's my affair; you mustn't meddle with what you don't understand. Look sharp; put on your things, and come along."

What was the wife to do? She had to obey her husband, whether she liked it or not.

On the way to the field, the Hedgehog said:

"Now, listen to what I'm going to tell you. Do you see that plowed field over there? That's where we're to run our race. The hare will run in one furrow, and I in the other. Now, all you've got to do is hide yourself at the other end of my furrow and, directly the Hare comes up to you, you pop your head up and say:

"'Here I am already!'"

With that they reached the field. The Hedgehog told his wife where to stand, and went on to the other end.

The Hare was there waiting for him.

"Shall we start?" asked the Hare.

"Right," said the Hedgehog.

"Now then!"

Each took up his place.

The Hare counted:

"One, two, three!"

And away he went like the wind.

But the Hedgehog took about three paces, then he went back, ducked down in his furrow, and stood there as comfortably as you please, and laughing as if he would split his sides.

Now, the moment the Hare came rushing up to the other end, the Hedgehog's wife called out to him:

"Here I am already!"

The Hare was quite taken aback, though he made sure it was the Hedgehog himself who was sitting there calling to him. But, as everyone knows, a hedgehog's wife looks exactly like her husband.

"There's something not quite right here," said the Hare. "We must run again back to the starting point."

And away he flew like the wind, and his ears floated behind him. But the Hedgehog's wife never moved.

When the Hare got to the other end, the Hedgehog called out:

"Here I am already!"

Then the Hare, quite beside himself with jealousy, shouted:

"We must run again!"

"Right!" said the Hedgehog. "As often as you like."

And so the Hare went on, running backward and forward seventy-three times, and every time he was beaten. Every time the Hare arrived at one end or the other, the Hedgehog or his wife called out:

"Here I am already!"

But the seventy-fourth time the Hare dropped down dead tired before he got half-way. So the Hedgehog took his golden guinea, and he and his wife went home very well pleased with themselves. And so my tale is finished.

Peter Pan has become known as the boy who refused
to grow up. Many of us know about him—
his relations with Tinker Bell and his struggles
with Captain Hook—through stage plays, motion pictures,
and television. But there is an earlier Peter, a
somewhat different Peter Pan, whom J. M. Barrie
created in The Little White Bird
and who became the hero of the later adventures. In the
following chapters, we see the original Peter Pan,
making his home in Kensington Gardens,
one of London's favorite parks. There, after the gates are shut
tight every evening at Lock-out Time, the birds
and fairies take possession.

Peter Pan

From The Little White Bird

BY J. M. BARRIE
Illustrated by JEAN WINSLOW

IF YOU ASK your mother whether she knew about Peter Pan when she was a little girl she will say, "Why, of course, I did, child," and if you ask her whether he rode on a goat in those days she will say, "What a foolish question to ask; certainly he did." Then if you ask your grandmother whether she knew about Peter Pan when she was a girl, she also says, "Why, of course, I did, child," but if you ask her whether he rode on a goat in those days, she says she never heard of his having a goat. Perhaps she has forgotten, just as she sometimes forgets your name and calls you Mildred, which is your mother's name. Still, she could hardly forget such an important thing as the goat. Therefore there was no goat when your grandmother was a little girl. This shows that, in telling the story of Peter Pan, to begin with the goat (as most people do) is as silly as to put on your jacket before your vest.

Of course, it also shows that Peter is ever so old, but he is really always the same age, so that does not matter in the least. His age is one week, and though he was born so long ago he has never had a birthday, nor is there the slightest chance of his ever having one. The reason is that he escaped from being a human when he was seven days' old; he escaped by the window and flew back to the Kensington Gardens.

If you think he was the only baby who ever wanted to escape, it shows how completely you have forgotten your own young days. When David[1] heard this story first he was quite certain that he had never tried to escape, but I told him to think back hard, pressing his hands to his temples, and when he had done this hard, and even harder, he distinctly remembered a youthful desire to return to the tree-tops, and with that memory came others, as that he had lain in bed planning to escape as soon as his mother was asleep, and how she had once caught him half-way up the chimney. All children could have such recollections if they would press their hands hard to their temples, for, having been birds before they were human, they are naturally a little

wild during the first few weeks, and very itchy at the shoulders, where their wings used to be. So David tells me.

I ought to mention here that the following is our way with a story: First, I tell it to him, and then he tells it to me, the understanding being that it is quite a different story; and then I retell it with his additions, and so we go on until no one could say whether it is more his story or mine. In this story of Peter Pan, for instance, the bald narrative and most of the moral reflections are mine, though not all, for this boy can be a stern moralist, but the interesting bits about the ways and customs of babies in the bird-stage are mostly reminiscences of David's, recalled by pressing his hands to his temples and thinking hard.

Well, Peter Pan got out by the window, which had no bars. Standing on the ledge he could see trees far away, which were doubtless the Kensington Gardens, and the moment he saw them he entirely forgot that he was now a little boy in a nightgown, and away he flew, right over the houses to the Gardens. It is wonderful that he could fly without wings, but the

---

[1] David is the little boy to whom the author first told this story.

place itched tremendously, and perhaps we could all fly if we were as dead-confident-sure of our capacity to do it as was bold Peter Pan that evening.

He alighted gaily on the open sward, between the Baby's Palace and the Serpentine, and the first thing he did was to lie on his back and kick. He was quite unaware already that he had ever been human, and thought he was a bird, even in appearance, just the same as in his early days, and when he tried to catch a fly he did not understand that the reason he missed it was because he had attempted to seize it with his hand, which, of course, a bird never does. He saw, however, that it must be past Lock-out Time, for there were a good many fairies about, all too busy to notice him; they were getting breakfast ready, milking their cows, drawing water, and so on, and the sight of the water-pails made him thirsty, so he flew over to the Round Pond to have a drink. He stooped, and dipped his beak in the pond; he thought it was his beak, but, of course, it was only his nose, and, therefore, very little water came up, and that not so refreshing as usual, so next he tried a puddle, and he fell flop into it. When a real bird falls in flop, he spreads out his feathers and pecks them dry, but Peter could not remember what was the thing to do, and he decided, rather sulkily, to go to sleep on the weeping beech in the Baby Walk.

At first he found some difficulty in balancing himself on a branch, but presently he remembered the way, and fell asleep. He awoke long before morning, shivering, and saying to himself, "I never was out in such a cold night;" he had really been out in colder nights when he was a bird, but,

408

of course, as everybody knows, what seems a warm night to a bird is a cold night to a boy in a night-gown. Peter also felt strangely uncomfortable, as if his head was stuffy, he heard loud noises that made him look round sharply, though they were really himself sneezing. There was something he wanted very much, but, though he knew he wanted it, he could not think what it was. What he wanted so much was his mother to blow his nose, but that never struck him, so he decided to appeal to the fairies for enlightenment. They are reputed to know a good deal.

There were two of them strolling along the Baby Walk, with their arms round each other's waists, and he hopped down to address them. The fairies have their tiffs with the birds, but they usually give a civil answer to a civil question, and he was quite angry when these two ran away the moment they saw him. Another was lolling on a garden-chair, reading a postage-stamp which some human had let fall, and when he heard Peter's voice he popped in alarm behind a tulip.

To Peter's bewilderment he discovered that every fairy he met fled from him. A band of workmen, who were sawing down a toadstool, rushed away, leaving their tools behind them. A milkmaid turned her pail upside down and hid in it. Soon the Gardens were in an uproar. Crowds of fairies were running this way and that, asking each other stoutly who was afraid, lights were extinguished, doors barricaded, and from the grounds of Queen Mab's palace came the rubadub of drums, showing that the royal guard had been called out. A regiment of Lancers came charging down the Broad Walk, armed with holly-leaves, with which they jog the enemy horribly in passing. Peter heard the little people crying everywhere that there was a human in the Gardens after Lock-out Time, but he never thought for a moment that he was the human. He was feeling stuffier and stuffier, and more and more wistful to learn what he wanted done to his nose, but he pursued them with the vital question in vain; the timid creatures ran from him, and even the Lancers, when he approached them up the Hump, turned swiftly into a side-walk, on the pretence that they saw him there.

Despairing of the fairies, he resolved to consult the birds, but now he remembered, as an odd thing, that all the birds on the weeping beech had flown away when he alighted on it, and though that had not troubled him at the time, he saw its meaning now. Every living thing was shunning him. Poor little Peter Pan, he sat down and cried, and even then he did not know that, for a bird, he was sitting on his wrong part. It is a blessing that he did not know, for otherwise he would have lost faith in his power to fly, and the moment you doubt whether you can fly, you cease forever to be able to do it. The reason birds can fly and we can't is simply that they have perfect faith, for to have faith is to have wings.

Now, except by flying, no one can reach the island in the Serpentine, for the boats of humans are forbidden to land there, and there are stakes round it, standing up in the water, on each of which a bird-sentinel sits by day and night. It was to the island that Peter now flew to put his strange case before old Solomon Caw, and he alighted on it with relief, much heartened to find himself at last at home,

as the birds call the island. All of them
were asleep, including the sentinels, except Solomon, who was wide awake on
one side, and he listened quietly to Peter's
adventures, and then told him their true
meaning.

"Look at your night-gown, if you don't
believe me," Solomon said, and with staring eyes Peter looked at his night-gown,
and then at the sleeping birds. Not one
of them wore anything.

"How many of your toes are thumbs?"
said Solomon, a little cruelly, and Peter
saw to his consternation that all his toes
were fingers. The shock was so great that
it drove away his cold.

"Ruffle your feathers," said that grim
old Solomon, and Peter tried most desperately hard to ruffle his feathers, but he
had none. Then he rose up, quaking, and
for the first time since he stood on the
window-ledge, he remembered a lady
who had been very fond of him.

"I think I shall go back to mother," he
said timidly.

"Good-bye," replied Solomon Caw with
a queer look.

But Peter hesitated. "Why don't you
go?" the old one asked politely.

"I suppose," said Peter huskily, "I suppose I can still fly?"

You see, he had lost faith.

"Poor little half-and-half," said Solomon, who was not really hard-hearted,
"you will never be able to fly again, not
even on windy days. You must live here
on the island always."

"And never even go to the Kensington
Gardens?" Peter asked tragically.

"How could you get across?" said Solomon. He promised very kindly, however,
to teach Peter as many of the bird ways
as could be learned by one of such an
awkward shape.

"Then I shan't be exactly a human?"
Peter asked.

"No."

"Nor exactly a bird?"

"No."

"What shall I be?"

"You will be a Betwixt-and-Between,"
Solomon said, and certainly he was a wise
old fellow, for that is exactly how it
turned out.

The birds on the island never got used
to him. His oddities tickled them every
day, as if they were quite new, though it
was really the birds that were new. They
came out of the eggs daily, and laughed
at him at once, then off they soon flew to
be humans, and other birds came out of
other eggs, and so it went on forever. The
crafty mother-birds, when they tired of
sitting on their eggs, used to get the
young ones to break their shells a day before the right time by whispering to them
that now was their chance to see Peter
washing or drinking or eating. Thousands

gathered round him daily to watch him do these things, just as you watch the peacocks, and they screamed with delight when he lifted the crusts they flung him with his hands instead of in the usual way with the mouth. All his food was brought to him from the Gardens at Solomon's orders by the birds. He would not eat worms or insects (which they thought very silly of him), so they brought him bread in their beaks. Thus, when you cry out, "Greedy! Greedy!" to the bird that flies away with the big crust, you know now that you ought not to do this, for he is very likely taking it to Peter Pan.

Peter wore no night-gown now. You see, the birds were always begging him for bits of it to line their nests with, and, being very good-natured, he could not refuse, so by Solomon's advice he had hidden what was left of it. But, though he was now quite naked, you must not think that he was cold or unhappy. He was usually very happy and gay, and the reason was that Solomon had kept his promise and taught him many of the bird ways. To be easily pleased, for instance, and always to be really doing something, and to think that whatever he was doing was a thing of vast importance. Peter became very clever at helping the birds to build their nests; soon he could build better than a wood-pigeon, and nearly as well as a blackbird, though never did he satisfy the finches, and he made nice little water-troughs near the nests and dug up worms for the young ones with his fingers. He also became very learned in bird-lore, and knew an east-wind from a west-wind by its smell, and he could see the grass growing and hear the insects walking about inside the tree-trunks. But the best thing

Solomon had done was to teach him to have a glad heart. All birds have glad hearts unless you rob their nests, and so as they were the only kind of heart Solomon knew about, it was easy to him to teach Peter how to have one.

Peter's heart was so glad that he felt he must sing all day long, just as the birds sing for joy, but, being partly human, he needed an instrument, so he made a pipe of reeds, and he used to sit by the shore of the island of an evening, practising the sough of the wind and the ripple of the water, and catching handfuls of the shine of the moon, and he put them all in his pipe and played them so beautifully that even the birds were deceived, and they would say to each other, "Was that a fish leaping in the water or was it Peter playing leaping fish on his pipe?" and sometimes he played the birth of birds, and then the mothers would turn round in their nests to see whether they had laid an egg. If you are a child of the Gardens you must know the chestnut-tree near the bridge, which comes out in flower first of all the chestnuts, but perhaps you have not heard why this tree leads the way. It is because Peter wearies for summer and plays that it has come, and the chestnut being so near, hears him and is cheated.

But as Peter sat by the shore tootling divinely on his pipe he sometimes fell into sad thoughts and then the music became sad also, and the reason of all this sadness was that he could not reach the Gardens, though he could see them through the arch of the bridge. He knew he could never be a real human again, and scarcely wanted to be one, but oh, how he longed to play as other children play, and of course there is no such lovely place to play in as the Gardens. The birds brought him news of how boys and girls play, and wistful tears started in Peter's eyes.

Perhaps you wonder why he did not swim across. The reason was that he could not swim. He wanted to know how to swim, but no one on the island knew the way except the ducks, and they are so stupid. They were quite willing to teach him, but all they could say about it was, "You sit down on the top of the water in this way, and then you kick out like that." Peter tried it often, but always before he could kick out he sank. What he really needed to know was how you sit on the water without sinking, and they said it was quite impossible to explain such an easy thing as that. Occasionally swans touched on the island, and he would give them all his day's food and then ask them how they sat on the water, but as soon as he had no more to give them the hateful things hissed at him and sailed away.

Once he really thought he had discovered a way of reaching the Gardens. A wonderful white thing, like a runaway newspaper, floated high over the island and then tumbled, rolling over and over after the manner of a bird that has broken its wing. Peter was so frightened that he hid, but the birds told him it was only a kite, and what a kite is, and that it must have tugged its string out of a boy's hand, and soared away. After that they laughed at Peter for being so fond of a kite: he loved it so much that he even slept with one hand on it; and I think this was pathetic and pretty, for the reason he loved it was because it had belonged to a real boy.

To the birds this was a very poor reason, but the older ones felt grateful to him at this time because he had nursed a number of fledglings through the German measles, and they offered to show him how birds fly a kite. So six of them took the end of the string in their beaks

414

and flew away with it; and to his amazement it flew after them and went even higher than they.

Peter screamed out, "Do it again!" and with great good-nature they did it several times, and always instead of thanking them he cried, "Do it again!" which shows that even now he had not quite forgotten what it was to be a boy.

At last, with a grand design burning within his brave heart, he begged them to do it once more with him clinging to the tail, and now a hundred flew off with the string, and Peter clung to the tail, meaning to drop off when he was over the Gardens. But the kite broke to pieces in the air, and he would have drowned in the Serpentine had he not caught hold of two indignant swans and made them carry him to the island. After this the birds said that they would help him no more in his mad enterprise.

Nevertheless, Peter did reach the Gardens at last by the help of Shelley's boat, as I am now to tell you.

The Thrush's Nest

SHELLEY was a young gentleman and as grown-up as he need ever expect to be. He was a poet; and they are never exactly grown-up. They are people who despise money except what you need for to-day, and he had all that and five pounds over. So, when he was walking in the Kensington Gardens, he made a paper boat of his bank-note, and sent it sailing on the Serpentine.

It reached the island at night: and the look-out brought it to Solomon Caw, who thought at first that it was the usual thing, a message from a lady, saying she would be obliged if he could let her have a good one. They always ask for the best one he has, and if he likes the letter he sends one from Class A; but if it ruffles him he sends very funny ones indeed. Sometimes he sends none at all, and at another time he sends a nestful; it all depends on the mood you catch him in. He likes you to leave it all to him, and if you mention particularly that you hope he will see his way to making it *a boy this time,* he is almost sure to send another girl. And whether you are a lady or only a little boy who wants a baby-sister, always take pains to write your address clearly. You can't think what a lot of babies Solomon has sent to the wrong house.

Shelley's boat, when opened, completely puzzled Solomon, and he took counsel of his assistants, who, having walked over it twice, first with their toes pointed out, and then with their toes pointed in, decided that it came from some greedy person who wanted five. They thought this because there was a large five printed on it. "Preposterous!" cried Solomon in a rage, and he presented it to Peter; anything useless which drifted upon the island was usually given to Peter as a play-thing.

But he did not play with his precious bank-note, for he knew what it was at once, having been very observant during the week when he was an ordinary boy. With so much money, he reflected, he could surely at last contrive to reach the Gardens, and he considered all the possible ways, and decided (wisely, I think) to choose the best way. But, first, he had to tell the birds of the value of Shelley's boat; and though they were too honest to demand it back, he saw that they were galled, and they cast such black looks at Solomon, who was rather vain of his cleverness, that he flew away to the end of the island, and sat there very depressed with his head buried in his wings. Now Peter knew that unless Solomon was on your side, you never got anything done for you in the island, so he followed him and tried to hearten him.

Nor was this all that Peter did to gain the powerful old fellow's good will. You must know that Solomon had no intention of remaining in office all his life. He looked forward to retiring by-and-by, and devoting his green old age to a life of pleasure on a certain yew-stump in the Figs which had taken his fancy, and for years he had been quietly filling his stocking. It was a stocking belonging to some bathing person which had been cast upon the island, and at the time I speak of it contained a hundred and eighty crumbs, thirty-four nuts, sixteen crusts, a penwiper and a bootlace. When his stocking was full, Solomon calculated that he would be able to retire on a competency. Peter now gave him a pound. He cut it off his bank-note with a sharp stick.

This made Solomon his friend for ever, and after the two had consulted together they called a meeting of the thrushes. You will see presently why thrushes only were invited. The scheme to be put before them was really Peter's, but Solomon did most of the talking, because he soon became irritable if other people talked. He began by saying that he had been much impressed by the superior ingenuity shown by the thrushes in nest-building, and this put them into good-humour at once, as it was meant to do; for all the quarrels between birds are about the best way of building nests. Other birds, said Solomon, omitted to line their nests with mud, and as a result they did not hold water. Here he cocked his head as if he had used an unanswerable argument; but, unfortunately, a Mrs. Finch had come to the meeting uninvited, and she squeaked out, "We don't build nests to hold water, but to hold eggs," and then the thrushes stopped cheering, and Solomon was so perplexed that he took several sips of water.

"Consider," he said at last, "how warm the mud makes the nest."

417

"Consider," cried Mrs. Finch, "that when water gets into the nest it remains there and your little ones are drowned."

The thrushes begged Solomon with a look to say something crushing in reply to this, but again he was perplexed.

"Try another drink," suggested Mrs. Finch pertly. Kate was her name, and all Kates are saucy.

Solomon did try another drink, and it inspired him. "If," said he, "a finch's nest is placed on the Serpentine it fills and breaks to pieces, but a thrush's nest is still as dry as the cup of a swan's back."

How the thrushes applauded! Now they knew why they lined their nests with mud, and when Mrs. Finch called out, "We don't place our nests on the Serpentine," they did what they should have done at first: chased her from the meeting. After this it was most orderly. What they had been brought together to hear, said Solomon, was this: their young friend, Peter Pan, as they well knew, wanted very much to be able to cross to the Gardens, and he now proposed, with their help, to build a boat.

At this the thrushes began to fidget, which made Peter tremble for his scheme.

Solomon explained hastily that what he meant was not one of the cumbrous boats that humans use; the proposed boat was to be simply a thrush's nest large enough to hold Peter.

But still, to Peter's agony, the thrushes were sulky. "We are very busy people," they grumbled, "and this would be a big job."

"Quite so," said Solomon, "and, of course, Peter would not allow you to work for nothing. You must remember that he is now in comfortable circumstances, and

he will pay you such wages as you have never been paid before. Peter Pan authorizes me to say that you shall all be paid sixpence a day."

Then all the thrushes hopped for joy, and that very day was begun the celebrated Building of the Boat. All their ordinary business fell into arrears. It was the time of year when they should have been pairing, but not a thrush's nest was built except this big one, and so Solomon soon ran short of thrushes with which to supply the demand from the mainland. The stout, rather greedy children, who look so well in perambulators but get puffed easily when they walk, were all young thrushes once, and ladies often ask specially for them. What do you think Solomon did? He sent over to the house-tops for a lot of sparrows and ordered them to lay their eggs in old thrushes' nests and sent their young to the ladies and swore they were all thrushes! It was known afterward on the island as the Sparrows' Year, and so, when you meet, as you doubtless sometimes do, grown-up people who puff and blow as if they thought themselves bigger than they are, very likely they belong to that year. You ask them.

Peter was a just master, and paid his work-people every evening. They stood in rows on the branches, waiting politely while he cut the paper sixpences out of his bank-note, and presently he called the roll, and then each bird, as the names were mentioned, flew down and got sixpence. It must have been a fine sight.

And at last, after months of labor, the boat was finished. Oh, the deportment of Peter as he saw it growing more and more like a great thrush's nest! From the very beginning of the building of it he slept by its side, and often woke up to say sweet things to it, and after it was lined with mud and the mud had dried he always slept in it. He sleeps in his nest still, and has a fascinating way of curling round in it, for it is just large enough to hold him comfortably when he curls round like a kitten. It is brown inside, of course, but outside it is mostly green, being woven

of grass and twigs, and when these wither or snap the walls are thatched afresh. There are also a few feathers here and there, which came off the thrushes while they were building.

The other birds were extremely jealous and said that the boat would not balance on the water, but it lay most beautifully steady; they said the water would come into it, but no water came into it. Next they said that Peter had no oars, and this caused the thrushes to look at each other in dismay, but Peter replied that he had no need of oars, for he had a sail, and with such a proud, happy face he produced a sail which he had fashioned out of his night-gown, and though it was still rather like a night-gown it made a lovely sail.

And that night, the moon being full, and all the birds asleep, he did enter his coracle (as Master Francis Pretty would have said) and depart out of the island. And first, he knew not why, he looked upward, with his hands clasped, and from that moment his eyes were pinned to the west.

He had promised the thrushes to begin by making short voyages, with them as his guides, but far away he saw the Kensington Gardens beckoning to him beneath the bridge, and he could not wait. His face was flushed, but he never looked back; there was an exultation in his little breast that drove out fear. Was Peter the least gallant of the English mariners who have sailed westward to meet the Unknown?

At first, his boat turned round and round, and he was driven back to the place of his starting, whereupon he shortened sail, by removing one of the sleeves, and was forthwith carried backward by a contrary breeze, to his no small peril. He now let go the sail, with the result that he was drifted toward the far shore, where are black shadows he knew not the dangers of, but suspected them, and so once more hoisted his night-gown and went roomer of the shadows until he caught a favouring wind, which bore him westward, but at so great a speed that he was like to be broke against the bridge. Which, having avoided, he passed under the bridge and came, to his great rejoicing, within full sight of the delectable Gardens. But having tried to cast anchor, which was a stone at the end of a piece of the kite-string, he found no bottom,

and was fain to hold off, seeking for moorage, and, feeling his way, he buffeted against a sunken reef that cast him overboard by the greatness of the shock, and he was near to being drowned, but clambered back into the vessel. There now arose a mighty storm, accompanied by roaring of waters, such as he had never heard the like, and he was tossed this way and that, and his hands so numbed with the cold that he could not close them. Having escaped the danger of which, he was mercifully carried into a small bay, where his boat rode at peace.

Nevertheless, he was not yet in safety; for, on pretending to disembark, he found a multitude of small people drawn up on the shore to contest his landing, and shouting shrilly to him to be off, for it was long past Lock-out Time. This, with much brandishing of their holly-leaves, and also

a company of them carried an arrow which some boy had left in the Gardens, and this they were prepared to use as a battering-ram.

they gathered around him with intent to slay him, but there then arose a great cry among the women, and it was because they had now observed that his sail was

Then Peter, who knew them for the fairies, called out that he was not an ordinary human and had no desire to do them displeasure, but to be their friend; nevertheless, having found a jolly harbour, he was in no temper to draw off therefrom, and he warned them if they sought to mischief him to stand to their harms.

So saying, he boldly leapt ashore, and

a baby's night-gown. Whereupon, they straightway loved him, and grieved that their laps were too small, the which I cannot explain, except by saying that such is the way of women. The men-fairies now sheathed their weapons on observing the behaviour of their women, on whose intelligence they set great store, and they led him civilly to their queen, who conferred upon him the courtesy of the Gardens after Lock-out Time, and henceforth Peter could go whither he chose, and the fairies had orders to put him in comfort.

Such was his first voyage to the Gardens, and you may gather from the antiquity of the language that it took place a long time ago. But Peter never grows any older, and if we could be watching for him under the bridge to-night (but, of course, we can't), I daresay we should see him hoisting his night-gown and sailing or paddling toward us in the Thrush's Nest. When he sails, he sits down, but he stands up to paddle. I shall tell you presently how he got his paddle.

Long before the time for the opening of the gates comes he steals back to the island, for people must not see him (he is not so human as all that), but this gives him hours for play, and he plays exactly as real children play. At least he thinks so, and it is one of the pathetic things about him that he often plays quite wrongly.

You see, he had no one to tell him how children really play, for the fairies were all more or less in hiding until dusk, and so know nothing, and though the birds pretended that they could tell him a great deal, when the time for telling came, it was wonderful how little they really knew. They told him the truth about hide-and-seek, and he often plays it by himself, but even the ducks on the Round Pond could not explain to him what it is that makes the pond so fascinating to boys. Every night the ducks have forgotten all the events of the day, except the number of pieces of cake thrown to them. They are gloomy creatures, and say that cake is not what it was in their young days.

So Peter had to find out many things for himself. He often played ships at the Round Pond, but his ship was only a hoop which he had found on the grass. Of course, he had never seen a hoop, and he wondered what you play at with them, and decided that you play at pretending they are boats. This hoop always sank at once, but he waded in for it, and sometimes he dragged it gleefully round the rim of the pond, and he was quite proud to think that he had discovered what boys do with hoops.

Another time, when he found a child's pail, he thought it was for sitting in, and he sat so hard in it that he could scarcely get out of it. Also he found a balloon. It was bobbing about on the Hump, quite as if it was having a game by itself, and he caught it after an exciting chase. But he thought it was a ball, and Jenny Wren had told him that boys kick balls, so he kicked it; and after that he could not find it anywhere.

Perhaps the most surprising thing he found was a perambulator. It was under a lime-tree, near the entrance to the Fairy Queen's Winter Palace (which is within the circle of the seven Spanish chestnuts), and Peter approached it warily, for the birds had never mentioned such things to him. Lest it was alive, he addressed it politely, and then, as it gave no answer, he went nearer and felt it cautiously. He gave it a little push, and it ran from him, which made him think it must be alive after all; but, as it had run from him, he was not afraid. So he stretched out his hand to pull it to him, but this time it ran

at him, and he was so alarmed that he leapt the railing and scudded away to his boat. You must not think, however, that he was a coward, for he came back next night with a crust in one hand and a stick in the other, but the perambulator had gone, and he never saw another one. I have promised to tell you also about his paddle. It was a child's spade which he had found near St. Govor's Well, and he thought it was a paddle.

Do you pity Peter Pan for making these mistakes? If so, I think it rather silly of you. What I mean is that, of course, one must pity him now and then, but to pity him all the time would be impertinence. He thought he had the most splendid time in the Gardens, and to think you have it is almost quite as good as really to have it. He played without ceasing, while you often waste time by being mad-dog or Mary-Annish. He could be neither of these things, for he had never heard of them, but do you think he is to be pitied for that?

Oh, he was merry. He was as much merrier than you, for instance, as you are merrier than your father. Sometimes he fell, like a spinning-top, from sheer merriment. Have you seen a greyhound leaping the fences of the Gardens? That is how Peter leaps them.

And think of the music of his pipe. Gentlemen who walk home at night write to the papers to say they heard a nightingale in the Gardens, but it is really Peter's pipe they hear. Of course, he had no mother— at least, what use was she to him? You can be sorry for him for that, but don't be too sorry, for the next thing I mean to tell you is how he revisited her. It was the fairies who gave him the chance.

Lock-out Time

IT IS frightfully difficult to know much about the fairies, and almost the only thing known for certain is that there are fairies wherever there are children. Long ago children were forbidden the Gardens, and at that time there was not a fairy in the place; then the children were admitted, and the fairies came trooping in that very evening. They can't resist following the children, but you seldom see them, partly because they live in the daytime behind the railings, where you are not allowed to go, and also partly because they are so cunning. They are not a bit cunning after Lock-out, but until Lock-out, my word!

When you were a bird you knew the fairies pretty well, and you remember a good deal about them in your babyhood, which it is a great pity you can't write down, for gradually you forget, and I have heard of children who declared that they had never once seen a fairy. Very likely if they said this in the Kensington Gardens, they were standing looking at a fairy all the time. The reason they were cheated was that she pretended to be something else. This is one of their best tricks. They usually pretend to be flowers, because the court sits in the Fairies' Basin, and there are so many flowers there, and all along the Baby Walk, that a flower is the thing least likely to attract attention. They dress exactly like flowers, and change with the seasons, putting on white when lilies are in and blue for blue-bells, and so on. They like crocus and hyacinth time best of all, as they are partial to a bit of colour, but tulips (except white ones, which are the fairy-cradles) they consider garish, and they sometimes put off dressing like tulips for days, so that the beginning of the tulip weeks is almost the best time to catch them.

When they think you are not looking they skip along pretty lively, but if you look and they fear there is no time to hide, they stand quite still, pretending to be flowers. Then, after you have passed without knowing that they were fairies, they rush home and tell their mothers they have had such an adventure. The Fairies' Basin, you remember, is all covered with ground-ivy (from which they make their castor-oil), with flowers growing in it here and there. Most of them really are flowers, but some of them are fairies. You never can be sure of them, but a good plan is to walk by looking the other way, and then turn round sharply. Another good plan, which David and I sometimes follow, is to stare them down. After a long time they can't help winking, and then you know for certain that they are fairies.

There are also numbers of them along the Baby Walk, which is a famous gentle place, as spots frequented by fairies are called. Once twenty-four of them had an extraordinary adventure. They were a girls' school out for a walk with the governess, and all wearing hyacinth gowns, when she suddenly put her finger to her mouth, and then they all stood still on an empty bed and pretended to be hyacinths. Unfortunately, what the governess had heard was two gardeners coming to plant new flowers in that very bed. They were wheeling a handcart with the flowers in it, and were quite surprised to find the bed occupied. "Pity to lift them hyacinths," said the one man. "Duke's orders," replied the other, and, having emptied the cart, they dug up the boarding-school and put the poor, terrified things in it in five rows. Of course, neither the governess nor the girls dare let on that they were fairies, so they were carted far away to a potting-shed, out of which they escaped in the night without their shoes, but there was a great row about it among the parents, and the school was ruined.

As for their houses, it is no use looking for them, because they are the exact opposite of our houses. You can see our houses by day but you can't see them by dark. Well, you can see their houses by dark, but you can't see them by day, for they are the colour of night, and I never heard of anyone yet who could see night in the daytime. This does not mean that they are black, for night has its colours just as day has, but ever so much brighter. Their blues and reds and greens are like ours with a light behind them. The palace is entirely built of many-coloured glasses, and is quite the loveliest of all royal residences, but the queen sometimes complains because the common people will peep in to see what she is doing. They are very inquisitive folk, and press quite hard against the glass, and that is why their noses are mostly snubby. The streets are miles long and very twisty, and have paths on each side made of bright worsted. The birds used to steal the worsted for their nests, but a policeman has been appointed to hold on at the other end. One of the great differences between the fairies and us is that they never do anything useful. When the first baby laughed for the first time, his laugh broke into a million pieces, and they all went skipping about. That was the beginning of fairies. They look tremendously busy, you know, as if they had not a moment to spare, but if you were to ask them what they are doing, they could not tell you in the least. They are frightfully ignorant, and everything they do is make-believe. They have a postman, but he never calls except at Christmas with his little box, and though they have beautiful schools, nothing is taught in them; the youngest child being chief person is always elected mistress, and when she has called the roll, they all go out for a walk and never come back. It is a very noticeable thing that, in fairy families, the youngest is always chief person, and usually becomes a prince or princess, and children remember this and think it must be so among

humans also, and that is why they are often made uneasy when they come upon their mother furtively putting new frills on the bassinet.

You have probably observed that your baby-sister wants to do all sorts of things

that your mother and her nurse want her not do do: to stand up at sitting-down time, and to sit down at standing-up time, for instance, or to wake up when she should fall asleep, or to crawl on the floor when she is wearing her best frock, and so on, and perhaps you put this down to naughtiness. But it is not; it simply means that she is doing as she has seen the fairies do; she begins by following their ways, and it takes about two years to get her into the human ways. Her fits of passion, which are awful to behold, and are usually called teething, are no such thing; they are her natural exasperation, because we don't understand her, though she is talking an intelligible language. She is talking fairy. The reason mothers and nurses know what her remarks mean, before other people know, as that "Guch" means "Give it to me at once," while "Wa" is "Why do you wear such a funny hat?" is because, mixing so much with babies, they have picked up a little of the fairy language.

Of late David has been thinking back hard about the fairy tongue, with his hands clutching his temples, and he has remembered a number of their phrases which I shall tell you some day if I don't forget. He had heard them in the days when he was a thrush, and though I suggested to him that perhaps it is really bird language he is remembering, he says not, for these phrases are about fun and adventures, and the birds talked of nothing but nest-building. He distinctly remembers that the birds used to go from spot to spot like ladies at shop-windows, looking at the different nests and saying, "Not my colour, my dear," and "How would that do with a soft lining?" and "But will it wear?" and "What hideous trimming!" and so on.

The fairies are exquisite dancers, and that is why one of the first things the baby does is to sign to you to dance to him and then to cry when you do it. They hold their great balls in the open air, in what is called a fairy-ring. For weeks afterward you can see the ring on the grass. It is not there when they begin, but they make it by waltzing round and round. Sometimes you will find mushrooms inside the ring, and these are fairy chairs that the servants have forgotten to clear away. The chairs and the rings are the only tell-tale marks these little people leave behind them, and they would remove even these were they not so fond of dancing that they toe it till the very moment of the opening of the gates. David and I once found a fairy-ring quite warm.

But there is also a way of finding out about the ball before it takes place. You know the boards which tell at what time the Gardens are to close to-day. Well, these tricky fairies sometimes slyly change the board on a ball night, so that it says the Gardens are to close at six-thirty for instance, instead of at seven. This enables them to get begun half an hour earlier.

If on such a night we could remain behind in the Gardens, as the famous Maimie Mannering did, we might see delicious sights, hundreds of lovely fairies hastening to the ball, the married ones wearing their wedding-rings round their waists, the gentlemen, all in uniform, holding up the ladies' trains, and linkmen running in front carrying winter cherries, which are the fairy-lanterns, the cloak-room where they put on their silver slippers and get a ticket for their wraps, the flowers streaming up from the Baby Walk to look on, and always welcome because they can lend a pin, the supper-table, with Queen Mab at the head of it, and behind her chair the Lord Chamberlain, who carries a dandelion on which he blows when Her Majesty wants to know the time.

The table-cloth varies according to the seasons, and in May it is made of chestnut-blossom. The way the fairy-servants do is this: The men, scores of them, climb up the trees and shake the branches, and the blossom falls like snow. Then the lady servants sweep it together by whisking their skirts until it is exactly like a table-cloth, and that is how they get their table-cloth.

They have real glasses and real wine of three kinds, namely, blackthorn wine, berberris wine, and cowslip wine, and the Queen pours out, but the bottles are so heavy that she just pretends to pour out. There is bread and butter to begin with, of the size of a threepenny bit; and cakes to end with, and they are so small that they have no crumbs. The fairies sit round on mushrooms, and at first they are very well-behaved and always cough off the table, and so on, but after a bit they are not so well-behaved and stick their fingers into the butter, which is got from the roots of old trees, and the really horrid ones crawl over the table-cloth chasing sugar or other delicacies with their tongues. When the Queen sees them doing this she signs to the servants to wash up and put away, and then everybody adjourns to the dance, the Queen walking in front while the Lord Chamberlain walks behind her, carrying two little pots, one of which contains the juice of wall-flower and the other the juice of Solomon's Seals. Wall-flower juice is good for reviving dancers who fall to the ground in a fit, and Solomon's Seals juice is for bruises. They bruise very easily and when Peter plays faster and faster they foot it till they fall down in fits. For, as you know without my telling you, Peter Pan is the fairies' orchestra. He sits in the middle of the ring, and they would never dream of having a smart dance nowadays without him. "P. P." is written on the corner of the invitation-cards sent out by all really good families. They are grateful little people, too, and at the princess's coming-of-age ball (they come of age on their second birthday and have a birthday every month) they gave him the wish of his heart.

The way it was done was this. The Queen ordered him to kneel, and then said that for playing so beautifully she would give him the wish of his heart. Then they all gathered round Peter to hear what was the wish of his heart, but for a long time he hesitated, not being certain what it was himself.

"If I chose to go back to mother," he asked at last, "could you give me that wish?"

Now this question vexed them, for were he to return to his mother they should lose his music, so the Queen tilted her nose contemptuously and said, "Pooh, ask for a much bigger wish than that."

"Is that quite a little wish?" he inquired.

"As little as this," the Queen answered, putting her hands near each other.

"What size is a big wish?" he asked.

She measured it off on her skirt and it was a very handsome length.

Then Peter reflected and said, "Well, then, I think I shall have two little wishes instead of one big one."

Of course, the fairies had to agree, though his cleverness rather shocked them, and he said that his first wish was to go to his mother, but with the right to return to the Gardens if he found her disappointing. His second wish he would hold in reserve.

They tried to dissuade him, and even put obstacles in the way.

431

"I can give you the power to fly to her house," the Queen said, "but I can't open the door for you."

"The window I flew out at will be open," Peter said confidently. "Mother always keeps it open in the hope that I may fly back."

"How do you know?" they asked, quite surprised, and, really, Peter could not explain how he knew.

"I just do know," he said.

So as he persisted in his wish, they had to grant it. The way they gave him power to fly was this: They all tickled him on the shoulder, and soon he felt a funny itching in that part and then up he rose higher and higher and flew away out of the Gardens and over the house-tops.

It was so delicious that instead of flying straight to his old home he skimmed away over St. Paul's to the Crystal Palace and back by the river and Regent's Park, and by the time he reached his mother's window he had quite made up his mind that his second wish should be to become a bird.

The window was wide open, just as he knew it would be, and in he fluttered, and there was his mother lying asleep. Peter alighted softly on the wooden rail at the foot of the bed and had a good look at her. She lay with her head on her hand, and the hollow in the pillow was like a nest lined with her brown wavy hair. He remembered, though he had long forgotten it, that she always gave

her hair a holiday at night. How sweet the frills of her nightgown were. He was very glad she was such a pretty mother.

But she looked sad, and he knew why she looked sad. One of her arms moved as if it wanted to go round something, and he knew what it wanted to go round.

"Oh, mother," said Peter to himself, "if you just knew who is sitting on the rail at the foot of the bed."

Very gently he patted the little mound that her feet made, and he could see by her face that she liked it. He knew he had but to say "Mother" ever so softly, and she would wake up. They always wake up at once if it is you that says their name. Then she would give such a joyous cry and squeeze him tight. How nice that would be to him, but oh, how exquisitely delicious it would be to her. That I am afraid is how Peter regarded it. In returning to his mother he never doubted that he was giving her the greatest treat a woman can have. Nothing can be more splendid, he thought, than to have a little boy of your own. How proud of him they are; and very right and proper, too.

But why does Peter sit so long on the rail; why does he not tell his mother that he has come back?

I quite shrink from the truth, which is that he sat there in two minds. Sometimes he looked longingly at his mother, and sometimes he looked longingly at the window. Certainly it would be pleasant to be her boy again, but, on the other hand, what times those had been in the Gardens!

Was he so sure that he would enjoy wearing clothes again? He popped off the bed and opened some drawers to have a look at his old garments. They were still

there, but he could not remember how you put them on. The socks, for instance, were they worn on the hands or on the feet? He was about to try one of them on his hand, when he had a great adventure. Perhaps the drawer had creaked; at any rate, his mother woke up, for he heard her say "Peter," as if it was the most lovely word in the language. He remained sitting on the floor and held his breath, wondering how she knew that he had come back. If she said "Peter" again, he meant to cry "Mother" and run to her. But she spoke no more, she made little moans only, and when next he peeped at her she was once more asleep, with tears on her face.

It made Peter very miserable, and what do you think was the first thing he did? Sitting on the rail at the foot of the bed, he played a beautiful lullaby to his mother on his pipe. He had made it up himself out of the way she said "Peter," and he never stopped playing until she looked happy.

He thought this so clever of him that he could scarcely resist wakening her to hear her say, "Oh, Peter, how exquisitely you play." However, as she now seemed comfortable, he again cast looks at the window. You must not think that he meditated flying away and never coming back. He had quite decided to be his mother's boy, but hesitated about beginning tonight. It was the second wish which troubled him. He no longer meant to make it a wish to be a bird, but not to ask for a second wish seemed wasteful, and, of course, he could not ask for it without returning to the fairies. Also, if he put off asking for his wish too long it might go bad. He asked himself if he had not been hard-hearted to fly away without saying good-bye to Solomon. "I should like awfully to sail in my boat just once more," he said wistfully to his sleeping mother. He quite argued with her as if she could hear him. "It would be so splendid to tell the birds of this adventure," he said coaxingly. "I promise to come back," he said solemnly and meant it, too.

And in the end, you know, he flew away. Twice he came back from the window, wanting to kiss his mother, but he feared the delight of it might waken her, so at last he played her a lovely kiss on his pipe, and then he flew back to the Gardens.

Many nights and even months passed before he asked the fairies for his second wish; and I am not sure that I quite know why he delayed so long. One reason was that he had so many good-byes to say, not only to his particular friends, but to a hundred favourite spots. Then he had his last sail, and his very last sail, and his last sail of all, and so on. Again, a number of farewell feasts were given in his honour; and another comfortable reason was that, after all, there was no hurry, for his mother would never weary of waiting for him. This last reason displeased old Solomon, for it was an encouragement to the birds to procrastinate. Solomon had several excellent mottoes for keeping them at their work, such as "Never put off laying to-day, because you can lay to-morrow," and "In this world there are no second chances," and yet here was Peter gaily putting off and none the worse for it. The birds pointed this out to each other, and fell into lazy habits.

But, mind you, though Peter was so slow in going back to his mother, he was quite decided to go back. The best proof of this was his caution with the fairies. They were most anxious that he should remain in the Gardens to play to them, and to bring this to pass they tried to trick him into making such a remark as "I wish the grass was not so wet," and some of them danced out of time in the hope that he might cry, "I do wish you would keep time!" Then they would have said that this was his second wish. But he smoked their design, and though on occasions he began, "I wish—" he always stopped in time. So when at last he said to them bravely, "I wish now to go back to mother for ever and always," they had to tickle his shoulders and let him go.

He went in a hurry in the end because he had dreamt that his mother was crying, and he knew what was the great thing she cried for, and that a hug from her splendid Peter would quickly make her smile. Oh, he felt sure of it, and so eager was he to be nestling in her arms that this time he flew straight to the window, which was always to be open for him.

But the window was closed, and there were iron bars on it, and peering inside he saw his mother sleeping peacefully with her arm round another little boy.

Peter called, "Mother! mother!" but she heard him not; in vain he beat his little limbs against the iron bars. He had to fly back, sobbing, to the Gardens, and he never saw his dear again. What a glorious boy he had meant to be to her. Ah, Peter, we who have made the great mistake, how differently we should all act at the second chance. But Solomon was right; there is no second chance, not for most of us. When we reach the window it is Lockout Time. The iron bars are up for life.

Kenneth Grahame was an important Secretary
of the Bank of England,
but his most important work was a story about some
animals who lived on the bank of a river.
He had written two delightful books, The Golden Age and
Dream Days, based on his childhood.
In letters to his small son who was away at school, he
began a tale about a Water Rat,
a Badger, and a Mole who dreamed of the Wild Wood and,
urged by a pompous Toad, took to the open road.
Just as Lewis Carroll fashioned Alice's Adventures in Wonderland out of a story he told three little girls,
so Kenneth Grahame made a book out of adventures he
had thought up to please a little boy.
He called it The Wind in the Willows when
it was published in 1908.
Everyone who read it loved everything about it. A.A.Milne,
the creator of Winnie-the-Pooh, made a play around it
called "Mr. Toad of Toad Hall."
The book became almost as great a favorite as the Alice books.
The opening chapter, which follows,
gaily introduces the main characters.
It also gives the very feel and smell of spring, the
wet earth, the happy rush of waters,
and the wandering wind singing quietly in the reeds.

The River Bank

From The Wind in the Willows

BY KENNETH GRAHAME
Illustrated by E. H. SHEPARD

THE MOLE had been working very hard all the morning, spring-cleaning his little home. First with brooms, then with dusters; then on ladders and steps and chairs, with a brush and a pail of whitewash; till he had dust in his throat and eyes, and splashes of whitewash all over his black fur, and an aching back and weary arms. Spring was moving in the air above and in the earth below and around him, penetrating even his dark and lowly little house with its spirit of divine discontent and longing. It was small wonder, then, that he suddenly flung down his brush on the floor, said "Bother!" and "O blow!" and also "Hang spring-cleaning!" and bolted out of the house without even waiting to put on his coat. Something up above was calling him imperiously, and he made for the steep little tunnel which

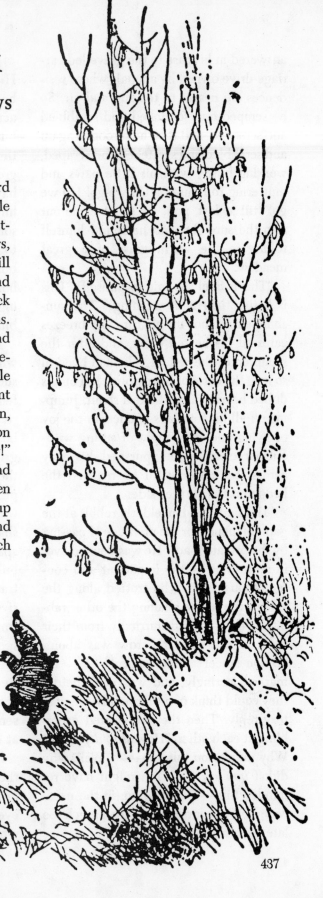

437

answered in his case to the gravelled carriage-drive owned by animals whose residences are nearer to the sun and air. So he scraped and scratched and scrabbled and scrooged, and then he scrooged again and scrabbled and scratched and scraped, working busily with his little paws and muttering to himself, "Up we go! Up we go!" till at last, pop! his snout came out into the sunlight, and he found himself rolling in the warm grass of a great meadow.

"This is fine!" he said to himself. "This is better than whitewashing!" The sunshine struck hot on his fur, soft breezes caressed his heated brow, and after the seclusion of the cellarage he had lived in so long the carol of happy birds fell on his dulled hearing almost like a shout. Jumping off all his four legs at once, in the joy of living and the delight of spring without its cleaning, he pursued his way across the meadow till he reached the hedge on the further side.

"Hold up!" said an elderly rabbit at the gap. "Sixpence for the privilege of passing by the private road!" He was bowled over in an instant by the impatient and contemptuous Mole, who trotted along the side of the hedge chaffing the other rabbits as they peeped hurriedly from their holes to see what the row was about. "Onion-sauce! Onion-sauce!" he remarked jeeringly, and was gone before they could think of a thoroughly satisfactory reply. Then they all started grumbling at each other. "How *stupid* you are! Why didn't you tell him——" "Well, why didn't *you* say——" "You might have reminded him——" and so on, in the usual way; but, of course, it was then much too late, as is always the case.

It all seemed too good to be true. Hither and thither through the meadows he rambled busily, along the hedgerows, across the copses, finding everywhere birds building, flowers budding, leaves thrusting—everything happy, and progressive, and occupied. And instead of having an uneasy conscience pricking him and whispering "Whitewash!" he somehow could only feel how jolly it was to be the only idle dog among all these busy citizens. After all, the best part of a holiday is perhaps not so much to be resting yourself, as to see all the other fellows busy working.

He thought his happiness was complete when, as he meandered aimlessly along, suddenly he stood by the edge of a full-fed river. Never in his life had he seen a river before—this sleek, sinuous, full-bodied animal, chasing and chuckling, gripping things with a gurgle and leaving them with a laugh, to fling itself on fresh playmates that shook themselves free, and were caught and held again. All was a-shake and a-shiver—glints and gleams and sparkles, rustle and swirl, chatter and bubble. The Mole was bewitched, entranced, fascinated. By the side of the river he trotted as one trots, when very small, by the side of a man who holds one spellbound by exciting stories; and when tired at last, he sat on the bank, while the river still chattered on to him, a babbling procession of the best stories in the world, sent from the heart of the earth to be told at last to the insatiable sea.

As he sat on the grass and looked across the river, a dark hole in the bank opposite, just above the water's edge, caught his eye, and dreamily he fell to considering what a nice snug dwelling-place it would make for an animal with few wants and fond of a bijou riverside residence, above flood level and remote from noise and dust. As he gazed, something bright and small seemed to twinkle down in the heart of it, vanished, then twinkled once more like a tiny star. But it could hardly be a star in such an unlikely situation; and it was too glittering and small for a glow-worm. Then, as he looked, it winked at him, and so declared itself to be an eye; and a small face began gradually to grow up round it, like a frame round a picture.

A brown little face, with whiskers.

A grave round face, with the same twinkle in its eye that had first attracted his notice.

Small neat ears and thick silky hair.

It was the Water Rat!

Then the two animals stood and regarded each other cautiously.

"Hullo, Mole!" said the Water Rat.

"Hullo, Rat!" said the Mole.

"Would you like to come over?" inquired the Rat presently.

"Oh, it's all very well to *talk*," said the Mole, rather pettishly, he being new to a river and riverside life and its ways.

The Rat said nothing, but stooped and unfastened a rope and hauled on it; then lightly stepped into a little boat which the Mole had not observed. It was painted blue outside and white within, and was just the size for two animals; and the Mole's whole heart went out to it at once, even though he did not yet fully understand its uses.

The Rat sculled smartly across and made fast. Then he held up his fore-paw as the Mole stepped gingerly down. "Lean on that!" he said. "Now then, step lively!" and the Mole to his surprise and rapture found himself actually seated in the stern of a real boat.

"This has been a wonderful day!" said he, as the Rat shoved off and took to the sculls again. "Do you know, I've never been in a boat before in all my life."

"What?" cried the Rat, open-mouthed: "Never been in a—you never—well, I—what have you been doing, then?"

"Is it so nice as all that?" asked the Mole shyly, though he was quite prepared to believe it as he leant back in his seat and surveyed the cushions, the oars, the rowlocks, and all the fascinating fittings, and felt the boat sway lightly under him.

"Nice? It's the *only* thing," said the Water Rat solemnly, as he leaned forward for his stroke. "Believe me, my young friend, there is *nothing*—absolutely nothing—half so much worth doing as simply messing about in boats. Simply messing," he went on dreamily: "messing—about—in—boats; messing——"

"Look ahead, Rat!" cried the Mole suddenly.

It was too late. The boat struck the bank full tilt. The dreamer, the joyous oarsman, lay on his back at the bottom of the boat, his heels in the air.

"—about in boats—or *with* boats," the Rat went on composedly, picking himself up with a pleasant laugh. "In or out of 'em, it doesn't matter. Nothing seems really to matter, that's the charm of it. Whether you get away, or whether you don't; whether you arrive at your destination or whether you reach somewhere else, or whether you never get anywhere at all, you're always busy, and you never do anything in particular; and when you've done it there's always something else to do, and you can do it if you like, but you'd much better not. Look here! If you've really nothing else on hand this morning, supposing we drop down the river together, and have a long day of it?"

The Mole waggled his toes from sheer happiness, spread his chest with a sigh of full contentment, and leaned back blissfully into the soft cushions. "*What* a day I'm having!" he said. "Let us start at once!"

"Hold hard a minute, then!" said the Rat. He looped the painter through a ring in his landing-stage, climbed up into his hole above, and after a short interval reappeared staggering under a fat, wicker luncheon-basket.

"Shove that under your feet," he observed to the Mole, as he passed it down into the boat. Then he untied the painter and took the sculls again.

"What's inside it?" asked the Mole, wriggling with curiosity.

"There's cold chicken inside it," replied the Rat briefly; "coldtonguecoldhamcold-beefpickledgherkinssaladfrenchrollscress-andwidgespottedmeatgingerbeerlemon-adesodawater——"

"O stop, stop," cried the Mole in ecstasies: "This is too much!"

"Do you really think so?" inquired the Rat seriously. "It's only what I always take on these little excursions; and the other animals are always telling me that I'm a mean beast and cut it *very* fine!"

The Mole never heard a word he was saying. Absorbed in the new life he was entering upon, intoxicated with the sparkle, the ripple, the scents and the sounds and the sunlight, he trailed a paw in the water and dreamed long waking dreams. The Water Rat, like the good fellow he was, sculled steadily on and forebore to disturb him.

"I like your clothes awfully, old chap," he remarked after some half an hour or so had passed. "I'm going to get a black velvet smoking suit myself some day, as soon as I can afford it."

"I beg your pardon," said the Mole, pulling himself together with an effort. "You must think me very rude; but all this is so new to me. So—this– is–a—River!"

"*The* River," corrected the Rat.

"And you really live by the river? What a jolly life!"

"By it and with it and on it and in it," said the Rat. "It's brother and sister to me, and aunts, and company, and food and drink, and (naturally) washing. It's my world, and I don't want any other. What it hasn't got is not worth having, and what it doesn't know is not worth knowing. Lord! the times we've had together! Whether in winter or summer, spring or autumn, it's always got its fun and its excitements. When the floods are on in February, and my cellars and basement are brimming with drink that's no good to me, and the brown water runs by my best bedroom window; or again when it all drops away and shows patches of mud that smells like plum-cake, and the rushes and weed clog the channels, and I can potter about dry-shod over most of the bed of it and find fresh food to eat, and things careless people have dropped out of boats!"

"But isn't it a bit dull at times?" the Mole ventured to ask. "Just you and the river, and no one else to pass a word with?"

"No one else to—well, I mustn't be hard on you," said the Rat with forbearance. "You're new to it, and of course you don't know. The bank is so crowded nowadays that many people are moving away altogether. O no, it isn't what it used to be, at all. Otters, kingfishers, dabchicks, moor-hens, all of them about all day long and always wanting you to *do* something—as if a fellow had no business of his own to attend to!"

"What lies over *there?*" asked the Mole, waving a paw towards a background of woodland that darkly framed the water-meadows on one side of the river.

"That? O, that's just the Wild Wood," said the Rat shortly. "We don't go there very much, we river-bankers."

"Aren't they—aren't they very *nice* peo-ple in there?" said the Mole a trifle ner-vously.

"W-e-ll," replied the Rat, "let me see. The squirrels are all right. *And* the rabbits —some of 'em, but rabbits are a mixed lot. And then there's Badger, of course. He lives right in the heart of it; wouldn't live anywhere else, either, if you paid him to do it. Dear old Badger! Nobody interferes with *him*. They'd better not," he added significantly.

"Why, who *should* interfere with him?" asked the Mole.

"Well, of course—there—are others," ex-plained the Rat in a hesitating sort of way. "Weasels—and stoats—and foxes—and so on. They're all right in a way—I'm very good friends with them—pass the time of day when we meet, and all that—but they break out sometimes, there's no denying it, and then—well, you can't really trust them, and that's the fact."

The Mole knew well that it is quite against animal-etiquette to dwell on pos-sible trouble ahead, or even to allude to it; so he dropped the subject.

"And beyond the Wild Wood again?" he asked: "Where it's all blue and dim, and one sees what may be hills or perhaps they mayn't, and something like the smoke of towns, or is it only cloud-drift?"

"Beyond the Wild Wood comes the Wide World," said the Rat. "And that's something that doesn't matter, either to you or me. I've never been there, and I'm never going, nor you either, if you've got any sense at all. Don't ever refer to it again, please. Now then! Here's our back-water at last, where we're going to lunch."

Leaving the main stream, they now passed into what seemed at first sight like a little land-locked lake. Green turf sloped down to either edge, brown snaky tree-roots gleamed below the surface of the quiet water, while ahead of them the sil-very shoulder and foamy tumble of a weir, arm-in-arm with a restless dripping mill-wheel, that held up in its turn a grey-gabled mill-house, filled the air with a soothing murmur of sound, dull and smothery, yet with little clear voices speaking up cheerfully out of it at inter-vals. It was so very beautiful that the Mole could only hold up both forepaws and gasp, "O my! O my! O my!"

The Rat brought the boat alongside the bank, made her fast, helped the still awk-ward Mole safely ashore, and swung out the luncheon-basket. The Mole begged as a favour to be allowed to unpack it all by himself; and the Rat was very pleased to indulge him, and to sprawl at full length on the grass and rest, while his ex-cited friend shook out the table-cloth and spread it, took out all the mysterious packets one by one and arranged their contents in due order, still gasping, "O my! O my!" at each fresh revelation. When all was ready, the Rat said, "Now, pitch in, old fellow!" and the Mole was indeed very glad to obey, for he had

started his spring-cleaning at a very early hour that morning, as people *will* do, and had not paused for bite or sup; and he had been through a very great deal since that distant time which now seemed so many days ago.

"What are you looking at?" said the Rat presently, when the edge of their hunger was somewhat dulled, and the Mole's eyes were able to wander off the table-cloth a little.

"I am looking," said the Mole, "at a streak of bubbles that I see travelling along the surface of the water. That is a thing that strikes me as funny."

"Bubbles? Oho!" said the Rat, and chirruped cheerily in an inviting sort of way.

A broad glistening muzzle showed itself above the edge of the bank, and the Otter hauled himself out and shook the water from his coat.

"Greedy beggars!" he observed, making for the provender. "Why didn't you invite me, Ratty?"

"This was an impromptu affair," explained the Rat. "By the way—my friend Mr. Mole."

"Proud, I'm sure," said the Otter, and the two animals were friends forthwith.

"Such a rumpus everywhere!" continued the Otter. "All the world seems out on the river to-day. I came up this backwater to try and get a moment's peace, and then stumble upon you fellows!—At least—I beg pardon—I don't exactly mean that, you know."

There was a rustle behind them, proceeding from a hedge wherein last year's leaves still clung thick, and a stripy head, with high shoulders behind it, peered forth on them.

"Come on, old Badger!" shouted the Rat.

The Badger trotted forward a pace or two; then grunted, "H'm! Company," and turned his back and disappeared from view.

"That's *just* the sort of fellow he is!" observed the disappointed Rat. "Simply hates Society! Now we shan't see any more of him to-day. Well, tell us *who's* out on the river?"

"Toad's out, for one," replied the Otter. "In his brand-new wager-boat; new togs, new everything!"

The two animals looked at each other and laughed.

"Once, it was nothing but sailing," said the Rat. "Then he tired of that and took to punting. Nothing would please him but to punt all day and every day, and a nice mess he made of it. Last year it was house-boating, and we all had to go and stay with him in his house-boat, and pretend we liked it. He was going to spend the rest of his life in a house-boat. It's all the same, whatever he takes up; he gets tired of it, and starts on something fresh."

"Such a good fellow, too," remarked the Otter reflectively: "But no stability—especially in a boat!"

From where they sat they could get a glimpse of the main stream across the island that separated them; and just then a wager-boat flashed into view, the rower —a short, stout figure—splashing badly and rolling a good deal, but working his hardest. The Rat stood up and hailed him, but Toad—for it was he—shook his head and settled sternly to his work.

"He'll be out of the boat in a minute if he rolls like that," said the Rat, sitting down again.

"Of course he will," chuckled the Otter. "Did I ever tell you that good story about

444

Toad and the lock-keeper? It happened this way. Toad . . ."

An errant May-fly swerved unsteadily athwart the current in the intoxicated fashion affected by young bloods of May-flies seeing life. A swirl of water and a "cloop!" and the May-fly was visible no more.

Neither was the Otter.

The Mole looked down. The voice was still in his ears, but the turf whereon he had sprawled was clearly vacant. Not an Otter to be seen, as far as the distant horizon.

But again there was a streak of bubbles on the surface of the river.

The Rat hummed a tune, and the Mole recollected that animal-etiquette forbade any sort of comment on the sudden disappearance of one's friends at any moment, for any reason or no reason whatever.

"Well, well," said the Rat, "I suppose we ought to be moving. I wonder which of us had better pack the luncheon-basket?" He did not speak as if he was frightfully eager for the treat.

"O, please let me," said the Mole. So, of course, the Rat let him.

Packing the basket was not quite such pleasant work as unpacking the basket. It never is. But the Mole was bent on enjoying everything, and although just when he had got the basket packed and strapped up tightly he saw a plate staring up at him from the grass, and when the job had been done again the Rat pointed out a fork which anybody ought to have seen, and last of all, behold! the mustard pot, which he had been sitting on without knowing it—still, somehow, the thing got finished at last, without much loss of temper.

The afternoon sun was getting low as the Rat sculled gently homewards in a dreamy mood, murmuring poetry-things over to himself, and not paying much attention to Mole. But the Mole was very full of lunch, and self-satisfaction, and pride, and already quite at home in a boat (so he thought) and was getting a bit restless besides: and presently he said, "Ratty! Please, *I* want to row, now!"

The Rat shook his head with a smile. "Not yet, my young friend," he said— "wait till you've had a few lessons. It's not so easy as it looks."

The Mole was quiet for a minute or two. But he began to feel more and more jealous of Rat, sculling so strongly and so easily along, and his pride began to whisper that he could do it every bit as well. He jumped up and seized the sculls, so suddenly, that the Rat, who was gazing out over the water and saying more poetry-things to himself, was taken by surprise and fell backwards off his seat with his legs in the air for the second time, while the triumphant Mole took his place and grabbed the sculls with entire confidence.

"Stop it, you *silly* ass!" cried the Rat, from the bottom of the boat. "You can't do it! You'll have us over!"

The Mole flung his sculls back with a flourish, and made a great dig at the water. He missed the surface altogether, his legs flew up above his head, and he found himself lying on the top of the prostrate Rat. Greatly alarmed, he made a grab at the side of the boat, and the next moment—Sploosh!

Over went the boat, and he found himself struggling in the river.

O my, how cold the water was, and O,

how *very* wet it felt. How it sang in his ears as he went down, down, down! How bright and welcome the sun looked as he rose to the surface coughing and spluttering! How black was his despair when he felt himself sinking again! Then a firm paw gripped him by the back of his neck. It was the Rat, and he was evidently laughing—the Mole could *feel* him laughing, right down his arm and through his paw, and so into his—the Mole's—neck.

The Rat got hold of a scull and shoved it under the Mole's arm; then he did the same by the other side of him and, swimming behind, propelled the helpless animal to shore, hauled him out, and set him down on the bank, a squashy, pulpy lump of misery.

When the Rat had rubbed him down a bit, and wrung some of the wet out of him, he said, "Now, then, old fellow! Trot up and down the towing-path as hard as you can, till you're warm and dry again, while I dive for the luncheon-basket."

So the dismal Mole, wet without and ashamed within, trotted about till he was fairly dry, while the Rat plunged into the water again, recovered the boat, righted her and made her fast, fetched his floating property to shore by degrees, and finally dived successfully for the luncheon-basket and struggled to land with it.

When all was ready for a start once more, the Mole, limp and dejected, took his seat in the stern of the boat; and as they set off, he said in a low voice, broken with emotion, "Ratty, my generous friend! I am very sorry indeed for my foolish and ungrateful conduct. My heart quite fails me when I think how I might

446

have lost that beautiful luncheon-basket. Indeed, I have been a complete ass, and I know it. Will you overlook it this once and forgive me, and let things go on as before?"

"That's all right, bless you!" responded the Rat cheerily. "What's a little wet to a Water Rat? I'm more in the water than out of it most days. Don't you think any more about it; and, look here! I really think you had better come and stop with me for a little time. It's very plain and rough, you know—not like Toad's house at all—but you haven't seen that yet; still, I can make you comfortable. I'll teach you to row, and to swim, and you'll soon be as handy on the water as any of us."

The Mole was so touched by his kind manner of speaking that he could find no voice to answer him; and he had to brush away a tear or two with the back of his paw. But the Rat kindly looked in another direction, and presently the Mole's spirits revived again, and he was even able to give some straight back-talk to a couple of moorhens who were sniggering to each other about his bedraggled appearance.

When they got home, the Rat made a bright fire in the parlour, and planted the Mole in an arm-chair in front of it, having fetched down a dressing-gown and slippers for him, and told him river stories till supper-time. Very thrilling stories they were, too, to an earth-dwelling animal like Mole. Stories about weirs, and sudden floods, and leaping pike, and steamers that flung hard bottles—at least bottles were certainly flung, and *from* steamers, so presumably *by* them; and about herons, and how particular they were whom they spoke to; and about adventures down drains, and night-fishings with Otter, or excursions far afield with Badger. Supper was a most cheerful meal; but very shortly afterwards a terribly sleepy Mole had to be escorted upstairs by his considerate host, to the best bedroom, where he soon laid his head on his pillow in great peace and contentment, knowing that his new-found friend the River was lapping the sill of his window.

This day was only the first of many similar ones for the emancipated Mole, each of them longer and fuller of interest as the ripening summer moved onward. He learnt to swim and to row, and entered into the joy of running water; and with his ear to the reed-stems he caught, at intervals, something of what the wind went whispering so constantly among them.

It is hard to believe that
the worldly and cynical poet and playwright, Oscar Wilde,
was the same man who wrote some of the simplest and most
beautiful of modern fairy tales.
"The Selfish Giant" is one of these.
It is a touching tale of an overgrown and overbearing creature
who built a high wall to keep children out of his garden and,
as a consequence, shut out the sunshine and all happiness.
How the song of a small bird made him break down the wall,
and how a boy he comes to love suddenly disappears—
this is the secret of a story that
turns into much more than a story.

The Selfish Giant

BY OSCAR WILDE

Illustrated by DENVER GILLEN

EVERY AFTERNOON, as they were coming from school, the children used to go and play in the Giant's garden.

It was a large lovely garden, with soft green grass. Here and there over the grass stood beautiful flowers like stars, and there were twelve peach-trees that in the springtime broke out into delicate blossoms of pink and pearl, and in the autumn bore rich fruit. The birds sat on the trees and sang so sweetly that the children used to stop their games in order to listen to them. "How happy we are here!" they cried to each other.

One day the Giant came back. He had been to visit his friend the Cornish ogre, and had stayed with him for seven years. After the seven years were over he had said all that he had to say, for his conversation was limited, and he determined to return to his own castle. When he arrived he saw the children playing in the garden.

"What are you doing there?" he cried in a very gruff voice, and the children ran away.

"My own garden is my own garden," said the Giant; "any one can understand that, and I will allow nobody to play in it but myself." So he built a high wall all around it, and put up a notice-board.

TRESPASSERS
WILL BE
PROSECUTED

He was a very selfish Giant.

The poor children had now nowhere to play. They tried to play on the road, but the road was very dusty and full of hard stones, and they did not like it. They used to wander round the high wall when their lessons were over, and talk about the beautiful garden inside. "How happy we were there," they said to each other.

Then the Spring came, and all over the country there were little blossoms and little birds. Only in the garden of the selfish Giant it was still winter. The birds did not care to sing in it as there were no children, and the trees forgot to blossom. Once a beautiful flower put its head out from the grass, but when it saw the notice-board it was so sorry for the children that it slipped back into the ground again, and went off to sleep. The only people who were pleased were the Snow and the Frost. "Spring has forgotten this garden," they cried, "so we will live here all the year round." The Snow covered up the grass with her great white cloak, and the Frost painted all the trees silver. Then they invited the North Wind to stay with them, and he came. He was wrapped in furs, and he roared all day about the garden, and blew the chimney-pots down. "This is a delightful spot," he said, "we must ask the Hail on a visit." So the Hail came. Every day for three hours he rattled on the roof of the castle till he broke most of the slates, and then he ran round and round the garden as fast as he could go.

He was dressed in grey, and his breath was like ice.

"I cannot understand why the Spring is so late in coming," said the Selfish Giant, as he sat at the window and looked out at his cold white garden; "I hope there will be a change in the weather."

But the Spring never came, nor the Summer. The Autumn gave golden fruit to every garden, but to the Giant's garden she gave none. "He is too selfish," she said. So it was always Winter there, and the North Wind, and the Hail, and the Frost, and the Snow danced about through the trees.

One morning the Giant was lying awake in bed when he heard some lovely music. It sounded so sweet to his ears that he thought it must be the King's musicians passing by. It was really only a little linnet singing outside his window, but it was so long since he had heard a bird sing in his garden that it seemed to him to be the most beautiful music in the world. Then the Hail stopped dancing over his head, and the North Wind ceased roaring, and a delicious perfume came to him through the open casement. "I believe the Spring has come at last," said the Giant; and he jumped out of bed and looked out.

What did he see?

He saw a most wonderful sight. Through a little hole in the wall the children had crept in, and they were sitting in the branches of the trees. In every tree that he could see there was a little child. And the trees were so glad to have the children back again that they had covered themselves with blossoms, and were waving their arms gently

above the children's heads. The birds were flying about and twittering with delight, and the flowers were looking up through the green grass and laughing. It was a lovely scene; only in one corner it was still winter. It was the farthest corner of the garden, and in it was standing a little boy. He was so small that he could not reach up to the branches of the tree, and he was wandering all around it, crying bitterly. The poor tree was still quite covered with frost and snow, and

the North Wind was blowing and roaring about it. "Climb up! little boy," said the tree, and it bent its branches down as low as it could; but the boy was too tiny.

And the Giant's heart melted as he looked out. "How selfish I have been!" he said; "now I know why the Spring would not come here. I will put that poor little boy on the top of the tree, and then I will knock down the wall, and my garden shall be the children's playground for ever and ever."

He was really very sorry for what he had done.

So he crept downstairs and opened the front door quite softly, and went out into the garden. But when the children saw him they were so frightened that they all ran away, and the garden became winter again. Only the little boy did not run, for his eyes were so full of tears that he did not see the Giant coming. And the Giant stole up behind him and took him gently in his hand, and

451

put him up into the tree. And the tree broke at once into blossom, and the birds came and sang on it, and the little boy stretched out his two arms and flung them round the Giant's neck, and kissed him. And the other children, when they saw that the Giant was not wicked any longer, came running back, and with them came the Spring. "It is your garden now, little children," said the Giant, and he took a great axe and knocked down the wall. And when the people were going to market at twelve o'clock they found the Giant playing with the children in the most beautiful garden they had ever seen. All day long they played, and in the evening they came to the Giant to bid him good-bye.

"But where is your little companion?" he said, "the boy I put into the tree?" The Giant loved him the best because he had kissed him.

"We don't know," answered the children; "he has gone away."

"You must tell him to be sure and come here tomorrow," said the Giant. But the children said that they did not know where he lived, and had never seen him before; and the Giant felt very sad.

Every afternoon, when school was over, the children came and played with the Giant. But the little boy whom the Giant loved was never seen again. The Giant was very kind to all the children, yet he longed for his first little friend, and often spoke of him. "How I would like to see him!" he used to say.

Years went over, and the Giant grew very old and feeble. He could not play about any more, so he sat in a huge armchair, and watched the children at their games, and admired his garden. "I have many beautiful flowers," he said; "but the children are the most beautiful flowers of all."

One winter morning he looked out of his window as he was dressing. He did not hate the Winter now, for he knew that is was merely the Spring asleep, and that the flowers were resting.

Suddenly he rubbed his eyes in wonder, and looked and looked. It certainly was a marvellous sight. In the farthest corner of the garden was a tree quite covered with lovely white blossoms. Its branches were all golden, and silver fruit hung down from them, and underneath it stood the little boy he had loved.

Downstairs ran the Giant in great joy, and out into the garden. He hastened across the grass, and came near to the child. And when he came quite close his face grew red with anger, and he said, "Who hath dared to wound thee?" For on the palms of the child's hands were the prints of two nails, and the prints of two nails were on the little feet.

"Who hath dared to wound thee?" cried the Giant; "tell me, that I may take my sword and slay him."

"Nay!" answered the child; "but these are the wounds of Love."

"Who art thou?" said the Giant, and a strange awe fell on him, and he knelt before the little child.

And the child smiled on the Giant, and said to him, "You let me play once in your garden; today you shall come with me to my garden, which is Paradise."

And when the children ran in that afternoon, they found the Giant lying dead under the tree, all covered with white blossoms.

"Count Beet" is a most unusual fairy tale.
It is a story in which the chief character is an earth spirit
who tries to understand
the world of men and falls in love with a human princess.
Another peculiar thing about this story is
that our sympathy is not
with the abducted princess but with the unhappy gnome—
it is hard to decide whether he is a mistaken hero
or a defeated villain.
Written especially for this collection,
the story is a free adaptation of an old German folk tale.

453

Count Beet

RETOLD BY LOUIS UNTERMEYER
Illustrated by ROBERT J. LEE

MILLIONS and millions of years ago, deep
down in the earth under a huge mountain, there lived an elemental and
powerful gnome. The world was still
new; it had not yet cooled off; there was
nothing on it but barren land and steaming water. Every ten thousand years or
so, the gnome would come up and look
over the slowly changing world. It did
not interest him very much, and there
were not many changes during ten
thousand years. He was the lord of a
vast subterranean kingdom; he had
countless slaves to do his bidding and
work wonders for him. Still, he was
curious about what was happening—
or going to happen—on the surface of
the earth. More than a million years
passed before there was any sign of
change; many more millions before

things began to grow, to come to life,
crawl out of the great seas, learn to
walk, to leap, and even to fly.

Ages were added to ages, and then
one day the gnome saw a new world. He
saw men. He watched them, wondering,
while they built houses, made fires,
tamed animals, sowed seeds, harvested
crops, and raised families.

"That must be a fine way to live,"
thought the gnome. "I must try it. I must
learn what these creatures are like, how
they live, and how they think."

Disguising himself as a plowman, he
applied for work to a rich landowner.
Everything he did went well, for the soil
obeyed him. The crops grew rapidly, and
he was considered the best worker in
the village. But the landowner was a
spendthrift; he never had money for his

454

workers and barely paid them enough to keep them from starvation.

The gnome refused to work for an employer who cheated him, so he hired himself out as a shepherd to the land-owner's neighbor. He took excellent care of the flock. He guarded the ewes and lambs better than they had ever been cared for; he found places where there were sweet grasses and health-giving plants. Not one sheep fell from the cliffs; no single lamb was torn by a wolf. But his employer was a miser. He refused to give the shepherd his rightful share. On the contrary, he claimed that several of the sheep had been lost, and he deducted their value from the shepherd's wages.

Cheated for the second time, the gnome thought more carefully what sort of man he should work for next. He decided to enter an honored profession and, as a law student, became clerk to a judge. Soon, however, the transformed gnome found out that the judge was not only unrighteous but actually dishonest, that he paid no attention to the laws, was hard on the poor but was always ready to do favors for the rich. When the clerk refused to carry out one of the judge's cruel orders he was put in jail. It was, however, an easy matter for the gnome to escape. He merely changed into a breath of air and wafted himself through the keyhole.

Disappointed and disillusioned, he sank back into the depths of the earth. His first experience with men had been unhappy and he resolved to have nothing more to do with them. He marvelled that Mother Nature permitted such creatures to exist, and could even be kind to them.

Yet he continued to be curious and, after staying underground many, many years, he resolved once more to try to understand the human race.

This time he was more cautious. He did not join people at their work, but watched them from a safe distance. He hid himself on the edge of dark forests, peered at them from behind bushes, and drifted noiselessly through valleys and little villages.

Then, one day he happened to spy a group of girls. One of them was the loveliest thing his eyes had ever seen, so young and beautiful that he could not believe her to be one of the daughters of men. She was a king's daughter, be-trothed to the knight, Roland, and she and her six companions often went into the woods to pick wild strawberries, mushrooms, and rare flowers which she brought back to the castle. In the warm weather she loved to linger in the cool shadows of the trees and, when the days were hot with summer, bathe in a pool beneath a waterfall.

This was one of those days. The gnome, who had often observed the princess and her six companions, re-mained hidden as the group came to the pool. He heard their low voices change to cries of delight and astonishment. The pool was there, but everything about it had changed. The rough boulders were now smooth marble and gleaming agate. The water no longer gushed wildly from a hole in the rocks; instead, it trickled gently down steps of carved stones like a miniature waterfall, making an ex-quisite music as it fell into a twenty-foot bowl of alabaster. The pebbly bottom had been turned into gold and silver sands, and from four directions came four soft breezes, each one carrying a different perfume. Daisies, buttercups, and pale blue forget-me-nots embroidered the border of the pool; wild jasmine, hedge-roses, and honeysuckle made a living curtain, and every bush held a shower of many-colored blooms. There were niches in the marble background, and these contained delicious cakes and sweetmeats in dishes made of ivory; crystal goblets glistened with cooling drinks. A path of sparkling mica and mosaic pictures led to the pool where the water flickered with all the colors of the rainbow.

Overcome with surprise, the girls stared, clapped their hands, and cried out their pleasure. Then, laughing in a dozen keys, they leaped into the pool. Playfully they swam about—until the princess gave a sudden shriek and sank out of sight. The other girls dived after her, but all they caught was a glimmer of golden hair. They saw a whirlpool forming at the bottom of the pool with an opening like an endless funnel, and down this the princess disappeared.

There was nothing left to do but to inform her father, the king. As they drew near the castle, they met him returning from a hunt. After he had learned what had happened, his grief could not be controlled. He tore his clothes, buried his face in his purple mantle, and groaned: "My lost darling, my lovely Lora—I am the most miserable of men. I will not rest until she is found." Then suddenly he cried out, "What am I doing? Why are we staying here? Take me to the spot and show me that treacherously enchanted place!"

But when they came to the pool, it was as wild as it was before it had been transformed. The water tumbled through raw rocks. There was not a trace of marble or agate or alabaster; there were no forget-me-nots, no roses, no bowers of jasmine and honeysuckle. A cold wind rattled dry branches. Sick at heart, the king turned back to the castle, and the girls followed sadly.

Meanwhile, Lora was safe in the gnome's kingdom. She did not know how long she had been asleep nor who had worked a magic spell; when she woke she had no idea where she was. She reclined on a luxurious sofa covered in rose-colored satin with a ruffle of sky-blue silk. A young man stood before her, and in this guise the gnome told her about his mysterious origin, his powers, his possessions, and his desire that she should be his bride. Saying that he had built this palace for her, he led her through huge halls, magnificent chambers, and richly decorated rooms. He showed her a pleasure garden with summer-houses, terraces, and grassy turf as smooth as a dance floor. In the center of the garden stood a fountain that spread itself into opening and folding fans of spray or shot up into a thin spire of dazzling diamonds. There were strange trees that shed continually changing shadows, and each tree bore a new and different kind of fruit. There were peaches sprinkled with flecks of silver; there were apples that were purple on one side and pink on the other; there were nectarines with skins of gold, cool and crisp to the taste. Each tree housed a hundred birds, and when they sang their many-toned voices made a symphony sweeter than anything ever heard on earth.

In spite of all these wonders, the princess shuddered at the thought of marrying the gnome. She grew listless and melancholy. She barely glanced at the beautiful things, but sighed deeply and disconsolately. The gnome did everything he could to divert and please her, but it was useless. Finally he thought of a plan. Human beings, he said to himself, are like bees and ants; they need company. If she had her own kind to talk to, to entertain and play with, she would be happy.

He did not hesitate another moment. He went into the field and dug up six large beets, put them in a basket, and brought them to the lovely Lora, who was sitting sad-eyed in a rose-shaded arbor.

"Put all gloomy thoughts out of your mind," he said, "and open your heart to joy. In this basket is everything you need to make you happy here. Take this striped little wand, wave it gently in the air, and these earth-grown things will turn to any earthly creatures you desire." And with these words he left the princess.

The moment he was out of sight, she opened the basket and waved the magic wand over it. "Bella! Bertha! Brenda! Bona! Bryna! Brynnhilde!" she cried. And before the wand stopped waving, Lora's six companions stood before her. They cried out, kissed and clasped her, and she kissed and embraced each one in turn. Lora could not tell whether she had summoned her playmates from their places on earth or whether she had really changed the six vegetables into her six playmates. But she was too happy to trouble her mind about it. All she cared about was that she had company, the company she loved best. She showed the girls the garden, made them taste the silver peaches and the golden nectarines, took them through all the rooms of the gnome's palace, and displayed all the treasures. They admired the gowns made of the finest tissues and the richest velvets, wound the moonbeam-sheer scarves around their shoulders, put the necklaces and enamelled lockets about their throats, and tried on every jewelled ring, brooch, bracelet, diadem, and earring.

The gnome, who had spied upon them, was delighted with what he had done. "Now," he reflected, "I am beginning to understand the nature of mankind—and womankind. All you have to do to make them happy is give them what they want."

He noticed that Lora looked more amiably upon him; she smiled whenever they met. She was truly a princess again, for she was surrounded by her court-maidens, and no queen was ever better served.

For a while everything was perfect. The gnome's kingdom was transformed by a flurry of laughing girls. There were songs, dances, and the sound of stringed instruments from morning to night. Then one day Lora noticed that Bella was looking pale. When she looked closely at the others, she saw that Bertha seemed tired, Brenda's full color was fading, Bona could not dance, Bryna's quick laughter ceased, and Brynnhilde was always asking to be excused from play. When Lora inquired if anything had happened to displease them, they assured her that nothing was wrong. Yet, though the princess thought up new amusements and the gnome supplied them with every delicacy for their delight, the six maidens grew thinner day by day. They lost their high spirits and their youth; their whole personalities changed.

One sunny morning, after a worried sleep, the princess thought of a way to bring her handmaidens back to their former selves. But as she entered the reception room, she was terrified. She saw, to her horror, six old women hobbling about on crutches, coughing and groaning, unable to hold themselves erect. Shuddering, she ran from the room to the portals of the palace and commanded the gnome to appear. When, at her first outcry, he came, she stamped her foot in rage and screamed at him: "You hideous creature! Why have you robbed me of the only pleasure I have in life here! Why did you bewitch my six carefree companions! Do you want me to go mad in this forsaken place! Give me back my girls and my happiness at once, or you'll have nothing from me but scorn and hatred!"

"Mistress," replied the gnome, "do not be angry. Everything in my power is yours to command—you have only to ask—but do not expect me to do the impossible. Nature is kind to me and will let me change some of her features, but only if I do not try to break her first law, the law of life. As long as strength and sap were in the beets, the magic wand could transform them into other things that had strength and vitality. But when the life-giving element dwindles and dies, whatever shape it has

assumed must also die. Do not grieve. Another basketful of beets will undo the harm, and you can summon all the faces and figures you desire. Give Nature's wornout gifts back to Nature, and try again. In the large field beyond the garden you will find lively company." And with these words the gnome again disappeared.

As soon as he was out of sight, Lora seized the striped wand and waved it over the withered old crones. Nothing happened. So, with a shrug, she did what children do who have no further use for a broken toy—she threw the shriveled vegetables out with the rest of the rubbish.

With a light heart she ran quickly over the greensward to pick up the basket and fill it again, but it was nowhere to be found. She raced back and forth across the garden without discovering a sign of it. At the edge of the grape arbor she saw the gnome, very disturbed. Ignoring his embarrassment, she said, "You have cheated me again! Where have you hidden the basket? I've been searching for it more than an hour!"

"Mistress," he answered humbly, "please forgive my thoughtlessness. I promised more than I could perform. I've looked everywhere, but the harvest has been gathered, the crops have been stripped, the root vegetables have been dug up, and all the beets have been stored in dark cellars. The fields lie fallow, for the growing season is over. It is winter, and only your presence makes it seem like spring. Your warm heart keeps the ice from forming, and flowers grow to greet you wherever your foot touches the ground. Wait three months and you will be able to play with as many smiling and dancing dolls as you please."

Lora did not thank him for his advice. Before he finished she turned her back on him, walked away without a word, and shut herself in her room. He, however, went to a market-town within his kingdom and sent her, as a peace offering, a velvet-gray donkey laden with all manner of gay silks, brilliant brocades, and glowing satins, so that the beast and his burden looked as though they had come straight from the sunny Orient. Moreover, he gave orders to plow the fields, to plant seeds, and build an underground fire so that the seeds would develop roots and grow as rapidly as in a greenhouse.

Soon the beets began to put forth little shoots and promised an early crop. Lora watched the progress of their growth more eagerly than if she were waiting for the ripening of the golden apples of the Hesperides. But discontent clouded her cornflower-blue eyes. Restlessly she wandered among dark trees, and her tears softened the cold ground as she thought of Roland, the young knight she was to have married. Then one dusky evening that showed promise of winter's ending, she thought of a plan.

Spring came back to the mountain kingdom deep in the earth. The gnome let the underground fires die; and there, before any flower had dared to blossom, was a magnificent, full-grown field of beets. Lora, who rejoiced in the quick growth, was now ready to try her experiment. She dug up a small beet, waved the magic wand, and changed the beet into a bee.

"Fly away, little messenger," she said, "fly to Roland, who is mourning for me, and tell him that his Lora is still alive. Tell him that she is held captive by a powerful gnome, but she is planning a way to escape. Whisper this in his ear and bring back word. Then I will tell him more."

The bee buzzed his understanding of the message and flew straight from Lora's finger. But his flight had scarcely begun when a greedy swallow caught him and gulped him down. Lora saw the unfortunate mishap, but she did not grieve more than a moment.

She took another beet and changed it into a cricket. Giving the same directions, she said, "Hop off, little one. You are too small to be seen threading your way through the dark subterranean passages. When you come to Roland, tell him to be ready to rescue me."

Obedient to her command, the cricket hopped away. But a sharp-eyed, long-legged stork spotted the little chirper and, with a sudden snap of his bill, swallowed him whole.

This second misfortune disappointed Lora, but it did not discourage her. "All good things come in threes," she said to herself, and changed the third beet into a magpie. "Spread your wings, you lively chatterer," she commanded the bird, after repeating the instructions, "until you come to Roland. Tell him exactly where I am, and everything else you have heard from me. Then tell him to have men and horses waiting at the very edge of the hole leading down into the earth and be ready to carry me off should I be pursued."

The clever black and white bird

whistled sharply, rose into the air, and soared through one twisting passage after another. Lora watched him anxiously until his shining tail and white-patched wings were out of sight.

Meanwhile, Roland continued to grieve for his lost sweetheart. The coming of spring did not cheer him; on the contrary, it made him still more doleful. He wandered through the woods, ignored the bright-colored wildflowers, sat under heavy oak trees and sighed "Lora!" The woods echoed the sad syllables: "Lora! Lora! For Lora! Forlorn!" Suddenly he realized that it was not an echo he heard but another voice. He started up in amazement, and saw the magpie hopping from bough to bough. "Unhappy chatterbox," said Roland, "who taught you to utter the name which makes this listener so sorrowful?" Picking up a stone, he cried angrily, "If I hear it once more you will not live to say it again." At that moment, the magpie spoke. "Hold your hand! Lora sent me!" And the bird related everything he had learned to the last word.

The moment Roland the knight heard these tidings his soul leaped with joy; the death-like melancholy which had settled on his spirit vanished. Eagerly he asked for more details; but the bird, clever though magpies are, could only repeat the lesson Lora had taught him. He said it once more and flew away. Roland rushed back to his residence, summoned his retainers and, with a squadron of horsemen, rode off to the mountain fastness.

Next morning, shortly after dawn, Lora appeared attired like a bride. Her dress, of the purest whitest satin, shone as if it were woven with moonbeams; a necklace of fire-opals burned about her neck; her head was crowned with a diadem of a hundred gems, and ropes of pearls were twisted in the braids of her golden hair. "Yes," she said softly to the astonished gnome, "I am now ready to become the queen of your kingdom. But first I must ask you for one more proof of your desire to please me. I must know the number—the exact amount—of beets growing in that acre. I want my marriage to be the biggest and most beautiful in the world—I will need dozens of bridesmaids to attend me, many little flower-girls; and hundreds of other witnesses. I must know *exactly* how many to be sure of, so do not deceive me. Count the beets to the last one and bring me the total—that will be the last test of your devotion."

The gnome listened eagerly. Then, without waiting to reply, he rushed off to the beet-field and began the allotted task. It was, as the sly Lora meant it to be, a long and difficult assignment, and the gnome was so anxious to complete it that he continually made mistakes. Five times he counted the beets—and got five different results. Then, more slowly and more uncertainly, he started over again.

As soon as the gnome was out of sight, Lora busied herself with her plans for flight. She had hidden a particularly large beet, and this she changed into a swift, red steed with saddle, reins, and stirrups. Quickly she swung herself upon the horse's back and rode down the dark passages, over rocks and rivers, hedges and heights, until they came to the chasm in the mountain and, without a change in pace, Lora dashed up the sides to the very top. There Roland and his men were waiting for her.

The gnome was still so occupied with his work that he saw nothing, heard nothing, and suspected nothing. Finally, after much trouble and many mistakes, he finally arrived at the correct total of all the beets, large and small, down to the last leafy sprout. Having completed the labor, he hurried happily back to claim his bride. But Lora was nowhere to be found. He ran anxiously through the meadow, peered into the flowery arbors, but there was no sign of her. He searched throughout the palace, looked through every room, but he could not find what he sought. He called "Lora! Lora!" but the only answer was the echo of her name.

Then he noticed the disorder of her room—and he saw how he had been fooled. Casting off his bodily form the way a man throws off a coat, the gnome resumed his phantom shape and rose into the air. But when he issued from the depths of the mountain all he could see was his intended bride far in the distance, vanishing beyond his power, crossing the border of his rulership into her father's kingdom. Frantic with disappointment and trembling with rage, he reached up into the sky, clapped two black clouds together and hurled a bolt of lightning at the fleeing girl and her escort. But he was so overcome with emotion that his aim was poor and he struck only a thousand-year-old oak.

At that moment his mood changed, for his grief was far greater than his anger. He returned to the palace and went from room to room, sighing and weeping. He wandered through the great pleasure garden, but nothing in it gave him the least pleasure. He cursed himself bitterly. "It is my own fault," he cried. "What insane curiosity drove me to try to understand the ways of men and women. It is a good-looking but cruel and treacherous race, and, henceforth, I will have nothing more to do with it!"

Uttering these harsh words, he stamped violently upon the ground— stamped three times—and the palace, the pleasure garden, and all the other wonders vanished. He closed up the chasm, blocked all the passages, and, opening a path through the rocks for himself, sank deeper and deeper until he reached the center of the earth, taking with him his hurt as well as his hatred.

After Lora and Roland had reached her father's castle there was no end to the rejoicing. There were feasts and festivals, carnivals all day and fireworks at night. There was a resplendent wedding. Lora's father shared his throne with his daughter and, when the monarch died, Lora reigned as queen.

Lora never tired of relating the story of her adventures in the gnome's mountain kingdom, her clever ruse, and her bold escape. The tale grew with each retelling—it became a popular legend —and people found Lora's trickery so amusing that they called her foolish victim "The Beet-Counter." Later generations mockingly shortened it to "Count Beet." As the years passed, they even forgot that he was a gnome, an unearthly spirit who had once tried to understand human beings but, having failed, never again visited the disenchanting world of mortal men.

461

Unfamiliar though he may be,
there is no need for us to describe a hobbit.
The author has done that in the fourth paragraph
of his opening chapter.
The hero, a hobbit named Bilbo Baggins, lives
a quiet, ordinary life, until one morning
a wizard named Gandalf comes along
and involves him in a quest for stolen treasure.
He is captured by goblins, almost eaten by savage trolls,
and goes through one hair-raising adventure
after another until, with the help of a host of eagles,
the gold is recovered and, with his share,
Bilbo returns safely home. The story takes place
in a world of its own. It has iron hills,
lonely mountains, and withered heaths, populated
by dragons, dwarfs, and monster worms.
Although it is a land of magic, the hobbit finds
it conventional and is quite at home in it.
You will be, too.

An Unexpected Party

From The Hobbit

BY J. R. R. TOLKIEN
Illustrated by ROBERT J. LEE

IN A hole in the ground there lived a hobbit. Not a nasty, dirty, wet hole, filled with the ends of worms and an oozy smell, nor yet a dry, bare, sandy hole with nothing in it to sit down on or to eat. It was a hobbit-hole, and that means comfort.

It had a perfectly round door like a porthole, painted green, with a shiny yellow brass knob in the exact middle. The door opened on to a tube-shaped hall like a tunnel: a very comfortable tunnel without smoke, with panelled walls, and floors

463

tiled and carpeted, provided with polished chairs, and lots and lots of pegs for hats and coats—the hobbit was fond of visitors. The tunnel wound on and on, going fairly but not quite straight into the side of the hill—The Hill, as all the people for many miles round called it—and many little round doors opened out of it, first on one side and then on another. No going upstairs for the hobbit: bedrooms, bathrooms, cellars, pantries (lots of these), wardrobes (he had whole rooms devoted to clothes), kitchens, dining-rooms, all were on the same floor, and indeed on the same passage. The best rooms were all on the lefthand side (going in), for these were the only ones to have windows, deep-set round windows looking over his garden, and meadows beyond, sloping down to the river.

This hobbit was a very well-to-do hobbit, and his name was Baggins. The Bagginses had lived in the neighbourhood of The Hill for time out of mind, and people considered them very respectable, not only because most of them were rich, but

also because they never had any adventures or did anything unexpected: you could tell what a Baggins would say on any question without the bother of asking him. This is a story of how a Baggins had an adventure, and found himself doing and saying things altogether unexpected. He may have lost the neighbours' respect, but he gained—well, you will see whether he gained anything in the end.

The mother of our particular hobbit—what is a hobbit? I suppose hobbits need some description nowadays, since they have become rare and shy of the Big People, as they call us. They are (or were) small people, smaller than dwarves (and they have no beards) but very much larger than Lilliputians. There is little or no magic about them, except the ordinary everyday sort which helps them to disappear quietly and quickly when large stupid folk like you and me come blundering along, making a noise like elephants which they can hear a mile off. They are inclined to be fat in the stomach; they dress in bright colours (chiefly green and yellow); wear no shoes, because their feet grow natural leathery soles and thick warm brown hair like the stuff on their heads (which is curly); have long clever brown fingers, good-natured faces, and laugh deep fruity laughs (especially after dinner, which they have twice a day when they can get it). Now you know enough to go on with. As I was saying, the mother of this hobbit—of Bilbo Baggins, that is—was the famous Belladonna Took, one of the three remarkable daughters of the Old Took, head of the hobbits who lived across The Water, the small river that ran at the foot of The Hill. It had always been said that long ago one or other of the

Tooks had married into a fairy family (the less friendly said a goblin family); certainly there was still something not entirely hobbitlike about them, and once in a while members of the Took-clan would go and have adventures. They discreetly disappeared, and the family hushed it up; but the fact remained that the Tooks were not as respectable as the Bagginses, though they were undoubtedly richer.

Not that Belladonna Took ever had any adventures after she became Mrs. Bungo Baggins. Bungo, that was Bilbo's father, built the most luxurious hobbit-hole for her (and partly with her money) that was to be found either under The Hill or over The Hill or across The Water, and there they remained to the end of their days. Still it is probable that Bilbo, her only son, although he looked and behaved exactly like a second edition of his solid and comfortable father, got something a bit queer in his make-up from the Took side, something that only waited for a chance to come out. The chance never arrived, until Bilbo Baggins was grown up, being about fifty years old or so, and living in the beautiful hobbit-hole built by his father, which I have just described for you, until he had in fact apparently settled down immovably.

By some curious chance one morning long ago in the quiet of the world, when there was less noise and more green, and the hobbits were still numerous and prosperous, and Bilbo Baggins was standing at his door after breakfast smoking an enormous long wooden pipe that reached nearly down to his woolly toes (neatly brushed)—Gandalf came by. Gandalf! If you had heard only a quarter of what I have heard about him, and I have only

heard very little of all there is to hear, you would be prepared for any sort of remarkable tale. Tales and adventures sprouted up all over the place wherever he went, in the most extraordinary fashion. He had not been down that way under The Hill for ages and ages, not since his friend the Old Took died, in fact, and the hobbits had almost forgotten what he looked like. He had been away over The Hill and across The Water on businesses of his own since they were all small hobbit-boys and hobbit-girls.

All that the unsuspecting Bilbo saw that morning was a little old man with a tall pointed blue hat, a long grey cloak, a silver scarf over which his long white beard hung down below his waist, and immense black boots.

"Good morning!" said Bilbo, and he meant it. The sun was shining, and the grass was very green. But Gandalf looked at him from under long bushy eyebrows that stuck out further than the brim of his shady hat.

"What do you mean?" he said. "Do you wish me a good morning, or mean that it is a good morning whether I want it or not; or that you feel good this morning; or that it is a morning to be good on?"

"All of them at once," said Bilbo. "And a very fine morning for a pipe of tobacco out of doors, into the bargain. If you have a pipe about you, sit down and have a fill of mine! There's no hurry, we have all the day before us!" Then Bilbo sat down on a seat by his door, crossed his legs, and blew out a beautiful grey ring of smoke that sailed up into the air without breaking and floated away over The Hill.

"Very pretty!" said Gandalf. "But I have no time to blow smoke-rings this morning. I am looking for someone to share in an adventure that I am arranging, and it's very difficult to find anyone."

"I should think so—in these parts! We are plain quiet folk and have no use for adventures. Nasty disturbing uncomfortable things! Make you late for dinner! I can't think what anybody sees in them," said our Mr. Baggins, and stuck one thumb behind his braces, and blew out another even bigger smoke-ring. Then he took out his morning letters, and began to read, pretending to take no more notice of the old man. He had decided that he was not quite his sort, and wanted him to go away. But the old man did not move. He stood leaning on his stick and gazing at the hobbit without saying anything, till Bilbo got quite uncomfortable and even a little cross.

"Good morning!" he said at last. "We don't want any adventures here, thank you! You might try over The Hill or across The Water." By this he meant that the conversation was at an end.

"What a lot of things you do use *Good morning* for!" said Gandalf. "Now you mean that you want to get rid of me, and that it won't be good till I move off."

"Not at all, not at all, my dear sir! Let

466

me see, I don't think I know your name?"

"Yes, yes, my dear sir!—and I do know your name, Mr. Bilbo Baggins. And you do know my name, though you don't remember that I belong to it. I am Gandalf, and Gandalf means me! To think that I should have lived to be good-morninged by Belladonna Took's son, as if I was selling buttons at the door!"

"Gandalf, Gandalf! Good gracious me! Not the wandering wizard that gave Old Took a pair of magic diamond studs that fastened themselves and never came undone till ordered? Not the fellow who used to tell such wonderful tales at parties, about dragons and goblins and giants and the rescue of princesses and the unexpected luck of widows' sons? Not the man that used to make such particularly excellent fireworks! I remember those! Old Took used to have them on Midsummer's Eve. Splendid! They used to go up like great lilies and snapdragons and laburnums of fire and hang in the twilight all evening!" You will notice already that Mr. Baggins was not quite so prosy as he liked to believe, also that he was very fond of flowers. "Dear me!" he went on. "Not the Gandalf who was responsible for so many quiet lads and lasses going off into the Blue for mad adventures, anything from climbing trees to stowing away aboard the ships that sail to the Other Side? Bless me, life used to be quite inter— I mean, you used to upset things badly in these parts once upon a time. I beg your pardon, but I had no idea you were still in business."

"Where else should I be?" said the wizard. "All the same I am pleased to find you remember something about me. You seem to remember my fireworks kindly, at any rate, and that is not without hope. Indeed for your old grandfather Took's sake, and for the sake of poor Belladonna, I will give you what you asked for."

"I beg your pardon, I haven't asked for anything!"

"Yes, you have! Twice now. My pardon. I give it you. In fact I will go so far as to send you on this adventure. Very amusing for me, very good for you—and profitable too, very likely, if you ever get over it."

"Sorry! I don't want any adventures, thank you. Not today. Good morning! But please come to tea—any time you like! Why not tomorrow? Come tomorrow! Good-bye!" With that the hobbit turned and scuttled inside his round green door, and shut it as quickly as he dared, not to seem rude. Wizards after all are wizards.

"What on earth did I ask him to tea for!" he said to himself, as he went to the pantry. He had only just had breakfast,

but he thought a cake or two and a drink of something would do him good after his fright.

Gandalf in the meantime was still standing outside the door, and laughing long but quietly. After a while he stepped up, and with the spike on his staff scratched a queer sign on the hobbit's beautiful green front-door. Then he strode away, just about the time when Bilbo was finishing his second cake and beginning to think that he had escaped adventures very well.

The next day he had almost forgotten about Gandalf. He did not remember things very well, unless he put them down on his Engagement Tablet: like this: *Gandalf Tea Wednesday*. Yesterday he had been too flustered to do anything of the kind.

Just before tea-time there came a tremendous ring on the front-door bell, and

then he remembered! He rushed and put on the kettle, and put out another cup and saucer, and an extra cake or two, and ran to the door.

"I am so sorry to keep you waiting!" he was going to say, when he saw that it was not Gandalf at all. It was a dwarf with a blue beard tucked into a golden belt, and very bright eyes under his dark-green hood. As soon as the door was opened, he pushed inside, just as if he had been expected.

He hung his hooded cloak on the nearest peg, and "Dwalin at your service!" he said with a low bow.

"Bilbo Baggins at yours!" said the hobbit, too surprised to ask any questions for the moment. When the silence that followed had become uncomfortable, he added: "I am just about to take tea; pray come and have some with me." A little stiff perhaps, but he meant it kindly. And what would you do, if an uninvited dwarf came and hung his things up in your hall without a word of explanation?

They had not been at table long, in fact they had hardly reached the third cake, when there came another even louder ring at the bell.

"Excuse me!" said the hobbit, and off he went to the door.

"So you have got here at last!" what was what he was going to say to Gandalf this time. But it was not Gandalf. Instead there was a very old-looking dwarf on the step with a white beard and a scarlet hood; and he too hopped inside as soon as the door was open, just as if he had been invited.

"I see they have begun to arrive already," he said when he caught sight of Dwalin's green hood hanging up. He

hung his red one next to it, and "Balin at your service!" he said with his hand on his breast.

"Thank you!" said Bilbo with a gasp. It was not the correct thing to say, but *they have begun to arrive* had flustered him badly. He liked visitors, but he liked to know them before they arrived, and he preferred to ask them himself. He had a horrible thought that the cakes might run short, and then he—as the host: he knew his duty and stuck to it however painful —he might have to go without.

"Come along in, and have some tea!" he managed to say after taking a deep breath.

"A little beer would suit me better, if it is all the same to you, my good sir," said Balin with the white beard. "But I don't mind some cake—seed-cake, if you have any."

"Lots!" Bilbo found himself answering, to his own surprise; and he found himself scuttling off, too, to the cellar to fill a pint beer-mug, and to the pantry to fetch two beautiful round seed-cakes which he had

baked that afternoon for his after-supper
morsel.

When he got back Balin and Dwalin
were talking at the table like old friends
(as a matter of fact they were brothers).
Bilbo plumped down the beer and the
cake in front of them, when loud came a
ring at the bell again, and then another
ring.

"Gandalf for sure this time," he thought
as he puffed along the passage. But it was
not. It was two more dwarves, both with
blue hoods, silver belts, and yellow

beards; and each of them carried a bag of
tools and a spade. In they hopped, as soon
as the door began to open—Bilbo was
hardly surprised at all.

"What can I do for you, my dwarves?"
he said.

"Kili at your service!" said the one.
"And Fili!" added the other; and they
both swept off their blue hoods and
bowed.

"At yours and your family's!" replied
Bilbo, remembering his manners this
time.

"Dwalin and Balin here already, I see," said Kili. "Let us join the throng!"

"Throng!" thought Mr. Baggins. "I don't like the sound of that. I really must sit down for a minute and collect my wits, and have a drink." He had only just had a sip—in the corner, while the four dwarves sat round the table, and talked about mines and gold and troubles with the goblins, and the depredations of dragons, and lots of other things which he did not understand, and did not want to, for they sounded much too adventurous—when, *ding-dong-a-ling-dang*, his bell rang again, as if some naughty little hobbit-boy was trying to pull the handle off.

"Someone at the door!" he said, blinking.

"Some four, I should say by the sound," said Fili. "Besides, we saw them coming along behind us in the distance."

The poor little hobbit sat down in the hall and put his head in his hands, and wondered what had happened, and what was going to happen, and whether they would all stay to supper. Then the bell rang again louder than ever, and he had to run to the door. It was not four after all, it was FIVE. Another one had come along while he was wondering in the hall. He had hardly turned the knob, before they were all inside, bowing and saying "at your service" one after another. Dori, Nori, Ori, Oin, and Gloin were their names; and very soon two purple hoods, a grey hood, a brown hood, and a white hood were hanging on the pegs, and off they marched with their broad hands stuck in their gold and silver belts to join the others. Already it had almost become a throng. Some called for ale, and some for porter, and one for coffee, and all of them for cakes; so the hobbit was kept very busy for a while.

A big jug of coffee had just been set in the hearth, the seed-cakes were gone, and the dwarves were starting on a round of buttered scones, when there came—a loud knock. Not a ring, but a hard rat-tat on the hobbit's beautiful green door. Somebody was banging with a stick!

Bilbo rushed along the passage, very angry, and altogether bewildered and bewuthered—this was the most awkward

Wednesday he ever remembered. He pulled open the door with a jerk, and they all fell in, one on top of the other. More dwarves, four more! And there was Gandalf behind, leaning on his staff and laughing. He had made quite a dent on the beautiful door; he had also, by the way, knocked out the secret mark that he had put there the morning before.

"Carefully! Carefully!" he said. "It is not like you, Bilbo, to keep friends waiting on the mat, and then open the door like a pop-gun! Let me introduce Bifur, Bofur, Bombur, and especially Thorin!"

"At your service!" said Bifur, Bofur, and Bombur standing in a row. Then they hung up two yellow hoods and a pale green one; and also a sky-blue one with a long silver tassel. This last belonged to Thorin, an enormously important dwarf, in fact no other than the great Thorin Oakenshield himself, who was not at all pleased at falling flat on Bilbo's mat with Bifur, Bofur, and Bombur on top of him. For one thing Bombur was immensely fat and heavy. Thorin indeed was very haughty, and said nothing about *service*; but poor Mr. Baggins said he was sorry so many times, that at last he grunted "pray don't mention it," and stopped frowning.

"Now we are all here!" said Gandalf, looking at the row of thirteen hoods—the best detachable party hoods—and his own hat hanging on the pegs. "Quite a merry gathering! I hope there is something left for the late-comers to eat and drink! What's that? Tea! No thank you! A little red wine, I think, for me."

"And for me," said Thorin.

"And raspberry jam and apple-tart," said Bifur.

"And mince-pies and cheese," said Bofur.

"And pork-pie and salad," said Bombur.

"And more cakes—and ale—and coffee, if you don't mind," called the other dwarves through the door.

"Put on a few eggs, there's a good fellow!" Gandalf called after him, as the hobbit stumped off to the pantries. "And just bring out the cold chicken and tomatoes!"

"Seems to know as much about the inside of my larder as I do myself!" thought Mr. Baggins, who was feeling positively flummoxed, and was beginning to wonder whether a most wretched adventure had not come right into his house. By the time he had got all the bottles and dishes and knives and forks and glasses and plates and spoons and things piled up on big trays, he was getting very hot, and red in the face, and annoyed.

474

"Confusticate and bebother these dwarves!" he said aloud. "Why don't they come and lend a hand?" Lo and behold! there stood Balin and Dwalin at the door of the kitchen, and Fili and Kili behind them, and before he could say *knife* they had whisked the trays and a couple of small tables into the parlour and set out everything afresh.

Gandalf sat at the head of the party with the thirteen dwarves all round: and Bilbo sat on a stool at the fireside, nibbling at a biscuit (his appetite was quite taken away), and trying to look as if this was all perfectly ordinary and not in the least an adventure. The dwarves ate and ate, and talked and talked, and time got on. At last they pushed their chairs back, and Bilbo made a move to collect the plates and glasses.

"I suppose you will all stay to supper?" he said in his politest unpressing tones.

"Of course!" said Thorin. "And after. We shan't get through the business till late, and we must have some music first. Now to clear up!"

Thereupon the twelve dwarves—not Thorin, he was too important, and stayed talking to Gandalf—jumped to their feet, and made tall piles of all the things. Off they went, not waiting for trays, balancing columns of plates, each with a bottle on the top, with one hand, while the hobbit ran after them almost squeaking with fright: "please be careful!" and "please, don't trouble! I can manage." But the dwarves only started to sing:

Chip the glasses and crack the plates!
  Blunt the knives and bend the forks!
That's what Bilbo Baggins hates—
  Smash the bottles and burn the corks!

Cut the cloth and tread on the fat!
  Pour the milk on the pantry floor!
Leave the bones on the bedroom mat!
  Splash the wine on every door!

Dump the crocks in a boiling bowl;
  Pound them up with a thumping pole;
And when you've finished, if any are
    whole,
  Send them down the hall to roll!

That's what Bilbo Baggins hates!
So, carefully! carefully with the plates!

And of course they did none of these dreadful things, and everything was cleaned and put away safe as quick as lightning, while the hobbit was turning round and round in the middle of the kitchen trying to see what they were doing. Then they went back, and found Thorin with his feet on the fender smoking a pipe. He was blowing the most enormous smoke-rings, and wherever he told one to go, it went—up the chimney, or behind the clock on the mantelpiece, or under the table, or round and round the ceiling; but wherever it went it was not quick enough to escape Gandalf. Pop! he sent a smaller smoke-ring from his short clay-pipe straight through each one of Thorin's. Then Gandalf's smoke-ring would go green with the joke and come back to hover over the wizard's head. He had quite a cloud of them about him already, and it made him look positively sorcerous. Bilbo stood still and watched—he loved smoke-rings—and then he blushed to think how proud he had been yesterday morning of the smoke-rings he had sent up the wind over The Hill.

"Now for some music!" said Thorin. "Bring out the instruments!"

Kili and Fili rushed for their bags and brought back little fiddles; Dori, Nori, and Ori brought out flutes from somewhere inside their coats; Bombur produced a drum from the hall; Bifur and Bofur went out too, and came back with clarinets that they had left among the walking-sticks. Dwalin and Balin said: "Excuse me, I left mine in the porch!" "Just bring mine in with you!" said Thorin. They came back with viols as big as themselves, and with Thorin's harp wrapped in a green cloth. It was a beautiful golden harp, and when Thorin struck it the music began all at once, so sudden and sweet that Bilbo forgot everything else, and was swept away into dark lands under strange moons, far over The Water and very far from his hobbit-hole under The Hill.

The dark came into the room from the little window that opened in the side of The Hill; the firelight flickered—it was April—and still they played on, while the shadow of Gandalf's beard wagged against the wall.

The dark filled all the room, and the fire died down, and the shadows were lost, and still they played on. And suddenly first one and then another began to sing as they played, deep-throated singing of the dwarves in the deep places of their ancient homes; and this is like a fragment of their song, if it can be like their song without their music.

Far over the misty mountains cold
To dungeons deep and caverns old
We must away, ere break of day,
To seek the pale enchanted gold.

The dwarves of yore made mighty
*   spells,*
While hammers fell like ringing bells
In places deep, where dark things
*   sleep,*
In hollow halls beneath the fells.

For ancient king and elvish lord
There many a gleaming golden hoard
They shaped and wrought, and light
*   they caught*
To hide in gems on hilt of sword.

On silver necklaces they strung
The flowering stars, on crowns they
*   hung*
The dragon-fire, in twisted wire
They meshed the light of moon and
*   sun.*

Far over the misty mountains cold
To dungeons deep and caverns old
We must away, ere break of day,
To claim our long-forgotten gold.

Goblets they carved there for
*   themselves*
And harps of gold; where no man
*   delves*
There lay they long, and many a song
Was sung unheard by men or elves.

The pines were roaring on the height,
The winds were moaning in the night.
The fire was red, it flaming spread;
The trees like torches blazed with light.

The bells were ringing in the dale
And men looked up with faces pale;
The dragon's ire more fierce than fire
Laid low their towers and houses frail.

*The mountain smoked beneath the
   moon;
The dwarves, they heard the tramp of
   doom.
They fled their hall to dying fall
Beneath his feet, beneath the moon.*

*Far over the misty mountains grim
To dungeons deep and caverns dim
We must away, ere break of day,
To win our harps and gold from him!*

As they sang the hobbit felt the love of beautiful things made by hands and by cunning and by magic moving through him, a fierce and a jealous love, the desire of the hearts of dwarves. Then something Tookish woke up inside him, and he wished to go and see the great mountains, and hear the pine-trees and the waterfalls, and explore the caves, and wear a sword instead of a walking-stick. He looked out of the window. The stars were out in a dark sky above the trees. He thought of the jewels of the dwarves shining in dark caverns. Suddenly in the wood beyond The Water a flame leapt up—probably somebody lighting a wood-fire—and he thought of plundering dragons settling on

his quiet Hill and kindling it all to flames. He shuddered; and very quickly he was plain Mr. Baggins of Bag-End, Under-Hill, again.

He got up trembling. He had less than half a mind to fetch the lamp, and more than half a mind to pretend to, and go and hide behind the beer-barrels in the cellar, and not come out again until all the dwarves had gone away. Suddenly he found that the music and the singing had stopped, and they were all looking at him with eyes shining in the dark.

"Where are you going?" said Thorin, in a tone that seemed to show that he guessed both halves of the hobbit's mind.

"What about a little light?" said Bilbo apologetically.

"We like the dark," said all the dwarves. "Dark for dark business! There are many hours before dawn."

"Of course!" said Bilbo, and sat down in a hurry. He missed the stool and sat in the fender, knocking over the poker and shovel with a crash.

"Hush!" said Gandalf. "Let Thorin speak!" And this is how Thorin began:

"Gandalf, dwarves and Mr. Baggins! We are met together in the house of our

477

friend and fellow conspirator, this most excellent and audacious hobbit—may the hair on his toes never fall out! all praise to his wine and ale!—" He paused for breath and for a polite remark from the hobbit, but the compliments were quite lost on poor Bilbo Baggins, who was wagging his mouth in protest at being called *audacious* and worst of all *fellow conspirator*, though no noise came out, he was so flummoxed. So Thorin went on:

"We are met to discuss our plans, our ways, means, policy and devices. We shall soon before the break of day start on our long journey, a journey from which some of us, or perhaps all of us (except our friend and counsellor, the ingenious wizard Gandalf) may never return. It is a solemn moment. Our object is, I take it, well known to us all. To the estimable Mr. Baggins, and perhaps to one or two of the younger dwarves (I think I should be right in naming Kili and Fili, for instance), the exact situation at the moment may require a little brief explanation—"

This was Thorin's style. He was an important dwarf. If he had been allowed, he would probably have gone on like this until he was out of breath, without telling any one there anything that was not known already. But he was rudely interrupted. Poor Bilbo couldn't bear it any longer. At *may never return* he began to feel a shriek coming up inside, and very soon it burst out like the whistle of an engine coming out of a tunnel. All the dwarves sprang up, knocking over the table. Gandalf struck a blue light on the end of his magic staff, and in its firework glare the poor little hobbit could be seen kneeling on the hearthrug, shaking like a jelly that was melting. Then he fell flat on the floor, and kept on calling out "struck by lightning, struck by lightning!" over and over again; and that was all they could get out of him for a long time. So they took him and laid him out of the way on the drawing-room sofa with a drink at his elbow, and they went back to their dark business.

"Excitable little fellow," said Gandalf, as they sat down again. "Gets funny queer fits, but he is one of the best, one of the best—as fierce as a dragon in a pinch."

If you have ever seen a dragon in a pinch, you will realize that this was only poetical exaggeration applied to any hobbit, even to Old Took's great-grand-uncle Bullroarer, who was so huge (for a hobbit) that he could rise a horse. He charged the ranks of the goblins of Mount Gram in the Battle of the Green Fields, and knocked their king Golfimbul's head clean off with a wooden club. It sailed a hundred yards through the air and went down a rabbit-hole, and in this way the battle was won and the game of Golf invented at the same moment.

In the meanwhile, however, Bullroarer's gentler descendant was reviving in the drawing-room. After a while and a drink he crept nervously to the door of the parlour. This is what he heard, Gloin speaking: "Humph!" (or some snort more or less like that). "Will he do, do you think? It is all very well for Gandalf to talk about this hobbit being fierce, but one shriek like that in a moment of excitement would be enough to wake the dragon and all his relatives, and kill the lot of us. I think it sounded more like fright than excitement! In fact, if it had not been for the sign on the door, I should have been sure we had come to the wrong house. As soon as I clapped eyes on the little fellow bobbing and puffing on the mat, I had my doubts. He looks more like a grocer than a burglar!"

Then Mr. Baggins turned the handle and went in. The Took side had won. He suddenly felt he would go without bed and breakfast to be thought fierce. As for *little fellow bobbing on the mat* it almost made him really fierce. Many a time afterwards the Baggins part regretted what he did now, and he said to himself: "Bilbo, you were a fool; you walked right in and put your foot in it."

"Pardon me," he said, "if I have overheard words that you were saying. I don't pretend to understand what you are talking about, or your reference to burglars, but I think I am right in believing" (this is what he called being on his dignity) "that you think I am no good. I will show you. I have no signs on my door—it was painted a week ago—and I am quite sure you have come to the wrong house. As soon as I saw your funny faces on the door-step, I had my doubts. But treat it as the right one. Tell me what you want done, and I will try it, if I have to walk from here to the East of East and fight the wild Wereworms in the Last Desert. I had a great-great-great-grand-uncle once, Bullroarer Took, and—"

"Yes, yes, but that was long ago," said Gloin. "I was talking about *you*. And I assure you there is a mark on this door— the usual one in the trade—or used to be. *Burglar wants a good job, plenty of Excitement and reasonable Reward,* that's how it is usually read. You can say *Expert Treasure-hunter*, instead of *Burglar* if you like. Some of them do. It's all the same to us. Gandalf told us that there was a man of the sort in these parts looking for a Job at once, and that he had arranged for a meeting here this Wednesday tea-time."

"Of course there is a mark," said Gandalf. "I put it there myself. For very good reasons. You asked me to find the fourteenth man for your expedition, and I chose Mr. Baggins. Just let any one say I chose the wrong man or the wrong house, and you can stop at thirteen and have all the bad luck you like, or go back to digging coal."

He scowled so angrily at Gloin that the dwarf huddled back in his chair; and when Bilbo tried to open his mouth to ask a question, he turned and frowned at him and stuck out his bushy eyebrows, till Bilbo shut his mouth tight with a snap. "That's right," said Gandalf. "Let's have no more argument. I have chosen Mr. Baggins and that ought to be enough for all of you. If I say he is a Burglar, a Burglar he is, or will be when the time comes. There is a lot more in him than you guess, and a deal more than he has any idea of himself. You may (possibly) all live to thank me yet. Now Bilbo, my boy, fetch the lamp, and let's have a little light on this!"

On the table in the light of a big lamp with a red shade he spread a piece of parchment rather like a map.

"This was made by your grandfather, Thorin," he said in answer to the dwarves'

excited questions. "It is a plan of the Mountain."

"I don't see that this will help us much," said Thorin disappointedly after a glance. "I remember the Mountain well enough and the lands about it. And I know where Mirkwood is, and the Withered Heath where the great dragons bred."

"There is a dragon marked in red on the Mountain," said Balin, "but it will be easy enough to find him without that, if ever we arrive there."

"There is one point that you haven't noticed," said the wizard, "and that is the secret entrance. You see that rune on the West side, and the hand pointing to it from the other runes? That marks a hidden passage to the Lower Halls." (Look at the map at the beginning of this book, and you will see there the runes in red.)

"It may have been secret once," said Thorin, "but how do we know that it is secret any longer? Old Smaug has lived there long enough now to find out anything there is to know about those caves."

"He may—but he can't have used it for years and years."

"Why?"

"Because it is too small. 'Five feet high the door and three may walk abreast' say the runes, but Smaug could not creep into a hole that size, not even when he was a young dragon, certainly not after devouring so many of the maidens of the valley."

"It seems a great big hole to me," squeaked Bilbo (who had no experience of dragons and only of hobbit-holes). He was getting excited and interested again, so that he forgot to keep his mouth shut. He loved maps, and in his hall there hung a large one of the Country Round with all his favourite walks marked on it in red

ink. "How could such a large door be kept secret from everybody outside, apart from the dragon?" he asked. He was only a little hobbit you must remember.

"In lots of ways," said Gandalf. "But in what way this one has been hidden we don't know without going to see. From what it says on the map I should guess there is a closed door which has been made to look exactly like the side of the Mountain. That is the usual dwarves' method—I think that is right, isn't it?"

"Quite right," said Thorin.

"Also," went on Gandalf, "I forgot to mention that with the map went a key, a small and curious key. Here it is!" he said, and handed to Thorin a key with a long barrel and intricate wards, made of silver. "Keep it safe!"

"Indeed I will," said Thorin, and he fastened it upon a fine chain that hung about his neck and under his jacket. "Now things begin to look more hopeful. This news alters them much for the better. So far we have had no clear idea what to do. We thought of going East, as quiet and careful as we could, as far as the Long Lake. After that the trouble would begin—."

"A long time before that, if I know any-thing about the roads East," interrupted Gandalf.

"We might go from there up along the River Running," went on Thorin taking no notice, "and so to the ruins of Dale—the old town in the valley there, under the shadow of the Mountain. But we none of us liked the idea of the Front Gate. The river runs right out of it through the great cliff at the South of the Mountain, and out of it comes the dragon too—far too often, unless he has changed his habits."

"That would be no good," said the wiz-ard, "not without a mighty Warrior, even a Hero. I tried to find one; but warriors are busy fighting one another in distant lands, and in this neighbourhood heroes are scarce, or simply not to be found. Swords in these parts are mostly blunt, and axes are used for trees, and shields as cradles or dishcovers; and dragons are comfortably far-off (and therefore legen-dary). That is why I settled on *burglary*—especially when I remembered the exist-ence of a Side-door. And here is our little Bilbo Baggins, *the* burglar, the chosen and selected burglar. So now let's get on and make some plans."

"Very well then," said Thorin, "suppos-ing the burglar-expert gives us some ideas or suggestions."

He turned with mock-politeness to Bilbo.

"First I should like to know a bit more about things," said he, feeling all con-fused and a bit shaky inside, but so far still Tookishly determined to go on with things. "I mean about the gold and the dragon, and all that, and how it got there, and who it belongs to, and so on and further."

"Bless me!" said Thorin, "haven't you got a map? and didn't you hear our song? and haven't we been talking about all this for hours?"

"All the same, I should like it all plain and clear," said he obstinately, putting on his business manner (usually reserved for people who tried to borrow money off him), and doing his best to appear wise and prudent and professional and live up to Gandalf's recommendation. "Also I should like to know about risks, out-of-pocket expenses, time required and remu-neration, and so forth"—by which he meant: "What am I going to get out of it? and am I going to come back alive?"

"O very well," said Thorin. "Long ago in my grandfather's time some dwarves were driven out of the far North, and came with all their wealth and their tools to this Mountain on the map. There they mined and they tunnelled and they made huge halls and great workshops—and in addition I believe they found a good deal of gold and a great many jewels too. Anyway, they grew immensely rich and famous, and my grandfather was King under the Mountain, and treated with great reverence by the mortal men, who lived to the South, and were gradually spreading up the Running River as far as the valley overshadowed by the Mountain. They built the merry town of Dale there in those days. Kings used to send for our smiths, and reward even the least skilful most richly. Fathers would beg us to take their sons as apprentices, and pay us handsomely, especially in food-supplies, which we never bothered to grow or find for ourselves. Altogether those were good days for us, and the poorest of us had money to spend and to lend, and leisure to make beautiful things just for the fun of it, not to speak of the most marvellous and magical toys, the like of which is not to be found in the world now-a-days. So my grandfather's halls became full of wonderful jewels and carvings and cups, and the toyshops of Dale were a sight to behold.

"Undoubtedly that was what brought the dragon. Dragons steal gold and jewels, you know, from men and elves and dwarves, wherever they can find them; and they guard their plunder as long as they live (which is practically for ever, unless they are killed), and never enjoy a brass ring of it. Indeed they hardly know a good bit of work from a bad, though they usually have a good notion of the current market value; and they can't make a thing for themselves, not even mend a little loose scale of their armour. There were lots of dragons in the North in those days, and gold was probably getting scarce up there, with the dwarves flying south or getting killed, and all the general waste and destruction that dragons make going from bad to worse. There was a most specially greedy, strong and wicked worm called Smaug. One day he flew up into the air and came south. The first we heard of it was a noise like a hurricane coming from the North, and the pine-trees on the Mountain creaking and cracking in the wind. Some of the dwarves who happened to be outside (I was one luckily—a fine adventurous lad in those days, always wandering about, and it saved my life that day)—well, from a good way off we saw the dragon settle on our mountain in a spout of flame. Then he came down the slopes and when he reached the woods they all went up in fire. By that time all the bells were ringing in Dale and the

warriors were arming. The dwarves rushed out of their great gate; but there was the dragon waiting for them. None escaped that way. The river rushed up in steam and a fog fell on Dale, and in the fog the dragon came on them and destroyed most of the warriors—the usual unhappy story, it was only too common in those days. Then he went back and crept in through the Front Gate and routed out all the halls, and lanes, and tunnels, alleys, cellars, mansions and passages. After that there were no dwarves left alive inside, and he took all their wealth for himself. Probably, for that is the dragons' way, he has piled it all up in a great heap far inside, and sleeps on it for a bed. Later he used to crawl out of the great gate and come by night to Dale, and carry away people, especially maidens, to eat, until Dale was ruined, and all the people dead or gone. What goes on there now I don't know for certain, but I don't suppose any one lives nearer to the Mountain than the far edge of the Long Lake now-a-days.

"The few of us that were well outside sat and wept in hiding, and cursed Smaug; and there we were unexpectedly joined by my father and my grandfather with singed beards. They looked very grim but they said very little. When I asked how they had got away, they told me to hold my tongue, and said that one day in the proper time I should know. After that we went away, and we have had to earn our livings as best we could up and down the lands, often enough sinking as low as blacksmith-work or even coal mining. But we have never forgotten our stolen treasure. And even now, when

I will allow we have a good bit laid by and are not so badly off"—here Thorin stroked the gold chain round his neck—"we still mean to get it back, and to bring our curses home to Smaug—if we can.

"I have often wondered about my father's and my grandfather's escape. I see now they must have had a private Side-door which only they knew about. But apparently they made a map, and I should like to know how Gandalf got hold of it, and why it did not come down to me, the rightful heir."

"I did not 'get hold of it,' I was given it," said the wizard. "Your grandfather was killed, you remember, in the mines of Moria by a goblin—"

"Curse the goblin, yes," said Thorin.

"And your father went away on the twenty-first of April, a hundred years ago last Thursday, and has never been seen by you since—"

"True, true," said Thorin.

"Well, your father gave me this to give to you; and if I have chosen my own time and way for handing it over, you can hardly blame me, considering the trouble I had to find you. Your father could not remember his own name when he gave me the paper, and he never told me yours; so on the whole I think I ought to be praised and thanked! Here it is," said he handing the map to Thorin.

"I don't understand," said Thorin, and Bilbo felt he would have liked to say the same. The explanation did not seem to explain.

"Your grandfather," said the wizard slowly and crossly, "gave the map to his son for safety before he went to the mines of Moria. Your father went away to try his luck with the map after your grand-father was killed; and lots of adventures of a most unpleasant sort he had, but he never got near the Mountain. How he got there I don't know, but I found him a prisoner in the dungeons of the Necro-mancer."

"Whatever were you doing there?" asked Thorin with a shudder, and all the dwarves shivered.

"Never you mind. I was finding things out, as usual; and a nasty dangerous business it was. Even I, Gandalf, only just escaped. I tried to save your father, but it was too late. He was witless and wandering, and had forgotten almost everything except the map and the key."

"We have long ago paid the goblins of Moria," said Thorin; "we must give a thought to the Necromancer."

"Don't be absurd! That is a job quite beyond the powers of all the dwarves put together, if they could all be collected again from the four corners of the world. The one thing your father wished was for you to read the map and use the key. The dragon and the Mountain are more than big enough tasks for you!"

"Hear, hear!" said Bilbo, and accidentally said it aloud.

"Hear what?" they all said turning suddenly towards him, and he was so flustered that he answered, "Hear what I have got to say!"

"What's that?" they asked.

"Well, I should say that you ought to go East and have a look round. After all there is the Side-door, and dragons must sleep sometimes, I suppose. If you sit on the door-step long enough, I daresay you will think of something. And well, don't you know, I think we have talked long enough for one night, if you see what

I mean. What about bed, and an early start, and all that? I will give you a good breakfast before you go."

"Before *we* go, I suppose you mean," said Thorin. "Aren't you the burglar? And isn't sitting on the door-step your job, not

his mind up about was not to bother to get up very early and cook everybody else's wretched breakfast. The Tookishness was wearing off, and he was not now quite so sure that he was going on any journey in the morning.

to speak of getting inside the door? But I agree about bed and breakfast. I like six eggs with my ham, when starting on a journey: fried not poached, and mind you don't break 'em."

After all the others had ordered their breakfasts without so much as a please (which annoyed Bilbo very much), they all got up. The hobbit had to find room for them all, and filled all his spare-rooms and made beds on chairs and sofas, before he got them all stowed and went to his own little bed very tired and not altogether happy. One thing he did make

As he lay in bed he could hear Thorin still humming to himself in the best bedroom next to him:

Far over the misty mountains cold
To dungeons deep and caverns old
We must away, ere break of day,
To find our long-forgotten gold.

Bilbo went to sleep with that in his ears, and it gave him very uncomfortable dreams.

It was long after the break of day, when he woke up.

"Hungry Hans" is a little known story
that comes from Switzerland—it is, in fact,
so little known even in its native country
that it cannot be found in many editions
of the author's works.
The translator found it while traveling
in Europe and published it in a book
of fables and fairy tales called
The Fat of the Cat.
It has been made into a ballet
and a one-act comic opera.

Hungry Hans

From The Fat of the Cat and Other Stories

BY GOTTFRIED KELLER, ADAPTED BY LOUIS UNTERMEYER
Illustrated by JEAN WINSLOW

CLOSE to Seldwyla there lived an apothecary who could always be found hard at work. Early and late, he busied himself with pills and powders and potions and drugs and ointments and salves. He mixed medicines, distilled extracts, registered letters and never gave himself a moment's leisure. He never invited company to his house, never accepted any invitations, refused to go to places of amusement. Year in, year out, he never set foot in a tavern, and he abused anybody who, after his day's work, sat down to a glass of country-wine. His beloved better half attended to the house. She kept no maid, did everything herself: scouring and scrubbing, baking and broiling, mending and knitting—she attended to every detail. Like her husband, she stayed at home; never went to pay visits or attend the dances in Seldwyla. The only time she left the house was on Sunday, when, with her husband, she walked stiffly to church.

487

Clever though they were in many ways, they had one fault which everyone noticed at once—and which you have already guessed—their stinginess. They were, so ran the gossip, the stingiest couple in Switzerland. But they were not miserly with themselves. Far from it! They enjoyed the best of food. The most delicate dishes came to their table every day, the finest wines trickled down their throats every evening, the most expensive tobacco was crammed into the apothecary's pipe after every meal. But when it came to sharing anything with someone else, they would not part with the tiniest morsel. She cooked the richest meats—and refused to give the ragged beggars an old crust of bread. He finished a whole bottle of rare claret every night—and wouldn't move from his chair to oblige thirsty travellers with a glass of water.

When I tell you that they did not keep a maid, do not think that they did their own work because they believed in hard work for its own sake. No, the reason is much simpler. They kept no maid because no maid would stay with them. And no maid would stay with them because she never got enough to eat.

While these two gluttons gorged themselves, all they ever gave the servants (when they had them!) was a plate of wretched soup, a piece of old bread and, once a week, a few greasy scraps of left-over meat. Because of this kind of treat-

ment, the apothecary's staff of assistants had been reduced to one apprentice, a lean and starved-looking boy who had twice run away from his master, but who was bound by contract to serve four years and who had been brought back each time. He was six feet high—for the only way he could grow was up. This poor youngster was made to do the work of half a dozen able-bodied men; he was continually being called from the laboratory to the kitchen, from the kitchen to the store-room, from the attic to the cellar and back again—all in a few minutes. Often his master in the work-room, and his mistress in the pantry, would call for him at once. And then he would be thrashed for not being in both places at the same time!

Hans—for this was the name of the lanky apprentice—was always hungry. Ever since he could remember, he had not had enough to eat. He had been born hungry. He went about his work in a daze, thinking of nothing but food. The only dreams he had were about wonderful feasts; he imagined Heaven as a place where the good souls ate and ate through all eternity. All day long he went sniffing through the rooms, and if there was anything to eat anywhere in sight, you can be sure his five fingers were in it. He had been caught and whipped hundreds of times. His back was black and blue from the marks of his master's brown-lacquered cane; his face showed scratches from his mistress's sharp claws. But hunger is greater than fear. He dipped into everything; his muscles seemed to move by themselves, without his will. Often he peeked through the keyhole where his greedy employers were devouring some

fragrant repast, and his jaws began working up and down of their own accord, even though the poor boy had nothing in his mouth except his tongue and his teeth.

His favorite place was, as you might imagine, the pantry. Here were kept cocoa, sugar, cookies, chocolate, syrups, delicious flavouring extracts, honey, and so forth. And here, whenever he got a chance, Hans would come, tasting, chewing and swallowing, no matter how often the brown-lacquered cane fell on him in the midst of his stolen sweets. Even when his bruises hurt him most, he would come back to this enchanting spot and console himself with some of the famous goose-liver paste, which was his master's chief pride. This paste was packed in layers in a large case and Hans, by loosening one of the boards at the bottom, would take out a bit now and then to comfort himself. He only allowed himself this delicacy once in a while, and did not indulge himself oftener for a peculiar reason. He was fond enough of it, you may be sure, but he had to overcome a horrible feeling every time he came near the case which contained the dainties. On top of this case stood three wide-necked, carefully sealed, white glass jars which contained (in his opinion) the juiciest, most appetizing preserved fruits he had ever seen. He felt terribly unhappy because he could never taste these lovely morsels—and it was not his conscience that made him keep his hands off. It was something stronger than his appetite that made him tremble whenever he happened to touch these jars. For, pasted on the glass, was a label, and on the label was a grinning skull and two crossed bones next to the one word "Poison"! Hans shook his head every time he saw the word. "What a pity," he would murmur. "What a shame to use such beautiful fruit for such a terrible purpose." And, with a sigh of disappointment, he would go back to his work.

One morning—it was a Sunday—as Hans was helping himself to the goose-liver, he heard the harsh voice of his mistress calling him to the kitchen. His bad conscience almost made him feel her outstretched claws dig into him as he ran down the steps, choking down the last bite of his stolen breakfast. But a great surprise was awaiting him; an entirely different sight than he expected met his astonished eyes. There stood the apothecary in a cinnamon-brown coat trimmed with steel-blue buttons; he had on narrow nankeen trousers, white silk stockings, fancy buckled shoes, and the hated cane swung from his hand. Next to him stood his owl-faced wife in a bright green dress with a large fur collar. Her fingers were not preparing to scratch him as usual, but were busy sorting out the bad coins from her purse so she could put these—which were not worth anything—in the poor-box at church.

"Hans," the apothecary said, "to-day is the birthday of your indulgent mistress, my dear wife, and so, as a special holiday, we are going to church together."

"And here," that generous lady chimed in, "so that you won't be lonely, here is some work for you to keep you busy while we are away." And a poke in his ribs directed him to the hearth where a suckling-pig was beginning to be broiled on the spit. Already a magical fragrance

was rising from it and Hans's thirsty nostrils started to drink it in. But—"Don't stand there all day like a ninny!" came the commanding voice of the mistress of the household. "Here is what you have to do: Keep turning the spit so that the meat gets good and brown all over, pour the gravy over it every few seconds so that it stays moist and tender, don't forget to rake the coals so that the fire is the right heat, but if it gets too hot and you burn any part of the meat, I'll box your ears till the blood comes!" This pleasant speech—which was all delivered in one breath—was scarcely out of her mouth before his master continued, "And I'll do my share, you young rascal! If the Sunday dinner is spoiled, I'll broil *you* on the spit instead of the pig that's on it now! Understand?" And with this sweet farewell, the gentle pair left the house and walked to church, where they sang the sacred hymns louder than anyone in the congregation.

After the lock had turned and the backs of his two slave-drivers had disappeared down the street, Hans began to feel better and, coming nearer the hearth, to breathe deeper.

The wonderful, sweet smell—sweeter than heavenly incense—bewitched his senses. His teeth ached for a single bite and his jaws began to work up and down over their painful emptiness. The pigling grew browner and tenderer, and a thousand little fat bubbles, like tiny pearls, leaped and danced and disappeared and sprang up again on the smooth surface of the roast. The meat crisped and crackled and hummed and hissed, as if something alive were talking to him from the spit. And poor Hans sat there, turn-

ing and ladling and dipping and poking the fire, while the crust on the grilled meat grew more tempting and Hans's eyes began to have a glassy stare. Finally, when his mouth watered so that he could not sit there any longer, it seemed as if a voice spoke to him from the hissing spit. "Every cook has the right to taste what he is preparing," said the voice in a juicy whisper, "why shouldn't *you?* How can you tell if I'm cooked properly unless you see how I taste. Here is a tiny crust toward the back; nobody will ever miss that. Besides, it's loose and is just about to fall into the fire, so you may as well have it."

"And why shouldn't I?" said Hans to himself. "The place will get smooth and brown in a minute." No sooner said than done—and down went a good-sized crust into Hans's bottomless pit. . . .

It would be hard to describe the effect of the taste of this morsel on Hans. He sat there, licking his lips, his eyes sparkling, while a tiny trickle of fat crept out of the corners of his mouth.

"Whoever says A must say B and C," runs an old saying. So with Hans. Almost beside himself with the taste of that first scrap, he heard the tempting voice again. "Come," it seemed to say in rich, fat tones, "enjoy yourself, you poor fellow. You have nothing else in the world except your watery soup and mouldy bread and a back that's beaten black and blue. You never have an hour of pleasure; never a decent satisfying meal. Therefore, take another little piece from me— the place will get smooth and brown again—no one will notice it."

And Hans, the poor chap, listened and obeyed. You can imagine he did not need much urging. The second piece tasted better than the first, the third still better, the fourth better still, and soon—("that's all right, the place will get brown quickly")—the entire crust had disappeared. The taste of this rich food affected him like strong wine, lifting him into another world, far away from the kitchen. Strange visions came to him: He dreamed of all the great feasts in history. He fancied himself at these great banquets, helped to all the rare sweetmeats of the olden world. He was at Alexander's feast, at the great tables of the Roman Emperors, at all the festivals mentioned in the Bible. He imagined he was one of the guests at the famous Marriage at Cana and had just devoured an entire game-pie of stuffed capon, as the chief-cook, splendid in scarlet, helped by fourteen assistant-cooks, placed a whole roast ox in front of him, upright on the table.... And he ate this colossal dish down to the very bones! Again, he dreamed that he was one of the seven lean Egyptian oxen in the story of Joseph and, after eating all of the fat cattle, he found himself in an enormous wheat-field, which he devoured until nothing was left standing but a few rocks.

During these fantastic visions, Hans had been helping himself to what was in front of him, and, naturally, by this time, there was very little left of the pig. As Hans searched for more, his eyes suddenly caught sight of the one thing that remained, and its appearance made him tremble all over. It was the stiff, little, brown-toasted tail, which stuck out from the bones exactly like a tiny copy of the brown-lacquered cane of his master. As quick as lightning, he was hurled back to his present surroundings. The lovely dreams were scattered. The game-pie, the roast ox, the great wheat-field went the way of soap-bubbles. And all Hans saw before him was the bare skeleton of the young pig, which grinned at him as though to say, "Now, my friend, *you* will have to take my place here on the spit!"

This was too much for unhappy Hans. He believed that the apothecary would do exactly what he threatened. The beating he would get would be terrible enough. But to be put on the spit—! No, that was too much. If he had to die, rather than suffer such torture, he would kill himself! But how? He had no gun, and, as he hated water, he could not drown himself. But poison—ah, that was an idea! Poison was the easiest way—and what could be better than the poisoned fruit! So Hans fetched the three glass jars, made himself comfortable, and stuffed himself with preserved oranges, apples, pears, plums, peaches and pineapples. "Ah, delicious fruit," he sighed, "too bad that you are poisonous," and sank, tired and filled to the brim, in front of the hearth. There he lay, with closed eyes, awaiting death.

Suddenly, he heard the door slam, and there stood—not Death—but his master, who stared at him with open mouth and eyes popping out of his head. The apothecary thought he must be dreaming, as he looked first at what remained of the Sunday dinner and then at Hans, who, instead of being frightened, merely smiled at the furious man. "You won't have to cut my throat," murmured Hans, in a weak voice, "let me alone. I will die soon enough. Let me alone. I have poisoned myself."

"Poisoned yourself?" cried the astonished apothecary. "How? When? With what?"

"With the poisoned fruit, master. I ate all of it. The three jars are empty. Three jars, master."

"You idiot, you rascal, you outrageous villain!" shrieked the apothecary, whose face had gone purple. "That was not poison! I only pasted the labels on so that people would keep their hands off! Those three jars contained my most delicate desserts! I was keeping them for some great occasion! You thief, you scoundrel, you unspeakable robber!"—and blow after blow of the brown-lacquered cane fell on Hans's back, till his whole body shook.

But Hans's back was shaking with laughter not with sobs. This was more than the outraged apothecary could stand. When he saw that the more he whipped the boy, the louder Hans laughed and that, to make matters worse, his precious cane snapped in two, his rage knew no bounds. "Get out of my sight!" he screamed, "get out of my sight, you plunderer, and never let me see you again!"

And you can be sure that Hans did not wait for the order to be repeated. By the time the apothecary had calmed himself, Hans, although he was almost too full to move, was halfway to Goldach.

And there, a prosperous dealer in medicines, you can find him to-day. Any time you are passing through the town, you will see his peculiar sign-board. Above a picture of two enormous jars, one on each side of a roasted pig, is this curious inscription: *"At the Sign of The Poisoned Fruit.* Everything in Food and Drugs. Cure Guaranteed."

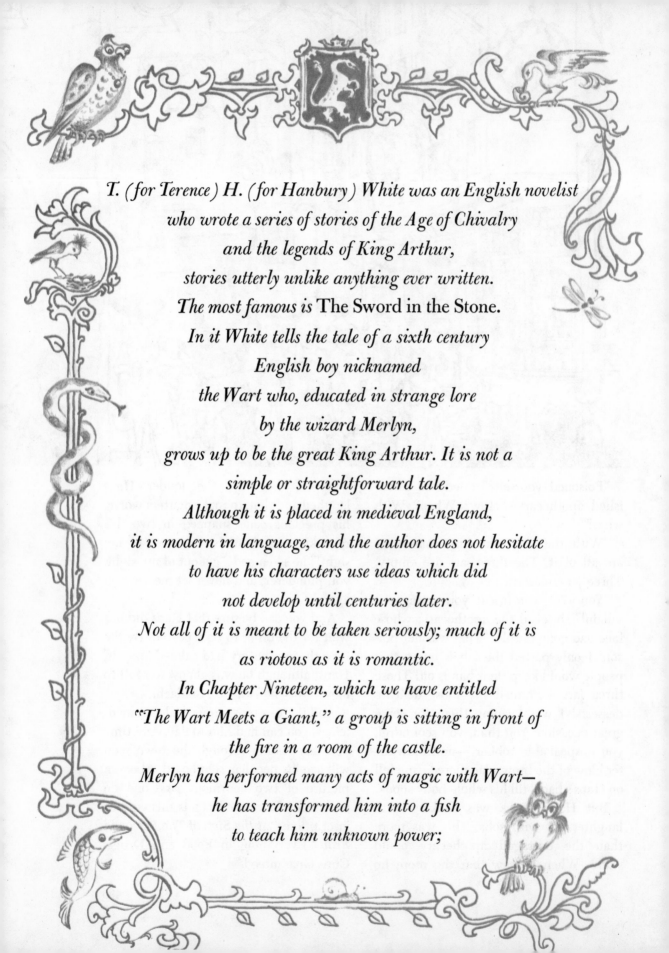

*T. (for Terence) H. (for Hanbury) White was an English novelist
who wrote a series of stories of the Age of Chivalry
and the legends of King Arthur,
stories utterly unlike anything ever written.
The most famous is* The Sword in the Stone.
*In it White tells the tale of a sixth century
English boy nicknamed
the Wart who, educated in strange lore
by the wizard Merlyn,
grows up to be the great King Arthur. It is not a
simple or straightforward tale.
Although it is placed in medieval England,
it is modern in language, and the author does not hesitate
to have his characters use ideas which did
not develop until centuries later.
Not all of it is meant to be taken seriously; much of it is
as riotous as it is romantic.
In Chapter Nineteen, which we have entitled
"The Wart Meets a Giant," a group is sitting in front of
the fire in a room of the castle.
Merlyn has performed many acts of magic with Wart—
he has transformed him into a fish
to teach him unknown power;*

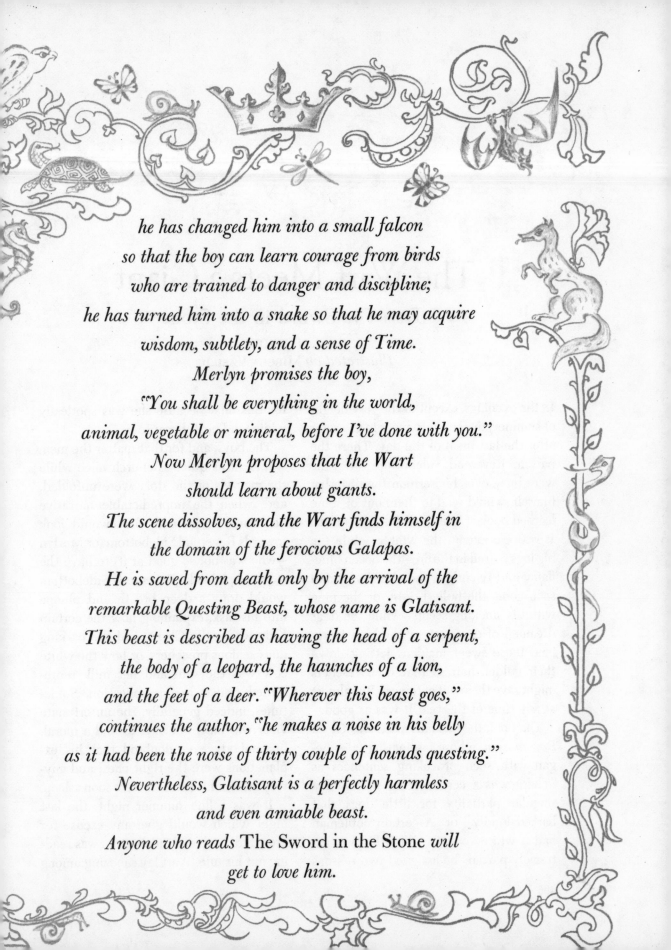

he has changed him into a small falcon
so that the boy can learn courage from birds
who are trained to danger and discipline;
he has turned him into a snake so that he may acquire
wisdom, subtlety, and a sense of Time.
Merlyn promises the boy,
"You shall be everything in the world,
animal, vegetable or mineral, before I've done with you."
Now Merlyn proposes that the Wart
should learn about giants.
The scene dissolves, and the Wart finds himself in
the domain of the ferocious Galapas.
He is saved from death only by the arrival of the
remarkable Questing Beast, whose name is Glatisant.
This beast is described as having the head of a serpent,
the body of a leopard, the haunches of a lion,
and the feet of a deer. "Wherever this beast goes,"
continues the author, "he makes a noise in his belly
as it had been the noise of thirty couple of hounds questing."
Nevertheless, Glatisant is a perfectly harmless
and even amiable beast.
Anyone who reads The Sword in the Stone will
get to love him.

The Wart Meets a Giant

From The Sword in the Stone

BY T. H. WHITE

Illustrated by MIRCEA VASILIU

IN the evenings, except in the very height of summer, they used to meet in the solar after the last meal of the day. There the parson, Reverend Sidebottom, or if he were busy over his sermon then Merlyn himself, would read to them out of some learned book of tales, to calm their spirits. It was glorious in the winter, while the big logs roared in the fire—the beech blue-flamy and relentless, the elm showy and soon gone, the holly bright, or the pine with his smoking scents—while the dogs dreamed of conquest, or the boys imagined those sweet maidens letting down their golden hair so that their rescuers might save them out of towers. But almost at any time of the year it was as good.

The book they usually used was *Gesta Romanorum,* whose fascinating tales began with such provoking sentences as "There was a certain King who had a singular partiality for little dogs that barked loudly," or "A certain nobleman had a white cow, to which he was extremely partial: he assigned two reasons

for this, first because she was spotlessly white, and next, because . . ."

The boys, and for that matter the men, would sit as quiet as church mice while the marvels of the story were unfolded, and, when the unpredictable narrative had come to an end, they would look towards Reverend Sidebottom (or Merlyn —who was not so good at it) to have the story explained. Reverend Sidebottom would draw a deep breath and plunge into his task, explaining how the certain King was really Christ, and the barking dogs zealous preachers, or how the white cow was the soul and her milk represented prayer and supplication. Sometimes, indeed generally, the unfortunate vicar was hard put to it to find a moral, but nobody ever doubted that his explanations were the right ones; and anyway most of his listeners were soon asleep.

It was a fine summer night, the last night which would give any excuse for fires, and Reverend Sidebottom was reading out his tale. Wart lay snoozing among the lean ribs of the gazehounds: Sir Ector sipped his wine with his eyes brooding on the logs which lit the evening: Kay played chess with himself rather badly: and Merlyn, with his long beard saffron in the firelight, sat cross-legged knitting, beside the Wart.

"There was once discovered at Rome," read Reverend Sidebottom through his nose, *"an uncorrupted body, taller than the wall of the city, on which the following words were inscribed—'Pallas, the son of Evander, whom the lance of a crooked soldier slew, is interred here.' A candle burned at his head which neither water nor wind could extinguish, until air was admitted through a hole made with the point of a needle beneath the flame. The wound of which this giant had died was four feet and a half long. Having been killed after the overthrow of Troy, he remained in his tomb two thousand two hundred and forty years."*

"Have you ever seen a giant?" asked Merlyn softly, so as not to interrupt the reading. "No, I remember you haven't. Just catch hold of my hand a moment, and shut your eyes."

The vicar was droning on about the gigantic son of Evander, Sir Ector was staring into the fire, and Kay was making a slight click as he moved one of the chessmen, but the Wart and Merlyn were immediately standing hand in hand in an unknown forest.

"This is the Forest of the Burbly Water," said Merlyn, "and we are going to visit the giant Galapas. Now listen. You are invisible at the moment, because you are holding my hand. I am able to keep myself invisible by an exercise of will-power—an exceedingly exhausting job it is—and I can keep you invisible so long as you hold on to me. It takes twice as much will-power, but there. If, however, you let go of me even for a moment, during that moment you will become visible, and, if you do it in the presence of Galapas, he will munch you up in two bites. So hold on."

"Very well," said the Wart.

"Don't say 'Very well.' It isn't very well at all. On the contrary, it is very ill indeed. And another thing. The whole of this beastly wood is dotted with pitfalls and I shall be grateful if you will look where you are going."

"What sort of pitfalls?"

"He digs a lot of pits about ten feet deep, with smooth clay walls, and covers them over with dead branches, pine needles and such-like. Then, if people walk

about, they tumble into them, and he goes round with his bow every morning to finish them off. When he has shot them dead, he climbs in and collects them for dinner. He can hoist himself out of a ten-foot pit quite easily."

"Very well," said the Wart again, and corrected himself to, "I will be careful."

Being invisible is not so pleasant as it sounds. After a few minutes of it you forget where you last left your hands and legs—or at least you can only guess to within three or four inches—and the result is that it is by no means easy to make your way through a brambly wood. You can see the brambles all right, but where exactly you are in relation to them becomes more confusing. The only guide to your legs, for the feeling in them soon becomes complicated, is by looking for your footprints—these you can see in the neatly flattened grass below you—and, as for your arms and hands, it becomes hopeless unless you concentrate your mind to remember where you put them last. You can generally tell where your body is, either by the unnatural bend of a thorn branch, or by the pain of one of its thorns, or by the strange feeling of *centralness* which all human beings have, because we keep our souls in the region of our liver.

"Hold on," said Merlyn, "and for glory's sake don't trip up."

They proceeded to tread their tipsy way through the forest, staring carefully at the earth in front of them in case it should give way, and stopping very often when an extra large bramble fastened itself in their flesh. When Merlyn was stuck with a bramble, he swore, and when he swore he lost some of his concentration

and they both became dimly visible, like autumn mist. The rabbits upwind of them stood on their hind legs at this, and exclaimed, "Good gracious!"

"What are we going to do?" asked the Wart.

"Well," said Merlyn, "here we are at the Burbly Water. You can see the giant's castle on the opposite bank, and we shall have to swim across. It may be difficult to walk when you are invisible, but to swim is perfectly impossible, even with years of practice. You are always getting your nose under water. So I shall have to let go of you until we have swum across in our own time. Don't forget to meet me quickly on the other bank."

The Wart went down into the warm starlit water, which ran musically like a real salmon stream, and struck out for the other side. He swam fast, across and down river, with a kind of natural dog-stroke, and he had to go about a quarter of a mile below his landing-place along the bank before Merlyn also came out to meet him, dripping. Merlyn swam the breast-stroke, very slowly and with great precision, watching ahead of him over the bow wave of his beard, with that faintly anxious expression of a faithful retriever.

"Now," said Merlyn, "catch hold again, and we will see what Galapas is about."

They walked invisible across the sward, where many unhappy-looking gardeners with iron collars round their necks were mowing, weeding and sweeping by torchlight, although it was so late, in what had begun to be a garden. They were slaves.

"Talk in whispers," said Merlyn, "if you have to talk."

There was a brick wall in front of them, with fruit trees nailed along it, and this they were forced to climb. They did so by the usual methods of bending over, climbing on each other's backs, giving a hand up from on top, and so forth, but every time that the Wart was compelled to let go of his magician for a moment he became visible. It was like an early cinematograph flickering very badly, or one of those magic lanterns where you put in slide after slide. A slave gardener, looking at that part of the wall, sadly tapped himself on the head and went away into a shrubbery to be sick.

"Hush," whispered Merlyn from the top of the wall, and they looked down upon the giant in person, as he took his evening ease by candlelight upon the bowling green.

"But he's not big at all," whispered the Wart disappointedly.

"He is ten feet high," hissed Merlyn, "and that is *extremely* big for a giant. I chose the best one I knew. Even Goliath was only six cubits and a span—or nine feet four inches. If you don't like him you can go home."

"I'm sorry. I didn't mean to be ungrateful, Merlyn, only I thought they were sixty feet long and that sort of thing."

"Sixty feet!" sniffed the necromancer.

The giant had heard something at the top of the wall, and looked up towards them, remarking in a rumbling tone, "How the bats squeak at night!" Then he poured himself out another hornful of madeira and tossed it off in one draught.

Merlyn lowered his voice and explained: "People find the teeth and bones of creatures like your friend Atlantosau-

rus, and then they tell stories about human giants. One of them found a tooth weighing two hundred ounces. It's dragons, not giants, that grow really big."

"But can't humans grow big, too?"

"I don't understand it myself, but it is something about the composition of their bones. If a human was to grow sixty feet high, he would simply snap his bones with the weight of their own gravity. The biggest real giant was Eleazer, and he was only ten feet and a half."

"Well," said the Wart, "I must say it is rather a disappointment."

"I don't mean being brought to see him," he added hastily, "but that they don't grow like I thought. Still, I suppose ten feet is quite big when you come to think of it."

"It is twice as high as you are," said Merlyn. "You would just come up to his navel, and he could pitch you up to a corn rick about as high as you can throw a sheaf."

They had become interested in this discussion, so that they got less and less careful of their voices, and now the giant rose up out of his easy-chair. He came towards them with a three-gallon bottle of wine in his hand, and stared earnestly at the wall on which they were sitting. Then he threw the bottle at the wall rather to their left, said in an angry voice, "Beastly screech owls!" and proceeded to stump off into the castle.

"Follow him," cried Merlyn quickly.

They scrambled down off the wall, joined hands, and hurried after the giant by the garden door.

In the beginning the downstairs parts were reasonably civilized, with green baize doors behind which butlers and footmen—though with iron collars round their necks—were polishing silver and finishing off the decanters. Later on there were strong-rooms with ancient safes in them, that contained the various gold cups, épergnes and other trophies won at jousts and horse-races by the giant. Next there were dismal cellars with cobwebs over the wine bins, and dreary-looking rats peeping thoughtfully at the bodiless footprints in the dust, and several corpses of human beings hanging up in the game cupboards until they should be ready to eat. It was like the place for adults only in the Chamber of Horrors at Madame Tussaud's.

At the very bottom of the castle they came upon the dungeons. Here the chalky walls dripped with greasy moisture, and there were pathetic messages and graffiti scratched upon the stone. "Pray for poor Priscilla," said one, and another said, "Oh, if I had only paid for my dog license honestly, I should never have come to this pass." There was a picture of a man hanging from a gallows, with arms and legs sticking out like those of a Guy Fawkes in all directions, and another of a demon with horns. A fifth carving said, "Midnight Sun for the two-thirty," while a sixth said, "Oh, yeah?" and a seventh exclaimed, "Alas, that I should have forgotten to feed my poor canary: now I am in the same dread doom." A message which had been scratched out said, "Beastly old Galapas loves Madame Mim, the dirty hound," and somebody else had written, "Repent and be saved for the Kingdom of Hell is at hand." There were kisses, dates, pious ejaculations, mottoes such as "Waste not, want not," and "Good night, ladies," also hearts

with arrows in them, skulls and crossbones, pictures of pigs drawn with the eyes shut, and pathetic messages such as, "Don't forget to take the potatoes off at half-past twelve," "The key is under the geranium," "Revenge me on stinking Galapas, by whom I am foully slain," or merely "Mazawatee Mead for Night Starvation." It was a grimly place.

"Ha!" cried Galapas, stopping outside one of his cells. "Are you going to give me back my patent unbreakable helm, or make me another one?"

"It's not your helm," answered a feeble voice. "I invented it, and I patented it, and you can go sing for another one, you beast."

"No dinner tomorrow," said Galapas cruelly, and went on to the next cell.

"What about that publicity?" asked the giant. "Are you going to say that the Queen of Sheba made an unprovoked attack upon me and that I took her country in self-defense?"

"No, I'm not," said the journalist in the cell.

"Rubber truncheons for you," said Galapas, "in the morning."

"Where have you hidden my elastic stays?" thundered the giant at the third cell.

"I shan't tell you," said the cell.

"If you don't tell me," said Galapas, "I shall have your feet burnt."

"You can do what you like."

"Oh, come on," pleaded the giant. "My stomach hangs down without them. If you will tell me where you put them I will make you a general, and you shall go hunting in Poland in a fur cap. Or you can have a pet lion, or a comic beard, and you can fly to America with an Armada.

Would you like to marry any of my daughters?"

"I think all your propositions are foul," said the cell. "You had better have a public trial of me for propaganda."

"You are just a mean, horrible bully," said the giant, and went on to the next cell.

"Now then," said Galapas. "What about that ransom, you dirty English pig?"

"I'm not a pig," said the cell, "and I'm not dirty, or I wasn't until I fell into that beastly pit. Now I've got pine needles all down my back. What have you done with my tooth-brush, you giant, and where have you put my poor brachet, what?"

"Never mind your brachet and your tooth-brush," shouted Galapas, "what about that ransom, you idiot, or are you too steeped in British sottishness to understand anything at all?"

"I want to brush my teeth," answered King Pellinore obstinately. "They feel funny, if you understand what I mean, and it makes me feel not very well."

"Uomo bestiale," cried the giant. "Have you no finer feelings?"

"No," said King Pellinore, "I don't think I have. I want to brush my teeth, and I am getting cramp through sitting all the time on this bench, or whatever you call it."

"Unbelievable sot," screamed the master of the castle. "Where is your soul, you shop-keeper? Do you think of nothing but your teeth?"

"I think of lots of things, old boy," said King Pellinore. "I think how nice it would be to have a poached egg, what?"

"Well, you shan't have a poached egg, you shall just stay there until you pay my ransom. How do you suppose I am to run my business if I don't have my ransoms?

What about my concentration camps, and my thousand-dollar wreaths at funerals? Do you suppose that all this is run on nothing? Why, I had to send a wreath for King Gwythno Garanhir which consisted of a Welsh Harp forty feet long, made entirely out of orchids. It said, 'Melodious Angels Sing Thee to Thy Rest.' "

"I think that was a very good wreath," said King Pellinore admiringly. "But couldn't I have my tooth-brush, what? Dash it all, really, it isn't much compared with a wreath like that. Or is it?"

"Imbecile," exclaimed the giant, and moved on to the next cell.

"We shall have to rescue him," whispered the Wart. "It is poor old King Pellinore, and he must have fallen into one of those traps you were telling me about, while he was after the Questing Beast."

"Let him stay," said Merlyn. "A chap who doesn't know enough to keep himself out of the clutches of one of these giants isn't worth troubling about."

"Perhaps he was thinking of something else," whispered the Wart.

"Well, he shouldn't have been," hissed the magician. "Giants like this do absolutely no harm in the long run, and you can keep them quite quiet by the smallest considerations, such as giving them back their stays. Anybody knows that. If he has got himself into trouble with Galapas, let him stay in it. Let him pay the ransom."

"I know for a fact," said the Wart, "that he hasn't got the money. He can't even afford to buy himself a feather bed."

"Then he should be polite," said Merlyn doubtfully.

"He is trying to be," said the Wart. "He doesn't understand very much. Oh, please, King Pellinore is a friend of mine

501

and I don't like to see him in these forbidding cells without a single helper."

"Whatever can we do?" cried Merlyn angrily. "The cells are firmly locked."

There was really nothing to do, but the magician's louder cry had altered matters into a crisis. Forgetting to be silent as well as invisible, Merlyn had spoken too loudly for the safety of his expedition.

"Who's there?" shrieked Galapas, wheeling round at the fifth cell.

"It's nothing," cried Merlyn. "Only a mouse."

The giant Galapas whipped out his mighty sword, and stared backwards down the narrow passage with his torch held high above his head. "Nonsense," he pronounced. "Mouses don't talk in human speech."

"Eek," said Merlyn, hoping that this would do.

"You can't fool me," said Galapas. "Now I shall come for you with my shining blade, and I shall see what you are, by yea or by nay."

He came down towards them, holding the blue glittering edge in front of him, and his fat eyes were brutal and piggish in the torchlight. You can imagine that it was not very pleasant having a person who weighed five hundred pounds looking for you in a narrow passage, with a sword as long as yourself, in the hopes of sticking it into your liver.

"Don't be silly," said Merlyn. "It is only a mouse, or two mice. You ought to know better."

"It is an invisible magician," said Galapas. "And as for invisible magicians, I slit them up, see? I shed their bowels upon the earth. see? I rip them and tear them, see, so that their invisible guts fall out

upon the earth. Now, where are you, magician, so that I may slice and zip?"

"We are behind you," said Merlyn anxiously. "Look, in that further corner behind your back."

"Yes," said Galapas grimly, "except for your voice."

"Hold on," cried Merlyn, but the Wart in the confusion had slipped his hand.

"A visible magician," remarked the giant, "this time. But only a small one. We shall see whether the sword goes in with a slide."

"Catch hold, you idiot," cried Merlyn frantically, and with several fumblings they were hand in hand.

"Gone again," said Galapas, and swiped with his sword towards where they had been. It struck blue sparks from the stones.

Merlyn put his invisible mouth right up to the Wart's invisible ear, and whispered, "Lie flat in the passage. We will press ourselves one to each side, and hope that he will go beyond us."

This worked; but the Wart, in wriggling along the floor, lost contact with his protector once again. He groped everywhere but could not find him, and of course he was now visible again, like any other person.

"Ha!" cried Galapas. "The same small one, equally visible."

He made a swipe into the darkness, but Merlyn had snatched his pupil's hand again, and just dragged him out of danger.

"Mysterious chaps," said the giant. "The best thing would be to go snip-snap along the floor. That's the way they cut up spinach, you know," added the giant, "or anything you have to chip small."

Merlyn and the Wart crouched hand in

502

hand at the furthest corner of the corridor, while the horrible giant Galapas slowly minced his way towards them, laughing from the bottom of his thunderous belly, and not sparing a single inch of the ground. Click, click, went his razor sword upon the brutal stones, and there seemed to be no hope of rescue. He was behind them now and had cut them off.

"Good-by," whispered the Wart. "It was worth it."

"Good-by," said Merlyn. "I don't think it was at all."

"You may well say Good-by," sneered the giant, "for soon this choppy blade will rip you."

"My dear friends," shouted King Pellinore out of his cell, "don't you say Good-by at all. I think I can hear something coming, and while there is life there is hope."

"Yah," cried the imprisoned inventor, also coming to their help. He feebly rattled the bars of his cell. "You leave those persons alone, you grincing giant, or I won't make you an unbreakable helmet, ever."

"What about your stays?" exclaimed the next cell fiercely, to distract his attention. "Fatty!"

"I am not fat," shouted Galapas, stopping half-way down the passage.

"Yes, you are," replied the cell. "Fatty!"

"Fatty!" shouted all the prisoners together. "Fat old Galapas.

"Fat old Galapas cried for his mummy.

"He couldn't find his stays and down fell his tummy!"

"All right," said the giant, looking perfectly blue in the face. "All right, my beauties. I'll just finish these two off and then it will be truncheons for supper."

"Truncheons yourself," they answered. "You leave those two alone."

"Truncheons," was all the giant said. "Truncheons and a few little thumbscrews to finish up with. Now then, where are we?"

There was a distant noise, a kind of barking; and King Pellinore, who had been listening at his barred window while this was going on, began to jump and hop.

"It's it!" he shouted in high delight. "It's it!"

"What's it?" they asked him.

"It!" explained the King. "It, itself."

While he was explaining, the noise had come nearer and now was clamoring just outside the dungeon door, behind the giant. It was a pack of hounds.

"Wouff!" cried the door, while the giant and all his victims stood transfixed.

"Wouff!" cried the door again, and the hinges creaked.

"Wouff!" cried the door for the third time, and the hinges broke.

"Wow!" cried the giant Galapas, as the door crashed to the stone flags with a tremendous slap, and the Beast Glatisant bounded into the corridor.

"Let go of me, you awful animal," cried the giant, as the Questing Beast fixed its teeth into the seat of his pants.

"Help! Help!" squealed the giant, as the monster ran him out of the broken door.

"Good old Beast!" yelled King Pellinore, from behind his bars. "Look at that, I ask you! Good old Beast. Leu, leu, leu, leu! Fetch him along then, old lady: bring him on, then, bring him on. Good old girl, bring him on: bring him on, then, bring him on."

"Dead, dead," added King Pellinore

rather prematurely. "Bring him on dead, then: bring him on dead. There you are then, good old girl. Hie lost! Hie lost! Leu, leu, leu, leu! What do you know about that, for a retriever entirely self-trained?"

"Hourouff," barked the Questing Beast in the far distance. "Hourouff, hourouff." And they could just hear the giant Galapas running round and round the circular stairs, towards the highest turret in his castle.

Merlyn and the Wart hurriedly opened all the cell doors with the keys which the giant had dropped—though the Beast would no doubt have been able to break them down even if he had not—and the pathetic prisoners came out blinking into the torchlight. They were thin and bleached like mushrooms, but their spirits were not broken.

"Well," they said. "Isn't this a bit of all right?"

"No more thumbscrews for supper."

"No more dungeons, no more stench," sang the inventor. "No more sitting on this hard bench."

"I wonder where he can have put my tooth-brush?"

"That's a splendid animal of yours, Pellinore. We owe her all our lives."

"Three cheers for Glatisant!"

"And the brachet must be somewhere about."

"Oh, come along, my dear fellow. You can clean your teeth some other time, with a stick or something, when we get out. The thing to do is to set free all the slaves and to run away before the Beast lets him out of the Tower."

"As far as that goes, we can pinch the épergnes on the way out."

"Lordy, I shan't be sorry to see a nice

fire again. That place fair gave me the rheumatics."

"Let's burn all his truncheons, and write what we think of him on the walls."

"Good old Glatisant!"

"Three cheers for Pellinore!"

"Three cheers for everybody else!"

"Huzza! Huzza! Huzza!"

Merlyn and the Wart slipped away invisibly from the rejoicings. They left the slaves thronging out of the Castle while King Pellinore carefully unlocked the iron rings from their necks with a few appropriate words, as if he were distributing the prizes on speech day. Glatisant was still making a noise like thirty couple of hounds questing, outside the Tower door, and Galapas, with all the furniture piled against the door, was leaning out of the Tower window shouting for the fire brigade. The slaves giggled at him as they went out. Downstairs the occupant of cell No. 3 was busily collecting the Ascot Gold Cup and other trophies out of the giant's safe, while the publicity man was having a splendid time with a bonfire of truncheons, thumbscrews and anything else that looked as if it would melt the instruments of torture. Across the corridor of the now abandoned dungeons the inventor was carving a rude message with hammer and chisel, and this said, "Nuts to Galapas." The firelight and the cheering, with King Pellinore's encouraging remarks, such as "Britons never shall be slaves," or "I hope you will never forget the lessons you have learned while you were with us here," or "I shall always be glad to hear from any Old Slaves, how they get on in life," or "Try to make it a rule always to clean your teeth twice a day," combined to make the leave-taking a festive one, from which the two invisible visitors were sorry to depart. But time was precious, as Merlyn said, and they hurried off towards the Burbly Water.

Considering the things that had happened, there must have been something queer about Time, as well as its preciousness, for when the Wart opened his eyes in the solar, Kay was still clicking his chessmen and Sir Ector still staring into the flames.

"Well," said Sir Ector, "what about the giant?"

Merlyn looked up from his knitting, and the Wart opened a startled mouth to speak, but the question had been addressed to the vicar.

Reverend Sidebottom closed his book about Pallas, the son of Evander, rolled his eyeballs wildly, clutched his thin beard, gasped for breath, shut his eyes, and exclaimed hurriedly, "My beloved, the giant is Adam, who was formed free from all corruption. The wound from which he died is transgression of the divine command."

Then he blew out his cheeks, let go of his beard and glanced triumphantly at Merlyn.

"Very good," said Merlyn. "Especially that bit about remaining uncorrupted. But what about the candle and the needle?"

The vicar closed his eyes again, as if in pain, and all waited in silence for the explanation.

After they had waited for several minutes, Wart said, "If I were a knight in armor, and met a giant, I should smite off both his legs by the knees, saying, 'Now art thou better of a size to deal with than thou were,' and after that I should swish off his head."

"Hush," said Sir Ector. "Never mind about that."

"The candle," said the vicar wanly, "is eternal punishment, extinguished by means of a needle—that is, by the passion of Christ."

"Very good indeed," said Merlyn, patting him on the back.

The fire burned merrily, as if it were a bonfire which some slaves were dancing round, and one of the gazehounds next to the Wart now went "Hourouff, hourouff" in its sleep, so that it sounded like a pack of thirty couple of hounds questing in the distance, very far away beyond the night-lit woods.

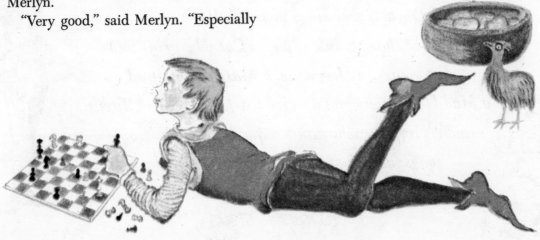

The man who wrote one of the world's favorite books was really two men. As Charles Lutwidge Dodgson he was a deacon who spent his life at Christ Church College in Oxford teaching mathematics; as Lewis Carroll he created the immortal foolishness of Alice's Adventures in Wonderland and Through the Looking Glass.

The first story was told to a real Alice (Alice Pleasance Liddel) and two other girls while they were boating on the river Cherwell, near Oxford. That was about a hundred years ago.

The Reverend Mr. Dodgson liked telling the story so well that he made a note of it and put down the exact date: July 4, 1862. Three years later he expanded it and had it published. Since that time it has been translated into every language of the civilized world.

Alice's Adventures in Wonderland is full of the queerest characters who ever came alive—a Rabbit who carries a watch in his pocket and loses his kid gloves; a Caterpillar who quotes poetry; a Duchess who sings violent lullabies to a baby who changes into a pig; a Cat who grins and disappears; a Dormouse, a March Hare, and a Mad Hatter who give a weird tea-party; a Mock Turtle and a Gryphon who dance a quadrille to their own songs; a pack of playing cards that hold a topsy-turvy trial in a crazy court.

It is also full of the most beautiful nonsense ever
written, nonsense that is surprising, lively, and, somehow,
logical. It needs no explanation.
As the author said: "Take care of the sounds and
the sense will take care of itself."
Through the Looking Glass *is a rare thing:*
a sequel which is as good as, if not better than, the
book which preceded it. Like Alice's Adventures in
Wonderland *it is peopled with strange creatures:*
flowers that talk; comic insects like Rocking-horse-flies,
Bread-and-butter-flies, and Snap-dragon-flies;
a goat that rides on a train; a train that jumps brooks;
a sheep that tends a shop; a White Knight who keeps
falling off his horse; and a set of chess pieces that are very
much alive. The story itself is a kind of disguise.
Lewis Carroll *planned it in the form of a*
chess problem—as a mathematician he was fond
of games and tricks—and Alice turns out to be a White
Pawn who wins the game. One of Alice's moves
across the animated chess board brings her to the
Eighth Square, *where "she came upon two fat little men,*
so suddenly that she could not help starting back,
but in another moment she recovered herself..."

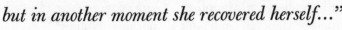

Tweedledum and Tweedledee

From Through the Looking-Glass

BY LEWIS CARROLL

Illustrated by SIR JOHN TENNIEL

THEY were standing under a tree, each with an arm round the other's neck, and Alice knew which was which in a moment, because one of them had "DUM" embroidered on his collar, and the other "DEE." "I suppose they've each got 'TWEEDLE' round at the back of the collar," she said to herself.

They stood so still that she quite forgot they were alive, and she was just going round to see if the word "TWEEDLE" was written at the back of each collar, when she was startled by a voice coming from the one marked "DUM."

"If you think we're wax-works," he said, "you ought to pay, you know. Wax-works weren't made to be looked at for nothing. Nohow!"

"Contrariwise," added the one marked "DEE," "if you think we're alive, you ought to speak."

"I'm sure I'm very sorry," was all Alice could say; for the words of the old song kept ringing through her head like the

508

ticking of a clock, and she could hardly help saying them out loud:

"Tweedledum and Tweedledee
　　Agreed to have a battle;
For Tweedledum said Tweedledee
　　Had spoiled his nice new rattle.

Just then flew down a monstrous crow
　　As black as a tar-barrel;
Which frightened both the heroes so,
　　They quite forgot their quarrel."

"I know what you're thinking about," said Tweedledum; "but it isn't so, nohow."

"Contrariwise," continued Tweedledee, "if it was so, it might be; and if it were so, it would be; but as it isn't, it ain't. That's logic."

"I was thinking," Alice said very politely, "which is the best way out of this wood: it's getting so dark. Would you tell me, please?"

But the fat little men only looked at each other and grinned.

They looked so exactly like a couple of great schoolboys, that Alice couldn't help pointing her finger at Tweedledum, and saying "First Boy!"

"Nohow!" Tweedledum cried out briskly, and shut his mouth up again with a snap.

"Next Boy!" said Alice, passing on to Tweedledee, though she felt quite certain he would only shout out "Contrariwise!" and so he did.

"You've begun wrong!" cried Tweedledum. "The first thing in a visit is to say 'How d'ye do?' and shake hands!" And here the two brothers gave each other a hug, and then they held out the two hands that were free, to shake hands with her.

Alice did not like shaking hands with either of them first, for fear of hurting the other one's feelings; so, as the best way out of the difficulty, she took hold of both hands at once: the next moment they were dancing round in a ring. This seemed quite natural (she remembered afterwards), and she was not even surprised to hear music playing; it seemed to come from the tree under which they were dancing, and it was done (as well as she could make it out) by the branches rubbing one across the other, like fiddles and fiddle-sticks.

"But it certainly *was* funny" (Alice said afterwards, when she was telling her sister the history of all this), "to find myself singing '*Here we go round the mulberry bush.*' I don't know when I began it, but somehow I felt as if I'd been singing it a long, long time!"

The other two dancers were fat, and very soon out of breath. "Four times round is enough for one dance," Tweedledum panted out, and they left off dancing as suddenly as they had begun; the music stopped at the same moment.

Then they let go of Alice's hands, and stood looking at her for a minute; there was a rather awkward pause, as Alice didn't know how to begin a conversation with people she had just been dancing with. "It would never do to say 'How d'ye do?' *now*," she said to herself; "we seem to have got beyond that, somehow!"

"I hope you're not much tired," she said at last.

"Nohow. And thank you *very* much for asking," said Tweedledum.

"So *much* obliged!" added Tweedledee. "You like poetry?"

"Ye-es, pretty well—*some* poetry," Alice said doubtfully. "Would you tell me which road leads out of the wood?"

"What shall I repeat to her?" said Tweedledee, looking round at Tweedledum with great solemn eyes, and not noticing Alice's question.

"*The Walrus and the Carpenter* is the longest," Tweedledum replied, giving his brother an affectionate hug.

Tweedledee began instantly:

"*The sun was shining—*"

Here Alice ventured to interrupt him. "If it's *very* long," she said, as politely as she could, "would you please tell me first which road—"

Tweedledee smiled gently, and began again:

> "*The sun was shining on the sea,*
> *Shining with all his might;*
> *He did his very best to make*
> *The billows smooth and bright—*
> *And this was odd, because it was*
> *The middle of the night.*

> *The moon was shining sulkily,*
> *Because she thought the sun*
> *Had got no business to be there*
> *After the day was done—*
> *'It's very rude of him,' she said,*
> *'To come and spoil the fun!'*

> *The sea was wet as wet could be,*
> *The sands were dry as dry.*
> *You could not see a cloud, because*
> *No cloud was in the sky;*
> *No birds were flying overhead—*
> *There were no birds to fly.*

> *The Walrus and the Carpenter*
> *Were walking close at hand;*
> *They wept like anything to see*
> *Such quantities of sand:*
> *'If this were only cleared away,'*
> *They said, 'it would be grand!'*

'If seven maids with seven mops
　　Swept it for half a year,
Do you suppose,' the Walrus said,
　　'That they could get it clear?'
'I doubt it,' said the Carpenter,
　　And shed a bitter tear.

'O Oysters, come and walk with us!'
　　The Walrus did beseech.
'A pleasant walk, a pleasant talk,
　　Along the briny beach;
We cannot do with more than four,
　　To give a hand to each.'

The eldest Oyster looked at him
　　But never a word he said;
The eldest Oyster winked his eye,
　　And shook his heavy head—
Meaning to say he did not choose
　　To leave the oyster-bed.

But four young Oysters hurried up,
　　All eager for the treat;
Their coats were brushed, their faces
　　washed,
　　Their shoes were clean and neat—
And this was odd, because, you know,
　　They hadn't any feet.

Four other Oysters followed them,
　　And yet another four;
And thick and fast they came at last,
　　And more, and more, and more—
All hopping through the frothy waves,
　　And scrambling to the shore.

The Walrus and the Carpenter
　　Walked on a mile or so,
And then they rested on a rock
　　Conveniently low;
And all the little Oysters stood
　　And waited in a row.

511

'The time has come,' the Walrus said,
  'To talk of many things:
Of shoes—and ships—and sealing-wax
  Of cabbages—and kings—
And why the sea is boiling hot—
  And whether pigs have wings.'

'But wait a bit,' the Oysters cried,
  'Before we have our chat;
For some of us are out of breath,
  And all of us are fat!'
'No hurry!' said the Carpenter.
  They thanked him much for that.

'A loaf of bread,' the Walrus said,
  'Is what we chiefly need;
Pepper and vinegar besides
  Are very good indeed—
Now, if you're ready, Oysters dear,
  We can begin to feed.'

'But not on us!' the Oysters cried,
  Turning a little blue.
'After such kindness, that would be
  A dismal thing to do!'
'The night is fine,' the Walrus said.
  'Do you admire the view?'

'It was so kind of you to come!
  And you are very nice!'
The Carpenter said nothing but
  'Cut us another slice.
I wish you were not quite so deaf—
  I've had to ask you twice!'

'It seems a shame,' the Walrus said,
  'To play them such a trick,
After we've brought them out so far,
  And made them trot so quick!'
The Carpenter said nothing but
  'The butter's spread too thick!'

'I weep for you,' the Walrus said;
    'I deeply sympathise.'
With sobs and tears he sorted out
    Those of the largest size,
Holding his pocket-handkerchief
    Before his streaming eyes.

'O Oysters,' said the Carpenter,
    'You've had a pleasant run!
Shall we be trotting home again?'
    But answer came there none—
And this was scarcely odd, because
    They'd eaten every one."

"I like the Walrus best," said Alice: "because he was a little sorry for the poor oysters."

"He ate more than the Carpenter, though," said Tweedledee. "You see he held his handkerchief in front, so that the Carpenter couldn't count how many he took: contrariwise."

"That was mean!" Alice said indignantly. "Then I like the Carpenter best—if he didn't eat so many as the Walrus."

"But he ate as many as he could get," said Tweedledum.

This was a puzzler. After a pause, Alice began, "Well! They were *both* very unpleasant characters—" Here she checked herself in some alarm, at hearing something that sounded to her like the puffing of a large steam-engine in the wood near them, though she feared it was more likely to be a wild beast. "Are there any lions or tigers about here?" she asked timidly.

"It's only the Red King snoring," said Tweedledee.

"Come and look at him!" the brothers cried, and they each took one of Alice's hands, and led her up to where the King was sleeping.

"Isn't he a *lovely* sight?" said Tweedledum.

Alice couldn't say honestly that he was. He had a tall red nightcap on, with a tassel, and he was lying crumpled up into a sort of untidy heap, and snoring loud—"fit to snore his head off!" as Tweedledum remarked.

"I'm afraid he'll catch cold with lying on the damp grass," said Alice, who was a very thoughtful little girl.

"He's dreaming now," said Tweedledee: "and what do you think he's dreaming about?"

Alice said, "Nobody can guess that."

"Why, about *you!*" Tweedledee exclaimed, clapping his hands triumphantly. "And if he left off dreaming about you, where do you suppose you'd be?"

"Where I am now, of course," said Alice.

"Not you!" Tweedledee retorted contemptuously. "You'd be nowhere. Why, you're only a sort of thing in his dream!"

"If that there King was to wake," added Tweedledum, "you'd go out—bang!—just like a candle!"

"I shouldn't!" Alice exclaimed indignantly. "Besides, if *I'm* only a sort of thing in his dream, what are *you,* I should like to know?"

"Ditto," said Tweedledum.

"Ditto, ditto!" cried Tweedledee.

He shouted this so loud that Alice couldn't help saying, "Hush! You'll be waking him, I'm afraid, if you make so much noise."

"Well, it's no use *your* talking about waking him," said Tweedledum, "when you're only one of the things in his dream. You know very well you're not real."

"I *am* real!" said Alice, and began to cry.

"You won't make yourself a bit realler by crying," Tweedledee remarked. "There's nothing to cry about."

"If I wasn't real," Alice said — half laughing through her tears, it all seemed so ridiculous—"I shouldn't be able to cry."

"I hope you don't suppose those are *real* tears?" Tweedledum interrupted her in a tone of great contempt.

"I know they're talking nonsense," Alice thought to herself; "and it's foolish to cry about it." So she brushed away her tears, and went on, as cheerfully as she could, "At any rate I'd better be getting out of the wood for really it's coming on very dark. Do you think it's going to rain?"

Tweedledum spread a large umbrella over himself and his brother, and looked up into it. "No, I don't think it is," he said. "At least, not under *here*. Nohow."

"But it may rain *outside*?"

"It may—if it chooses," said Tweedledee. "We've no objection. Contrariwise."

"Selfish things!" thought Alice, and she was just going to say "Good-night" and leave them, when Tweedledum sprang out from under the umbrella and seized her by the wrist.

"Do you see *that*?" he said, in a voice choking with passion, and his eyes grew large and yellow all in a moment, as he pointed with a trembling finger at a small white thing lying under the tree.

"It's only a rattle," Alice said, after a careful examination of the little white thing. "Not a rattle-*snake*, you know," she added hastily, thinking that he was frightened—"only an old rattle—quite old and broken."

"I knew it was!" cried Tweedledum beginning to stamp about wildly and tear his hair. "It's spoilt, of course!" Here he looked at Tweedledee, who immediately sat down on the ground and tried to hide himself under the umbrella.

Alice laid her hand upon his arm and said, in a soothing tone, "You needn't be so angry about an old rattle."

"But it *isn't* old!" Tweedledum cried, in a greater fury than ever. "It's *new*, I tell you—I bought it yesterday—my nice NEW RATTLE!" and his voice rose to a perfect scream.

All this time Tweedledee was trying his best to fold up the umbrella, with himself in it; which was such an extraordinary thing to do, that it took off Alice's attention from the angry brother. But he couldn't quite succeed, and it ended in his rolling over, bundled up in the umbrella, with only his head out, and there he lay, opening and shutting his mouth and his large eyes—"looking more like a fish than anything else," Alice thought.

"Of course you agree to have a battle?" Tweedledum said in a calmer tone.

"I suppose so," the other sulkily replied, as he crawled out of the umbrella: "only *she* must help us to dress up, you know."

So the two brothers went off hand-in-hand into the wood, and returned in a minute with their arms full of things—such as bolsters, blankets, hearth-rugs, table-cloths, dish-covers, and coal-scuttles. "I hope you're a good hand at pinning and tying strings?" Tweedledum remarked. "Every one of these things has got to go on, somehow or other."

Alice said afterwards she had never seen such a fuss made about anything in all her life—the way those two bustled about—and the quantity of things they put on—and the trouble they gave her in tying strings and fastening buttons—"Really, they'll be more like bundles of old clothes than anything else, by the time they're ready!" she said to herself, as she arranged a bolster round the neck of Tweedledee, "to keep his head from being cut off," as he said.

"You know," he added very gravely, "it's one of the most serious things that can possibly happen to one in a battle—to get one's head cut off."

Alice laughed loud, but she managed to turn it into a cough, for fear of hurting his feelings.

"Do I look very pale?" said Tweedledum, coming up to have his helmet tied on. (He *called* it a helmet, though it certainly looked much more like a saucepan.)

"Well—yes—a *little*," Alice replied gently.

"I'm very brave, generally," he went on in a loud voice; "only to-day I happen to have a headache!"

"And *I've* got toothache!" said Tweedledee, who had overheard the remark. "I'm far worse than you."

"Then you'd better not fight to-day," said Alice, thinking it a good opportunity to make peace.

"We *must* have a bit of a fight, but I don't care about going on long," said Tweedledum. "What's the time now?"

Tweedledee looked at his watch and said, "Half-past four."

"Let's fight till six, and then have dinner," said Tweedledum.

"Very well," the other said, rather sadly; "and *she* can watch us—only you'd better not come *very* close," he added. "I generally hit everything I can see—when I get really excited."

"And *I* hit everything within reach," cried Tweedledum, "whether I can see it or not!"

Alice laughed. "You must hit the *trees* pretty often, I should think," she said.

Tweedledum looked round him with a satisfied smile. "I don't suppose," he said, "there'll be a tree left standing, for ever so far round, by the time we've finished!"

"And all about a rattle!" said Alice, still hoping to make them a *little* ashamed of fighting for such a trifle.

"I shouldn't have minded it so much," said Tweedledum, "if it hadn't been a new one."

"I wish the monstrous crow would come!" thought Alice.

"There's only one sword, you know," Tweedledum said to his brother; "but *you* can have the umbrella—it's quite as sharp. Only we must begin quick. It's getting as dark as it can."

"And darker," said Tweedledee.

It was getting dark so suddenly that Alice thought there must be a thunderstorm coming on. "What a thick black cloud that is!" she said. "And how fast it comes! Why, I do believe it's got wings!"

"It's the crow!" Tweedledum cried out in a shrill voice of alarm; and the two brothers took to their heels and were out of sight in a moment.

A Mad Tea-Party
From Alice's Adventures in Wonderland

BY LEWIS CARROLL
Illustrated by Sir John Tenniel

THERE was a table set out under a tree in front of the house, and the March Hare and the Hatter were having tea at it: a Dormouse was sitting between them fast asleep, and the other two were using it as a cushion, resting their elbows on it, and talking over its head. "Very uncomfortable for the Dormouse," thought Alice; "only, as it's asleep, I suppose it doesn't mind."

The table was a large one, but the three were all crowded together at one corner of it: "No room! No room!" they cried out when they saw Alice coming.

"There's *plenty* of room!" said Alice, indignantly, and she sat down in a large arm-chair at one end of the table.

"Have some wine," the March Hare said in an encouraging tone.

Alice looked all round the table, but there was nothing on it but tea. "I don't see any wine," she remarked.

"There isn't any," said the March Hare.

"Then it wasn't very civil of you to offer it," said Alice angrily.

"It wasn't very civil of you to sit down without being invited," said the March Hare.

"I didn't know it was *your* table," said Alice; "it's laid for a great many more than three."

"Your hair wants cutting," said the Hatter. He had been looking at Alice for some time with great curiosity, and this was his first speech.

"You should learn not to make personal remarks," Alice said with some severity: "it's very rude."

The Hatter opened his eyes very wide on hearing this; but all he *said* was, "Why is a raven like a writing-desk?"

"Come, we shall have some fun now!" thought Alice. "I'm glad they've begun asking riddles—I believe I can guess that," she added aloud.

"Do you mean that you think you can find out the answer to it?" said the March Hare.

"Exactly so," said Alice.

"Then you should say what you mean," the March Hare went on.

"I do," Alice hastily replied; "at least— at least I mean what I say—that's the same thing, you know."

"Not the same thing a bit!" said the Hatter. "Why, you might just as well say that 'I see what I eat' is the same thing as 'I eat what I see'!"

"You might just as well say," added the March Hare, "that 'I like what I get' is the same thing as 'I get what I like'!"

"You might just as well say," added the Dormouse, who seemed to be talking in his sleep, "that 'I breathe when I sleep' is the same thing as 'I sleep when I breathe'!"

"It *is* the same thing with you," said the Hatter, and here the conversation dropped, and the party sat silent for a minute, while Alice thought over all she could remember about ravens and writing-desks, which wasn't much.

The Hatter was the first to break the silence.

"What day the month is it?" he said, turning to Alice: he had taken his watch out of his pocket, and was looking at it uneasily, shaking it every now and then, and holding it to his ear.

Alice considered a little, and said, "The fourth."

"Two days wrong!" sighed the Hatter. "I told you butter wouldn't suit the works!" he added, looking angrily at the March Hare.

"It was the *best* butter," the March Hare meekly replied.

"Yes, but some crumbs must have got in as well," the Hatter grumbled: "you shouldn't have put it in with the bread-knife."

The March Hare took the watch and looked at it gloomily: then he dipped it into his cup of tea, and looked at it again: but he could think of nothing better to say than his first remark, "It was the *best* butter, you know."

Alice had been looking over his shoulder with some curiosity. "What a funny watch!" she remarked. "It tells the day of the month, and doesn't tell what o'clock it is!"

"Why should it?" muttered the Hatter. "Does *your* watch tell you what year it is?"

"Of course not," Alice replied very readily: "but that's because it stays the same year for such a long time together."

"Which is just the case with *mine*," said the Hatter.

Alice felt dreadfully puzzled. The Hatter's remark seemed to her to have no sort of meaning in it, and yet it was certainly English. "I don't quite understand you," she said, as politely as she could.

"The Dormouse is asleep again," said the Hatter, and he poured a little hot tea on to its nose.

The Dormouse shook its head impatiently, and said, without opening its eyes, "Of course, of course; just what I was going to remark myself."

"Have you guessed the riddle yet?" the Hatter said, turning to Alice again.

"No, I give it up," Alice replied: "what's the answer?"

"I haven't the slightest idea," said the Hatter.

"Nor I," said the March Hare.

Alice sighed wearily. "I think you might do something better with the time," she said, "than wasting it in asking riddles that have no answers."

"If you knew Time as well as I do," said the Hatter, "you wouldn't talk about wasting *it*. It's *him*."

"I don't know what you mean," said Alice.

"Of course you don't," the Hatter said, tossing his head contemptuously. "I dare say you never even spoke to Time!"

"Perhaps not!" Alice cautiously replied: "but I know I have to beat time when I learn music."

"Ah! that accounts for it," said the Hatter. "He won't stand beating. Now, if you only kept on good terms with him, he'd do almost anything you liked with the clock. For instance, suppose it were nine o'clock in the morning, just time to begin lessons:

you'd only have to whisper a hint to Time, and round goes the clock in a twinkling! Half-past one, time for dinner!"

("I only wish it was," the March Hare said to itself in a whisper.)

"That would be grand, certainly," said Alice thoughtfully: "but then—I shouldn't be hungry for it, you know."

"Not at first, perhaps," said the Hatter: "but you could keep it to half-past one as long as you liked."

"Is that the way *you* manage?" Alice asked.

The Hatter shook his head mournfully. "Not I!" he replied. "We quarrelled last March—just before *he* went mad, you know—" (pointing with his teaspoon at the March Hare), "—it was at the great con-

cert given by the Queen of Hearts, and I had to sing

'Twinkle, twinkle, little bat!

How I wonder what you're at!'

You know the song, perhaps?"

"I've heard something like it," said Alice.

"It goes on, you know," the Hatter continued, "in this way:

'Up above the world you fly,

Like a tea-tray in the sky.

Twinkle, twinkle—'"

Here the Dormouse shook itself, and began singing in its sleep *"Twinkle, twinkle, twinkle—"* and went on so long that they had to pinch it to make it stop.

"Well, I'd hardly finished the first verse," said the Hatter, "when the Queen

bawled out, 'He's murdering the time! Off with his head!' "

"How dreadfully savage!" exclaimed Alice.

"And ever since that," the Hatter went on in a mournful tone, "he won't do a thing I ask! It's always six o'clock now."

A bright idea came into Alice's head. "Is that the reason so many tea-things are put out here?" she asked.

"Yes, that's it," said the Hatter with a sigh: "it's always tea-time, and we've no time to wash the things between whiles."

"Then you keep moving round, I suppose?" said Alice.

"Exactly so," said the Hatter: "as the things get used up."

"But when you come to the beginning again?" Alice ventured to ask.

"Suppose we change the subject," the March Hare interrupted, yawning. "I'm getting tired of this. I vote the young lady tells us a story."

"I'm afraid I don't know one," said Alice, rather alarmed at the proposal.

"Then the Dormouse shall!" they both cried. "Wake up, Dormouse!" And they pinched it on both sides at once.

The Dormouse slowly opened his eyes. "I wasn't asleep," he said in a hoarse, feeble voice: "I heard every word you fellows were saying."

"Tell us a story!" said the March Hare.

"Yes, please do!" pleaded Alice.

"And be quick about it," added the Hatter, "or you'll be asleep again before it's done."

"Once upon a time there were three little sisters," the Dormouse began in a great hurry; "and their names were Elsie, Lacie, and Tillie and they lived at the bottom of a well—"

"What did they live on?" said Alice, who always took a great interest in questions of eating and drinking.

"They lived on treacle," said the Dormouse, after thinking a minute or two.

"They couldn't have done that, you know," Alice gently remarked: "they'd have been ill."

"So they were," said the Dormouse; "*very* ill."

Alice tried a little to fancy to herself what such an extraordinary way of living would be like, but it puzzled her too much, so she went on:

"But why did they live at the bottom of a well?"

"Take some more tea," the March Hare said to Alice, very earnestly.

"I've had nothing yet," Alice replied in an offended tone, "so I can't take more."

"You mean you can't take *less*," said the Hatter: "it's very easy to take *more* than nothing."

"Nobody asked *your* opinion," said Alice.

"Who's making personal remarks now?" the Hatter asked triumphantly.

Alice did not quite know what to say to this: so she helped herself to some tea and bread-and-butter, and then turned to the Dormouse, and repeated her question. "Why did they live at the bottom of a well?"

The Dormouse again took a minute or two to think about it, and then said, "It was a treacle-well."

"There's no such thing!" Alice was beginning very angrily, but the Hatter and the March Hare went "Sh! sh!" and the Dormouse sulkily remarked, "If you can't be civil, you'd better finish the story for yourself."

"No, please go on!" Alice said very humbly: "I won't interrupt you again. I dare say there may be *one*."

"One, indeed!" said the Dormouse indignantly. However, he consented to go on. "And so these three little sisters—they were learning to draw, you know—"

"What did they draw?" said Alice, quite forgetting her promise.

"Treacle," said the Dormouse, without considering at all this time.

"I want a clean cup," interrupted the Hatter: "let's all move one place on."

He moved on as he spoke, and the Dormouse followed him: the March Hare moved into the Dormouse's place, and Alice rather unwillingly took the place of the March Hare. The Hatter was the only one who got any advantage from the change: and Alice was a good deal worse off than before, as the March Hare had just upset the milk-jug into his plate.

Alice did not wish to offend the Dormouse again, so she began very cautiously: "But I don't understand. Where did they draw the treacle from?"

"You can draw water out of a water-

well," said the Hatter; "so I should think you could draw treacle out of a treacle-well—eh, stupid?"

"But they were *in* the well," Alice said to the Dormouse, not choosing to notice this last remark.

"Of course they were," said the Dormouse, "well in."

This answer so confused poor Alice, that she let the Dormouse go on for some time without interrupting it.

"They were learning to draw," the Dormouse went on, yawning and rubbing its eyes, for it was getting very sleepy; "and they drew all manner of things—everything that begins with an M—"

"Why with an M?" said Alice.

"Why not?" said the March Hare.

Alice was silent.

The Dormouse had closed its eyes by this time, and was going off into a doze; but, on being pinched by the Hatter, it woke up again with a little shriek, and went on: "—that begins with an M, such as mouse-traps, and the moon, and memory, and muchness—you know you say things are 'much of a muchness'—did you ever see such a thing as a drawing of a muchness?"

"Really, now you ask me," said Alice, very much confused, "I don't think—"

"Then you shouldn't talk," said the Hatter.

This piece of rudeness was more than Alice could bear: she got up in great disgust, and walked off; the Dormouse fell asleep instantly, and neither of the others took the least notice of her going, though she looked back once or twice, half hoping that they would call after her: the last time she saw them, they were trying to put the Dormouse into the teapot.

When we speak of heroic deeds
we think often—perhaps too often
—of mortal combats, bitter struggles,
and battlefields. But there are also acts
of heroism, quiet and unaccompanied by loud acclaim,
which deserve to be celebrated.
"The Boy Who Kept His Finger in the Dike,"
a popular legend that comes from Holland,
is about one of these humble
but gallant deeds.

The Boy Who Kept His Finger in the Dike

RETOLD BY MICHAEL LEWIS
Illustrated by PETER SPIER

HENDRIK had not lived much of his life as yet—when asked his age he said he would be ten in about ten months—but, during all the life he had lived so far, he had heard about the dikes. He knew that half of Holland, his homeland, lay below the level of the sea and the only things that protected it from being flooded were the dunes and dikes. The dikes, which were made by man, were the most important. Long ago, long before historians kept records, Hollanders put up great mounds of earth and sods to save their land from the tides. It was a cruel war, a constant battling between the rising of the sea and the strength of the dikes, and for many years the sea threatened to be the victor. But the Hollanders were determined not to be driven out of the country they loved. Stubbornly they fought back the waters that roared in from the North Sea; they protected the soil with longer and larger dikes, using barriers of clay and stone as well as bricks.

Most Dutch boys were aware of this, but they seldom gave it a thought. Hendrik, however, thought about it all the time, for it was, so to speak, in his family. His grandfather had been a dike-builder; his father looked after dike repairs; his uncle was in charge of a polder, an area of reclaimed land, surrounded by dikes. On his way to and from school Hendrik walked as close to the dike as possible. It was not only a protection but his pride; it was a sort of family possession as well as a family responsibility. He admired the way the dike was constructed; its tall grassy flanks and the great stone blocks on the sea's side, put there to break the violence of the onrushing waves. He would imagine himself swarming to the top and, standing on the wall as if it were a rampart, hurling cries of defiance and holding off the enemy. He would make expeditions into the countryside, exploring the turns and twists of the walls, examining the ways in which they were built, trying to guess their age.

One day he roamed further than he had ever gone, much further than he had intended. The sky was darkening when he turned toward home; there was no time to watch anything except the shady, unfamiliar road. It was a still, chill, stormy evening; the birds had gone to their nests; there was no sound in the air except . . . Hendrik listened intently. He did not want to believe what he heard, but he knew only too well what it was. It was the sound of water. Nothing much— only a trickle—but Hendrik knew what it would mean. He knew that the trickle would soon become a gurgle, then there would be a gush, then a rush, a roar, and the North Sea would sweep in.

For a moment he stood bewildered. It was growing dark, hard to see, harder to locate a small leak in the dike. Finally he found it—a few feet from the ground— he could just reach it. It was, as he suspected, a small leak, small enough to be stopped with one finger.

At first he was not worried. He even felt a little heroic, elated to see that the finger of one small boy could hold the mighty waters in check. Besides, he thought, it will not be long; someone is sure to pass by, see what is happening, and get men to repair the damage. But the stillness continued, stillness and loneliness. As the night came on Hendrik grew colder. His hand pained him; there were cramps in his arm; soon his entire side felt numb. He could not tell how long he had hunched there; hours seemed to pass; he called and cried, but there was no answer. No help came.

The pains frightened him, but he could not take his finger from the dike. The air was freezing; he was afraid he would drop from fatigue. He stamped his feet to stamp out the cold. He rubbed his stiff arm with the fingers of his other hand to keep the blood flowing. He was dizzy; shooting nerves stabbed every part of his body. But he would not take his finger from the dike.

When he saw the man with a lantern in his hand, Hendrik fainted. His parents had been searching for him; but it was a laborer, returning late from work, who found the boy. The leak was plugged, the dike strengthened, and a great part of Holland was saved.

Years passed, wars came and went, many things were forgotten. But the country remembered. Long after Hendrik became a storied figure, a hero without a name, he remained one of Holland's most cherished legends: The Boy Who Kept His Finger in the Dike.

Lafcadio Hearn loved everything that was odd,
strange, and exotic.
Son of an Irish doctor and a Greek mother,
he was born on one of the Greek islands,
became a journalist in America, and spent the last fifteen
years of his life in Japan.
There he taught English literature at the
Imperial University of Tokyo,
married the daughter of a noble Japanese family and,
when he died, was given a Buddhist funeral.
Hearn was always fascinated by folklore,
and he not only retold but added to the quaint
legends he collected.
Of these "The Boy Who Drew Cats" is one of
the most imaginative.

The Boy Who Drew Cats

BY LAFCADIO HEARN
Illustrated by GORDON LAITE

A LONG, LONG TIME AGO, in a small country village in Japan, there lived a poor farmer and his wife, who were very good people. They had a number of children, and found it very hard to feed them all. The elder son was strong enough when only fourteen years old to help his father; and the little girls learned to help their mother almost as soon as they could walk.

But the youngest child, a little boy, did not seem to be fit for hard work. He was very clever—cleverer than all his brothers and sisters, but he was quite weak and small, and people said he could never grow very big. So his parents thought it would be better for him to become a priest than to become a farmer. They took him with them to the village temple one day, and asked the good old priest who lived there, if he would have their little boy for his attendant, and teach him all that a priest ought to know.

The old man spoke kindly to the lad, and asked him some hard questions. So clever were the answers that the priest agreed to take the little fellow into the temple as an acolyte, and to educate him for the priesthood.

The boy learned quickly what the old priest taught him, and was very obedient in most things. But he had one fault. He liked to draw cats during study hours, and to draw cats even where cats ought not to have been drawn at all.

Whenever he found himself alone, he drew cats. He drew them on the margins of the priest's books, and on all the screens of the temple, and on the walls, and on the pillars. Several times the priest told him this was not right; but he did not stop drawing cats. He drew them because he could not really help it. He had what is called "the genius of an *artist*," and just for that reason he was not quite fit to be an acolyte; a good acolyte should study books.

One day after he had drawn some very clever pictures of cats upon a paper screen, the old priest said to him severely: "My boy, you must go away from this temple at once. You will never make a good priest, but perhaps you will become a great artist. Now let me give you a last piece of advice, and be sure you never forget it. *Avoid large places at night; keep to small!*"

The boy did not know what the priest meant my saying, *"Avoid large places; keep to small."* He thought and thought, while he was tying up his little bundle of clothes to go away. But he could not

understand those words, and he was afraid to speak to the priest any more, except to say good-bye.

He left the temple very sorrowfully, and began to wonder what he should do. If he went straight home he felt sure his father would punish him for having been disobedient to the priest: so he was afraid to go home. All at once he remembered that at the next village, twelve miles away, there was a very big temple. He had heard there were several priests at that temple, and he made up his mind to go to them and ask them to take him for their acolyte.

Now that big temple was closed up but the boy did not know this fact. The reason it had been closed up was that a goblin had frightened the priests away, and had taken possession of the place. Some brave warriors had afterward gone to the temple at night to kill the goblin; but they had never been seen alive again. Nobody had ever told these things to the boy—so he walked all the way to the village hoping to be kindly treated by the priests.

When he got to the village it was already dark, and all the people were in bed; but he saw the big temple on a hill at the other end of the principal street, and he saw there was a light in the temple. People who tell the story say the goblin used to make that light in order to tempt lonely travelers to ask for shelter. The boy went at once to the temple and knocked. There was no sound inside. He knocked and knocked again; but still nobody came. At last he pushed gently at the door, and was glad to find that it has not been fastened. So he went in, and saw a lamp burning—but no priest.

He thought some priest would be sure to come very soon, and he sat down and waited. Then he noticed that everything in the temple was gray with dust, and thickly spun over with cobwebs. So he thought to himself that the priests would certainly like to have an acolyte, to keep the place clean. He wondered why they had allowed everything to get so dusty. What most pleased him, however, were some big white screens, good to paint cats upon. Though he was tired, he looked at once for a writing-box, and found one, and ground some ink, and began to paint cats.

He painted a great many cats upon the screens; and then he began to feel very, very sleepy. He was just on the point of lying down to sleep beside one of the screens, when he suddenly remembered the words, *"Avoid large places; keep to small!"*

The temple was very large; he was all alone; and as he thought of these words —though he could not quite understand them—he began to feel for the first time a little afraid; and he resolved to look for a *small place* in which to sleep. He found a little cabinet with a sliding door, and went into it, and shut himself up. Then he lay down and fell fast asleep.

Very late in the night he was awakened by a most terrible noise—a noise of fighting and screaming. It was so dreadful that he was afraid even to look through a chink of the little cabinet: he lay very still, holding his breath for fright. The light that had been in the temple went out; but the awful sounds continued, and became more awful, and all the temple shook. After a long time silence came; but the boy was still afraid to move. He did not move until the light of the morning sun shone into the cabinet through the chinks of the little door.

Then he got out of his hiding-place very cautiously, and looked about. The first thing he saw was that all the floor of the temple was covered with blood. And then he saw, lying dead, in the middle of it, an enormous, monstrous rat —a goblin rat— bigger than a cow!

But who or what could have killed it? There was no man or other creature to be seen. Suddenly the boy observed that the mouths of all the cats he had drawn the night before were red and wet with blood. Then he knew that the goblin had been killed by the cats which he had drawn. And then also, for the first time, he understood why the wise old priest had said to him, *"Avoid large places at night; keep to small."*

Afterward that boy became a very famous artist. Some of the cats which he drew are still shown to travelers in Japan.

527

*The next three stories revolve around
the cleverness or character not of man but of the creatures
with which he shares the world. In each story there is a contest:
Who will win the Princess?
Will the wolf destroy the faithful dog?
Will the man tell his wife the secret that will cost him his life?
The answers lie in the instinctive wisdom of
animal, insect, and bird.*

The Leaping Match

BY HANS CHRISTIAN ANDERSEN
Illustrated by GORDON LAITE

THE FLEA, the grasshopper, and the frog once wished to try which of them could jump highest; so they invited the whole world, and anybody else who liked, to come and see the grand sight. They were all three first-rate jumpers, as every one saw when they met together in the room.

"I will give my daughter to him who shall jump highest," said the King. "It would be too bad for you to have to jump for nothing." The flea came first. He had very polite manners, and bowed to the company on every side, for he was

of noble blood; besides, he was accustomed to man, and that always makes a great difference.

Next came the grasshopper. He was certainly of a heavier build, but all the same he had a good figure and wore a green uniform, which belonged to him by right of birth. Besides, he was said to have sprung from a very high Egyptian family, and to be greatly thought of in that country. He had been taken out of the field where he learned to jump and put into a card house three stories high.

528

This house was built on purpose for him, and all of court-cards, the faces being turned inwards. As for the doors and windows, they were all cut out of the Queen of Hearts.

"And I can sing so well," said he, "that sixteen parlour-bred crickets, who have chirped and chirped and chirped ever since they were born, and yet could never get anybody to build them a card house, after hearing me, have fretted themselves ten times thinner than they were before, from jealousy."

Both the flea and the grasshopper knew how to make the most of themselves, and each thought himself quite a match for a Princess.

The frog said not a word; however, it might be that he thought the more. The house-dog, after sniffing about him carefully, stated that the frog must be of a good family. And the King's old and trusted councillor, who had received three medals for holding his tongue, declared that the frog must be gifted with the spirit of prophecy, and that one could tell from his back whether there was to be a severe or a mild winter, which was more than could be read from the back of the man who wrote the Almanac.

"I will say nothing for the present," said the old King, "but I will observe everything, and form my own opinion. Let them show us what they can do."

And now the match began.

The flea jumped so high that no one could see what had become of him, and so they insisted that he had not jumped at all, "which was disgraceful, after he had made such a fuss!"

The grasshopper only jumped half as high, but he jumped right into the King's face, and the King declared he was quite disgusted by his rudeness.

The frog stood still as if lost in thought; and people began to think he did not mean to jump at all.

"I'm afraid he is ill!" said the dog; and he went sniffing at him again to see if he could find out what was wrong, when, lo! all at once the frog made a little jump into the lap of the Princess, who was sitting on a low gold stool close by. Then the King gave his judgment.

"There is nothing higher than my daughter," said he; "therefore it is plain that he who jumps up to her jumps highest; but only a person of good understanding would ever have thought of that, so the frog has shown us that he has understanding."

And thus the frog won the Princess.

"I jumped highest, for all that!" said the flea. "But it's all the same to me. Let her have the stiff-legged, slimy creature, if she likes! I jumped highest; but dullness and heaviness win the day with people in this stupid world."

And so the flea went away and fought in foreign wars, where, it is said, he was killed.

As for the grasshopper, he sat on a green bank, and thought on the world and its strange goings on, and at length he repeated the flea's last words. "Yes," he said, "dullness and heaviness win the day! dullness and heaviness win the day!" And then he again began singing his own melancholy song, and it is from him that we have learnt this story, and yet, my friend, though you read it here in a printed book, it may not be perfectly true.

Old Sultan

BY JAKOB AND WILHELM GRIMM
Illustrated by GORDON LAITE

A SHEPHERD had a faithful dog, called Sultan, who was grown very old, and had lost all his teeth. And one day when the shepherd and his wife were standing together before the house the shepherd said, "I will shoot old Sultan tomorrow morning, for he is of no use now." But his wife said, "Pray let the poor faithful creature live; he has served us well a great many years, and we ought to give him a livelihood for the rest of his days." "But what can we do with him?" said the shepherd; "he has not a tooth in his head, and the thieves don't care for him at all. To be sure he has served us, but then he did it

to earn his livelihood; tomorrow shall be his last day, depend upon it."

Poor Sultan, who was lying close by them, heard all that the shepherd and his wife said to one another, and was very much frightened to think tomorrow would be his last day; so in the evening he went to his good friend the wolf, who lived in the wood, and told him all his sorrows, and how his master meant to kill him in the morning.

"Make yourself easy," said the wolf, "I will give you some good advice. Your master, you know, goes out every morning very early with his wife into the field; and they take their little child with them, and lay it down behind the hedge in the shade while they are at work. Now do you lie down close by the child, and pretend to be watching it, and I will come out of the wood and run away with it; you must run after me as fast as you can, and I will let it drop; then you may carry it back, and they will think you have saved their child, and will be so thankful to you that they will take care of you as long as you live." The dog liked this plan very well; and accordingly so it was managed. The wolf ran with the child a little way; the shepherd and his wife screamed out; but Sultan soon overtook him, and carried the poor little thing back to his master and mistress. Then the shepherd patted him on the head, and said, "Old Sultan has saved our child from the wolf, and therefore he shall live and be well taken care of, and have plenty to eat. Wife, go home, and give him a good dinner, and let him have my old cushion to sleep on as long as he lives." So from this time forward Sultan had all that he could wish for.

Soon afterwards the wolf came and wished him joy, and said, "Now, my good fellow, you must tell no tales, but turn your head the other way when I want to taste one of the old shepherd's fine sheep." "No," said Sultan; "I will be true to my master." However, the wolf thought he was joking, and came one night to get a dainty morsel. But Sultan had told his master what the wolf meant to do; so he laid in wait for him behind the barn-door, and when the wolf was busy looking out for a good sheep, he had a stout cudgel laid about his back, that combed his locks for him finely.

Then the wolf was very angry, and called Sultan "an old rogue," and swore he would have his revenge. So the next morning the wolf sent the boar to challenge Sultan to come into the wood to fight the matter out. Now Sultan had nobody he could ask to be his second but the shepherd's old three-legged cat; so he took her with him, and as the poor thing limped along with some trouble, she stuck up her tail straight in the air.

The wolf and the wild boar were first on the ground; and when they espied their enemies coming, and saw the cat's long tail standing straight in the air, they thought she was carrying a sword for Sultan to fight with; and every time she limped, they thought she was picking up a stone to throw at them; so they said they should not like this way of fighting, and the boar lay down behind a bush, and the wolf jumped up into a tree.

Sultan and the cat soon came up, and looked about, and wondered that no one was there. The boar, however, had not quite hidden himself, for his ears stuck out of the bush; and when he shook one of them a little, the cat, seeing something move, and thinking it was a mouse, sprang upon it, and bit and scratched it, so that the boar jumped up and grunted, and ran away, roaring out, "Look up in the tree; there sits the one who is to blame!"

So they looked up, and espied the wolf sitting amongst the branches; and they called him a cowardly rascal, and would not suffer him to come down till he was heartily ashamed of himself, and had promised to be good friends again with old Sultan.

The Language of Beasts

EDITED BY ANDREW LANG

Illustrated by GORDON LAITE

ONCE UPON a time a man had a shepherd who served him many years faithfully and honestly. One day, whilst herding his flock, this shepherd heard a hissing sound, coming out of the forest near by, which he could not account for. So he went into the wood in the direction of the noise to try to discover the cause. When he approached the place he found that the dry grass and leaves were on fire, and on a tree, surrounded by flames, a snake was coiled, hissing with terror.

The shepherd stood wondering how the poor snake could escape, for the wind was blowing the flames that way, and soon that tree would be burning like the rest. Suddenly the snake cried: "O shepherd! for the love of heaven save me from this fire!"

Then the shepherd stretched his staff out over the flames and the snake wound itself round the staff and up to his hand, and from his hand it crept up his arm, and twined itself about his neck. The shepherd trembled with fright, expecting every instant to be stung to death, and said: "What an unlucky man I am! Did I rescue you only to be destroyed myself?" But the snake answered: "Have no fear; only carry me home to my father who is the King of the Snakes." The shepherd, however, was much too frightened to listen, and said that he could not go away and leave his flock alone; but the snake said: "You need not be afraid to leave your flock, no evil shall befall them; but make all the haste you can."

So he set off through the wood carrying the snake, and after a time he came to a great gateway, made entirely of snakes intertwined one with another. The shepherd stood still with surprise, but the snake round his neck whistled, and immediately all the arch unwound itself.

"When we are come to my father's house," said his own snake to him, "he will reward you with anything you like to ask—silver, gold, jewels, or whatever on this earth is most precious. But take none of all these things; ask rather to understand the language of beasts. He will refuse it to you a long time, but in the end he will grant it to you."

Soon after that they arrived at the house of the King of the Snakes, who burst into tears of joy at the sight of his daughter, as he had given her up for dead. "Where have you been all this time?" he asked, directly he could speak, and she told him that she had been caught in a forest fire, and had been rescued from the flames by the shepherd. The King of the Snakes, then turning to the shepherd, said to him: "What reward will you choose for saving my child?"

"Make me to know the language of beasts," answered the shepherd, "that is all I desire."

The king replied: "Such knowledge would be of no benefit to you, for if I granted it to you and you told any one of it, you would immediately die; ask me rather for whatever else you would most like to possess, and it shall be yours."

But the shepherd answered him: "Sir, if you wish to reward me for saving your daughter, grant me, I pray you, to know the language of beasts. I desire nothing else"; and he turned as if to depart.

Then the king called him back, saying: "If nothing else will satisfy you, open your mouth." The man obeyed, and the king spat into it, and said: "Now spit into my mouth." The shepherd did as he was told; then the King of the Snakes spat again into the shepherd's mouth. When they had spat into each other's mouths three times, the king said: "Now you know the language of beasts, go in peace; but, if you value your life, beware lest you tell anyone of it, else you will immediately die."

So the shepherd set out for home, and on his way through the wood he heard and understood all that was said by the birds, and by every living creature. When he got back to his sheep he found the flock grazing peacefully, and as he was very tired he laid himself down by them to rest a little. Hardly had he done so when two ravens flew down and perched on a tree near by, and began to talk to each other in their own language: "If that shepherd only knew that there is a vault full of gold and silver beneath where that lamb is lying, what would he not do?" When the shepherd heard these words he went straight to his master and

told him, and the master at once took a wagon, and broke open the door of the vault, and they carried off the treasure. But instead of keeping it for himself, the master, who was an honourable man, gave it all up to the shepherd, saying: "Take it, it is yours. The gods have given it to you." So the shepherd took the treasure and built himself a house. He married a wife, and they lived in great peace and happiness, and he was acknowledged to be the richest man, not only in his native village, but of all the country-side. He had flocks of sheep, and cattle, and horses without end, as well as beautiful clothes and jewels.

One day, just before Christmas, he said to his wife: "Prepare everything for a great feast; to-morrow we will take things with us to the farm that the shepherds there may make merry." The wife obeyed, and all was prepared as he desired. Next day they both went to the farm, and in the evening the master said to the shepherds: "Now come, all of you, eat, drink, and make merry. I will watch the flocks myself to-night in your stead." Then he went out to spend the night with the flocks.

When midnight struck the wolves howled and the dogs barked, and the wolves spoke in their own tongue, saying:

"Shall we come in and work havoc, and you too shall eat flesh?" And the dogs answered in their tongue: "Come in, and for once we shall have enough to eat."

Now amongst the dogs there was one so old that he had only two teeth left in his head, and he spoke to the wolves, saying: "So long as I have my two teeth still in my head, I will let no harm be done to my master."

All this the master heard and understood, and as soon as morning dawned he ordered all the dogs to be killed excepting the old dog. The farm servants wondered at this order, and exclaimed: "But surely, sir, that would be a pity!"

The master answered: "Do as I bid you"; and made ready to return home with his wife, and they mounted their horses, her steed being a mare." As they went on their way, it happened that the husband rode on ahead, while the wife was a little way behind. The husband's horse, seeing this, neighed, and said to the mare: "Come along, make haste; why are you so slow?" And the mare answered: "It is very easy for you. You carry only your master, who is a thin man, but I carry my mistress, who is so fat that she weighs as much as three." When the husband heard that, he looked back and laughed, which the wife perceiving, she urged on the mare till she caught up with her husband, and asked him why he laughed. "For nothing at all," he answered; "just because it came into my head."

She would not be satisfied with this answer, and urged him more and more to tell her why he had laughed. But he controlled himself and said: "Let me be, wife; what ails you? I do not know myself why I laughed." But the more he put her off, the more she tormented him to tell her the cause of his laughter. At length he said to her: "Know, then, that if I tell it you I shall immediately and surely die." But even this did not quiet her; she only besought him the more to tell her. Meanwhile they had reached home, and before getting down from his horse the man called for a coffin to be

brought; and when it was there he placed it in front of the house, and said to his wife:

"See, I will lay myself down in this coffin, and will then tell you why I laughed, for as soon as I have told you I shall surely die." So he lay down in the coffin, and while he took a last look around him, his old dog came out from the farm and sat down by him, and whined. When the master saw this, he called to his wife: "Bring a piece of bread to give to the dog." The wife brought some bread and threw it to the dog, but he would not look at it. Then the farm cock came and pecked at the bread; but the dog said to it: "Wretched glutton, you can eat like that when you

536

see that your master is dying?" The cock answered: "Let him die, if he is so stupid. I have a hundred wives, which I call together when I find a grain of corn, and as soon as they are there I swallow it myself; should one of them dare to be angry, I would give her a lesson with my beak. He has only one wife, and he cannot keep her in order."

As soon as the man understood this, he got up out of the coffin, seized a stick, and called his wife into the room, saying: "Come, and I will tell you what you so much want to know"; and then he began to beat her with the stick, saying with each blow: "It is that, wife, it is that!" And in this way he taught her never again to ask why he had laughed.

The tale of Androcles and the Lion
is one of the oldest of animal stories.
Variations of it are found in Aesop, who lived
six centuries before the Christian era, in Roman folklore,
and in modern retellings.
In 1912 George Bernard Shaw turned
it into one of his wittiest and most charming plays.
Part fable and part parable, the tale delivers its lesson lightly;
without preaching it says something unforgettable
about gratitude and the surprising
rewards of kindness.

Androcles and the Lion

RETOLD BY LOUIS UNTERMEYER

Illustrated by HARLOW ROCKWELL

ANDROCLES was a slave. His father had been a slave, and so had his grandfather. All his family had come to accept slavery as something which they had to endure. But not Androcles. He hated being overworked and underfed; he loathed the idea that the masters not only compelled the slaves to labor endlessly without payment but that they held the power of life and death over their unhappy serving men who were treated worse than dogs. Dogs and horses were well cared for. Most of all, Androcles hated confinement. He loved the idea of liberty; he did not dare plan for it, but he never stopped dreaming about a day of freedom.

One day the dream became reality. It was a spring morning when Androcles could no longer bear the hardships and cruelties of his condition. Working in the field he somehow managed to break the chain that held him. He knew that there was little chance for an escaping slave; he knew that if one were captured he would be tortured and put to death as an example to other slaves. But, without further thought and against all reason, he ran away.

He ran all day and all night—ran without stopping to eat or drink—ran from the fields into the forest—ran until he could run no more. Exhausted, he sank into lifelessness, but just before losing consciousness, he realized, with the instinct of an animal, that he must find shelter somewhere. Dragging himself along the ground he saw a hole among the rocks, crept in, and fell asleep.

When he woke he could not tell where he was; it was even hard for him to recognize himself. Briars had torn his clothes to rags; there was blood where his body had been scratched by thorns, bruises where he had run against boughs, a swelling where a stone had struck his ankle. He could tell it was nearly dawn, for a thin light trickled through the branches that framed the hole, and the birds were waking each other. Raising himself, he saw he had crawled into a cavern and, from the strong smell which penetrated his nostrils, he knew it was a cave belonging to some animal. "I could scarcely have chosen a worse place," he thought. "I must not stay here another minute." He rose shakily to his feet and stumbled toward the light. Then he was aware that the light had gone. A monstrous form had blacked out the opening.

It was a huge lion returning from his nightly hunt. He stood there roaring. "This is the end," thought Androcles. "Too bad it had to come so soon. But," he added with painful philosophy, "I'd rather be eaten, especially if the creature is as hungry as I am, than be tortured to death."

The lion continued to roar, but he did not spring; he did not even show his teeth. Slowly it occurred to Androcles that it was not a roar of anger but a roar of pain, an almost plaintive roar, more of a moan than a menace.

"Is something hurting you?" inquired Androcles politely.

The lion groaned.

539

"I thought so," said Androcles in a consoling tone. "Let's see what it is."

The lion lifted a great hairy paw.

"Oh," sympathized Androcles, "that's it—a long, nasty thorn. No wonder you're crying. I'm surprised you can walk."

The lion, full of self-pity, moaned again. He moved a step closer.

"Now, don't be frightened," said Androcles who was still trembling. "We'll see what we can do. It is going to hurt a little, but you must—er—grit your teeth. No biting, remember, and keep your claws to yourself. Now let's have the poor foot."

The lion, whimpering softly, held out the injured paw. Androcles took it in his hand, stroked it for a moment, and then tugged at the thorn. The lion pulled back and let out another roar, this time a roar of unmistakable rage.

"Now, now," said Androcles, "you mustn't talk like that to the doctor. You must be a big, brave lion, not a cowardly little cub. We'll have it all out the next try. Once more, now—ready?" Androcles' fingers tightened around the thorn, the lion held still, his eyes shut, and suddenly the thorn was out.

"There," said Androcles, as the lion shook himself. "It didn't hurt so much, did it? Now let's see how it feels when you walk."

Gingerly the lion put the sore paw upon the ground; then he took a step or two; then he bounded up to Androcles and licked his face.

— 2 —

Life with the lion was a continual pleasure. There was no question as to who was the master and who was the

slave; there was not even a distinction between man and beast. They were companions, friends in the forest, safe, secure, and serene in their happiness. They were well nourished with a variety of food. Every morning the lion would bring home his kill—a plump rabbit, a young deer, a wild turkey—and Androcles would catch fish and gather berries, which he taught the lion to like. It was a rare thing, this understanding between a naturally wild creature and the man who had gone back to nature. The two were united by a bond of mutual respect and something close to love. They roamed the woods, swam streams and, after Androcles had cooked the meal, sat about the fire together. Androcles talked, and the lion listened attentively, purring to show he agreed with every word.

Things went on like this for a long while—a year, two years, three years, Androcles could not tell, for he had stopped counting the days. Then the companionship came to a sudden end. One afternoon he was tempted to stray a little beyond the forest toward an orchard where fruit was ripening. It was then he heard a sound that alarmed him more than the roaring of any animal. It was the sound of human voices, and Androcles turned to run to the cave which had become his home and his haven. But it was too late. There were six armed men searching for fugitive slaves. They spread out, cut off his retreat, and without a struggle, captured him.

"A dirty-looking specimen," grumbled the leader. "More like a beast than a man. I've half a mind to let him go. No one would want him around the house, not even in the workrooms."

"There can't be too many slaves, and we can't be too particular about them," said one of the other men. "Besides, those who aren't fit for work can be used for sport in the arena."

"That's so," replied the leader. "The Emperor has just declared another big holiday—free bread and circuses for everybody—and," he laughed unpleasantly, "free food for the wild beasts in the Colosseum"

And they snapped the chains on Androcles.

— 3 —

The Colosseum was crowded to the last seat; fifty thousand spectators had come to witness their favorite spectacle. They had been promised a gala Roman holiday, and they cheered lustily when the Emperor, robed in purple, entered the royal platform and seated himself on the imperial couch. All the first-ranking nobles were there: Senators, Pontiffs, Magistrates, and the holy Vestals. The Emperor raised his hand and the performance began.

First there was a parade to dazzle the eye and indicate the excitement to come. At the head of the procession, accompanied by a military band, marched the Praetorian Guard, the Emperor's own soldiers, clad in scarlet embroidered with gold. There followed the captains of the regular army in shining armor, troops from occupied territories, regiments newly arrived from abroad carrying their trophies, embattled veterans and beardless young volunteers. Another band separated the conquerors from the conquered —prisoners of foreign wars, men and women to be put to work, traitors and captured slaves to be put to death. Some shambled past, with their eyes on the dust; others, in spite of the chains, carried their heads high; but all knew that the drums were pronouncing their doom. This was the part of the spectacle that the crowd enjoyed least; although it displayed the power of Rome, people were glad when it was over and the gay part of the pageant was resumed.

There was a new burst of music as the gladiators swept into the amphitheatre. Those on foot flourished their swords and bucklers; those in chariots whipped up the horses, while their brilliantly colored scarves streamed into the wind. Then came the other combatants: fighters carrying daggers or short swords; retiarii with nets to entangle their victims and with tridents to stab them; fire-throwers; spear-hurlers; lancers; archers with bows and arrows.

Last of all came the beasts: elephants who were to be pitted against horned rhinoceri; bears that were trained to attack buffalo; wild horses that were to be matched against savage boars; bulls that were to be goaded and killed by men brandishing pieces of red cloth. The only animals missing were the lions—these were too ferocious to be let loose, for they had been confined in dark pits and starved for days to make them more bloodthirsty.

There was a fanfare of trumpets and the parade stopped. All the combatants faced the Emperor's box and, raising their right hands, cried as with one voice: "Hail, Caesar! We who are ready to die salute thee!"

Then the games began. They began harmlessly enough with a series of char-iot races—the deadly gladiatorial combats were always kept for the climax—and the spectators cheered their favorites. Every charioteer had his group of admirers; even the horses had their ardent followers. Exhibitions of skill and danger came next: Egyptians who juggled naked swords, swords that were so sharpened that they would cut to the bone; wrestlers whose bodies were smeared with oil and who fought in a small square lined with knives; boxers wearing brass knuckles studded with nails; bowmen who used small torches instead of arrows, and whose targets were human beings.

An intermission allowed black attendants to mop up the blood, strew fresh sand, carry off the dead and dying, while the onlookers refreshed themselves with wine and sweet drinks. Then, as a diversion before the struggles of beast against beast, a few runaway slaves were to be thrown to the lions. The first of those chosen was Androcles.

Thrust into the middle of the colossal arena, he stood helpless. He had been given a cudgel, but it was so pitiful a defense against a starved and ravening lion that it seemed an added cruelty. He stood up straight—at least he would not die like a slave grovelling on the ground. He heard a gate being swung back on its hinges, and he closed his eyes. He heard a tremendous roar, but he did not see the lion that was looking for its prey. He did not see the leaps with which the lion sprang furiously across the sand, nor did he understand why the lion suddenly stopped and the spectators grew quiet. In the hush he was aware of a curious sniffing and he felt something rubbing his ankles. He opened his eyes — and could not believe them. For there was the lion—his lion—brushing a paw against his clothes, fawning on him, standing up to lick his face, purring and rolling over with joy.

The crowd went wild. "Magnificent!" "Marvellous!" "A miracle!" they shouted, holding out their fists with the thumbs pressed back to show that the man's life should be spared. The Emperor stood up. A life, especially the life of a slave, lost or saved, meant nothing to him, but he liked the approval of the crowd.

"Come here," he called to Androcles. "You are either a brave man or a lucky one. Or you are a magician. It does not matter to me. But it seems to matter to my people. They want you to live. You shall be my Chief Keeper of Animals."

"Oh, your majesty, I couldn't do that," said Androcles. "Thank you all the same, but I couldn't. I—I am afraid of animals."

The Emperor smiled. "That is amusing enough to earn you something extra. This great beast here acts as though he were your loyal, long-lost dog. Would you, perhaps, like to be set up in business as a caretaker and doctor of pets? It's a pleasant way of living, I'm told, and profitable, too."

"Thank you again, your majesty, but no. There's only one thing I would like to do."

"And what is that?" asked the Emperor.

"I would like to go back to the forest, and live there—with the lion, of course."

"If that is all—and it is little enough— you are free to go, free in every sense. The gods have been kind to a slave, and I, who do their bidding, can do no less. Go," said the Emperor, "and our protection goes with you."

Not as a master and his creature, but side by side, Androcles and the lion walked out of the Colosseum. Through the streets of Rome they went, across the fields and, quickening their pace, into the forest.

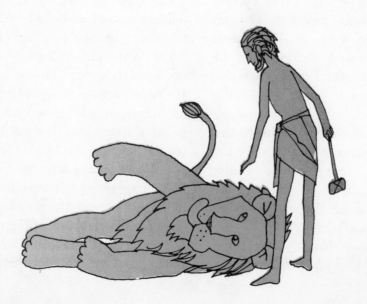